What's New in This Edition

Sams Teach Yourself HTML 4 in 24 Hours has been extensively revised and updated for the fourth edition!

- Many of the example Web pages illustrated in this edition are new and the accompanying Web site (`http://24hourHTMLcafe.com/`) now contains more than 250 online example pages for you to explore, modify, and reuse.

- All examples have been thoroughly tested with both Netscape Navigator 4.5 and Microsoft Internet Explorer 5. For maximum compatibility, every example was also tested with earlier versions of Navigator and Internet Explorer, as well as Opera 3.21. The examples were also checked against the official HTML 4 standard and Netscape's stated goals for Navigator 5. The HTML in this book is fully compatible with Windows 95 and 98, the Macintosh, and UNIX/X Window systems.

- Tips, notes, quiz questions, and exercises now incorporate feedback from more than 1,500 readers who sent in email suggestions and questions. Reader feedback has also influenced every aspect of the new edition, from the enhanced step-by-step instructions on creating your first Web page to the expanded coverage of advanced topics later in the book. You'll find answers to the most frequently asked reader questions in the new Appendix A, "Readers' Most Frequently Asked Questions."

- All code examples in the book and the accompanying Web site are updated for XML/XHTML compatibility—lowercase tags, closing tags, quotes around all attributes, and the use of both `id` and `name` attributes, for example. An emphasis on creating readable, maintainable HTML has been added throughout the book, which is not only good practice, but also will help keep your pages easily upgradable.

- Cautions have been added in most chapters noting potential incompatibilities between brower versions, including versions 3 through 5 of both Netscape Navigator and Microsoft Internet Explorer, as well as Windows CE and TV-based browsers. This edition also includes notes for users with visual disabilities and international users. The emphasis here is on how to stay widely compatible without giving up functionality.

Praise from Readers of *Sams Teach Yourself HTML in 24 Hours*

"I was recently offered a free homepage; however, the idiot-proof non-HTML text template would not save my work and I bought your book in desperation. Forget 24 hours! I was up and running in less than 4 hours! I am going to read this book from cover to cover and then I'm going to read it again and again until I can recite it in my sleep. This new skill is going to really help me in my computer business! Thanks so much for opening up a new world for me." —Jerry Pastore

"I'm halfway through *Sams Teach Yourself HTML 4 in 24 Hours*. It might as well be called *Sams Teach Yourself HTML 4 in 30 Seconds*—I can't believe how easy it is!" —Agricultor@aol.com

"I learned much more than I thought possible in such a short time!" —Scott A. Littfin

"You are a great teacher and your writing style made the book very difficult to put down when everyone said it was time to go to bed." —Barry Tattersall

"*Sams Teach Yourself HTML 4 in 24 Hours* is, without a doubt, the best computer book I've ever owned. I was about to invest in one of the more expensive Web Design packages when I purchased your book for a fraction of the price. In less then two weeks I have totally revamped my site, including brand new graphics and some JavaScript! I now have a homepage of which I am truly proud and it's all my own work." —mattyand-becky@dial.pipex.com

"My Web site has already gone through a dramatic metamorphosis and I'm only a third of the way through the book." —Kevin Wiesner

"Since I bought *Sams Teach Yourself HTML in 24 Hours* I have been a crazy man. We started our family Web site with 2 pages and because of my reading your book it has expanded to about 24 pages. I am still learning and using your book…You have made it fun." —John Ingalls

"Thanks a bunch for writing it in a way I could understand (and enjoy). Everything else makes my brain hurt!" —Mykayl Guerin

More Praise from Readers of *Sams Teach Yourself HTML in 24 Hours*

"I had been 'stalling' on learning HTML because it looked so hard, but your book made it easy…I especially like the clear examples you gave. It was a very short step from copying your examples to learning to use my own data! I also liked having this coordinating Web site and looking at the pages done by other 'newbies.' Thanks!" —Sue Powell

"I'll tell ya, I haven't been so engaged by material of this sort in a long time. Once I started I just couldn't put it down. Your book is great; well-written, engaging, and it walks you through HTML at just the right pace." —Nick Nagel

"…your book was an extraordinary resource. It had answers to just about all my questions in it, and if I couldn't find the answer in your book than your appendix enabled me to find it on the Web. It was easy to follow and hard to put down. My copy is incredibly dog-eared!" —Jim Kiley-Zufelt

"Add my name to the very long list of very satisfied readers…I will soon be completing my own Web site thanks to the invaluable information contained in your book…I found your writing style exceptional." —David E. Braund

"I really like your book. I can't put the crazy thing down." —Michael Odendahl

"…the most valuable computer book I have." —Jack Rumple

"I knew nothing about HTML before your book. Now I have a Web page up and running and am thrilled to death about how much I've learned in such a short amount of time…You have a wonderful way of explaining things." —Angie Sagan

"Simple and easy to comprehend for anyone. I enjoyed actually being able to sit down and understand something to do with computers for once." —Tony Yamada

"…very helpful and very well written. I was able to literally build a Web site for my company from scratch." —Sean McVay

"I loved the way you explained how to do everything and then showed what it should look like when it's typed in Notepad and then how it would look in a browser…I have recommended the book to all my friends on the Internet who want to create their own Web page but don't know the first thing about it." —Laurie Jersey

More Praise from Readers of *Sams Teach Yourself HTML in 24 Hours*

"I loved your book. It was so easy to follow. I got through Hour 10, then I just TOOK OFF and started doing all kinds of things on my own!! My site isn't completely finished yet, but I had a BLAST building it!" —Bonnie Richmond

"I had to learn fast, and your book did it for me! This old dog had to learn new tricks; the layout and step-by-step lessons were perfect for my needs." —David Cowlishaw

"Not only is your book an excellent resource, it is written with NON-programmers in mind! I really appreciate that. While I am interested in programming, I am not intrigued by lengthy lists of command definitions that have no context or examples as other books do. Your style is right on target." —Richard Rivette

"I could not believe how effective your method was until I gave it a try. Unlike other books that have currently flooded the market, yours cuts straight to the chase in a precise, easily understood text, with logical graphic illustrations, that is also an entertaining read." —Clark Thompson

"It was so effortless. After a couple of chapters I had created a page and could say, 'I wrote that.' There was a tremendous sense of achievement that really encouraged me to continue with the book. At the end of every chapter I could incorporate the new bit of knowledge into my Web page and see it change and grow." —Aidan Whitehall

"It has made it easy for me to cut loose from unsatisfactory HTML editors and just do things in straight HTML using Notepad. I now understand what I'm doing." —Kieran Loughran

"Today…I bought your book on a whim and am gleeful I did. It's dizzying to be able to boast already that I have created a Web page." —Paul Maglic

"I love this book. I am half way through it now and am making more progress than I ever thought possible." —Robert Doherty

"You write one mean book. I've purchased a bunch of them, and your book is the only one written from a practical point of view. It's so good that I told my local library I lost it and gave them full payment." —Al Jarvis

"It makes HTML coding so easy…the greatest beginner book I've ever read." —Mark Chang

Dick Oliver

SAMS
Teach Yourself
HMTL 4
in 24 Hours

FOURTH EDITION

SAMS

A Division of Macmillan USA
201 West 103rd St., Indianapolis, Indiana, 46290 USA

Sams Teach Yourself HTML 4 in 24 Hours, Fourth Edition

Copyright © 1999 by Sams Publishing

International Standard Book Number: 0-672-31724-9

Library of Congress Catalog Card Number: 99-63581

Printed in the United States of America

First Printing: September 1999

00   8   7

Trademarks

Warning and Disclaimer

ACQUISITIONS EDITOR
Randi Roger

DEVELOPMENT EDITOR
Damon Jordan

MANAGING EDITOR
Charlotte Clapp

PROJECT EDITOR
George E. Nedeff

COPY EDITOR
Tonya Maddox

INDEXER
Chris Barrick

PROOFREADERS
Louise Martin, BooksCraft, Inc.
Maryann Steinhart

TECHNICAL EDITOR
Sunil Hazari

INTERIOR DESIGN
Gary Adair

COVER DESIGN
Aren Howell

COPY WRITER
Eric Borgert

LAYOUT TECHNICIANS
Stacey DeRome
Ayanna Lacey
Heather Hiatt Miller

Contents at a Glance

Contents

About the Author

Dick Oliver (dicko@netletter.com) is the tall, dark, handsome author of lots of great books and software, including *Web Page Wizardry*, *Netscape Unleashed*, *Create Your Own Web Page Graphics*, and *Tricks of the Graphics Gurus*. He is also the president of Cedar Software and the warped mind behind the Nonlinear Nonsense Netletter at http://netletter.com (and many other Web sites). When he isn't banging on a keyboard, he's usually snowboarding, sledding, skiing, or warming up by the woodstove in his cozy Northern Vermont home (where they celebrate a day of summer each year, too). He likes writing HTML, eating killer-spicy Indian food, and waltzing wildly around the office with his daughters—not necessarily in that order. He also thinks it's pretty cool that authors get to write their own "About the Author" sections.

Dedication

This book is dedicated to my mother, Darlene Hewins, who had to teach herself HTML before the book was written, and told me in no uncertain terms that I'd better do a lot better job than those *other* books.

Acknowledgments

This book would certainly not exist today were it not for the author's loving family, who brought enough fresh carrot juice, tender popcorn, and buttery kisses to sustain him through the long hours of its creation.

Special thanks must also go to the folks at the Buffalo Mountain Food Cooperative in Hardwick, Vermont, for providing the carrots, popcorn, and butter.

Tell Us What You Think!

As the reader of this book, *you* are our most important critic and commentator. We value your opinion and want to know what we're doing right, what we could do better, what areas you'd like to see us publish in, and any other words of wisdom you're willing to pass our way.

You can fax, email, or write me directly to let me know what you did or didn't like about this book—as well as what we can do to make our books stronger.

Please note that I cannot help you with technical problems related to the topic of this book, and that due to the high volume of mail I receive, I might not be able to reply to every message.

When you write, please be sure to include this book's title and author as well as your name and phone or fax number. I will carefully review your comments and share them with the author and editors who worked on the book.

Fax: 317-581-4770

Email: webdev_sams@mcp.com

Mail: Mark Taber
          Associate Publisher
          Sams Publishing
          201 West 103rd Street
          Indianapolis, IN 46290 USA

Put Your HTML Page Online Today

In the next 24 hours, approximately 100,000 new Web pages will be posted in publicly accessible areas of the Internet. At least as many pages will be placed on private intranets to be seen by businesspeople connected to local networks. Every one of those pages—like over 100 million pages already online—will use Hypertext Markup Language, or HTML.

If you read on, your Web pages will be among those that appear on the Internet in the next 24 hours. This will also be the day that you gained one of the most valuable skills in the world today: mastery of HTML.

Can you really learn to create top-quality Web pages yourself, without any specialized software, in less time than it takes to schedule and wait for an appointment with a highly-paid HTML wizard? Can this thin, easy-to-read book really enable you to teach yourself state-of-the-art Web page publishing?

Yes. In fact, within two hours of starting this book, someone with no previous HTML experience at all can have a Web page ready to place on the Internet's World Wide Web.

How can you learn the language of the Web so fast? By example. This book breaks HTML down into simple steps that anyone can learn quickly, and shows you exactly how to take each step. Every HTML example pictured is followed by a picture of the Web page it will produce. You see it done, you read a brief, plain-English explanation of how it works, and you immediately do the same thing with your own page. Ten minutes later, you're on to the next step.

The next day, you're marveling at your own impressive pages on the Internet.

Beyond HTML

This book isn't just about HTML because HTML isn't the only thing you need to know to create Web pages today. My goal is to give you all the skills you need to create a stunning, state-of-the-art Web site in just 24 short, easy lessons. I've received literally thousands of email messages from readers telling me that the earlier editions of this book achieved that goal better than any other book available.

Go ahead and scan the bookstore shelves. You'll discover that the book you're holding now is the only on the market that covers all the following key skills and technologies in plain English that even beginners will understand.

- XHTML (extended HyperText Markup Language) and XML (eXtensible Markup Language) are the new standards for Web page creation. Every example in this book (and on the accompanying Web site) is fully XHTML and XML compatible, so you won't have to relearn anything as XHTML and XML replace old-fashioned HTML.

Do you have existing Web pages that you need to bring up to date so they're compatible with the new standards? If so, Hour 24, "Planning for the Future of HTML," gives you complete, easy-to-follow instructions for converting HTML pages into XHTML.

- At the same time, all the examples you learn here have been tested for compatibility with every major Web browser version in use today. That includes Microsoft Internet Explorer 3, 4, and 5 as well as Netscape Navigator 4 and Opera. You'll learn from the start to be compatible with the past, yet ready for the future.

- Hours 9 through 14 teach you to design and create your own Web page graphics (including animations) using industry-standard software you can download and try for free. Creating graphics is the single most important part of producing a great-looking site—and one that most HTML books leave out.

- Along with HTML, you'll learn cascading style sheets (CSS), JavaScript, and Dynamic HTML (DHTML) in Hours 16 through 20. Your Web pages will be interactive and enchanting, not static and unresponsive.

- The technical stuff is not enough, so I also include the advice you need when setting up a Web site to achieve your real-world goals. Key details—designing an effective page layout, posting your page to the Internet with FTP software, organizing and managing multiple pages, and getting your pages to appear high on the query lists at all the major Internet search sites—are all covered in enough depth to get you beyond the snags that often trip people up.

- A new generation of graphical Web site editors such as Microsoft FrontPage 2000 and Macromedia DreamWeaver have made Web design accessible to more people than ever—but these tools also make it more necessary than ever to understand HTML yourself so you can create pages that do exactly what you want and are easy to read and maintain. Throughout the book, I include notes telling you when the What-You-See-Is-What-You-Get editors are helpful and when they are dangerous, along with tips for fixing any mistakes or problems they may put into your pages.

All these essentials (which some authors treat like "extras," or don't discuss at all) are what made the first three editions of this book non-stop bestsellers. For this edition, I've incorporated the email feedback of thousands of readers to make every lesson easy, fast, and foolproof. I've also added even more hands-on examples for you to experience online and modify to suit your own purposes—nearly 300 example pages in all. The new, color quick-reference sheets and updated reference appendixes are sure to keep this volume at your side long after you've become an experienced Webmaster.

How to Use This Book

There are several ways to go through this book, and the best way for you depends on your situation. Here are five recommended options. Pick the one that matches your needs.

1. *"I need to get some text on the Internet today. Then I can worry about making it look pretty later."*

    - Read Hour 1, "Understanding HTML and XML."
    - Read Hour 2, "Create a Web Page Right Now."
    - Read Hour 4, "Publishing Your HTML Pages."
    - Put your first page on the Internet!

       (Total work time: 2–4 hours)

    - Read the rest of the book and update your pages as you learn more HTML.

2. *"I need a basic Web page with text and graphics on the Internet as soon as possible. Then I can work on improving it and adding more pages."*

    - Read Hour 1, "Understanding HTML and XML."
    - Read Hour 2, "Create a Web Page Right Now."
    - Read Hour 9, "Creating Your Own Web Page Graphics."
    - Read Hour 10, "Putting Graphics on a Web Page."
    - Read Hour 4, "Publishing Your HTML Pages."
    - Put your first page on the Internet!

       (Total work time: 4–8 hours)

    - Read the rest of the book and update your pages as you learn more HTML.

3. *"I need a professional-looking business Web site with an order form right away. Then I can continue to improve and develop my site over time."*

    - Read all four hours in Part I, "Your First Web Page."
    - Read Hour 8, "Creating HTML Forms."
    - Read Hour 9, "Creating Your Own Web Page Graphics."
    - Read Hour 10, "Putting Graphics on a Web Page."
    - Read Hour 11, "Custom Backgrounds and Colors."
    - Put your pages and order form on the Internet!

       (Total work time: 6–12 hours)

    - Read the rest of the book, and update your pages as you learn more HTML.

4. *"I need to develop a creative and attractive 'identity' Web site on a tight schedule. Then I need to develop many pages for our corporate intranet as well."*

- Read all four hours in Part I, "Your First Web Page."
- Read all four hours in Part II, "Web Page Text."
- Read all four hours in Part III, "Web Page Graphics."
- Read all four hours in Part IV, "Web Page Design."
- Put your pages on the Internet and your intranet!

  (Total work time: 8–16 hours)
- Read the rest of the book and update your pages as you learn more HTML.

5. *"I need to build a cutting-edge interactive Web site or HTML-based multimedia presentation—fast!"*

- Read this whole book.
- Put your pages on the Internet and/or CD-ROM!

  (Total work time: 12–24 hours)
- Review and use the techniques you've learned to continue improving and developing your site.

It may take a day or two for an Internet service provider to set up a host computer for your pages, as discussed in Hour 4. If you want to get your pages online immediately, read Hour 4 now so you can have a place on the Internet all ready for your first page.

No matter which of these approaches you take, you'll benefit from the unique presentation elements that make this book the fastest possible way to learn HTML.

Visual Examples

Like the Instant HTML reference card in the front of this book, every example is illustrated in two parts. The text you type in to make an HTML page is shown first, with all HTML commands highlighted. The resulting Web page is shown as it will appear to people who view it with the world's most popular Web browser, Microsoft Internet Explorer. You'll often be able to adapt the example to your own pages without reading any of the accompanying text at all.

(Although the figures use Microsoft Internet Explorer 5, I always tell you if the page will look different in other browsers or older versions. Everything in this book works with both Netscape Navigator and Microsoft Internet Explorer.)

Special Highlighted Elements

As you go through each hour, sections marked To Do guide you in applying what you just learned to your own Web pages at once.

 Whenever a new term is used, it is highlighted with a special icon like this one. No flipping back and forth to the Glossary!

 Tips and tricks to save you precious time are set aside so you can spot them quickly.

 Crucial information you should be sure not to miss is also highlighted.

 Coffee Break sections give you a chance to take a quick break and have some fun exploring online examples.

 When there's something you need to watch out for, you'll be warned about it in these sections.

Q&A, Quiz, and Exercises

Every hour ends with a short question-and-answer session that addresses the kind of "dumb questions" everyone wishes they dared to ask. A brief but complete quiz lets you test yourself to be sure you understand everything presented in the hour. Finally, one or two optional exercises give you a chance to practice your new skills before you move on.

The *24-Hour HTML Café*

Every example page illustrated in this book, plus over 150 more complete Web pages designed to reinforce and expand your knowledge of HTML, can be found at an Internet site called the *24-Hour HTML Café* (`http://24hourHTMLcafe.com/`). I built and opened the Café especially to provide readers of this book with oodles more examples and reusable HTML pages than I could ever picture in a short book.

You'll also get to have some fun with whimsical "edutainment" pages and break-time surprises, plus an extensive hotlist of links to a wide variety of Internet resources to help you produce your own Web pages even faster. See you there!

PART I

Your First Web Page

Hour

Understanding HTML and XML

Before you begin creating your own Web pages with HTML, you need a little background knowledge about what Web pages are, how to view and edit them, and what you can expect to achieve with them. This hour provides a quick summary of those basics, and some practical tips to make the most of your time as a Web page author and publisher.

To Do

Here's a review of what you need to do before you're ready to use the rest of this book.

1. Get a computer. I used a Windows 98 computer to create the figures in this book, but you can use any Windows, Macintosh, or UNIX machine to create your Web pages. The speed of the computer itself doesn't matter much for accessing Web pages, but the speed of the computer's modem or network interface card (NIC) should be at least 28.8Kbps, and faster is better. If you are buying a new modem, be sure it's compatible with the V.90 56Kbps standard.

▼   2. Get a connection to the Internet. You can either dial up an Internet service provider
        (ISP) by using the modem in your computer or connect through the local network
        of your school or business. An old UNIX shell account won't do the trick; it has to
        be a modern PPP (Point-to-Point Protocol) connection, which most ISP companies
        now offer for about $20 per month. The ISP, school, or business that provides your
        connection can help you with the details of setting it up properly.

> Not sure how to find an ISP? The best way is to comparison-shop online
> (using a friend's computer that's already connected to the Internet). You'll
> find a comprehensive list of all the national and regional ISPs at
> http://thelist.internet.com.

    3. Get a Web browser program. This is the software your computer needs to retrieve
        and display HTML Web pages. The most popular browser programs are currently
        Microsoft Internet Explorer 5 and Netscape Navigator 5. One or the other of these
        two Web browser programs is used by over 95 percent of the people who look at
        Web pages, so it's a good idea to get them both. You can buy them in software
        stores, or get them free through the Internet at http://www.microsoft.com and
        http://home.netscape.com.

    4. Explore! Use Microsoft Internet Explorer or Netscape Navigator to look around the
        Internet for Web pages that are similar in content or appearance to those you'd like
        to create. Note what frustrates you about some pages, what attracts you and keeps
▲   you reading, and what makes you come back to some pages over and over again.

> If you plan to put your HTML pages on the Internet (as opposed to publish-
> ing them on CD-ROM or a local intranet), you'll need to transfer them to a
> computer that is connected to the Internet 24 hours a day. The same com-
> pany or school that provides you with Internet access may also let you put
> Web pages on their computer; if not, you may need to pay another com-
> pany to host your pages.
>
> You can start learning HTML with this book right away and wait to find an
> Internet host for your pages when they're done. However, if you want to
> have a place on the Internet ready for your very first page as soon as it is
> finished, you may want to read Hour 4, "Publishing Your HTML Pages,"
> before you continue.

What Is a Web Page?

Once upon a time, back when there weren't any footprints on the moon, some far-sighted folks decided to see whether they could connect several major computer networks together. I'll spare you the names and stories (there are plenty of both), but the eventual result was the "mother of all networks," which we call the Internet.

Until 1990, accessing information through the Internet was a rather technical affair. It was so hard, in fact, that even Ph.D.-holding physicists were often frustrated when trying to swap data. One such physicist, the now famous Tim Berners Lee, cooked up a way to easily cross-reference text on the Internet through "hypertext" links. This wasn't a new idea, but his simple Hypertext Markup Language (HTML) managed to thrive while more ambitious hypertext projects floundered.

NEW TERM *Hypertext* means text stored in electronic form with cross-reference links between pages.

NEW TERM *Hypertext Markup Language (HTML)* is a language for describing how pages of text, graphics, and other information are organized, formatted, and linked together.

By 1993, almost 100 computers throughout the world were equipped to serve up HTML pages. Those interlinked pages were dubbed the *World Wide Web* (WWW), and several Web browser programs had been written to allow people to view Web pages. Because of the popularity of the Web, a few programmers soon wrote Web browsers that could view graphics images along with the text on a Web page. One of these programmers was Marc Andressen; he went on to become rich and famous, selling one of the world's most popular Web browsers, Netscape Navigator.

Today, HTML pages are the standard interface to the Internet. They can include animated graphics, sound and video, complete interactive programs, and good old-fashioned text. Millions of Web pages are retrieved each day from thousands of Web server computers around the world.

The Web is on the verge of becoming a mass-market medium, as high-speed Internet connections through TV cables, modernized phone lines, and direct satellite feeds become commonplace. You can already browse the Web using a $300 box attached to your television instead of using your computer, and the cost of such devices is likely to fall sharply over the next few years.

Yet the Internet is no longer the only place you'll find HTML. Most private corporate networks (called *intranets*), now use HTML to provide business information to employees and clients. HTML is now the interface of choice for publishing presentations on CD-ROM and the new high-capacity digital versatile disk (DVD) format. Microsoft is even integrating HTML directly into the Windows operating system, allowing every storage folder in your computer to be associated with an HTML page and hypertext links to other folders and pages.

In short, HTML is everywhere. Fortunately, you're in the right place to find out how HTML Web pages work and how to create them.

> There are actually two flavors of HTML. One is called HTML 4 and the other is called XHTML 1. The X stands for eXtensible, and you'll find out in Hour 24 of this book why it isn't called HTML 5. You'll also find out what all this has to do with another new language called XML.
>
> The most important thing to know from the outset is that all the examples in this book are compatible with both HTML 4 and XHTML 1 (as well as XML 1) and should be fully compatible with future versions of any software that interprets any Web page language.
>
> If you have other books on creating Web pages, the example HTML in those books may look slightly different than what you see in this one. Even though the old-fashioned format shown in those books will work in the current crop of Web browsers, I strongly recommend that you use the more modern approach shown in this book; this will ensure that your pages remain usable as far into the future as possible.

How Web Pages Work

When you are viewing Web pages, they look a lot like paper pages. At first glance, the process of displaying a Web page is simple: You tell your computer which page you want to see, and the page appears on your screen. If the page is stored on a disk inside your computer, it appears almost instantly. If it is located on some other computer, you might have to wait for it to be retrieved.

Of course, Web pages can do some very convenient things that paper pages can't. For example, you can't point to the words "continued on page 57" in a paper magazine and expect page 57 to automatically appear before your eyes. Nor can you tap your finger on the bottom of a paper order form and expect it to reach the company's order fulfillment

1

department five seconds later. You're not likely to see animated pictures or hear voices talk to you from most paper pages either (newfangled greeting cards aside). All these things are commonplace on Web pages.

But there are some deeper differences between Web pages and paper pages that you'll need to be aware of as a Web page author. For one thing, what appears as a single "page" on your screen may actually be an assembly of elements located in many different computer files. In fact, it's possible (though uncommon) to create a page that combines text from a computer in Australia with pictures from a computer in Russia and sounds from a computer in Canada.

Figure 1.1 shows a typical page as seen by Microsoft Internet Explorer, the world's most popular software for viewing Web pages. The page in Figure 1.1 would look just the same if viewed in Netscape Navigator, which runs a close second in popularity to Microsoft Internet Explorer.

A Web browser such as Internet Explorer does much more than just retrieve a file and put it on the screen. It actually assembles the component parts of a page and arranges those parts according to commands hidden in the text by the author. Those commands are written in HTML.

NEW TERM A *Web browser* is a computer program that interprets (HTML) commands to collect, arrange, and display the parts of a Web page.

FIGURE 1.1

A Web browser assembles separate text and image files to display them as an integrated page.

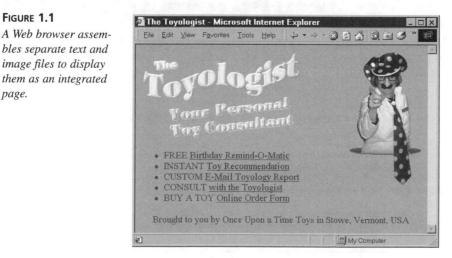

Figure 1.2 shows the text, including the HTML commands, I typed to create the page in
Figure 1.1. This text file can be read and edited with any word processor or text editor. It
looks a bit strange with all those odd symbols and code words, but the text file itself
doesn't include any embedded images, boldface text, or other special formatting.

Internet Explorer adds all the images and formatting you see in Figure 1.1. It reads the
coded HTML commands in the text, which tell it to look for separate image files and display them along with the text itself. Other commands tell it which text to display in boldface and how to break up the lines of text on the page.

> To see the HTML commands for any page on the Web, click with the right
> mouse button (or hold down the mouse button if you're using a Macintosh
> computer), and then select View Source from the pop-up menu. This is a great
> way to get an intuitive idea how HTML works and learn by others' examples.
>
> Some Web pages use an advanced feature called frames to display more
> than one HTML page at the same time. In Netscape Navigator and Microsoft
> Internet Explorer, you can view the HTML commands for any frame by right-
> clicking it and selecting View Frame Source.
>
> Other Web browsers have slightly different menu commands for viewing the
> HTML source code.

FIGURE 1.2

*This is the text I typed
to create the page in
Figure 1.1. The words
between < and > are
HTML tags.*

```
toyology.htm - Notepad
File  Edit  Search  Help
<html>
<head><title>The Toyologist</title></head>
<body background="toyback3.gif" bgcolor="magenta"
 text="blue" link="purple" vlink="white"
alink="magenta">
<img src="ologist4b.gif" align="right" />
<img src="toyolog7.gif" align="top" />
<ul>
<li>FREE
  <a href="remind.htm">Birthday Remind-O-Matic</a></li>
<li>INSTANT
  <a href="commend.htm">Toy Recommendation</a></li>
<li>CUSTOM
  <a href="report.htm">E-Mail Toyology Report</a></li>
<li>CONSULT
  <a href="consult.htm">with the Toyologist</a></li>
<li>BUY A TOY
  <a href="order.htm">Online Order Form</a></b></li>
</ul>
<div align="center">
Brought to you by Once Upon a Time Toys in Stowe,
Vermont, USA
</div></body></html>
```

How to Edit Web Pages

You'll learn how to understand and write HTML commands soon. The important point to note right now is that creating a Web page is just a matter of typing some text. You can type and save that text with any word processor or text editor you have on hand. You then open the text file with Microsoft Internet Explorer, Netscape Navigator, or any other HTML-compatible software to see it as a Web page.

When you want graphics, sound, animations, video, or interactive programming to appear on a Web page, you don't insert them into the text file directly, as you would if you were creating a document in most paper-oriented page layout programs. Instead, you type HTML text commands telling the Web browser where to find the media files. The media files themselves remain separate, even though the Web browser will make them *look* as if they're part of the same document when it displays the page.

For example, the HTML document in Figure 1.2 refers to three separate graphics images. Figure 1.3 shows these three image files being edited in the popular graphics program Paint Shop Pro.

FIGURE 1.3

Although text and graphics appear integrated in Figure 1.1, the graphics files are actually stored, and can be edited, separately.

You could use any graphics program you like to modify or replace these images at any time. Changing the graphics might make a big difference in how the page looks, even if you don't make any changes to the HTML text file. You can also use the same image on any number of pages while storing only one copy of the graphics file. You'll learn much more about incorporating graphics files into Web pages in Part III, "Web Page Graphics."

There are two basic approaches to making an HTML page: You can type out the text and HTML commands yourself with a text editor, or you can use graphical software that generates the HTML commands for you.

You will be able to follow along with this book and learn HTML much more easily if you work with an editor that shows the actual HTML text. Any word processor or text editor you already have—even the Windows Notepad or Macintosh SimpleText editor—will do nicely.

For now, I strongly recommend that you do not use a graphical, What-You-See-Is-What-You-Get Web page editor. Most graphical Web page editors currently suffer from at least two major problems: They often display pages incorrectly, and they generate very messy HTML that is difficult to read and maintain. The exception to this rule is FrontPage 2000, which makes it very easy to edit the HTML by hand when you want to and also use the graphical interface for routine tasks to save time. Unlike previous versions, FrontPage 2000 will not mutilate your handwritten HTML even if you add elements to the same page using its automated visual editor. Still, you may find it easier and more educational to start out with good old Windows Notepad when you're just learning HTML.

Software for Editing HTML

Lets You Edit HTML Code—Use These to Create Web Pages	Hides or Messes Up HTML Code—Do Not Use These to Create Web Pages
Windows Notepad (save as text)	Windows Wordpad (will not save text documents properly)
Microsoft FrontPage 2000 (click HTML tab)	Microsoft FrontPage 98 (will wreck your HTML)
Microsoft Word 6 or earlier (save as plain text)	Microsoft Word 95, 97, or 2000 (hides HTML code, rewrites your code)
WordPerfect, MS Works, or ClarisWorks (pre-1997 versions all okay)	WordPerfect 8/9 or Claris Home Page (won't let you write HTML without a fight)
Macintosh SimpleText (save as text)	HotMeTaL or InContext Spider (shareware editors that hide code)
S.H.E., Simple HTML Editor (Macintosh shareware editor)	Netscape Composer/Navigator Gold (replaces your code with a mess)
HTMLed, Hot Dog, or HTML Assistant (text-based shareware HTML editors)	Adobe PageMill (many bugs, hides HTML code)

HTML-Kit (freeware, helps verify code)	Symantec Visual Page (hides code, won't let you edit it)
Macromedia Dreamweaver (not ideal; hard to get to the HTML code)	AOL Press/NaviPress (hides HTML from you completely)
Any basic text editor	NetObjects Fusion (mangles any HTML you write yourself)
	Any graphical Web-page editor not listed to the left

The Many Faces of HTML

You'll find detailed, step-by-step instructions for creating, saving, and viewing your first Web page in the next hour.

You should be aware from the outset, however, that a single Web page can take on many different appearances, depending on who views it and with what they view it. Figure 1.4 is the same Web page pictured earlier in Figure 1.1, as seen with the text-based Lynx Web browser. Lynx users can only see the images if they click the [IMAGE] links at the top of the page.

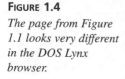
FIGURE 1.4

The page from Figure 1.1 looks very different in the DOS Lynx browser.

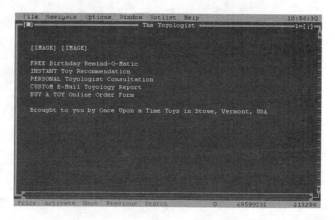

Not many people use text-based Web browsers like DOS Lynx these days. That's good news for Web page authors who want control over the appearance of their pages, and there's more good news to go with it: Most Web pages will look almost exactly the same in Netscape Navigator as they do in Microsoft Internet Explorer, and they will also look the same on PCs, Macintoshes, and UNIX machines. The page in Figure 1.1, for example, would look the same on any of these machines as long as the size of the viewing window, fonts, and program settings were the same on each machine.

Now for the bad news. Even users of the same version of the same Web browser can alter how a page appears by choosing different display options and/or changing the size of the viewing window. Both Netscape Navigator and Microsoft Internet Explorer allow users to override the background and fonts specified by the Web page author with those of their own choosing. Screen resolution, window size, and optional toolbars can also change how much of a page someone sees when it first appears.

The page in Figure 1.1 is shown in a 640×480 window, with the normal font settings. Figure 1.5 shows the same page at 800×600 resolution, with the Arial font at a large size. These are settings that you as a Web page author have no direct control over; each individual who looks at your pages can always choose whatever settings he or she prefers by selecting Edit, Preferences in Netscape Navigator or Internet Explorer 4, or by selecting Tools, Internet Options in Microsoft Internet Explorer 5.

Figure 1.5

The page from Figure 1.1, displayed by Microsoft Internet Explorer 5 at a higher resolution with larger fonts.

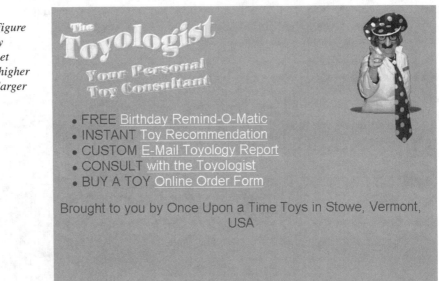

You can't even assume that people will be viewing your Web pages on a computer screen. The page in Figures 1.1, 1.4, and 1.5 might also be read on a low-resolution television screen (see Figure 1.6) or a high-resolution paper printout (see Figure 1.7).

FIGURE 1.6

Television screens may blur images, and TV Web browsers usually use a larger font to make text readable from a distance.

FIGURE 1.7

Web browsers usually change the background to white when sending pages to a printer.

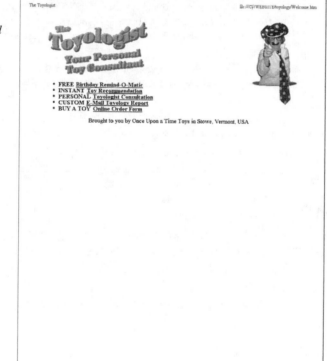

As you learn to make your own Web pages, remember how many different forms they can take when people view them. Some Web page authors fall into the trap of trying to make pages appear "perfect" on their computer and are sorely disappointed the first time they discover that it looks different on someone else's screen. (Even worse, some authors put silly messages on their pages demanding that everyone change the size of their viewing window and font settings to match the author's computer, or proclaiming "This page is best viewed by such-and-such." If you've ever encountered such messages, I'm sure you have ignored them just like everyone else does.)

In Part IV, "Web Page Design," you'll find many tips and tricks for ensuring that your pages look great in the widest variety of situations.

> In this book you encounter many example Web pages. At the accompanying *24-Hour HTML Café* Web site (`http://24hourHTMLcafe.com`), you'll find all those examples in living color, along with many more sample pages to explore.
>
> To get to the online examples for each hour in the book, click that hour number on the clock marked "Hour by Hour Examples from the Book" at `http://24hourHTMLcafe.com`.
>
> You can go directly to a specific hour by entering an address like the following into your Web browser:
>
> `http://24hourHTMLcafe.com/hour1/`

Summary

This hour introduced the basics of what Web pages are and how they work. You learned that coded HTML commands are included in the text of a Web page, but images and other media are stored in separate files. You also learned why typing HTML text yourself is often better than using a graphical editor to create HTML commands for you. Finally, you saw that a single Web page can look very different, depending on what software and hardware are used to display it.

Q&A

Q I'm stuck on my first page. It didn't work. What did I do wrong?

A That first page is always the hardest. For a step-by-step analysis of what might have gone wrong and how to fix it, refer to Appendix A, "Readers' Most Frequently Asked Questions." (You'll find that appendix handy anytime you have a question that doesn't seem to be answered elsewhere in the book.)

Q **I'm still not quite sure what the difference between a "Web page" and an "HTML page" is. And how are these different from a "home page" or a "Web site"?**

A If you want to get technical, I suppose a "Web page" would have to be from the Internet instead of a disk on your own computer. But in practice, the terms "Web page" and "HTML page" are used interchangeably. A "Web site" is one or more pages that are created together and related in content, like the pages of a book. "Home page" usually means the first page people visit when they look at a Web site, although some people use home page to mean any Web page. Others use home page to mean a personal page, as opposed to a corporate Web site.

Q **I've looked at the HTML "source" of some Web pages on the Internet, and it looks frighteningly difficult to learn. Do I have to think like a computer programmer to learn this stuff?**

A Although complex HTML pages can indeed look daunting, learning HTML is several orders of magnitude easier than other computer languages like BASIC, C, and Java. You don't need any experience or skill as a computer programmer to be a very successful HTML author.

Q **Do you need to be connected to the Internet constantly while you create HTML pages?**

A No. In fact, you don't need any Internet connection at all if you only want to produce Web pages for publication on a CD-ROM, zip or floppy disk, or local network. Hour 2, "Create a Web Page Right Now," gives more detailed instructions for working with Web pages offline.

Workshop

Quiz

1. Define the terms Internet, Web page, and World Wide Web.
2. How many files would you need to store on your computer to make a Web page with some text and two images on it?
3. Can you create Web pages with Microsoft Word or WordPerfect?

Answers

1. The Internet is the "network of networks" that connects millions of computers around the globe.

   A Web page is a text document that uses commands in a special language called HTML to add formatting, graphics and other media, and links to other pages.

   The World Wide Web is a collective name for all the Web pages on the Internet.

2. At least three files: one for the text (which includes the HTML commands), and one for each graphics image. In some cases, you might need more files to add a background pattern, sound, or interactive features to the page.

3. Yes, or with any other word processor on any computer (as long as the word processor will save plain text or ASCII files).

Exercise

- At the end of each hour in this book, you'll find some suggestions for optional exercises to reinforce and expand what you learned in the hour. However, because you're undoubtedly eager to get started learning HTML, let's skip the warm-up calisthenics and dive right into Hour 2, "Create a Web Page Right Now."

HOUR **2**

Create a Web Page Right Now

This hour guides you through the creation of your first Web page. The best way to follow along with this hour is to actually create a Web page as you read and model it after the example pages developed here in the book. If you're a little nervous about jumping right in, you might want to read this hour once to get the general idea and then go through it again at your computer while you work on your own page.

As mentioned in Hour 1, "Understanding HTML and XML," you can use any text editor or word processor to create HTML Web pages. Although you may eventually want to use an editor especially designed for HTML, for this hour I recommend you use Windows Notepad or the Macintosh SimpleText editor that came with your computer. That way you won't have to learn a new software program at the same time you're learning HTML.

Whatever you do, don't try making your first HTML page with Microsoft
Word 97, Word 2000, or any other recently released HTML-compatible word
processor; these programs may attempt to rewrite your HTML for you in
strange ways, leaving you totally confused.

Also be warned that the Wordpad program that comes with Windows contains a bug that prevents it from saving text files properly, making it useless
for editing HTML.

On the other hand, Notepad works just fine.

To Do

Before you begin working with this hour, you should start with some text that you want
to put on a Web page.

1. Find (or write) a few paragraphs of text about yourself, your company, or the
   intended subject.

2. Be sure to save it as plain, standard ASCII text. Notepad and most simple text editors always save files as plain text, but you may need to choose it as an option
   (after selecting File, Save As) if you're using another program.

3. As you go through this hour, you will add HTML commands (called *tags*) to the
   text file, making it into a Web page. Use Notepad or one of the editors mentioned
   in Hour 1 to do this; don't use Word or Wordpad!

4. Always give files containing HTML tags a name ending in .htm (or .html if you
   prefer) when you save them. This is important: If you forget to type the .htm or
   .html at the end of the filename when you save the file, most text editors will give
   it some other extension (such as .txt or .doc). If that happens, you won't be able to
   find it when you try to look at it with a Web browser.

A Simple Sample Page

Figure 2.1 shows the text you would type and save to create a simple HTML page. If you
opened this file with a Web browser such as Netscape Navigator, you would see the page
in Figure 2.2.

In Figure 2.1, as in every HTML page, the words starting with < and ending with > are
actually coded commands. These coded commands are called HTML tags because they

"tag" pieces of text and tell the Web browser what kind of text it is. This allows the Web browser to display the text appropriately.

NEW TERM   An HTML *tag* is a coded command used to indicate how part of a Web page should be displayed.

In Figure 2.1, and most other figures in this book, HTML tags are printed darker than the rest of the text so you can easily spot them. When you type your own HTML files, all the text will be the same color (unless you are using a special HTML editing program that uses color to highlight tags, such as HTML-Kit or FrontPage 2000).

2

FIGURE 2.1

Every Web page you create must include the <html>, <head>, <title>, *and* <body> *tags.*

```
<html>
<head>
<title>The First Web Page</title>
</head>
<body>
In the beginning, Tim created the HyperText Markup Language.
The Internet was without form and void, and text was upon
the face of the monitor and the Hands of Tim were moving over
the face of the keyboard. And Tim said, Let there be links;
and there were links. And Tim saw that the links were good;
and Tim separated the links from the text. Tim called the
links Anchors, and the text He called Other Stuff.
And the whole thing together was the first Web Page.
</body>
</html>
```

FIGURE 2.2

When you view the Web page in Figure 2.1 with a Web browser, only the actual title and body text are displayed.

The First Web Page - Microsoft Internet Explorer

File   Edit   View   Favorites   Tools   Help

In the beginning, Tim created the HyperText Markup Language. The Internet was without form and void, and text was upon the face of the monitor and the Hands of Tim were moving over the face of the keyboard. And Tim said, Let there be links; and there were links. And Tim saw that the links were good; and Tim separated the links from the text. Tim called the links Anchors, and the text He called Other Stuff. And the whole thing together was the first Web Page.

Done   My Computer

Figure 2.2 may look a little bit different than your Web browser does (even if you are using the same version of Netscape Navigator) because I have hidden all the button bars. All the figures in this book have the button bars hidden to leave more room for the Web pages themselves.

Before you learn what the HTML tags in Figure 2.1 mean, you might want to see exactly how I went about creating and viewing the document itself:

1. Type all the text in Figure 1.1, including the HTML tags, in Windows Notepad (or Macintosh SimpleText).

2. Select File, Save As and be sure to select Text Documents as the file type.

3. Name the file `myfirst.html`. (If you're using a Windows 3.1 or DOS program, you need to name it `myfirst.htm` instead because those old operating systems are too prudish to handle filenames ending in four-letter words.)

4. Choose the directory folder on your hard drive where you would like to keep your Web pages—and remember which one you choose! Click the Save or OK button to save the file.

5. Now start up Netscape Navigator or Microsoft Internet Explorer. (Leave Notepad running, too. That way you can easily switch back and forth between viewing and editing your page.)

You don't need to be connected to the Internet to view a Web page stored on your own computer. If your Web browser program tries to connect to the Internet every time you start it, it is being a bad browser and you must discipline it severely. The appropriate disciplinary action will depend on your breed of browser:

- In Microsoft Internet Explorer 5, select Tools, Internet Options; click the General tab and click Use Blank under Home page. (In Internet Explorer 4, this is on the View menu instead of the Tools menu.)

- In Netscape Navigator 5, select Edit, Preferences; choose the Navigator category and select Blank Page under Navigator Starts With.

This teaches your browser not to run off and fetch a page from the Internet every time it starts.

6. In Microsoft Internet Explorer 5, select File, Open and click Browse. If you're using Netscape Navigator 4 or 5, select File, Open Page and click the Choose File button. Navigate to the appropriate folder and select the `myfirst.html` file.

   Voilá! You should see the page in Figure 2.2.

Tags Every HTML Page Must Have

The time has come for the secret language of HTML tags to be revealed to you. When you understand this language, you will have creative powers far beyond those of other humans. Don't tell the other humans, but it's really pretty easy.

Most HTML tags have two parts: an *opening tag*, which indicates where a piece of text begins, and a *closing tag*, which indicates where the piece of text ends. Closing tags start with a / (forward slash) just after the < symbol.

For example, the <body> tag in Figure 2.1 tells the Web browser where the actual body text of the page begins, and </body> indicates where it ends. Everything between the <body> and </body> tags will appear in the main display area of the Web browser window, as you can see in Figure 2.2.

Netscape Navigator displays any text between <title> and </title> at the very top of the Netscape window, as you can also see in Figure 2.2. (Some very old Web browsers display the title in its own special little box instead.) The title text is also used to identify the page on the Netscape Navigator Bookmarks menu or in the Microsoft Internet Explorer Favorites list.

You will use the <body> and <title> tags in every HTML page you create because every Web page needs a title and some body text. You will also use the other two tags shown in Figure 2.1, <html> and <head>. Putting <html> at the very beginning of a document simply indicates that this is a Web page. The </html> at the end indicates that the Web page is over.

Don't ask me to explain why you have to put <head> in front of the <title> tag and </head> after the </title> tag. You just do. (Hour 22, "Organizing and Managing a Web Site," reveals some other advanced header information that can go between <head> and </head>, but none of it is necessary for most Web pages.)

> You may find it convenient to create and save a *bare-bones page* with just the opening and closing <html>, <head>, <title>, and <body> tags, similar to the document in Figure 2.1. You can then open that document as a starting point whenever you want to make a new Web page and save yourself from typing out all those obligatory tags every time.
>
> (This won't be necessary if you use a dedicated HTML editing program, which usually puts these tags in automatically when you begin a new page.)

Paragraphs and Line Breaks

When a Web browser displays HTML pages, it pays no attention to line endings or the number of spaces between words. For example, the top poem in Figure 2.3 appears with a single space between all words in Figure 2.4. When the text reaches the edge of the Netscape window, it automatically wraps down to the next line, no matter where the line breaks were in the original HTML file.

You must use HTML tags to control where line and paragraph breaks actually appear. To skip a line between paragraphs, put a <p> tag at the beginning of each paragraph and a </p> tag at the end.

The <br> tag forces a line break within a paragraph. Unlike the other tags you've seen so far, <br> doesn't require a closing </br> tag. To conform to the new XML and XHTML standards (see Hour 24, "Planning for the Future of HTML"), you should always include a / within any opening tag that doesn't have a closing tag, like this: <br />.

> Note that most Web pages you see on the Internet today use <br> instead of
 , and the current crop of Web browser software treats them both the same. However, you may save yourself a lot of work rewriting your pages in a year or two if you get in the habit of using the new <br /> form of the tag now.
>
> Likewise, the closing </p> tag is always optional in HTML 4 and is often left out by Web page authors today. Closing </p> tags are required by the new XHTML 1 standard, so I recommend that you always include them.

The second poem in Figures 2.3 and 2.4 shows the <br /> and <p> tags being used to separate the lines and verses of a nursery rhyme and to separate two paragraphs of text commenting on the rhyme.

You might have also noticed the <hr /> tag in Figure 2.3, which causes a horizontal rule line to appear in Figure 2.4. Inserting a horizontal rule with the <hr /> tag also causes a line break, even if you don't include a <br /> tag along with it. For a little extra blank space above or below a horizontal rule, you can put a <p> tag before the <hr /> tag and a </p> tag after it.

Like <br />, the <hr /> horizontal rule tag never gets a closing </hr> tag.

FIGURE 2.3

In HTML, extra spaces and line breaks (like those in the top poem here) are ignored.

```
<html>
<head>
<title>The Advertising Agency Song</title>
</head>
<body>
When your client's    hopping mad,
put his picture in the ad.

If he still should     prove refractory,
add a picture of his factory.

<hr />

<p>When your client's hopping mad,<br />
put his picture in the ad.</p>
<p>If he still should prove refractory,<br />
add a picture of his factory.</p>
</body>
</html>
```

FIGURE 2.4

When the HTML in Figure 2.3 is viewed as a Web page, line and paragraph breaks only appear where there are <br /> and <p> tags.

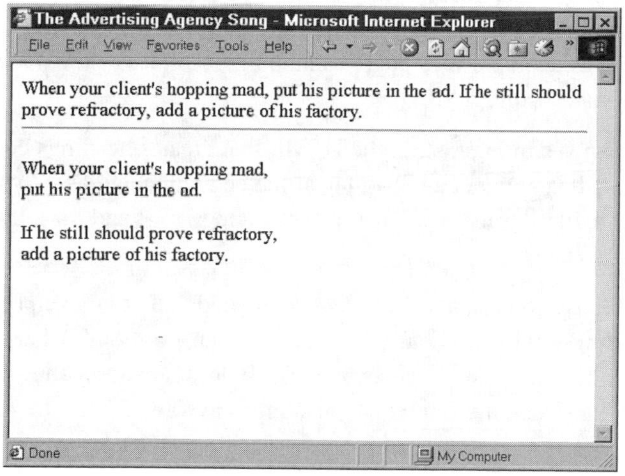

The Advertising Agency Song - Microsoft Internet Explorer

File Edit View Favorites Tools Help

When your client's hopping mad, put his picture in the ad. If he still should prove refractory, add a picture of his factory.

When your client's hopping mad,
put his picture in the ad.

If he still should prove refractory,
add a picture of his factory.

Done   My Computer

To Do

Take a passage of text and try your hand at formatting it as proper HTML:

1. Add **<html><head><title>***My Title***</title></head><body>** to the beginning of the text (using your own title for your page instead of *My Title*).

2. Add **</body></html>** to the very end of the text.

3. Add a **<p>** tag at the beginning of each paragraph and a **</p>** tag at the end of each paragraph.

4. Use **
** tags anywhere you want single-spaced line breaks.

5. Use **<hr />** to draw horizontal rules separating major sections of text, or wherever you'd like to see a line across the page.

▼   6. Save the file as ***mypage.htm*** (using your own filename instead of *mypage*). If you
        are using a word processor, always be sure to save HTML files in plain text or
        ASCII format.

     7. Open the file with Netscape Navigator or Microsoft Internet Explorer to see your
        Web page.

     8. If something doesn't look right, go back to the text editor to make corrections and
        save the file again. You then need to click Reload (in Netscape Navigator) or Refresh
▲   (in Microsoft Internet Explorer) to see the changes you made to the Web page.

Headings

When you browse through Web pages on the Internet, you can't help but notice that most
of them have a heading at the top that appears larger and bolder than the rest of the text.
Figure 2.6 is a simple Web page, containing examples of the three largest heading sizes
you can make with HTML.

As you can see in Figure 2.5, the HTML that creates headings couldn't be simpler. For a
big level 1 heading, put an <h1> tag at the beginning and an </h1> tag at the end. For a
slightly smaller level 2 heading, use <h2> and </h2>, and for a little level 3 heading, use
<h3> and </h3>.

Theoretically, you can also use <h4>, <h5>, and <h6> to make progressively less important headings, but nobody uses these very much—after all, what's the point of a heading
if it's not big and bold? Besides, most Web browsers don't show a noticeable difference
between these and the small <h3> headings anyway.

FIGURE 2.5

*Any text between <h1>
and </h1> tags will
appear as a large
heading. <h2> and
<h3> make smaller
headings.*

```
<html>
<head><title>Teach Yourself</title></head>
<body>
<h1>Teach Yourself Clock Programming in 13 Hours</h1>
<p>Tired of blinking VCRs and Microwaves? Embarrassed that
every fax from your office says it was sent from the year 1907?
Wondering whether you're ten, sixteen, or twenty-two minutes
late for work when all your LEDs and LCDs disagree?</p>
<h2>Take charge of your time.</h2>
<p>Pick up a copy of Teach Yourself Clock Programming in 13
Hours, and you'll never have to ignore another flashing
12:00AM again. In just 13 easy one-hour lessons, you'll learn
to set the time and date you want on any digital device, from
your bedside radio to the office copier.</p>
<h3>Complete, comprehensive, and FAST.</h3>
<p>Popular makes and models from every major appliance
manufacturer are covered, from convection ovens to car
stereos. PLUS special appendixes on VCR and fax programming
will take you beyond time, into the hallowed realms of
prescheduled recording and late-night "paper Spam".</p>
<p>Never ask your spouse how to reset the nuker again. Get
Teach Yourself Clock Programming in 13 Hours today.</p>
</body>
</html>
```

FIGURE 2.6

The <h1>, <h2>, and <h3> tags in Figure 2.5 make the three progressively smaller headings on this Web page.

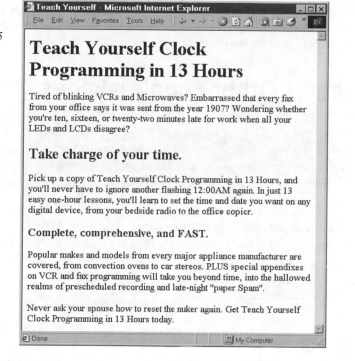

On many Web pages nowadays, graphical images of ornately rendered letters and logos are often used in place of the ordinary text headings discussed in this hour. You'll discover how to create graphics and put them on your pages in Part III, "Web Page Graphics." However, old-fashioned text headings are still widely used and have two major advantages over graphics headings:

- Text headings transfer and display almost instantly, no matter how fast or slow the reader's connection to the Internet is.
- Text headings can be seen in all Web browsers and HTML-compatible software, even old DOS and UNIX programs that don't show graphics.

It's important to remember the difference between a *title* and a *heading*. These two words are often interchangeable in day-to-day English, but when you're talking HTML, <title> gives the entire page an identifying name that isn't displayed on the page itself, but only on the window title bar. The heading tags, on the other hand, cause some text on the page to be displayed with visual emphasis. There can only be one <title> per page, but you can have as many <h1>, <h2>, and <h3> headings as you want, in any order that suits your fancy.

You'll learn to take complete control over the appearance of text on your Web pages in Part II, "Web Page Text." Yet headings provide the easiest and most popular way to draw extra attention to some important text.

Peeking at Other People's Pages

If you've even taken a quick peek at the World Wide Web, you know that the simple text pages described in this hour are only the tip of the HTML iceberg. Now that you know the basics, you may surprise yourself with how much of the rest you can pick up just by looking at other people's pages on the Internet. As mentioned in Hour 1, you can see the HTML for any page by right-clicking and selecting View, Source (or View, Frame Source) in Netscape Navigator or Microsoft Internet Explorer.

Don't worry if you aren't yet able to decipher what some HTML tags do or exactly how to use them yourself. You'll find out about all that in the next few hours. However, sneaking a preview now will show you the tags that you do know in action and give you a taste of what you'll soon be able to do with your Web pages.

The HTML goodies at my *24-Hour HTML Café* are especially designed to be intuitive and easy to understand.

The HTML used in the main entrance page at http://24houHTMLcafe.com may look a bit intimidating now, but you'll soon learn how to develop sophisticated sites like this yourself. For some less intimidating example pages, go to http://24hourHTMLcafe.com/hour2/.

Click the link to each example page, and then use View, Page Source in Netscape Navigator (View, Source in Microsoft Internet Explorer) to look at the HTML I wrote to create that page.

Summary

In this hour you've been introduced to the most basic and important HTML tags. By adding these coded commands to any plain text document, you can quickly transform it into a bona fide Web page.

The first step in creating a Web page is to put a few obligatory HTML tags at the beginning and end, including a title for the page. You then mark where paragraphs and lines end, and add horizontal rules and headings if you want them. Table 2.1 summarizes all the tags introduced in this hour.

TABLE 2.1   HTML Tags Covered in Hour 2

Tag	Function
`<html>...</html>`	Encloses the entire HTML document.
`<head>...</head>`	Encloses the head of the HTML document.
`<title>...</title>`	Indicates the title of the document. Used within `<head>`.
`<body>...</body>`	Encloses the body of the HTML document.
`<p>...</p>`	A paragraph; skips a line between paragraphs.
` `	A line break.
`<hr />`	A horizontal rule line.
`<h1>...</h1>`	A first-level heading.
`<h2>...</h2>`	A second-level heading.
`<h3>...</h3>`	A third-level heading.
`<h4>...</h4>`	A fourth-level heading (seldom used).
`<h5>...</h5>`	A fifth-level heading (seldom used).
`<h6>...</h6>`	A sixth-level heading (seldom used).

Q&A

Q When I open the file in my Web browser, I see all the text including the HTML tags. Sometimes I even see weird gobbledygook characters at the top of the page! What did I do wrong?

A You didn't save the file as plain text. Try saving the file again, being careful to save it as Text Only or ASCII Text. If you can't quite figure out how to get your word processor to do that, don't stress. Just type your HTML files in Notepad or SimpleText instead and everything should work just fine. (Also, always make sure the filename of your Web page ends in .htm or .html.)

Q I have this HTML Web page on my computer now. How do I get it on the Internet so everyone else can see it?

A Hour 4, "Publishing Your HTML Pages," explains how to put your pages on the Internet as well as how to get them ready for publishing on a local network or CD-ROM.

Q I want "Fred's Fresh Fish" to appear both at the top of my page and on people's bookmark (or favorites) lists when they bookmark my page. How can I get it to appear both places?

A Make a heading at the top of your page with the same text as the title, like this:

```
<html><head><title>Fred's Fresh Fish</title></head>
<body><h1>Fred's Fresh Fish</h1>
...the rest of the page goes here...
</body></html>
```

Q I've seen Web pages on the Internet that don't have `<html>` tags at the beginning. I've also seen pages with some other weird tags in front of the `<html>` tag. You said pages always have to start with `<html>`. What's the deal?

A Many Web browsers will forgive you if you forget to put in the `<html>` tag and will display the page correctly anyway. Yet it's a very good idea to include it because some software does need it to identify the page as valid HTML.

In fact, the official standard goes one step further and recommends that you put a tag at the beginning that looks like this: `<!DOCTYPE HTML PUBLIC "-//IETF//DTD HTML//EN//4.0">`. This indicates that your document conforms to the HTML 4 standard. No software that I've ever heard of pays any attention to this tag, however. Nor is it likely to be required in the near future, since so few of the millions of Web pages in the world include it.

Workshop

Quiz

1. What four tags are required in every HTML page?

2. Insert the appropriate line break and paragraph break tags to format the following poems with a blank line between them:

   Good night, God bless you,
   Go to bed and undress you.

   Good night, sweet repose,
   Half the bed and all the clothes.

3. Write the HTML for the following to appear one after the other:
   - A small heading with the words, "We are Proud to Present"
   - A horizontal rule across the page
   - A large heading with the one word, "Orbit"
   - A medium-sized heading with the words, "The Geometric Juggler"
   - Another horizontal rule

4. Write a complete HTML Web page with the title "Foo Bar" and a heading at the top which reads "Happy Hour at the Foo Bar", followed by the words "Come on down!" in regular type.

Answers

1. `<html>`, `<head>`, `<title>`, and `<body>` (along with their closing tags, `</html>`, `</head>`, `</title>`, and `</body>`).

2.
```
<p>Good night, God bless you,<br />
Go to bed and undress you.</p>
<p>Good night, sweet repose,<br />
Half the bed and all the clothes.</p>
```

3.
```
<h3>We are Proud to Present</h3>
<hr />
<h1>Orbit</h1>
<h2>The Geometric Juggler</h2>
<hr />
```

4.
```
<html>
<head><title>Foo Bar</title></head>
<body>
<h1>Happy Hour at the Foo Bar</h1>
Come on Down!
</body></html>
```

Exercises

- Even if your main goal in reading this book is to create Web pages for your business, you might want to make a personal Web page just for practice. Type a few paragraphs to introduce yourself to the world, and use the HTML tags you've learned in this hour to make them into a Web page.

- You'll be using the HTML tags covered in this hour so often that you'll want to commit them to memory. The best way to do that is to take some time now and create several Web pages before you go on. You can try creating some basic pages with serious information you want to post on the Internet, or just use your imagination and make some fun pages.

Linking to Other Web Pages

In the previous two hours you learned how to create an HTML page with some text on it. However, to make it a "real" Web page you need to connect it to the rest of the World Wide Web—or at least to your own personal or corporate web of pages.

This hour shows you how to create *hypertext links*—those words that take you from one Web page to another when you click them with your mouse. You learn how to create links that go to another part of the same page in Hour 7, "Email Links and Links Within a Page."

Although the same HTML tag you study in this hour is also used to make graphics images into clickable links, graphical links aren't explicitly discussed here. You'll find out about those in Hour 10, "Putting Graphics on a Web Page."

Linking to Another Web Page

The tag to create a link is called <a>, which stands for anchor. (Don't even try to imagine the thought process of the person who came up with this strange name for a link between pages. As Thomas Carlyle once said, "The coldest word was once a glowing new metaphor.") You put the address of the page to link to in quotes after href=, like the following:

```
<a href="http://netletter.com/dicko/index.htm">click here!</a>
```

This link displays the words click here! in blue with an underline. When a user clicks those, she would see the Web page named index.htm, which is located in the dicko folder on the Web server computer whose address is netletter.com—just as if she had typed the address into the Web browser by hand. (By the way, Internet addresses are also called *Uniform Resource Locators*, or *URLs*, by techie types.)

href stands for hypertext reference and is called an *attribute* of the <a> tag. You'll learn more about attributes in Hour 5, "Text Alignment and Lists."

As you may know, you can leave out the http:// at the front of any address when typing it into most Web browsers. You cannot leave that part out when you type an address into an <a href> link on a Web page, however.

One thing you can often leave out of an address is the actual name of the HTML page. Most computers on the Internet automatically pull up the home page for a particular address or directory folder. For example, you can use http://netletter.com to refer to the page located at http://netletter.com/index.htm because my server computer knows index.htm is the page you should see first (see Hour 4, "Publishing Your HTML Pages").

Figure 3.1 includes a number of <a> tags, which show up as underlined links in Figure 3.2. For example, clicking the words Alloway, New Jersey in Figure 3.2 will take you to the page located at http://www.accsyst.com/cow.html as shown in Figure 3.3.

You can easily transfer the address of a page from your Web browser to your own HTML page by using the Windows or Macintosh clipboard. Just highlight the address in the Location, Address, Bookmark Properties, or Edit Favorites box in your Web browser, and select Edit, Copy (or press Ctrl+C). Then type <a href=" and select Edit, Paste (Ctrl+V) in your HTML editor.

FIGURE 3.1

Words between <a> and </a> tags will become links to the addresses given in the HREF attributes.

```
<html>
<head><title>You Aren't There</title></head>
<body>
<h1>Wonders of the World</h1>
Vacations aren't cheap. But who needs them anymore, with so
many live cameras connected to the World Wide Web? Pack a
picnic, and you can visit spacious pastures (complete with
scenic cows) in
<a href="http://www.accsyst.com/cow.html">Alloway, New
Jersey</a> or, for the more scientifically minded, at
<a href=
"http://www.almaden.ibm.com/almaden/cattle/home_cow.htm">IBM's
Almaden Research Center</a>. Or if it's scenery you're
after, adventure to <a href="http://www.inwap.com/backyard/">a
half-paved backyard in Fremont, California.</a></p>
</body>
</html>
```

FIGURE 3.2

The HTML in Figure 3.1 produces this page, with links appearing as blue or purple underlined text.

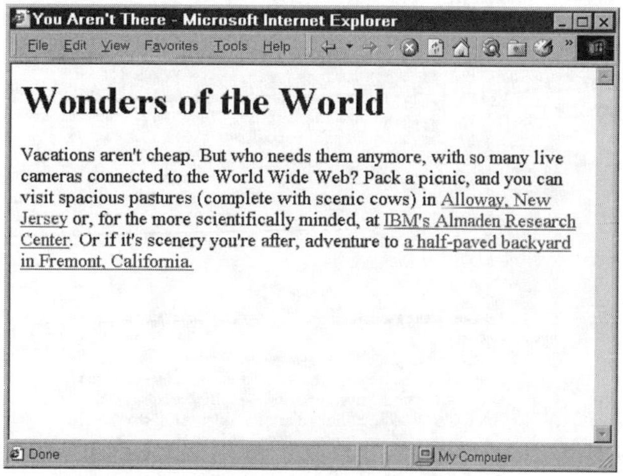

FIGURE 3.3

Clicking Alloway, New Jersey *in Figure 3.2 retrieves this page from the Internet.*

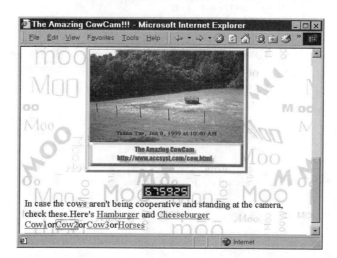

3

Linking Between Your Own Pages

When you create a link from one page to another page on the same computer, it isn't necessary to specify a complete Internet address. If the two pages are in the same directory folder, you can simply use the name of the HTML file:

```
<a href="pagetwo.htm">click here to go to page 2.</a>
```

As an example, Figures 3.4 and 3.6 show a quiz page with a link to the answers page in Figures 3.5 and 3.7. The answers page contains a link back to the quiz page.

FIGURE 3.4

Because this page links to another page in the same directory, the filename can be used in place of a complete address.

```
<html>
<head><title>History Quiz</title></head>
<body>
<h1>History Quiz</h1>
<p>Complete the following rhymes.
(Example: William the Conquerer played cruel tricks
on the Saxons in... ten sixty-six.)</p>
<p>1. Columbus sailed the ocean blue in...<br />
2. The Spanish Armada met its fate in...<br />
3. London burnt like rotten sticks in...<br />
4. Tricky Dickie served his time in...<br />
5. Billy C. went on a spree in...</p>
<p><a href="answers.htm">Click here for answers.</a></p>
</body>
</html>
```

FIGURE 3.5

This is the answers.htm *file. Figure 3.4 is* quizzer.htm, *to which this page links back.*

```
<html>
<head><title>History Quiz</title></head>
<body>
<h1>History Quiz Answers</h1>
<p>1. ...fourteen hundred and ninety-two.<br />
2. ...fifteen hundred and eighty eight.<br />
3. ...sixteen hundred and sixty-six.<br />
4. ...nineteen hundred and sixty-nine.<br />
5. ...nineteen hundred and ninety-three.</p>
<p><a href="quizzer.htm">Click here for the questions.</a></p>
</body>
</html>
```

FIGURE 3.6

This is the quizzer.htm *file listed in Figure 3.4 and referred to by the link in Figure 3.5.*

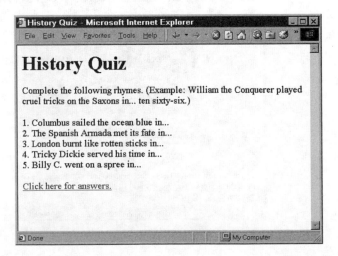

FIGURE 3.7

Click here for answers *in Figure 3.6 takes you here.* Click here for the questions *on this page is a link back to the page shown in Figure 3.6.*

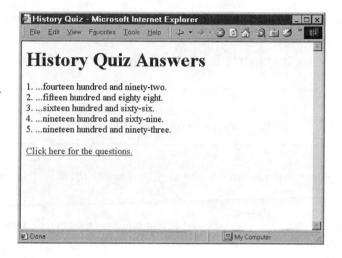

Using filenames instead of complete Internet addresses saves you a lot of typing. More importantly, the links between your pages will work properly no matter where the pages are located. You can test the links while the files are still on your computer's hard drive. You can then move them to a computer on the Internet, or to a CD-ROM or DVD disk, and all the links will still work correctly.

At the *24-Hour HTML Café*, you'll find some fun example pages demonstrating hypertext links, including a tour of Indigestible Ingestibles Research sites on the Internet and a light-hearted literary history quiz. These intriguing pages can be found, along with the other examples from this hour, at http://24hourhtmlcafe.com/hour3/.

Relative Addresses

If you have many pages, you'll want to put them in more than one directory folder. In that case, you still shouldn't use the full Internet address to link between them. You can use relative addresses, which include only enough information to find one page from another.

NEW TERM A *relative address* describes the path from one Web page to another, instead of a full (or *absolute*) Internet address.

For instance, suppose you are creating a page named zoo.htm in a directory folder named webpages on your hard drive. You want to include a link to a page named african.htm, which is in a subfolder named elephants within webpages. The link would look like the following:

```
<a href="elephants/african.htm">learn about african elephants.</a>
```

> The / forward slash is always used to separate directory folders in HTML.
> Don't use the \ backslash normally used in Windows and DOS!

The african.htm page might contain a link back to the main zoo.htm page:

```
<a href="../zoo.htm">return to the zoo.</a>
```

The double dot (..) is a special code that indicates the folder containing the current folder. (The .. means the same thing in DOS, Windows, Macintosh, and UNIX.)

You can then move these pages to another directory folder, disk drive, or Web server without changing the links, as long as you always put african.htm inside a subfolder named elephants.

Relative addresses can span quite complex directory structures if necessary; Hour 22, "Organizing and Managing a Web Site," offers more detailed advice for organizing and linking among large numbers of Web pages.

To Do

You probably created a page or two of your own while working through Hour 2, "Create a Web Page Right Now." Now is a great time to add a few more pages and link them together:

- Use a home page as a main entrance and central hub to which all your other pages are connected. If you created a page about yourself or your business in Hour 2, use that as your home page. You also might like to make a new page now for this purpose.

- On the home page, put a list of <a href> links to the other HTML files you've created (or plan to create soon). Be sure that the exact spelling of the filename, including any capitalization, is correct in every link.

- On each of the other pages, include a link at the bottom (or top) leading back to your home page. That makes it simple and easy to navigate around your site.

- You may also want to include a list of links to sites on the Internet, either on your home page or a separate hotlist page. People often include a list of their friends' personal pages on their own home page. (Businesses, however, should be careful not to lead potential customers away to other sites too quickly—there's no guarantee they'll come back!)

Remember to use only filenames (or *relative addressing*) for links between your own pages, but full Internet addresses for links to other sites.

> There is one good reason to sometimes use the complete address of your own pages in links. If someone saves one of your pages on his or her own hard drive, none of the links to your other pages from that page will work unless they include full Internet addresses.
>
> I like to include a link with the full address of my main home page at the bottom of every page, and use simple filenames or relative addresses in all the rest of the links.

Summary

The <a> tag is what makes hypertext "hyper." With it, you can create clickable links between pages, as well as links to specific anchor points on any page.

When creating links to other people's pages, include the full Internet address of each page in an <a href> tag. For links between your own pages, include just the filenames and enough directory information to get from one page to another.

Table 3.1 summarizes the <a> tag discussed in this hour.

TABLE 3.1 HTML Tag and Attribute Covered in Hour 3

Tag	Attribute	Function
<a>...</a>		With the href attribute, creates a link to another document or anchor.
	href="..."	The address of the document or anchor point to link to.

Q&A

Q When I make links, some of them are blue and some of them are purple. Why? How come most of the links I see on the Internet aren't blue and purple?

A A link appears blue to anyone who hasn't recently visited the page to which it points. Once you visit a page, any links to it turn purple. These colors can be (and often are) changed to match any color scheme a Web page author wants, so many links you see on the Web won't be blue and purple. (Hour 11, "Custom Backgrounds and Colors," tells how to change the colors of text and links on your Web pages.)

Q **What happens if I link to a page on the Internet and then the person who owns that page deletes or moves it?**

A That depends on how that person has set up his server computer. Usually, people see a message saying `page not found` or something to that effect when they click the link. They can still click the Back button to return to your page.

Q **One of my links works fine on my computer, but when I put the pages on the Internet it doesn't work anymore. What's up?**

A The most likely culprits are

- Capitalization problems. On Windows computers, linking to a file named `Freddy.htm` with `<a href="freddy.htm">` will work. On most Web servers (which are usually UNIX machines), the link must be `<a href="freddy.htm">` (or you must change the name of the file to `Freddy.htm`). To make matters worse, some text editors and file transfer programs actually change the capitalization without telling you!

- Spaces in filenames. Most Web servers don't allow filenames with spaces. For example, you should never name a Web page, `my page.htm`. Instead, call it `mypage.htm` or `MyPage.htm`.

  The next hour explains how to upload files to a Web site and how to rename files once they're online so that you can make sure the spelling and capitalization are perfect.

Workshop

Quiz

1. Your best friend from elementary school finds you on the Internet and says he wants to trade home page links. How do you put a link to his page at `www.cheapsuits.com/~billybob/` on your page?

2. Your home page will be at `http://www.mysite.com/home.htm` when you put it on the Internet. Write the HTML code to go on that page so that when someone clicks the words `all about me`, they see the page located at `http://www.mysite.com/mylife.htm`.

3. You plan to publish a CD-ROM disk containing HTML pages. How do you create a link from a page in the `\guide` directory folder to the `\guide\maine\katahdin.htm` page?

4. How about a link from `\guide\maine\katahdin.htm` to the `\guide\arizona\superstitions.htm` page?

Answers

1. Put the following on your page:

```
<a href="http://www.cheapsuits.com/~billybob/">
my buddy billy bob's page of inexpensive businesswear</a>
```

2. `<a href="mylife.htm">all about me</a>`

   The following would work equally well, although it would be harder to test on your hard drive:

   `<a href="http://www.mysite.com/mylife.htm">all about me</a>`

3. `<a href="maine/katahdin.htm">mount katahdin</a>`

4. `<a href="../arizona/superstitions.htm">`

   `the superstition range</a>`

Exercise

- To make a formatted list of your favorite sites, click the Bookmarks button in Netscape Navigator 4, click Edit Bookmarks, and then select File, Save As. You can then open that bookmark page in any text editor and add other text and HTML formatting as you prefer. (Alas, there's no easy way to export your Microsoft Internet Explorer favorites list as a single Web page.)

Hour **4**

Publishing Your HTML Pages

Here it is, the hour you've been waiting for! Your Web pages are ready for the world to see, and this hour explains how to get them to appear before the eyes of your intended audience.

The most obvious avenue for publishing Web pages is, of course, the Internet—but you may want to limit the distribution of your pages to a local intranet within your organization, instead of making them available to the general public. You may also choose to distribute your Web pages on CD-ROMs, floppy disks, Zip disks, or the new DVD-ROM disks.

This hour covers all of these options and offers advice for designing your pages to work best with whichever distribution method you choose.

NEW TERM An *intranet* is a private network with access restricted to one organization, but which uses the same technical standards and protocols as the global public Internet.

To Do

Before you read about publishing your pages, you should give some thought to which methods of distribution you will be using.

- If you want to reach only employees of your organization, publish on your local intranet only.

- If you want your pages to be visible to as many people as possible all over the world, Internet publishing is a must. However, don't rule out other distribution methods; you can easily adapt Internet-based pages for distribution on disks or local networks.

- If you want to provide very large graphics, multimedia, or other content that would be too slow to transfer over today's modems, consider publishing on a CD-ROM. You can easily link the CD-ROM to an Internet Web site and offer the CD-ROM to people who find you through the Internet, but want the "full experience."

- If you plan to make a presentation at a meeting and would also like to publish related material on the Internet or an intranet, why not use HTML instead of old-fashioned Powerpoint slides as a visual aid? I often give out floppy disks containing my HTML presentations to conference participants as well, with additional pages linked for them to explore on their own.

Setting Up an Internet Web Site

NEW TERM To make an HTML page part of the publicly accessible World Wide Web, you need to put it on a *Web server* (a computer permanently connected to the Internet and equipped to send out Web pages on request). If you run your own Web server, this procedure is simply a matter of copying the file to the right directory folder. Most people use a Web server run by an Internet service provider (ISP) to host their pages.

Almost all ISPs that offer Internet access also now offer space in which to place your own personal Web pages for little or no additional cost, though you may have to pay extra if your site attracts a huge number of visitors or includes very large multimedia files.

Prices for a business site start well under $100 per month, but you usually pay more when lots of people start viewing your pages. For a site with about a hundred different Web pages, I have paid as little as $20 per month when a few thousand people looked at my pages, and as much as $2,000 per month when hundreds of thousands of people looked at my pages.

Don't think that you have to use the same local company that provides you with Internet access to host your pages. If you run a high-traffic business Web site, you may save a lot of money and get more reliable service from a company in another city. For example, I use a company in Vermont to access the Internet, but a different company in Boston hosts my Web site.

To comparison shop the hosting services offered by various Internet service providers, go to the list of ISPs at `http://thelist.internet.com/`.

Free Web hosting services such as Geocities (`www.geocities.com`), Tripod (`www.tripod.com`), and Angelfire (`www.angelfire.com`) are very popular with Web page authors—and yes, they really are free—though most such services require that you include advertisements of their choosing on your pages.

One of the most important choices you'll need to make when you set up a Web site is the name you want to use as the site's address.

If you don't pay at least $70 up front and $35 a year to maintain your own domain name, your site's address will include the name of your Internet service provider (`http://www.shore.net/~smith/` is an example). If you're willing to pay for it, you can choose any name that isn't already used by another company (`http://mister-smith.com/` for example).

You can check to see if the name you want is already in use at `http://domain-registration.com/`. Once you find a name that isn't already taken, ask your Internet service provider to help you apply for that name as soon as possible.

Transferring Pages to a Web Server

When a Web server computer sends Web pages to people through the Internet, it uses an information exchange standard called Hypertext Transfer Protocol (HTTP). To upload a page to your Web site, however, you usually need software that uses an older communications standard called File Transfer Protocol (FTP).

New Term *File Transfer Protocol* is the standard that your file transfer software must adhere to when sending files to a Web server. The server then sends those files out to anyone who asks for them using the Hypertext Transfer Protocol.

You'll need to get four important pieces of information from your Web hosting service company before you can put pages up on your Web site:

1. Your *account name* (sometimes called a *username* or *user ID*). If the same company provides you with both Internet access and Web hosting, the account name for your Web site will probably be the same as your email account name.

2. Your *password*. This may also be the same as your email password.

3. The *FTP address* for your site. Note that this address may or may not be the same as the address people go to when they read your Web pages.

4. The *directory* folder where your Web page files should be placed. You can sometimes place them in the root directory, but often you need to go into a subdirectory named www or public, or the same as your domain name.

Next, you need to decide which software you'll use to send your pages to the Web server and maintain your site. This hour covers four options:

- Netscape Navigator
- Microsoft Internet Explorer
- Microsoft FrontPage (or similar Web site management software)
- CuteFTP (or similar FTP software)

Which of these do I recommend? It depends on your situation. If you plan on developing a complex Web site, you will find that a program such as Microsoft FrontPage saves you a lot of time by helping manage changing links between pages and automatically keeping track of which pages have changed and need updating. However, for the beginning Web page author and anyone who only plans to have a modest site with a few personal or business pages, it's easier to learn and use a simple program such as CuteFTP. If you just want to get your first page online without bothering to set up any new software at all, you can get the job done with the Web browser you already have. Microsoft Internet Explorer 5 is a better choice than Netscape Navigator 4 in this regard because Navigator doesn't yet allow you to delete and rename files once you put them online. (Navigator 5 should have this capability once it's released, though.)

If you're still not sure after reading the preceding paragraph, you should probably skip ahead to the section called "Publishing Pages with CuteFTP." For most readers of this book, that's likely to be the best choice overall.

Publishing Pages with Netscape Navigator

Many people don't realize that the Netscape Navigator Web browser can also upload pages to a Web server. Follow these steps:

1. Enter the address of your Web directory in Netscape Navigator's Location box, as in the following example:

`ftp://myname:mypassword@siteaddress.net/home/web/wherever/`

Put your account name and password for accessing the site instead of *myname* and *mypassword*, the FTP address for your site instead of *siteaddress.net*, and the top-level directory where your Web pages reside instead of */home/web/wherever/*.

2. Select File, Upload File, as shown in Figure 4.1. (If you are using Netscape Navigator version 2 or 3, you must drag the file into the Netscape window from Windows Explorer or another file management program because the Upload File menu choice is new in Navigator version 4.)

3. Choose the file you want to upload and click Open. Wait while the files are transferred.

4. Test your page by clicking the HTML file you just uploaded in the FTP directory listing (in the Netscape window). You're on the Web!

FIGURE 4.1

You can connect to your Web hosting service and publish your HTML pages using Netscape Navigator 4's Upload File feature.

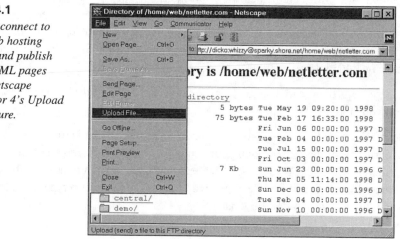

4

Even though Netscape Navigator can send files to any Web server on the Internet, specialized FTP programs such as CuteFTP and WS_FTP offer much more control for managing your Web pages. For example, Navigator doesn't give you any way to delete an old Web page or change the name of a Web page on the server computer. For these reasons, you'll definitely want something more than Navigator to maintain your Web site.

Netscape Composer is a Web page editing and publishing program designed to be tightly integrated with the Netscape Navigator Web browser. I don't recommend that you use Composer when learning HTML because the current version hides the actual HTML behind a complex graphical interface and often makes serious errors when creating HTML for you.

Once you finish this book, you will be savvy enough to correct the HTML errors Netscape Composer makes, and you may find it useful. Meanwhile, you will probably find it much less frustrating to publish your Web pages with a good old-fashioned text editor and one of the simple file transfer programs discussed in this hour.

Publishing Pages with Microsoft Internet Explorer

As you might guess from the name, Microsoft Internet Explorer was designed to work just like the Microsoft Explorer file manager that comes with Windows. When you enter an FTP address in the Address bar of Internet Explorer 5, you can cut, paste, delete, and rename any file or directory folder on the Web server just as if it were on your computer's own hard drive.

Follow these steps to upload a page you've created on your hard drive so that it will appear on your Internet Web site:

1. Start Microsoft Internet Explorer. In the Address bar, enter the drive letter and folder name of the directory on your computer where the page you created is currently located (`c:\webpages\` is an example), and press Enter. Note that going to the folder by selecting File, Open won't work—you have to type the folder name directly into the Address bar.

2. Click once on the file you want to upload to your Web site to highlight it. As in any Windows program, you can select multiple files by holding down the Shift or Ctrl key as you click on the files. Be sure to include any graphics files (see Hour 10) that need to go with the HTML file.

3. Select Edit, Copy (see Figure 4.2).

4. Now use the following format to enter your account name, password, and site address in the Address bar:

    `ftp://myname:mypassword@siteaddress.net/home/web/wherever/`

    Put your account name and password for accessing the site instead of *myname* and *mypassword*, the FTP address for your site instead of *siteaddress.net*, and the top-level directory where your Web pages go on the server instead of */home/web/wherever/*. Then press Enter.

FIGURE 4.2
To upload a page using Microsoft Internet Explorer, first go to the file folder where the files are on your own computer and select Edit, Copy.

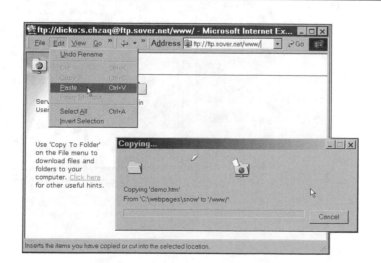

5. Select Edit, Paste. The file will be transferred from your hard drive to the Web server (see Figure 4.3).

To delete or rename a file or folder on the Web server, right-click it and select Delete or Rename, just as you would with local files in an Windows application.

You can take the first three steps described earlier with Windows Explorer instead of Internet Explorer. You can also drag and drop files from Windows Explorer into Internet Explorer.

FIGURE 4.3
Microsoft Internet Explorer uses the familiar Windows Explorer interface to paste files into folders on a distant Web server computer.

4

Okay, I lied. It isn't quite true that Internet Explorer treats FTP sites exactly the same as a local hard drive. The exception to this rule is that you cannot directly transfer a file from one folder on an FTP site to another folder on an FTP site. If you want to do that, you need to transfer the file to your hard drive first and then transfer it back to the new location on the FTP site.

Publishing Pages with Microsoft FrontPage

More sophisticated programs such as Microsoft FrontPage 2000 turn publishing your entire Web site into a one-step, automated process. Whether you've created one or one hundred pages, you can put them all online by selecting File, Publish Web (see Figure 4.4). The first time you do so, you are asked to specify the location to publish your Web to, which simply means to enter the FTP address your Web hosting service gave you (or the HTTP address, if the Web server has FrontPage extensions installed).

You are then asked to enter your account name and password. FrontPage automatically uploads all pages that you've changed since your last update. Other software—including Macromedia DreamWeaver, NetObjects Fusion, and Adobe PageMill—also offers automated uploading and site management features.

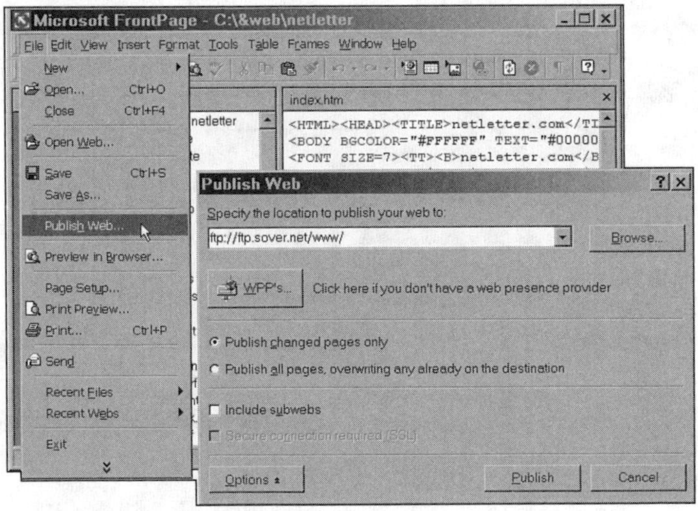

FIGURE 4.4

Microsoft FrontPage makes it easy to upload many pages at once—or to upload just those pages you made changes to.

Be very careful to include the correct subdirectory when you tell FrontPage where to publish the Web. For example, my Web host (sover.net) requires my pages to go in a directory folder named www, so I must publish to

ftp.sover.net/www/

I once forgot to include the www/ at the end, and before I knew it FrontPage had placed a large number of pages in the wrong directory. FrontPage does-n't offer any easy way to delete those pages without deleting them from my hard drive, so I ended up using another FTP program to get rid of them.

Publishing Pages with CuteFTP

Figure 4.5 shows one of the most popular FTP programs—CuteFTP for Windows. You can download a free copy of CuteFTP (see the following "To Do" section) although CuteFTP does require a modest registration fee for business users. (See the documentation that comes with the program for details.)

Similar programs are available for Macintosh computers (Fetch is a favorite), and FTP utilities come preinstalled on most UNIX computers. You can find these and other FTP programs at www.shareware.com.

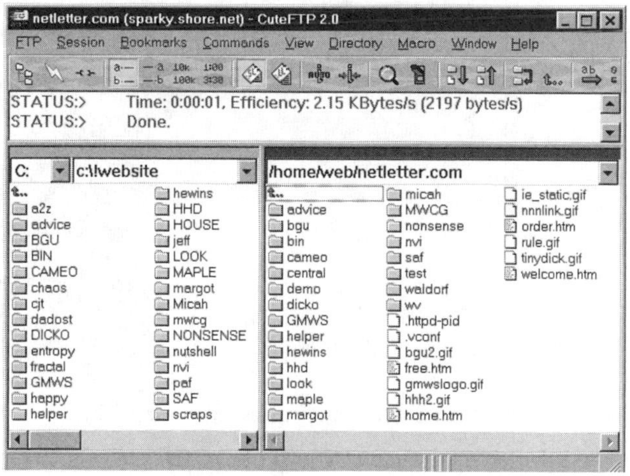

FIGURE 4.5

CuteFTP is a powerful and user-friendly FTP program that individuals can use for free.

4

To Do

I recommend that you download CuteFTP now and use it to send some files to your own Web site as you read on (if you have a Web site set up, that is).

- Go to the CuteFTP home page at `www.cuteftp.com/` and follow the "Download CuteFTP" links.

- Once the download is complete, run the self-extracting `.exe` program, which installs the CuteFTP program.

No matter which FTP program you choose, transferring your Web pages to a Web server involves the following steps. (The steps are illustrated here with CuteFTP, but other FTP programs work similarly.)

1. Before you can access the Web server, you must tell your FTP program its address, as well as your account name and password. In CuteFTP, select a category for your site in the FTP Site Manager window (Personal Web Sites in Figure 4.6), and click Add Site to access the Edit Host dialog box shown in Figure 4.7.

FIGURE 4.6

CuteFTP includes an intuitive FTP site manager although most Web page authors need only a single FTP site entry.

FTP Site Manager		×
🗀 FTP Sites	netletter.com	
⊞ 🗀 Public software archives		
├ 🗀 Company home sites		
├ 🗀 Applications home sites		
└ 🗀 **Personal FTP Sites**		

Add site   Delete site   Edit site
Comments
Host: sparky.share.net
My primary Web site

Add folder   Delete folder   Rename folder   Import   Connect   Exit

2. Here's how to fill in each of the items in Figure 4.7:

- Site Label is the name you'll use to refer to your own site. Nobody else will see this name, so enter whatever you want.

- Host Address is the FTP address of the Web server to which you need to send your Web pages. This usually (but not always) starts with `ftp`. Notice that it may or may not resemble the address that other people will use to view your Web pages. The ISP that runs your Web server will be able to tell you the correct address to enter here.

FIGURE 4.7

Clicking Add Site or Edit Site in Figure 4.3 brings up this dialog box.

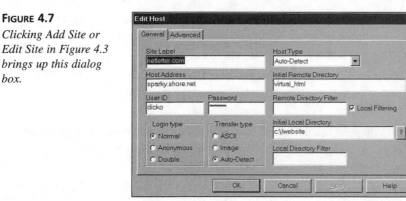

- The company that runs the Web server also issues User ID and Password. Be aware that CuteFTP (and most other FTP programs) remember your password automatically, which means that anyone who has physical access to your computer can modify your Web site.

- You should set the Login Type to Normal unless somebody important tells you otherwise. (The Anonymous setting is for downloading files from public FTP services that don't require user IDs or passwords.)

- Set the Transfer Type to Auto-Detect. (This automatically sends HTML and other text files using a slightly different protocol than images and other non-text files, to ensure complete compatibility with all types of computers.)

- The Host Type should also be set to Auto-Detect, unless you have trouble connecting. In that case, you need to find out what type of computer you're connecting to and pick the corresponding Host Type.

- For the Initial Remote Directory, fill in the name of the main directory folder on the Web server where your Web pages will be located. The people who run your Web server will tell you that directory's name. (In some cases, you don't need to enter anything here because the Web server computer will automatically put you in the directory when you connect to it.)

- You can leave Remote Directory Filter and Local Directory Filter both blank. (This is where you would enter wildcards such as *.htm* if you want to see files ending only in .htm or .html when you connect to this site. All other files, such as .gif and .jpg, would then be ignored.)

- For the Initial Local Directory, enter the drive and directory folder on your computer's hard drive where you keep your Web pages.

4

- Normally, you won't need to change any settings on the Advanced tab unless you experience problems with your connection. If that happens, have your ISP help you figure out the best settings.

3. When you click OK, you'll go back to the window shown in Figure 4.6. Make sure you are connected to the Internet; click Connect to establish a connection with the Web server computer.

   Most server computers issue a short message to everyone who connects to them. Many FTP programs ignore this message, but CuteFTP presents it to you. It seldom says anything important, so just click OK.

4. Once you're connected to the server, you'll see two lists of files, as shown earlier in Figure 4.5. The left window pane lists the files on your computer, while the right pane lists the files on the server computer.

   To transfer a Web page to the server, select the HTML file and any accompanying image files in the left window. (Remember that you can hold down the Ctrl key and click with the mouse to select multiple files in any Windows program.) Then select Commands, Upload (see Figure 4.8), or click the Upload button on the toolbar.

   As you can see, the same menu contains commands that delete or rename files (either on your computer or on the server), as well as commands to make and change directory folders.

> Most Web servers have a special name for the file that should be sent if a user doesn't include a specific filename when he requests a page. For example, if you go to http://netletter.com/, my Web server will automatically give you the welcome.htm file. Other Web servers use different names for the default file, such as index.html.
>
> Be sure to ask your ISP for the default filename so you can give your home page that name.

5. You can immediately view the page you just put on the Web server by using Netscape Navigator or Microsoft Internet Explorer.

6. When you're done sending and modifying files on the Web server, select FTP, Disconnect to close the connection.

The next time you need to upload some Web pages, you won't need to fill in all the information in step 2. You can just click Connect, select the pages you want to send, and click the Upload button.

FIGURE **4.8**

To send files to the server, select Commands, Upload in CuteFTP.

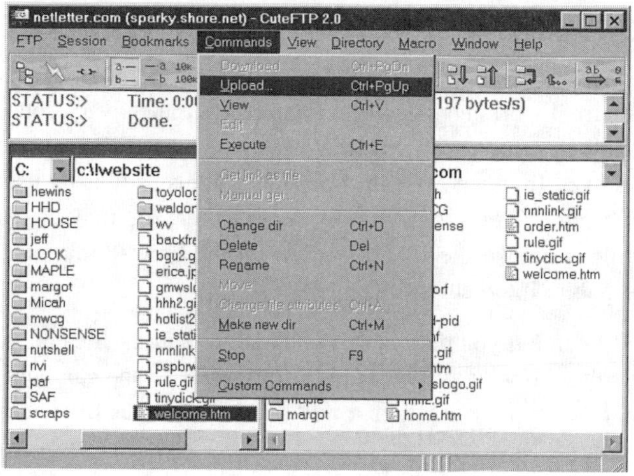

![CuteFTP window screenshot]

Most Web servers are set up so that any documents placed onto them are immediately made available to the entire World Wide Web. However, a few require that users manually change file permission settings, which control who is allowed to access individual files. Your ISP can tell you exactly how to change permission settings on its server and whether it's necessary to do so.

Making a File Available for Downloading

Many Web authors want to know how to make a file that isn't a Web page available for downloading from a Web site. A zip archive and an .exe program are good examples of such files.

Just upload the file to your Web site, following the instructions in this hour for uploading. Create a link to the file on one of your Web pages, as explained in Hour 3. For example, if the file were called neatgame.zip, the link would look like this:

```
<a href="neatgame.zip">Click here to download a neat game i wrote.</a>
```

You might want to put a reminder somewhere near the link telling people that the easiest way to download the file is to right-click (or, if you're a Macintosh user, hold down the mouse button) on the link and select Save Link As from the pop-up menu. (It also works fine if people just click the link normally.)

Remember that some Web host services charge by the number of bytes sent out, so if 10,000 people a day download a 2,000,000-byte file from your site, it might start costing you some serious money and overburden your Web server.

Putting Web Pages on an Intranet

The outlined procedure for sending pages to a public Internet server is fairly standard, but the internal workings of private corporate intranets vary considerably from company to company. In some cases, you may need to use an FTP program to send files to an intranet server. In others, you may be able to transfer files by using the same file management program you use on your own computer. You may also need to adjust permission settings or make special allowances for the firewall that insulates a private intranet from the public Internet.

About all I can tell you here in this book about putting files on your company's intranet is to consult with your systems administrator. He or she can help you put your Web pages on the company server in a way that best ensures their accessibility and security.

Publishing Web Pages on Disk

Unless you were hired to create documents for a company intranet, you have probably assumed that the Internet is the best way to get your pages in front of the eyes of the world. There are, however, three major incentives for considering distribution on some form of disk instead:

- Currently, more people have disk drives than Internet connections.
- Disks can deliver information to the computer screen much faster than people can download it from the Internet.
- You can distribute disks to a select audience, regardless of whether they are connected to the Internet or any particular intranet.

In the not-too-distant future, as Web-enabled televisions and high-speed networks become more commonplace, these advantages may disappear. For now, publishing on disk can be an excellent way to provide a bigger, faster, more tightly targeted Web presentation than you can on today's Internet.

Publishing on 1.44MB floppy disks or 100MB Zip disks is simply a matter of copying files from your hard disk with any file management program. You just need to keep in mind that any links starting with `http://` will work only if and when someone reading your pages is also connected to the Internet. The cost is currently about $0.50 per floppy disk, or $10 per Zip disk, plus any delivery or mailing costs.

> Never use drive letters (such as C:) in <a href> link tags on your Web pages;
> otherwise, they won't work when you copy the files to a different disk.
> Refer to Hour 3 for more details on how to make links that will work both
> on disk and on the Internet.

Publishing on CD-ROM or on the new DVD-ROM disks isn't much more complicated;
you either need a drive (and accompanying software) capable of creating the disks, or
you can send the files to a disk mastering and duplication company. Costs for CD-ROM
duplication vary a lot, depending on how many disks you need. If you buy fewer than a
hundred CD-ROMs, it may cost more than $10 per disk. For thousands of copies, expect
to pay less than $1 each plus delivery or mailing costs. DVD-ROM pricing hasn't settled
down yet, but it will eventually be similar to CD-ROM.

> Web browser software is always necessary for reading HTML pages.
> However, these days almost everyone has a Web browser, so you may not
> need to supply one with your Web pages. If you do want to include a
> browser, you might consider Opera, which includes most of the basic fea-
> tures of Netscape Navigator and Microsoft Internet Explorer but is small
> enough to fit on a single 1.44MB floppy disk and can be freely distributed in
> the form of a 30-day evaluation version. (You can download Opera at
> www.operasoftware.com.)
>
> Microsoft and Netscape are also often willing to allow their browsers to be
> included on CD-ROMs if you ask nicely in writing or pay them a licensing
> fee. Never give out copies of Microsoft or Netscape software without writ-
> ten permission, since these companies have Big Scary Lawyers who just love
> that sort of thing.

4

Testing Your Pages

Whenever you transfer Web pages to a disk, Internet site, or intranet server, you should
immediately test every page thoroughly.

The following checklist will help make sure everything on your pages behaves the way
you expected.

1. Before you transfer the pages, follow all of these steps to test the pages while
   they're on your hard drive. After you transfer the pages to the master disk or Web
   server, test them again—if your pages are on the Internet, preferably through a
   28.8Kbps modem connection.

2. Do each of the following steps with the latest version of Netscape Navigator, the latest Microsoft Internet Explorer, and at least one other browser such as DOS Lynx or Opera. Testing with an older version of Navigator or Internet Explorer isn't such a bad idea since many people still use outdated versions and some pages will appear differently.

3. Make sure the computer you're testing with is set to a 16-color video mode or, at most, a 256-color mode. (Pages look better in higher color modes, but you want to see the "bad news" of how they'll look to people with cheap video hardware.) Also, try several different brightness settings on your monitor and (if possible) change the color balance of your monitor to make sure your pages still look okay on displays that are more blue or red than yours.

4. If possible, use a computer with 800×600 resolution for testing purposes, but adjust the size of the browser window to exactly 640×480 pixels. On each page, use the maximize button on the corner of the window to switch back and forth between full 800×600 resolution and 640×480 resolution. If pages look good at these two resolutions, they'll probably look fine at larger resolutions, too. (Additional testing at 1,024×768 or 1,600×1,200 resolution can't hurt.)

5. Turn off auto image loading in Netscape Navigator before you start testing, so you can see what each page looks like without the graphics. Check your ALT tag messages and then click the Load Images button on the toolbar to load the graphics and review the page carefully again.

6. Use your browser's font size settings to look at each page in a variety of font sizes, to ensure that your careful layout doesn't fall to pieces.

7. Start at the home page and systematically follow every link. (Use the Back button to return after each link, and then click the next link on the page.)

8. Wait for each page to completely finish loading, and scroll all the way down to make sure all images appear where they should.

9. If you have a complex site, it may help to make a checklist of all the pages on your site to ensure they all get tested.

10. Time how long it takes each page to load through a 28.8Kbps modem, preferably when connected through a different ISP than the one that runs the Web server. Multiply that time by 2 to find out how long 14.4Kbps-modem users will have to wait to see the page. Is the information on that page valuable enough to keep them from going elsewhere before the page finishes loading?

If your pages pass all those tests, you can be pretty certain that they'll look great to every Internet surfer in the world.

Summary

This hour gave you the basic knowledge you need to choose among the most common distribution methods for Web pages. It also stepped you through the process of placing Web pages on a Web server computer by using commonly available file transfer software. Finally, it offered a checklist to help you thoroughly test your Web pages once they are in place.

Q&A

Q When I try to send pages to my Web site from home, it works fine. When I try it from the computer at work, I get error messages. Any idea what the problem might be?

A The company where you work probably has a *firewall*, which is a layer of security protecting their local network from tampering via the Internet. You need to set some special configuration options in your FTP program to help it get through the firewall when you send files. Your company's network administrator can help you with the details.

Q I don't know which ISP to choose—there are so many!

A Obviously, you should compare prices of the companies listed at `http://thelist.internet.com`. You should also ask for the names of some customers with sites about the same size you're planning on having; ask those customers (via email) how happy they are with the company's service and support. Also, make sure that your ISP has at least two major (T3 or bigger) links to the Internet, preferably provided to them by two different network companies.

Q All the tests you recommend would take longer than creating my pages! Can't I get away with less testing?

A If your pages aren't intended to make money or provide an important service, it's probably not a big deal if they look funny to some people or produce errors once in a while. In that case, just test each page with a couple of different window and font sizes and call it good. However, if you need to project a professional image, there is no substitute for rigorous testing.

Q I wanted to name my site `jockitch.com` but Proctor & Gamble beat me to it. Is there anything I can do?

A Well, if your company were named Jockitch, Inc., before Proctor & Gamble registered the domain name, you could always try suing them, but even if you don't have the budget to take on their legal army, you may still be able to register `jockitch.org` or `jockitch.net` (if P&G doesn't scoop you again).

4

Workshop

Quiz

1. How do you put a few Web pages on a floppy disk?

2. Suppose your ISP tells you to put your pages in the `/top/user/~elroy` directory at `ftp.bigisp.net`, that your username is `rastro`, and that your password is `rorry_relroy`. You have the Web pages all ready to go in the `\webpages` folder on your C drive. Where do you put all that information in CuteFTP so you can get the files on the Internet?

3. What address would you enter in Netscape Navigator to view the Web pages you uploaded in question 2?

4. If the following Web page is named `mypage.htm`, which files would you need to transfer to the Web server to put it on the Internet?

```
<html><head><title>My Page</title></head>
<body background="joy.gif">
<img src="me.jpg" align="right" />
<h1>My Web Page</h1>
<p>Oh happy joy I have a page on the Web!</p>
<a href="otherpage.htm">Click here for my other page.</a>
</body></html>
```

Answers

1. Just copy the HTML files and image files from your hard drive to the disk. Anyone can then insert the disk in his or her computer, start the Web browser, and open the pages right from the floppy.

2. Click Add Site in the FTP Site Manager window, and then enter the following information:

3. You can't tell from the information given in question 2. A good guess would be `http://www.bigisp.net/~elroy/`, but you might choose a completely different domain name, such as `http://elroy-and-astro.com/`.

4. You need to transfer all three of the following files into the same directory on the Web server:

   ```
   mypage.htm
   joy.jpg
   me.gif
   ```

   If you want the link on that page to work, you must also transfer this one, as well as any image files that are referred to in that HTML file:

   ```
   otherpage.htm
   ```

Exercise

- Put your pages on the Internet already!

4

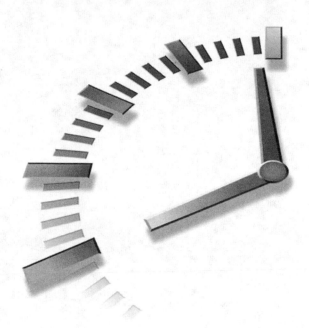

PART II

Web Page Text

Hour

Hour 5

Text Alignment and Lists

When you present information on paper (or with a good old-fashioned over-head projector), you probably often include lists of numbered steps or bullet points. You've also undoubtedly written many indented lists to organize information such as terms and their definitions or the outline of a business plan. Because lists are so common, HTML provides tags that automatically indent text and add numbers or bullets in front of each listed item.

In this hour you find out how to center text or align it to the right side of the page. You also see how to format numbered and bulleted lists, and how the HTML tags for creating definition lists can also be used for almost any other type of indentation you want on your Web pages.

To do these things, you need a few more HTML tags. You'll also need to learn how to control optional settings (called *attributes*) for some of the tags you already know.

To Do

You can make the most of this hour if you have some text that needs to be indented or centered to be presentable.

- Any type of outline, bullet points from a presentation, numbered steps, glossary, or list of textual information from a database will serve as good material with which to work.

- If the text you'll be using is from a word processor or database program, be sure to save it to a new file in plain text or ASCII format. You can then add the appropriate HTML tags to format it as you go through this chapter.

Text Alignment

Some HTML tags allow you to specify a variety of options, or attributes, along with the basic tag itself. For example, when you begin a paragraph with the <p> tag you can specify whether the text in that paragraph should be aligned to the left margin, right margin, or center of the page.

To align a paragraph to the right margin, you can put `align="right"` inside the <p> tag at the beginning of the paragraph. To center a paragraph, use `<p align="center">`. Similarly, the tag to align a paragraph to the left is `<p align="left">`. (This is seldom used because paragraphs are always aligned to the left when you use plain old <p>.)

The word `align` is called an attribute of the <p> tag. You can use the `align` attribute with just about any HTML tag that contains text, including <h1>, <h2>, the other heading tags, and some tags you will meet later. There are many other attributes besides `align`. You will find out how to use them as you learn more HTML tags.

NEW TERM   *Attributes* are special code words used inside an HTML tag to control exactly what the tag does.

According to the official HTML 4 standard, it doesn't matter whether tags and attributes are in uppercase or lowercase letters. However, the newer XHTML standard will require tags and attributes to be lowercase, so it's a very good idea to make all your HTML lowercase now for future compatibility. The new standard will also require quotation marks around attribute values.

For example, the following is technically okay now:

```
<P ALIGN=CENTER>
```

If you want to stay compatible with upcoming standards and software, you should always use the following instead:

```
<p align="center">
```

> Keep in mind that sometimes the same attribute word can have different meanings when used with different tags. For instance, you will discover in Hour 10, "Putting Graphics on a Web Page," that align="left" does something quite different when used with the <img> image tag than it does with the text tags discussed in this chapter.

When you want to set the alignment of more than one paragraph or heading at a time, you can use the align attribute with the <div>, or *division*, tag. By itself, <div> and its corresponding closing </div> tag actually don't do anything at all—which would seem to make it a peculiarly useless tag!

Yet if you include an align attribute, <div> becomes quite useful indeed. Everything you put between <div align="center"> and </div>, for example, is centered. This may include lines of text, paragraphs, headings, images, and all the other things you'll learn how to put on Web pages in upcoming chapters. Likewise, <div align="right"> will right-align everything down to the next </div> tag.

Figure 5.1 demonstrates the align attribute with both the <p> and <div> tags. The results are shown in Figure 5.2. You'll learn many more advanced uses of the <div> tag in Hour 16, "Using Style Sheets," and Hour 20, "Setting Pages in Motion with Dynamic HTML."

5

FIGURE 5.1

The align *attribute allows you to left-justify, right-justify, or center text.*

```
<html><head><title>Bohemia</title></head>
<body>
<div align="center">
   <h2>Bohemia</h2>
   <b>by Dorothy Parker</b>
</div>
<p align="left">
Authors and actors and artists and such<br />
Never know nothing, and never know much.<br />
Sculptors and singers and those of their kidney<br />
Tell their affairs from Seattle to Sydney.</p>
<p align="center">
Playwrights and poets and such horses' necks<br />
Start off from anywhere, end up at sex.<br />
Diarists, critics, and similar roe<br />
Never say nothing, and never say no.</p>
<p align="right">
People Who Do Things exceed my endurance;<br />
God, for a man that solicits insurance!</p>
</body></html>
```

The Three Types of HTML Lists

There are three basic types of HTML lists. All three are shown in Figure 5.3, and Figure
5.4 reveals the HTML to construct them:

- The bulleted list is called an *unordered list*. It opens with the `<ul>` tag and closes
  with `</ul>`. It looks just like an ordered list, except that bullets appear at each `<li>`
  tag instead of numbers.

- The numbered list at the top is called an *ordered list*. It begins with the `<ol>` tag
  and ends with a closing `</ol>` tag. Numbers and line breaks appear automatically
  at each `<li>` tag, and the entire list is indented.

- The list of terms and their meanings is called a *definition list*. It starts with the
  `<dl>` and ends with `</dl>`. The `<dt>` tag goes in front of each term to be defined,
  with a `<dd>` tag in front of each definition. Line breaks and indentations appear
  automatically.

NEW TERM   *Ordered lists* are indented lists that have numbers or letters in front of each item.
Unordered lists are indented lists with a special bullet symbol in front of each
item. *Definition lists* are indented lists without any number or symbol in front of each
item.

Figure 5.3

The three types of HTML lists, as they appear in Netscape Navigator.

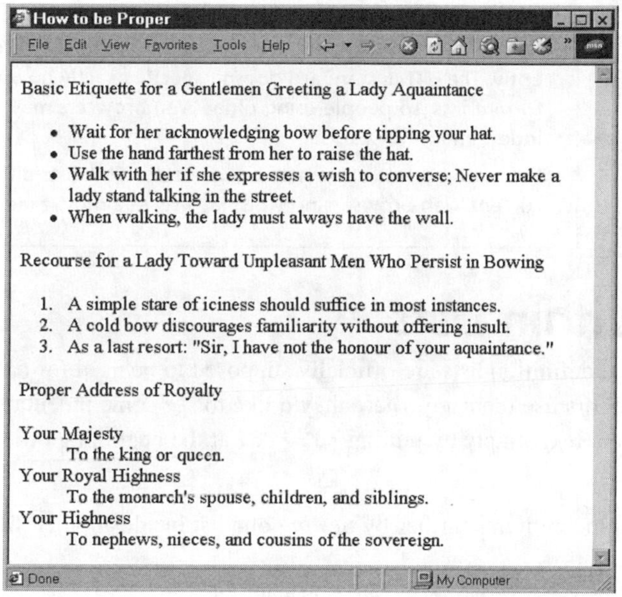

Figure 5.4

Use <ul> and <li> for unordered lists, <ol> and <li> for ordered lists, and <dl>, <dt>, and <dd> for definition lists.

```html
<html><head><title>How to be Proper</title></head>
<body>
Basic Etiquette for a Gentlemen Greeting a Lady Aquaintance
<ul>
<li>Wait for her acknowledging bow before tipping your
hat.</li>
<li>Use the hand farthest from her to raise the hat.</li>
<li>Walk with her if she expresses a wish to converse; Never
make a lady stand talking in the street.</li>
<li>When walking, the lady must always have the wall.</li>
</ul>
Recourse for a Lady Toward Unpleasant Men Who Persist in Bowing
<ol>
<li>A simple stare of iciness should suffice in most
instances.</li>
<li>A cold bow discourages familiarity without offering
insult.</li>
<li>As a last resort: "Sir, I have not the honour of your
aquaintance."</li>
</ol>
Proper Address of Royalty
<dl>
<dt>Your Majesty</dt>
<dd>To the king or queen.</dd>
<dt>Your Royal Highness</dt>
<dd>To the monarch's spouse, children, and siblings.</dd>
<dt>Your Highness</dt>
<dd>To nephews, nieces, and cousins of the sovereign.</dd>
</dl>
</body></html>
```

5

Remember that different Web browsers can display Web pages quite differently. The HTML standard doesn't specify exactly how Web browsers should
format lists, so people using older Web browsers may not see the same
indentation that you see.

Software of the future may also format HTML lists differently, although all
current Web browsers now display lists in almost exactly the same way.

Lists Within Lists

Although definition lists are officially supposed to be used for defining terms, many Web
page authors use them anywhere they'd like to see some indentation. In practice, you can
indent any text simply by putting <dl><dd> at the beginning of it and </dd></dl> at the
end.

You can indent items further by *nesting* one list inside another, like the following:

```
<dl><dd>this item will be indented</dd>
<dl><dd>this will be indented further</dd>
<dl><dl><dd>and this will be indented very far indeed</dd>
</dl></dl></dl></dl>
```

Just make sure you always have the same number of closing </dl> tags as opening <dl>
tags.

Ordered and unordered lists can also be nested inside one another, down to as many levels as you want. In Figure 5.5, a complex indented outline is constructed from several
unordered lists. You'll notice in Figure 5.6 that Netscape Navigator automatically uses a
different type of bullet for each of the first three levels of indentation, making the list
very easy to read.

As shown in Figure 5.6, Netscape Navigator (and Microsoft Internet Explorer) will normally use a solid disc for the first-level bullet, a hollow circle for the second-level bullet,
and a solid square for all deeper levels. However, you can explicitly choose which type
of bullet to use for any level by using <ul type="disc">, <ul type="circle">, or <ul
type="square"> instead of <ul>.

You can even change the bullet for any single point in an unordered list by using the
type attribute in the <li> tag. For example, the following would display a hollow circle
in front of the words Extra and Super, but a solid square in front of the word Special:

```
<ul type="circle">
<li>extra</li>
<li>super</li>
<li type="square">special</li>
</ul>
```

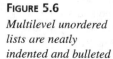

FIGURE 5.5

You can build elaborate outlines by placing lists within lists.

```
<html><head><title>Gloves</title></head>
<body>
<h2>Gloves</h2>
<ul><li><b>Power</b>
    <ul><li>Sega VR</li>
        <li>Surgical</li>
        <li>Elbow length, white</li>
    </ul></li>
    <li><b>Rec</b>
    <ul><li><b>Sporting</b>
        <ul><li>Boxing</li>
            <li>Driving</li>
            <li>Biking</li>
        </ul></li>
        <li><b>Evening</b>
        <ul><li>Elbow length, black</li>
            <li>Latex</li>
        </ul></li>
    </ul></li>
    <li><b>Cute</b>
    <ul><li>Swedish, fake fur</li>
        <li>Kid</li>
        <li>Golf</li>
    </ul></li>
</ul>
</body></html>
```

FIGURE 5.6

Multilevel unordered lists are neatly indented and bulleted for readability.

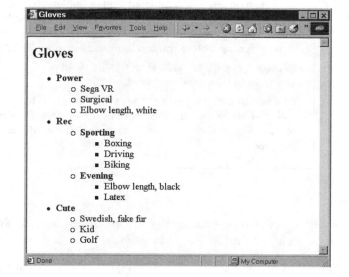

The type attribute also works with ordered lists, but instead of choosing a type of bullet, you choose the type of numbers or letters to place in front of each item. Figure 5.7 shows how to use roman numerals (`type="I"`), capital letters (`type="A"`), and lowercase letters (`type="a"`) along with ordinary numbers in a multilevel list. In Figure 5.8, you can see the resulting nicely formatted outline.

Although Figure 5.7 only uses the `type` attribute with the `<ol>` tag, you can also use it for specific `<li>` tags within a list (though it's hard to imagine a situation where you would want to). You can also explicitly specify ordinary numbering with `type="1"`, and you can make lowercase roman numerals with `type="i"`.

Here's one more seldom-used but handy-when-you-need-it trick: You can start an ordered list with any number (or letter) with the `start` attribute. `<ol start="3">`, for example, starts a numbered list at 3 instead of 1. Individual points can be renumbered with the `value` attribute (`<li value="12">` for example).

Note that you must always use numbers with the `start` and `value` attributes. To make a list that starts with the letter C, for example, you need to type `<ol type="A" start="3">`.

By combining ordered, unordered, and definition lists within one another, you can organize the most complex information in a readable and attractive way. To get your creative juices flowing, I've created a list of lists for you to browse through before you begin organizing your own HTML lists.

To check it out, go to the 24-Hour HTML Café at `http://24hourhtmlcafe.com/hour5/`.

Click the list-o-mania link and have some fun trying to figure out what the real titles of the example lists might be, based on the information they contain. Answers are given—as a nested HTML list, of course—at the end of the page.

To Do

Take a list or two of your own and try to find the best way to present the information so it can be easily understood.

1. Which type of list or combination of list types best suits your list? Use ordered lists only for lists that do actually have a natural order to them. Try to avoid more than seven bullet points in a row in any unordered list; otherwise, the list will be hard to read. Use definition lists whenever indenting is sufficient to convey the structure of your information.

FIGURE 5.7

The type *attribute lets you make multitiered lists with both numbered and lettered points.*

```html
<html><head><title>Advice from the Golf Guru</title></head>
<body>
<h2>How to Win at Golf</h2>
<ol type="I"><li>Training
  <ol><li>Mental prep
    <ol type="A"><li>Watch PGA on TV religiously</li>
      <li>Get that computer game with Jack whatsisname</li>
      <li>Rent "personal victory" subliminal tapes</li>
    </ol></li>
    <li>Equipage
    <ol type="A"><li>Make sure your putter has a pro autograph
                        on it</li>
      <li>Pick up a bargain bag of tees-n-balls at Costco</li>
    </ol></li>
    <li>Diet
    <ol type="A"><li>Avoid baseball or football food
      <ol type="a"><li>No hotdogs</li>
        <li>No pretzels</li>
        <li>No peanuts and Crackerjacks</li>
      </ol></li>
      <li>Drink cheap white wine only, no beer</li>
    </ol></li>
  </ol></li>
<li>Pre-game
<ol><li>Dress
  <ol type="A">
    <li>Put on shorts, even if it's freezing</li>
    <li>Buy a new hat if you lost last time</li>
  </ol></li>
  <li>Location and Scheduling
  <ol type="A">
    <li>Select a course where your spouse won't find you</li>
    <li>To save on fees, play where your buddy works</li>
  </ol></li>
  <li>Opponent
  <ol type="A">
    <li>Look for: obesity, femininity, alzheimers,
        inexperience</li>
    <li>Shun: suntan, stethescope, strident walk,
        florida accent</li>
    <li>Buy opponent as many pre-game drinks as possible</li>
  </ol></li>
</ol></li>
<li>On the Course
<ol><li>Tee first, then develop severe hayfever</li>
    <li>Drive cart over opponent's ball to degrade
        aerodynamics</li>
    <li>Say "fore" just before ball makes contact with
        opponent</li>
    <li>Always replace divots when putting</li>
    <li>Water cooler holes are a good time to correct any
        errors in ball placement</li>
    <li>Never record strokes taken when opponent is
        urinating</li>
</ol></li>
</ol>
</body></html>
```

5

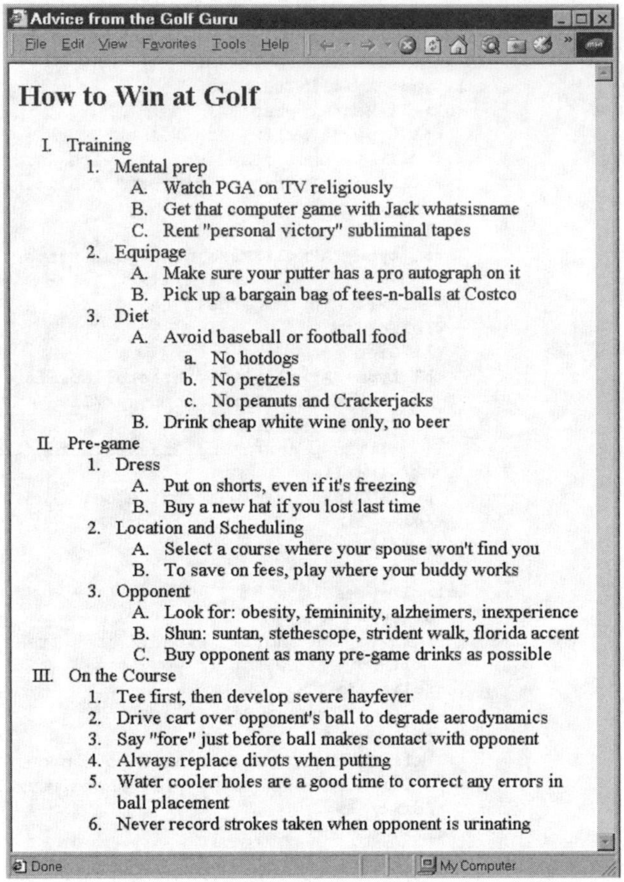

FIGURE 5.8

A well-formatted out-line can make almost any plan look more plausible.

> **Advice from the Golf Guru**
> File Edit View Favorites Tools Help
>
> ## How to Win at Golf
>
> I. Training
>   1. Mental prep
>   A. Watch PGA on TV religiously
>   B. Get that computer game with Jack whatsisname
>   C. Rent "personal victory" subliminal tapes
>   2. Equipage
>   A. Make sure your putter has a pro autograph on it
>   B. Pick up a bargain bag of tees-n-balls at Costco
>   3. Diet
>   A. Avoid baseball or football food
>   a. No hotdogs
>   b. No pretzels
>   c. No peanuts and Crackerjacks
>   B. Drink cheap white wine only, no beer
> II. Pre-game
>   1. Dress
>   A. Put on shorts, even if it's freezing
>   B. Buy a new hat if you lost last time
>   2. Location and Scheduling
>   A. Select a course where your spouse won't find you
>   B. To save on fees, play where your buddy works
>   3. Opponent
>   A. Look for: obesity, femininity, alzheimers, inexperience
>   B. Shun: suntan, stethescope, strident walk, florida accent
>   C. Buy opponent as many pre-game drinks as possible
> III. On the Course
>   1. Tee first, then develop severe hayfever
>   2. Drive cart over opponent's ball to degrade aerodynamics
>   3. Say "fore" just before ball makes contact with opponent
>   4. Always replace divots when putting
>   5. Water cooler holes are a good time to correct any errors in ball placement
>   6. Never record strokes taken when opponent is urinating
>
> Done   My Computer

2. Start each list (or new level within a multitiered list) with an `<ol>`, `<ul>`, or `<dl>`. Start each point within the list with `<li>`. Use the `type` attribute if you want non-standard bullets or letters instead of numbers.

3. If you want a blank line between list items, use `<li><p>` and `</p></li>` instead of just `<li>` and `</li>`.

4. Be very careful to close every `<li>` list item with a `</li>` tag. End every `<ol>` list with `</ol>`, and make sure that each `<ul>` or `<dl>` has a corresponding `</ul>` or `</dl>`. Unclosed lists can make pages look very strange, and can even cause some Web browsers not to display the list at all.

Summary

In this hour you learned that attributes are used to specify options and special behavior in many HTML tags, and you also learned to use the `align` attribute to center or right-align text.

You also found out how to create and combine three basic types of HTML list: ordered lists, unordered lists, and definition lists. Lists can be placed within other lists to create outlines and other complex arrangements of text.

Table 5.1 lists all the tags and attributes covered in this chapter.

TABLE 5.1 HTML Tags and Attributes Covered in Hour 5

Tag	Attribute	Function
`<div>...</div>`		A region of text to be formatted.
	`align="..."`	Align text to `center`, `left`, or `right`. (Can also be used with `<p>`, `<h1>`, `<h2>`, `<h3>`, and so on)
`<ol>...</ol>`		An ordered (numbered) list.
	`type="..."`	The type of numerals used to label the list. Possible values are `A`, `a`, `I`, `i`, `1`.
	`start="..."`	The value with which to start this list.
`<ul>...</ul>`		An unordered (bulleted) list.
	`type="..."`	The bullet dingbat used to mark list items. Possible values are `disc`, `circle`, and `square`.
`<li>...</li>`		A list item for use with `<ol>` or `<ul>`.
	`type="..."`	The type of bullet or number used to label this item. Possible values are `disc`, `circle`, `square`, `a`, `A`, `i`, `I`, `1`.
	`value="..."`	The numeric value this list item should have (affects this item and all below it in `<ol>` lists).
`<dl>...</dl>`		A definition list.
`<dt>...</dt>`		A definition term, as part of a definition list.
`<dd>...</dd>`		The corresponding definition to a definition term, as part of a definition list.

5

Q&A

Q Most Web pages I've seen on the Internet use `<center>` instead of `<div align="center">`. Should I be using `<center>` to make sure my pages are compatible with older Web browsers?

A For maximum compatibility, you might prefer to use both the obsolete `<center>` tag and the new `<div align="center">` tag, like this: `<div align="center"> <center>`. This text will be centered in both old and new browsers. Don't forget to end the centered section with `</center></div>`.

Q I used `<ul type="square">`, but the bullets came out round, not square.

A Are you using Netscape Navigator 2 or higher or Microsoft Internet Explorer 4 or higher? Alternate bullet types don't show up in any other Web browsers yet.

Q I've seen pages on the Internet that use three-dimensional little balls or other special graphics for bullets. How do they do that?

A That trick is a little bit beyond what this chapter covers. You'll find out how to do it yourself at the end of Chapter 10, "Putting Graphics on a Web Page."

Q How do I "full justify" text, so that both the left and right margins are flush?

A You don't. HTML 4 does not support full-justified text. You will be able to full-justify text in the future using style sheets (see Hour 16), although that feature of the style sheet standard isn't supported by any current Web browser.

Workshop

Quiz

1. How would you center everything on an entire page?

2. Write HTML to create the following ordered list:

   X. Xylophone

   Y. Yak

   Z. Zebra

3. How would you indent a single word and put a square bullet in front of it?

4. Use a definition list to show that the word "glunch" means "a look of disdain, anger, or displeasure" and that the word "glumpy" means "sullen, morose, or sulky."

5. Write the HTML to create the following indentation effect:

Apple pie,

   pudding,

      and pancake,

   All begin with an A.

Answers

1. Put `<div align="center">` immediately after the `<body>` tag at the top of the page, and `</div>` just before the `</body>` tag at the end of the page.

2. `<ol type="a" start="24"><li>xylophone</li><li>yak</li><li>zebra</li></ol>`

   The following alternative will also do the same thing:

   `<ol type="a"><li value="24">xylophone</li><li>yak</li><li>zebra</li></ol>`

3. `<ul type="square"><li>supercalifragilisticexpealidocious</li></ul>`

   (Putting the `type="square"` in the `<li>` tag would give the same result because there's only one item in this list.)

4.
```
<dl>
<dt>glunch</dt><dd>a look of disdain, anger, or displeasure</dd>
<dt>glumpy</dt><dd>sullen, morose, or sulky</dd>
</dl>
```

5.
```
<dl><dt>apple pie,</dt>
  <dd>pudding,</dd>
  <dl><dd>and pancake</dd></dl>
  all begin with an a.</dl>
```

   Note that blank lines will appear above and below and pancake in Microsoft Internet Explorer 3, but not in later versions or in any Netscape browser.

Exercise

- Try producing an ordered list outlining the information you'd like to put on your Web pages. This will give you practice formatting HTML lists and also give you a head start on thinking about the issues covered in Part VI, "Building a Web Site."

5

Hour 6

Text Formatting and Font Control

In this hour you learn to control the appearance of the text on your pages. You'll learn to incorporate boldface, italics, superscripts, subscripts, underlining, and strikethrough text into your pages, as well as how to choose typefaces and font sizes.

This chapter also shows you how to create special symbols, such as the copyright mark, and European language characters such as the é in Café.

There are two completely different approaches to controlling text formatting and alignment in HTML 4. The tags you study in this chapter (and the align attribute from Hour 5, "Text Alignment and Lists") are the "old way," which is actually officially discouraged. The "new way" is introduced in Hour 16, "Using Style Sheets."

Why learn something that's already out of date? Because a significant number of people still use Web browsers that don't support style sheets. If

> you want your pages to look right to everyone—not just those who use the latest software technology—you'll need to know everything in this chapter.
>
> All the tricks introduced in this chapter (and the previous one) will work with nearly any Web browser, old or new.

To Do

Before you proceed, you should get some text to work with so you can practice formatting it as you read this chapter.

- Any text will do, but try to find (or type) some text that you want to put onto a Web page. The text from a company brochure or from your personal résumé might be a good choice.
- If the text is from a word processor file, be sure to save it as plain text or ASCII text before adding any HTML tags.
- Add the `<html>`, `<head>`, `<title>`, and `<body>` tags (discussed in Hour 2, "Create a Web Page Right Now") before you use the tags introduced in this chapter to format the body text.

Boldface, Italics, and Special Formatting

Way back in the age of the typewriter, we were content with plain text and an occasional underline for emphasis. Today, **boldface** and *italicized* text have become de rigueur in all paper communication. Naturally, you can add bold and italic text to your Web pages too.

For boldface text, put the `<b>` tag at the beginning of the text and `</b>` at the end. Similarly, you can make any text italic by enclosing it between `<i>` and `</i>`.

You can *nest* one type of formatting inside another. For instance, if you want some text to be both bold and italic, put `<b><i>` in front of it and `</i></b>` after it. To avoid confusing some Web browsers, be careful to close the tags in the opposite order you opened them in. For example, don't do this:

```
<b>Bold, <i>bold and elegant,</b> or just plain elegant.</i>
```

Instead, do it this way:

```
<b>Bold, <i>bold and elegant,</i></b><i>or just plain elegant.</i>
```

Similarly, you should always close any `<b>`, `<i>`, or other formatting tags that occur within an `<li>` list item or heading before you end the `</li>`. Most of the `<b>` and `</b>`

tags in the following list may seem redundant, but adhering to this good form ensures that your pages fully meet the new XHTML and XML standards, which may save you having to rewrite them in the future.

```
<ul>
<li><b>Bold Men</b></li>
<li><b>Bold Women</b></li>
<li><b>Cool Cats</b></li>
<li>and Others</li>
</ul>
```

You can also use italics within headings, but boldface usually won't show in headings because they are already bold.

There are actually two ways to make text display as boldface; the `<b>` tag and the `<strong>` tag do the same thing in most Web browsers. Likewise, all popular browsers today interpret both `<i>` and `<em>` as italics.

Many purists prefer the `<strong>` and `<em>` tags because they imply only that the text should receive special emphasis, rather than dictating exactly how that effect should be achieved. Meanwhile, the vast majority of Web authors use the shorter and easier-to-remember `<b>` and `<i>` tags. I'll use `<b>` and `<i>` throughout this book, but if you like to be philosophically pure, by all means use `<strong>` and `<em>` instead.

In addition to `<b>`, `<i>`, `<em>`, and `<strong>`, there are several other HTML tags for adding special formatting to text. Table 6.1 summarizes all of them (including the bold-face and italic tags), and Figures 6.1 and 6.2 demonstrate each of them in action.

TABLE 6.1 HTML Tags That Add Special Formatting to Text

Tag	Function
`<small>`	Small text
`<big>`	Big Small text
`<sup>`	Superscript Small
`<sub>`	Subscript Small
`<strike>`	Strikethrough Small (draws a line through text)
`<u>`	Underline Small
`<em>` or `<i>`	Emphasized (italic) text
`<strong>` or `<b>`	Strong (boldface) text
`<tt>`	Monospaced Small typewriter font
`<pre>`	Monospaced Smallfont, preserving spaces and line breaks

6

Use the <u> tag sparingly, if at all. People expect underlined text to be a
link, and may get confused if you underline text that isn't a link.

If you're wondering how to get rid of the underlining for links, you can find
out in Hour 16.

FIGURE 6.1

*Each of the tags in
Table 6.1 is used in
this mock advertise-
ment.*

```
<html><head><title>The Micracle Product</title></head>
<body>
<u>New</u> <sup>Super</sup><strong>Strength</strong>
H<sub>2</sub>O <em>plus</em> will <strike>strike out</strike>
any stain, <big>big</big> or <small>small</small>.<br />
Look for new <sup>Super</sup><b>Strength</b> H<sub>2</sub>O
<i>plus</i> in a stream near you.
<p><tt>NUTRITION INFORMATION</tt> (void where prohibited)</p>
<pre>
            Calories   Grams    USRDA
            /Serving   of Fat   Moisture
Regular        3         4        100%
Unleaded       3         2        100%
Organic        2         3         99%
Sugar Free     0         1        110%
</pre>
</body></html>
```

FIGURE 6.2

*Here's what all char-
acter formatting from
Table 6.1 and Figure
6.3 looks like.*

The Micracle Product - Microsoft Internet Explorer

File   Edit   View   Favorites   Tools   Help

New ^{Super}**Strength** H_2O *plus* will ~~strike out~~ any stain, big or small.

Look for new ^{Super}**Strength** H_2O *plus* in a stream near you.

```
NUTRITION INFORMATION (void where prohibited)

            Calories   Grams    USRDA
            /Serving   of Fat   Moisture
Regular        3         4        100%
Unleaded       3         2        100%
Organic        2         3         99%
Sugar Free     0         1        110%
```

Done   My Computer

The <tt> tag usually changes the typeface to Courier New, a monospaced font.
(*Monospaced* means that all the letters and spaces are the same width.) However, Web
browsers let users change the monospaced <tt> font to the typeface of their choice
(under Tools, Internet Options, Fonts in Microsoft Internet Explorer 5 and Edit,
Preferences, Fonts in Netscape Navigator 4 or higher). The monospaced font may not

even be monospaced for some users, although the vast majority of people stick with the standard fonts that their browsers come set up with.

The `<pre>` tag causes text to appear in the monospaced font, but it also does something unique and useful. As you learned in Hour 2, multiple spaces and line breaks are normally ignored in HTML files, but `<pre>` causes exact spacing and line breaks to be preserved. For example, without `<pre>` the text at the end of Figure 6.3 would look like the following:

```
calories grams usrda /serving of fat moisture regular
3 4 100% unleaded 3 2 100% organic 2 3 99% sugar free 0 1 110%
```

Even if you added `<br />` tags at the end of every line, the columns wouldn't line up properly. However, when you put `<pre>` at the beginning and `</pre>` at the end, the columns line up properly—no `<br />` tags are needed.

There are fancier ways to make columns of text line up, and you learn all about them in Hour 15, "Advanced Layout with Tables." The `<pre>` tag gives you a quick and easy way to preserve the alignment of any monospaced text files you might want to transfer to a Web page with a minimum of effort.

> You can use the `<pre>` tag as a quick way to insert extra vertical space
> between paragraphs. For example, to put several blank lines between the
> words up and down, you could type this:
> up`<pre>`
>
>
> `</pre>`down

Font Size and Color

6

The `<big>`, `<small>`, and `<tt>` tags give you some rudimentary control over the size and appearance of the text on your pages. Generally, you should try sticking to those tags until you are ready for the advanced font formatting controls discussed in Hour 16.

However, there may be times when you'd just like a bit more control over the size and appearance of your text while maintaining as much compatibility with older Web browsers as possible. For those times, you can use the officially discouraged but widely used `<font>` tag.

For example, the following HTML will change the size and color of some text on a page:

```
<font size=5 color="purple">this text will be big and purple.</font>
```

The `size` attribute can take any value from 1 (tiny) to 7 (fairly big), with 3 being the default size. (If you need VERY big fonts, you'll need to use style sheets as explained in Hour 16.)

The `color` attribute can take any of the following standard color names: `black`, `white`, `red`, `green`, `blue`, `yellow`, `aqua`, `fuchsia`, `gray`, `lime`, `maroon`, `purple`, `navy`, `olive`, `silver`, or `teal`.

The actual size and exact color of the font depend on each reader's screen resolution and preference settings, but you can be assured that `size=6` is a lot bigger than `size=2` and that `color="red"` certainly shows its fire.

You learn more about controlling the color of the text on your pages in Hour 11, "Custom Backgrounds and Colors." That hour also shows you how to create your own custom colors and control the color of text links.

Choosing a Typeface

With the 3 and 4 versions of both Navigator and Internet Explorer, Netscape and Microsoft have added another extremely powerful form of font control: the `<font face>` attribute. This allows you to specify the actual typeface that should be used to display text—and has been the source of much rejoicing among Webmasters who are awfully sick of Times and Courier!

The page in Figures 6.3 and 6.4 uses these font controls to present a quick but colorful history lesson. Notice how `<font>` tags can be nested inside one another, changing some aspects of the font's appearance while leaving others the same; for example, even when `<font>` tags change the size and color of the letters in A HISTORY OF EVERYTHING, the typeface specified in the first `<font>` tag still applies. Likewise, the `<font>` tags that make small capital letters do not change the color, so the entire line ends up maroon.

The following is the code to set the typeface used for most of the text in Figure 6.3:

```
<font face="lucida sans unicode, arial, helvetica">
```

If Netscape Navigator or Microsoft Internet Explorer can find a font named Lucida Sans Unicode on a user's system, that font is used. Otherwise, the browser will look for Arial or Helvetica. Figure 6.5 shows how the page would look on a computer that didn't have Lucida Sans Unicode or Lucida Sans installed, but did have the Arial font.

FIGURE 6.3

The <font> tags give you control over the size, color, and type-face of any text.

```
<html><head><title>A History</title></head>
<body>
<font face="Lucida Sans Unicode, Arial, Helvetica">
  <font size="5" color="green">
    A H<font size="4"><b>ISTORY OF</b></font>
    E<font size="4"><b>VERYTHING</b></font>
  </font><br />
  <font face="Lucida Handwriting">
    It starts with a <b>bang</b>.
  </font>
Then everything <b>inflates</b> like a super-balloon tied up
with <b>super-strings</b>, until the whole mess curdles into
millions of <b>milky ways</b>. <b>Starlight</b> hits the <b>
volcanic rocks</b>, and cooks up some tasty <b>double-helix</b>
treats. They get eaten by each other, the <b>fittest</b> (and
least tasty) <b>survive</b>, a <b>meteor</b> kills the <b>
big</b> ones, and when it all <b>freezes over</b> the <b>
smart</b> ones move into <b>caves</b> and start a <b>fire</b>.
Growing <b>grass</b> turns out to be more fun than chasing <b>
woolly mammoths</b>, so the <b>agriculturalists</b> start a <b>
revolution</b>. The <b>pharoahs, ceasars, kings,</b> and <b>
fuhrers</b> mostly win but eventually lose, so the <b>
scientists</b> and <b>industrialists</b> revolt this time.
Japan gets <b>nuked</b> and takes over the <b>world
economy</b>, the <b>Berlin wall</b> and <b>Soviets</b> fall,
and the <b>United States</b> all sue <b>Microsoft</b> over
the <b>Internet</b>.
</font>
<font face="Lucida Handwriting"><i>The end.</i></font>
</body></html>
```

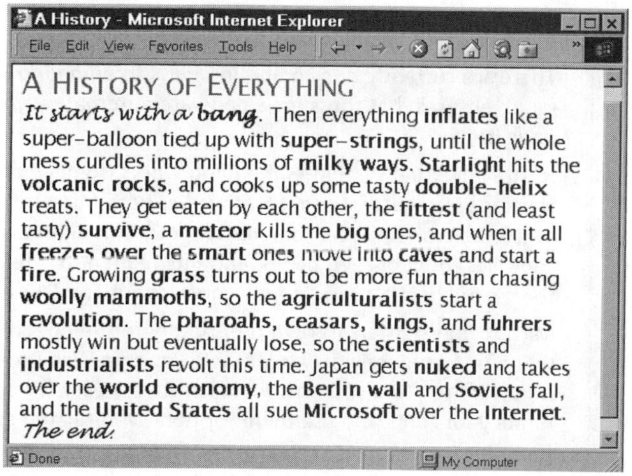

FIGURE 6.4

If you have the Lucida Sans Unicode and Lucida Sans fonts installed on your computer, they will be used to display the page. Now look at Figure 6.5.

6

If none of those fonts could be found, the browser would display the text using the default font (usually Times New Roman). Most browsers other than Navigator and Internet Explorer will ignore the font face attribute and display the fonts they always use.

FIGURE 6.5

If you didn't have Lucida Sans Unicode and Lucida Sans fonts installed, the text from Figure 6.3 would appear in Arial, if available, or in the default font, which is usually Times New Roman.

A History - Microsoft Internet Explorer

File Edit View Favorites Tools Help

A HISTORY OF EVERYTHING

It starts with a **bang**. Then everything **inflates** like a super-balloon tied up with **super-strings**, until the whole mess curdles into millions of **milky ways**. **Starlight** hits the **volcanic rocks**, and cooks up some tasty **double-helix** treats. They get eaten by each other, the **fittest** (and least tasty) **survive**, a **meteor** kills the **big** ones, and when it all **freezes over** the **smart** ones move into **caves** and start a **fire**. Growing **grass** turns out to be more fun than chasing **woolly mammoths**, so the **agriculturalists** start a **revolution**. The **pharoahs, ceasars, kings,** and **fuhrers** mostly win but eventually lose, so the **scientists** and **industrialists** revolt this time. Japan gets **nuked** and takes over the **world economy**, the **Berlin wall** and **Soviets** fall, and the **United States** all sue **Microsoft** over the **Internet**. *The end.*

Done   My Computer

Since only fonts that each user has on his system show up, you have no real control over which fonts appear on your pages. Furthermore, the exact spelling of the font names is important, and many common fonts go by several slightly different names. This means that about the only truly reliable choices are Arial (on Windows machines) and Helvetica (on Macintoshes). Don't be afraid to specify other fonts, but make sure your pages look acceptable in Times New Roman as well.

You'll find many additional tips on using typefaces in Hour 16.

There are currently two competing ways to *embed* fonts into a Web page, which ensures that fonts for a page are automatically sent along with the page itself.

Bitstream's TrueDoc font-embedding works (somewhat unreliably) with Netscape Navigator 4 and 4.5 as well as with Microsoft Internet Explorer 4 and 5. Several available commercial programs allow you to create TrueDoc font files for your Web pages, and Bitstream also offers several free fonts for use online. You can find out more about TrueDoc at www.truedoc.com.

Microsoft also offers its own proprietary font-embedding technology, which unfortunately only works with its own Web browser. Even more unfortunately, the technology makes it very easy for people to illegally pirate your fonts and use them for non–Web-related applications. For these reasons, industry acceptance of Microsoft's font-embedding solution has been lukewarm at best. If you'd like to know more about it, visit www.microsoft.com/truetype for details.

To see a list of the most common TrueType fonts, and to find out which of them are installed on your computer, visit the *24-Hour HTML Café* at `http://24hourhtmlcafe.com/hour6/`.

You'll also find some whimsical examples of how text formatting can liven up a page.

Special Characters

Most fonts now include special characters for European languages, such as the accented é in Café. There are also a few mathematical symbols and special punctuation marks such as the circular • bullet.

You can insert these special characters at any point in an HTML document by looking up the appropriate codes in Table 6.2 or in the complete list of character entities in Appendix D, "HTML Character Entities." You'll find an even more extensive list of codes for multiple character sets online at `http://www.w3.org/tr/rec-html40/sgml/entities.html`.

For example, the word Café would look like this:

café

Each symbol also has a mnemonic name that might be easier to remember than the number. Here is another way to write Café:

café

Notice that there are also codes for the angle brackets, quotation, and ampersand in Table 6.2. You need to use the codes if you want these symbols to appear on your pages; otherwise, the Web browser interprets them as HTML commands.

TABLE 6.2 Important English-Language Special Characters

Character	Numeric Code	Code Name	Description
"	&#34;	&quot;	Quotation mark
&	&#38;	&amp;	Ampersand
<	&#60;	&lt;	Less than
>	&#62;	&gt;	Greater than
¢	&#162;	&cent;	Cent sign
£	&#163;	&pound;	Pound sterling
¦	&#166;	¦ or brkbar;	Broken vertical bar

continues

6

TABLE 6.2 continued

Character	Numeric Code	Code Name	Description
§	§	§	Section sign
©	©	©	Copyright
®	®	®	Registered trademark
°	°	°	Degree sign
±	±	±	Plus or minus
^{2}	²	²	Superscript two
^{3}	³	³	Superscript three
·	·	·	Middle dot
^{1}	¹	¹	Superscript one
$^1/_4$	¼	¼	Fraction one-fourth
$^1/_2$	½	½	Fraction one-half
$^3/_4$	¾	¾	Fraction three-fourths
Æ	Æ	Æ	Capital AE ligature
æ	æ	æ	Small ae ligature
É	É	É	Accented capital E
é	é	é	Accented small e
×	×		Multiply sign
÷	÷		Division sign

Looking for the copyright © or registered trademark ® symbols? The codes you need are © and ® respectively.

To create an unregistered trademark ™ symbol, use ^{tm} or <small>^{tm}</small> for a smaller version.

In Figures 6.6 and 6.7, several more of the symbols from Table 6.2 and Appendix D are shown in use.

Some older Web browsers will not display many of the special characters in Table 6.2. Some fonts also may not include all of these characters.

FIGURE 6.6

Special character codes begin with & and end with ;.

```
<html><head><title>Punchuation Lines</title></head>
<body>
Q: What should you do when a British banker picks a fight with
you?<br />
A: &pound; some &cent;&cent; into him.
<hr />
Q: What do you call it when a judge takes part of a law off the
books?<br />
A: &sect; violence.
<hr />
Q: What did the football coach get from the locker room vending
machine in the middle of the game?<br />
A: A &frac14; back at &frac12; time.
<hr />
Q: How hot did it get when the police detective interrogated
the mathematician?<br />
A: x&sup3;&deg;
<hr />
Q: What does a punctilious plagarist do?<br />
A: &copy;
<hr />
</body></html>
```

FIGURE 6.7

This is how the HTML page in Figure 6.6 will look in most, but not all, Web browsers.

Punchuation Lines - Microsoft Internet Explorer

File Edit View Favorites Tools Help

Q: What should you do when a British banker picks a fight with you?
A: £ some ¢¢ into him.

Q: What do you call it when a judge takes part of a law off the books?
A: § violence.

Q: What did the football coach get from the locker room vending machine in the middle of the game?
A: A ¼ back at ½ time.

Q: How hot did it get when the police detective interrogated the mathematician?
A: x^{3o}

Q: What does a punctilious plagarist do?
A: ©

Done   My Computer

6

Summary

This hour showed you how to make text appear as boldface or italic, or with superscripts, subscripts, underlines, crossed-out text, special symbols, and accented letters. You saw how to make everything line up properly in preformatted passages of monospaced text and how to control the size, color, and typeface of any section of text on a Web page.

Table 6.3 summarizes the tags and attributes discussed in this hour. Don't feel like you have to memorize all these tags, by the way! That's why you have this book: You can look them up when you need them. Remember that all the HTML tags are listed in Appendix C, "Complete HTML 4 Quick Reference," and all the special character codes can be found in Appendix D.

TABLE 6.3 HTML Tags and Attributes Covered in Hour 6

Tag	Attribute	Function
`<em>...</em>`		Emphasis (usually italic).
`<strong>...</strong>`		Stronger emphasis (usually bold).
`<b>...</b>`		Boldface text.
`<i>...</i>`		Italic text.
`<tt>...</tt>`		Typewriter (monospaced) font.
`<pre>...</pre>`		Preformatted text (exact line endings and spacing will be preserved—usually rendered in a monospaced font).
`<big>...</big>`		Text is slightly larger than normal.
`<small>...</small>`		Text is slightly smaller than normal.
`<sub>...</sub>`		Subscript.
`<sup>...</sup>`		Superscript.
`<strike>...</strike>`		Puts a strikethrough in text.
`<font>...</font>`		Controls the appearance of the enclosed text.
	`size="..."`	The size of the font, from 1 to 7. Default is 3. Can also be specified as a value relative to the current size; for example, +2 or -1.
	`color="..."`	Changes the color of the text.
	`face="..."`	Name of font to use if it can be found on the user's system. Commas can separate multiple font names, and the first font on the list that can be found will be used.

Q&A

Q Other books talk about some text formatting tags that you didn't cover in this chapter, such as `<code>` and `<address>`. Shouldn't I know about them?

A There are a number of tags in HTML that indicate what kind of information is contained in some text. The `<address>` tag, for example, was supposed to be put around addresses. The only visible effect of `<address>` in most browsers, however, is making the text italic. Web page authors today most often simply use the `<i>` tag instead. Similarly, `<code>` and `<kbd>` do essentially the same thing as `<tt>`. You may also read about `<var>`, `<samp>`, or `<dfn>` in some older HTML references, but nobody uses them in ordinary Web pages.

One tag that you might occasionally find handy is `<blockquote>`, which indents all the text until the closing `</blockquote>`. Some Web page authors use `<blockquote>` on all or part of a page as a quick and easy way to widen the left and right margins.

Q How do I find out the exact name for a font I have on my computer?

A On a Windows or Macintosh computer, open the control panel and click the Fonts folder. The TrueType fonts on your system are listed. Use the exact spelling of font names when specifying them in the `<font face>` tag. If you use Adobe Type Manager, run the ATM Control Panel to find the name of Postscript fonts in Windows.

Q. How do I put Kanji, Arabic, Chinese, and other non-European characters on my pages?

A First of all, everyone you want to be able to read these characters on your pages must have the appropriate language fonts installed. They must also have selected that language character set and font under Options, General Preferences, Fonts in Netscape Navigator or View, Options, General, Fonts in Microsoft Internet Explorer. You can use the Character Map accessory in Windows 95 (or a similar program in other operating systems) to get the numerical codes for each character in any language font. If the character you want has a code of 214, use Ö to place it on a Web page.

The best way to include a short message in an Asian language (such as `we speak tamil—call us!`) is to include it as a graphics image. That way everyone will see it, even if they use English as their primary language for Web browsing.

6

Workshop

Quiz

1. Write the HTML to produce the following:

   Come for ~~cheap~~ free H$_2$O on May 7$^{\underline{th}}$ at 9:00PM

2. What's the difference between the following two lines of HTML?

   ```
   deep <tt>s p a   a  c e</tt> quest
   ```
   ```
   deep <pre>s p a   a  c e</pre> quest
   ```

3. How would you say, "We're having our annual Impeachment Day SALE today," in normal-sized blue text, but with the word "SALE" in the largest possible size in bright red?

4. How do you say "© 1996, Webwonks Inc." on a Web page?

Answers

1. ```
   come for <strike>cheap</strike> free h<sub>2</sub>o on may
   7<sup><u>th</u></sup> at 9:00<small>pm</small>
   ```

2. The line using `<tt>` will look like this:

   ```
   deep s p a a c e quest
   ```

   The line using `<pre>` will produce the following three lines of text on the Web page.

   ```
   deep
   s p a   a  c e
   quest
   ```

3. ```
   <font color="blue">We're having our annual Impeachment Day
   <font color="red" size=7>SALE</font> today!</font>
   ```

4. ```
   &copy; 1996, Webwonks Inc.
   ```

   The following produces the same result:

   ```
   &#169; 1996, Webwonks Inc.
   ```

Exercise

- Professional typesetters use small capitals for the AM and PM in clock times. They also use superscripts for dates like the 7th or 1st. Use the `<small>` and `<sup>` tags to typeset important dates and times correctly on your Web pages.
   ```

Hour 7

Email Links and Links Within a Page

In Hour 3, "Linking to Other Web Pages," you learned to use the <a> tag to create links between HTML pages. This hour shows you how to use the same tag to allow readers to jump between different parts of a single page. This gives you a convenient way to put a table of contents at the top of a long document, or to put a link at the bottom of a page that returns you to the top. You'll see how to link to a specific point within a separate page, too.

This hour also tells you how to embed a live link to your email address in a Web page, so readers can instantly compose and send messages to you from within most Web browsers.

Using Named Anchors

Figure 7.1 demonstrates the use of intrapage links. To see how such links are made, take a look at the first <a> tag in Figure 7.1:

```
<a name="top"></a>
```

FIGURE 7.1

An <a> tag with a name attribute acts as a marker, so <a> tags with href attributes can link to that specific point on a page.

```
<html><head><title>Alphabetical Shakespeare</title></head>
<body>
<a name="top"></a>
<h2>First Lines of Every Shakespearean Sonnet</h2>
Don't ya just hate when you go a-courting, and there you are
down on one knee about to rattle off a totally romantic
Shakespearean sonnet, and zap! You space it. <i>"Um... It was,
uh... I think it started with a B..."</i>
<p>Well, appearest thou no longer the dork. Simply pull this
page up on your laptop computer, click on the first letter of
the sonnet you want, and get an instant reminder of the first
line to get you started. <i>"Beshrew that heart that makes my
heart to groan..."</i> She's putty in your hands.</p>
<h3 align="center">Alphabetical Index<br />
(click on a letter)<br />
<a href="#A">A</a> <a href="#B">B</a> <a href="#C">C</a>
<a href="#D">D</a> <a href="#E">E</a> <a href="#F">F</a>
<a href="#G">G</a> <a href="#H">H</a> <a href="#I">I</a>
<a href="#J">J</a> <a href="#K">K</a> <a href="#L">L</a>
<a href="#M">M</a> <a href="#N">N</a> <a href="#O">O</a>
<a href="#P">P</a> <a href="#Q">Q</a> <a href="#R">R</a>
<a href="#S">S</a> <a href="#T">T</a> <a href="#U">U</a>
<a href="#V">V</a> <a href="#W">W</a> <a href="#X">X</a>
<a href="#Y">Y</a> <a href="#Z">Z</a></h3>
<p><hr /></p><a name="A"></a>
<h2>A</h2>
A woman's face with nature's own hand painted,<br />
Accuse me thus, that I have scanted all,<br />
Against my love shall be as I am now<br />
Against that time (if ever that time come)<br />
Ah wherefore with infection should he live,<br />
Alack what poverty my muse brings forth,<br />
Alas 'tis true, I have gone here and there,<br />
As a decrepit father takes delight,<br />
As an unperfect actor on the stage,<br />
As fast as thou shalt wane so fast thou grow'st,<br />
<p><a href="#top"><i>Return to Index.</i></a></p><hr />
<a name="B"></a><h2>B</h2>
Be wise as thou art cruel, do not press<br />
Being your slave what should I do but tend,<br />
Beshrew that heart that makes my heart to groan<br />
Betwixt mine eye and heart a league is took,<br />
But be contented when that fell arrest,<br />
But do thy worst to steal thy self away,<br />
But wherefore do not you a mightier way<br />
<p><a href="#top"><i>Return to Index.</i></a></p>

        ...Sonnets starting with C through X go here...

<a name="Y"></a><h2>Y</h2>
Your love and pity doth th' impression fill,<br />
<p><a href="#top"><i>Return to Index.</i></a></p><hr />
<a name="Z"></a><h2>Z</h2>
(No sonnets start with Z.)<br />
<p><a href="#top">Return to Index.</a></p><hr />
</body></html>
```

This is a different use of the <a> anchor tag; it simply gives a name to the specific point on the page where the tag occurs. The </a> tag must be included, but no text between <a> and </a> is necessary.

> For obscure technical reasons, the new XHTML and XML standards call for the use of id instead of name. If you want to give your pages the best chance of being compatible with all past and future software, you can include both name and id in your anchor tags, like this:
>
> <a name="top" id="top"></a>
>
> Even though I generally recommend conforming to the XHTML standard, this is one picky detail that I usually don't bother with. Maintaining the double name/id combination would not be fun, and it seems pretty unlikely that anyone would ever write software that doesn't recognize the old name attribute for named anchors.

Now look at the last <a> tag in Figure 7.1:

<a href="#top">Return to Index.</a>

The # symbol means that the word top refers to a named anchor point within the current document, rather than to a separate page. When a reader clicks Return to Index, the Web browser displays the part of the page starting with the <a name="top"> tag.

Here's an easy way to remember the difference between these two different types of <a> tags: <a href> is what you click, and <a name> is where you go when you click there.

NEW TERM An *anchor* is a named point on a Web page. The same tag is used to create hypertext links and anchors (which explains why the tag is named <a>).

Similarly, each of the <a href> links in Figure 7.1 makes an underlined link leading to a corresponding <a name> anchor. Clicking the letter B under alphabetical index in Figure 7.2, for instance, takes you to the part of the page shown in Figure 7.3.

7

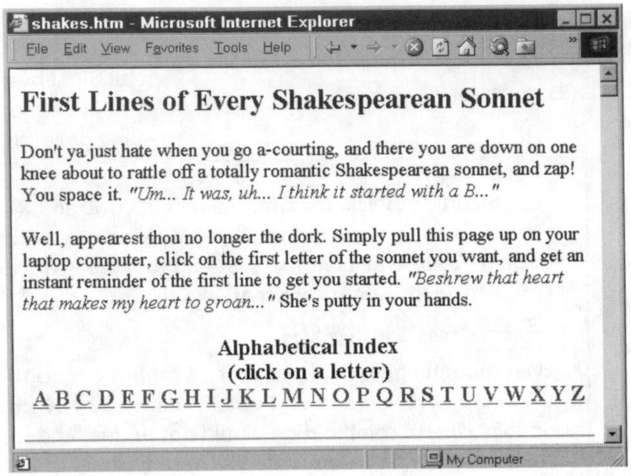

FIGURE 7.2

The <a name> tags in Figure 7.1 don't appear at all on the Web page. The <a href> tags appear as underlined links.

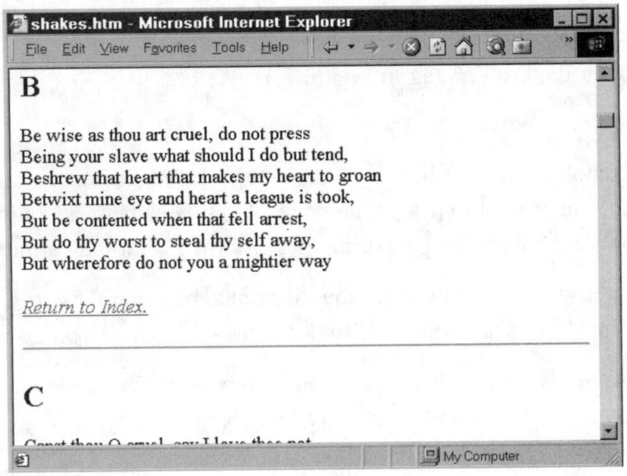

FIGURE 7.3

Clicking the letter B in Figure 7.2 takes you to the appropriate section of the same page.

To Do

Now that you have several pages of your own linked together, you might want to add an index at the top of your home page so people can easily get an overview of what your pages have to offer:

- Place <a name> tags in front of each major topic on your home page or any longish page you make.
- Copy each of the major topic headings to a list at the top of the page, and enclose each heading in an <a href> linking to the corresponding <a name> tag.

One of the most common uses for the <a name> tag is creating an alphabetical index. The bad news for anyone with an alphabetical list that he or she wants to index is that typing out 26 links to 26 anchors is a rather tedious endeavor. The good news is that I've already done it for you and dropped off the indexed page at the *24-Hour HTML Café*: http:// 24hourhtmlcafe.com/hour7/.

Click the Instant Alphabetical Index link and select File, Save As to save the document to your hard drive. You can then cut and paste your own alphabetical information after each letter.

Linking to a Specific Part of Another Page

You can even link to a named anchor on another page by including the address or name of that page followed by # and the anchor name.

Figure 7.4 shows several examples, such as the following:

```
<a href="sonnets.htm#131">
You're bossy, ugly and smelly, but I still love you.</a>
```

Clicking You're bossy, ugly and smelly, but I still love you, which is shown in Figure 7.5, brings up the page named sonnets.htm and goes directly to the point where <a name="131"></a> occurs on that page (see Figure 7.6). (The HTML for sonnets.htm is not listed here because it is quite long. It's just a bunch of sappy old sonnets with <a name> tags in front of each one.) Note that anchor names can be numbers, words, or any combination of letters and numbers. In this case, I used the sonnet number.

FIGURE 7.4

To link to a specific part of another page, put both the page address and anchor name in the <a href> tag.

```
<html><head><title>Topical Shakespeare</title></head>
<body>
<h2>Shakespearean Sonnets for Every Occasion</h2>
<p>Choose your message for a genuine Shakespearean sonnet which
expresses your feelings with tact and grace.</p>
<i><a href="sonnets.htm#131">
You're bossy, ugly and smelly, but I still love you.</a><br />
<a href="sonnets.htm#2">
Life is short. Let's make babies.</a><br />
<a href="sonnets.htm#140">
Say you love me or I'll tell lies about you.</a><br />
<a href="sonnets.htm#31">
You remind me of all my old girlfriends.</a><br />
<a href="sonnets.htm#57">
You abuse me, but you know I love it.</a><br />
<a href="sonnets.htm#141">
I think you're hideous, but I'm desperate.</a><br />
<a href="sonnets.htm#150">
You don't deserve me, but take me anyway.</a><br />
<a href="sonnets.htm#36">
I feel bad about leaving, but see ya later.</a></i>
</body></html>
```

7

FIGURE 7.5

This page is listed in Figure 7.4. All the links on this page go to different parts of a separate page named sonnets.htm.

Topical Shakespeare - Microsoft Internet Explorer

File Edit View Favorites Tools Help

Shakespearean Sonnets for Every Occasion

Choose your message for a genuine Shakespearean sonnet which expresses your feelings with tact and grace.

You're bossy, ugly and smelly, but I still love you.
Life is short. Let's make babies.
Say you love me or I'll tell lies about you.
You remind me of all my old girlfriends.
You abuse me, but you know I love it.
I think you're hideous, but I'm desperate.
You don't deserve me, but take me anyway.
I feel bad about leaving, but see ya later.

My Computer

FIGURE 7.6

Clicking the bossy link in Figure 7.4 brings you directly to this part of the sonnets.htm *page. HTML for this page isn't shown.*

Shakespeare's Sonnets - Microsoft Internet Explorer

File Edit View Favorites Tools Help

Sonnet 131

Thou art as tyrannous, so as thou art,
As those whose beauties proudly make them cruel;
For well thou know'st to my dear doting heart
Thou art the fairest and most precious jewel.
Yet in good faith some say that thee behold,
Thy face hath not the power to make love groan;
To say they err, I dare not be so bold,
Although I swear it to my self alone.
And to be sure that is not false I swear,
A thousand groans but thinking on thy face,
One on another's neck do witness bear
Thy black is fairest in my judgment's place.
In nothing art thou black save in thy deeds,
And thence this slander as I think proceeds.

Done   My Computer

Be sure to only include the # symbol in <a href> link tags. Don't put a # symbol in the <a name> tag; links to that name won't work in that case.

Linking Your Email Address into a Web Page

In addition to linking between pages and between parts of a single page, the <a> tag allows you to link to your email address. This is the simplest way to enable readers of your Web pages to "talk back" to you. Of course, you could just tell them your email address and trust them to type it into whatever email program they use if they want to say something to you. But you can make it almost completely effortless for them to send you messages by providing a clickable link to your email address.

An HTML link to my email address looks like the following:

```
<a href="mailto:dicko@netletter.com">Send me an email message.</a>
```

The words `Send me an email message` will appear just like any other `<a>` link (as underlined text in the color you set for links in the `link` or `vlink` attributes of the `<body>` tag). When someone clicks the link in most Web browsers, she gets a window in which to type a message that is immediately sent to you.

If you want people to see your actual email address (so they can make note of it or send a message using a different email program), type it both in the `href` attribute and as part of the message between the `<a>` and `</a>` tags.

For example, the HTML in Figure 7.7 is an email directory page for a club of aging German philosophers. (I know that Wittgenstein's English, but he was born in Austria, so they let him in the club anyway.) The resulting page in Figure 7.8 lists the club officers with a clickable email link for each.

FIGURE 7.7

Links to email addresses use the same `<a>` tag as links to Web pages.

```
<html><head><title>GPhC E-Mail Directory</title></head>
<body>
<h2>German Philosopher's Club<br />E-Mail Directory</h2>
<ul>
<li><p><a href="mailto:manny@netletter.com">
    <i>Emmanuel Kant, President</i><br />
    manny@netletter.com</a></p></li>
<li><p><a href="mailto:@martynetletter.com">
    <i>Martin Heidegger, Secretary</i><br />
    marty@netletter.com</a></p></li>
<li><p><a href="mailto:will-fred@netletter.com">
    <i>Georg Wilhelm Friedrick Hegel, Senior Officer</i><br />
    will-fred@netletter.com</a></p></li>
<li><p><a href="mailto:fred-will@netletter.com">
    <i>Friedrick Wilhelm Nietzche, Junior Officer</i><br />
    fred-will@netletter.com</a></p></li>
<li><p><a href="mailto:jj@netletter.com">
    <i>Ludwig J.J. Wittgenstein,
    Administrative Assistant</i><br />
    jj@netletter.com</a></p></li>
</ul>
</body></html>
```

7

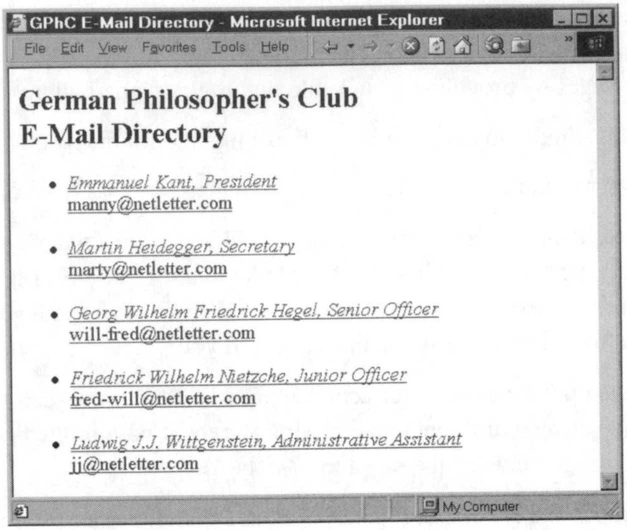

FIGURE **7.8**

The mailto: *links in Figure 7.7 look just like* http:// *links on the page.*

When someone clicks the top link in Figure 7.8, a separate window (see Figure 7.9) opens; the window has spaces for a subject line and email message. The email address from the link is automatically entered, and the user can simply click the mail button to send the message.

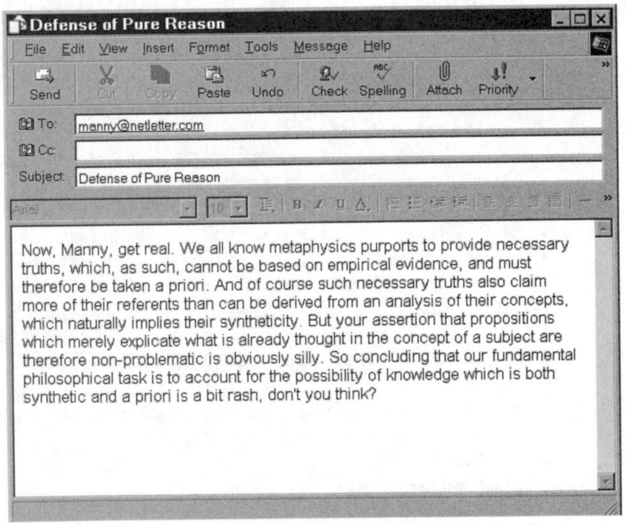

FIGURE **7.9**

Clicking the top link in Figure 7.8 brings up this email window (or the email software set up on your computer).

It is customary to put an email link to the Web page author at the bottom of every Web page. Not only does this make it easy for others to contact you, it also gives them a way to tell you about any problems with the page that your testing may have missed.

Summary

This hour has shown you two uses for the <a> tag not covered in Hour 3. You learned how to create named anchor points within a page and how to create links to a specific anchor. You also saw how to link to your email address so readers can easily send you messages. Table 7.1 summarizes the two attributes of the <a> tag discussed in this hour.

TABLE 7.1   HTML Tag and Attributes Covered in Hour 7

Tag	Attribute	Function
<a>...</a>		With the href attribute, creates a link to another document or anchor; with the name attribute, creates an anchor that can be linked to.
	href="..."	The address of the document or anchor point to which to link.
	name="..."	The name for this anchor point in the document.
	id="..."	Used exactly like name. (Include both name and id for maximum past and future compatibility.)

Q&A

Q Can I put both href and name in the same <a> tag? Would I want to for any reason?

A You can, and it might save you some typing if you have a named anchor point and a link right next to each other. It's generally better, however, to use <a href> and <a name> separately to avoid confusion because they play very different roles in an HTML document.

Q What happens if I accidentally spell the name of an anchor wrong or forget to put the # in front of it?

A If you link to an anchor name that doesn't exist within a page or misspell the anchor name, the link goes to the top of that page.

7

Q **When I test my intrapage links with Netscape Navigator 2 or 3, they don't seem to work quite right. Was there a change in the HTML standard?**

A The proper HTML hasn't changed, but there was a known bug in some older versions of Navigator that prevented links to anchors from working correctly in some (not all) situations. There's not much you can do about that other than encouraging people to upgrade to the latest version of their Web browser.

Q **What if I use a different company to handle my email than handles my Web pages? Will my email links still work?**

A Yes. You can put any email address on the Internet into a link, and it will work fine. The only situation where email links won't work is when the person who clicks the link hasn't set up the email part of his Web browser properly or is using an older version that isn't capable of sending email.

Workshop

Quiz

1. Write the HTML to make it possible for someone clicking the words "About the authors" at the top of the page to skip down to a list of credits at the bottom of the page.

2. Suppose your company has three employees and you want to create a company directory page listing some information about each of them. Write the HTML for that page and the HTML to link to one of the employees from another page.

3. If your email address is bon@soir.com, how would you make the text "goodnight greeting" into a link that people can click to compose and send you an email message?

Answers

1. Type this at the top of the page:

   ```
   <a href="#credits">About the authors</a>
   ```

   Type this at the beginning of the credits section:

   ```
   <a name="credits"></a>
   ```

2. The company directory page would look like the following:

   ```
   <html><head><title>company directory</title></head>
   <body><h1>Company Directory</h1>
   <a name="jones"><h2>Jane Jones</h2>
   Ms. Jones is our accountant... etc.
   <a name="smith"><h2>Sam Smith</h2>
   ```

```
Mr. Smith is our salesman.. etc.
<a name="bharwaniji"><h2>R.K. Satjiv Bharwahniji</h2>
Mr. Bharwahniji is our president... etc.
</body></html>
```

If the file were named `directory.htm`, a link to one employee's information from another page would look like the following:

```
<a href="directory.htm#bharwaniji">About our president</a>
```

3. Type the following on your Web page:

```
send me a <a href="mailto:bon@soir.com">goodnight greeting</a>!
```

Exercises

- When you link back to your home page from other pages, you might want to skip some of the introductory information at the top of the home page. Using a link to a named anchor just below that introductory information will avoid presenting it to people who have already read it, making your pages seem less repetitive. Also, if any pages on your site are longer than two screens of information when displayed in a Web browser, consider putting a link at the bottom of the page back up to the top.

- Look through your Web pages and consider whether there are any places in the text where you'd like to make it easy for people to respond to what you're saying. Include a link right there to your email address. You can never provide too many opportunities for people to contact you and tell you what they need or think about your products, especially if you're running a business.

7

HOUR 8

Creating HTML Forms

Up to this point, everything in this book has focused on getting information out to others. (Email links, introduced in Hour 7, "Email Links and Links Within a Page," are the one exception.) But HTML is a two-way street; you can use your Web pages to gather information from the people who read them as well.

Web forms allow you to receive feedback, orders, or other information from your Web pages readers. If you've ever used a Web search engine such as HotBot or Yahoo!, you're familiar with HTML forms. Product order forms are also an extremely popular use of forms.

This chapter shows you how to create your own forms and the basics of how to handle form submissions.

NEW TERM An HTML *form* is part of a Web page that includes areas where readers can enter information to be sent back to you, the publisher of the Web page.

How HTML Forms Work

Before you learn the HTML tags to make your own forms, you should understand how the information that someone fills out on a form makes its way back to you. You also need to have the person who runs your Web server computer set it up to process your forms.

Every form must include a button for the user to submit the form. When someone clicks that button, all the information he or she has filled in is sent (in a standard format) to an Internet address that you specify in the form itself. You have to put a special forms-processing program at that address in order for that information to get to you.

Almost all ISP companies that offer Web page hosting also provide preprogrammed scripts to their customers for processing forms. The most common thing that such a script would do is forward the information from the form to your email address, although it might also save the information to a file on the Web server or format the form data and make it easier for you to read. (Of course, if you happen to be a programmer, you can write your own scripts in any language supported on the server.)

A form-processing script also usually generates some sort of reply page and sends it back to be displayed for the user.

It's also possible to set things up so that much of the form information can be interpreted and processed automatically. For example, server software exists to authorize a credit card transaction automatically over the Internet, confirm an order to the customer's email address, and enter the order directly into your company's in-house database for shipment. Obviously, setting up that sort of thing can get quite complex, and it's beyond the scope of this book to explain all the things you can do with form data once it has been submitted.

Most ISPs that host Web pages already have a "generic" form-processing script set up and will happily tell you the exact HTML required to use it. If your ISP can't do this, or charges you an extra fee for it, you are frankly probably not using a very good ISP! In that case, you have the following choices:

- Switch to a more helpful Web hosting service.
- Learn advanced server programming.
- Use a form-creation service such as freedback.com to create and process your forms. (Although such services are free and work great, they will display other companies' advertising to everyone who uses your forms.)

To Do

Before you put a form online, you should do the following:

- Ask your ISP what it offers for form-processing scripts and the exact address to which your forms should send their information. Later in this chapter, you'll see where and how to put that address into your forms.

- If you run your own Web server computer, the server software probably came with some basic form-processing scripts. Consult your documentation to set them up properly and find the address on your server where each is located.

- If you have a choice of several form-processing scripts, I recommend starting with the script to simply send the "raw" form data to your email address. The examples in this chapter use such a script. You can experiment with fancier scripts later.

Creating a Form

Every form must begin with a `<form>` tag, which can be located anywhere in the body of the HTML document. The `form` tag normally has two attributes, `method` and `action`:

`<form method="post" action="mailto:me@mysite.com">`

Nowadays, the `method` is almost always `"post"`, which means to send the form entry results as a document. (In some special situations, you may need to use `method="get"`, which submits the results as part of the URL header instead. For example, `"get"` is sometimes used when submitting queries to search engines from a Web form. If you're not yet an expert on forms, just use `"post"` unless someone tells you to do otherwise.)

The `action` attribute specifies the address to which to send the form data. You have two options here:

- You can type the location of a form-processing program or script on a Web server computer, and the form data will then be sent to that program.

- You can type `mailto:` followed by your email address, and the form data will be sent directly to you whenever someone fills out the form.

Due to a bug in the Microsoft Windows messaging system, `action="mailto"` will not work properly for many people who use Microsoft Internet Explorer or Microsoft Outlook. Even when it does work, the form results come to you in a coded format that is very difficult to read. I therefore strongly recommend that you always use a form-processing script instead of the `mailto:` option.

The form in Figures 8.1 and 8.2 includes every type of input you can currently use on HTML forms (with one exception: the button tag is discussed in Hour 19, "Web Page Scripting for Non-Programmers"). Figure 8.3 shows how the form in Figure 8.2 might look after someone fills it out. Refer to these figures as you read the following explanations of each type of input element.

FIGURE 8.1

All parts of a form must fall between the <form> *and* </form> *tags.*

```
<html><head><title>Guest Book</title></head>
<body>
<h1>My Guest Book</h1>
<p>Please let me know what you think of my Web pages. Thanks!
<form method="POST" action="/htbin/generic">
<input type="hidden" name="mail_to" value="me@mysite.com" />
<pre>
  What is your name? <input type="text"
                            name="fullname" size="25" />
Your e-mail address: <input type="text"
                            name="e-address" size="25" />
</pre></p>
<p>Check all that apply:<br />
<input type="checkbox" name="likeit" checked="checked" />
I really like your Web site.<br />
<input type="checkbox" name="best" />
One of the best sites I've seen.<br />
<input type="checkbox" name="envy" />
I sure wish my pages looked as good as yours.<br />
<input type="checkbox" name="love" />
I think I'm in love with you.<br />
<input type="checkbox" name="idiot" />
I have no taste and I'm pretty dense,
so your site didn't do much for me.</p>

<p>Choose the one thing you love best about my pages:<br />
<input type="radio" name="lovebest" value="me" checked />
That gorgeous picture of you and your cats.<br />
<input type="radio" name="lovebest" value="cats" />
All those moving poems about your cats.<br />
<input type="radio" name="lovebest" value="burbs" />
The inspiring recap of your suburban childhood.<br />
<input type="radio" name="lovebest" value="treasures" />
The detailed list of all your Elvis memorabilia.</p>

<p>Imagine my site as a book, video, or album.<br />
Select the number of copies you think it would sell:<br />
<select size="3" name="potential">
<option selected>Million copy bestseller for sure!</option>
<option>100,000+ (would be Oprah's favorite)</option>
<option>Thousands (an under-appreciated classic)</option>
<option>Very few: not banal enough for today's public</option>
</select></p>

<p>How do you think I could improve my site?
<select name="suggestion">
<option selected>Couldn't be better</option>
<option>More about the cats</option>
<option>More Elvis stuff</option>
<option>More family pictures</option>
</select></p>

<p>Feel free to type more praise, marriage proposals,
gift offers, etc. below:<br />
<textarea name="comments" rows="4" cols="55">
I just want to thank you so much for touching my life.
</textarea>
<input type="submit" value="Click Here to Submit" />
<input type="reset" value="Erase and Start Over" /></p>
</form>
</body></html>
```

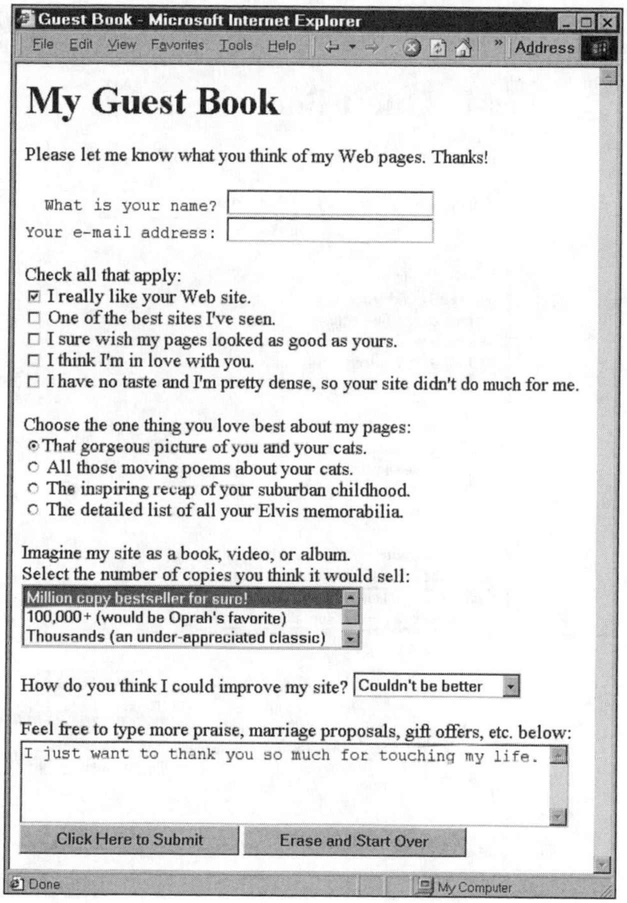

FIGURE 8.2

The form listed in Figure 8.1 uses nearly every type of HTML form input element.

Notice that some of the text in Figures 8.2 and 8.3 is monospaced, meaning that every letter is the same width. Monospaced text makes it easy to line up a form input box with the box above or below it and can make your forms look neater. To use monospaced text in all or part of a form, enclose the text between <pre> and </pre> tags. Using these tags also relieves you from having to put <br /> at the end of every line because the <pre> tag puts a line break on the page at every line break in the HTML document.

Text Input

To ask the user for a specific piece of information within a form, use the `<input />` tag. This tag must fall between the `<form>` and `</form>` tags, but it can be anywhere on the page in relation to text, images, and other HTML tags. For example, to ask for someone's name you could type the following:

```
What's your first name? <input type="text" size="20" maxlength="30"
name="firstname" />
What's your last name? <input type="text" size="20" maxlength="30"
name="lastname" />
```

The `type` attribute indicates what type of form element to display—a simple one-line text entry box in this case. (Each element type is discussed individually in the following sections.)

The size attribute indicates approximately how many characters wide the text input box should be. If you are using a proportionally spaced font, the width of the input will vary depending on what the user enters. If the input is too long to fit in the box, most Web browsers will automatically scroll the text to the left.

maxlength determines the number of characters the user is allowed to type into the text box. If someone tries to type beyond the specified length, the extra characters won't appear. You can specify a length that is longer, shorter, or the same as the physical size of the text box. size and maxlength are used only for type="text" because other input types (check boxes, radio buttons, and so on) have a fixed size.

> If you want the user to enter text without its being displayed on the screen, you can use `<input type="password" />` instead of `<input type="text" />`. Asterisks (***) are then displayed in place of the text the user types. The size, maxlength, and name attributes work exactly the same for type="password" as for type="text".

Identifying Each Piece of Form Data

No matter what type an input element is, you must give a name to the data it gathers. You can use any name you like for each input item, as long as each one on the form is different. When the form is sent to you (or to your form-processing script), each data item is identified by name.

For example, if someone entered Jane and Doe in the text box defined under Text Input previously, you would see something like the following two lines in the email message you get when she submits the form:

```
firstname=Jane
lastname=Doe
```

Figure 8.4 is a sample email message generated by the form-processing script specified in the form in Figure 8.3. Notice that each data element is identified by the name given to it in Figure 8.1.

> Depending on which form-processing script you use, you might see the data in a different format than that shown in Figure 8.4.

FIGURE 8.4

Clicking the Submit button in Figure 8.3 causes this information to be sent to me@mysite.com by the /htbin/generic form-processing script.

```
fullname=Bradley Pitt
e-address=brad@hollywood.com
likeit=on
best=on
envy=on
love=on
lovebest=cats
potential=Very few: not banal enough for today's public
suggestion=More about the cats
comments=Absolutely stunning. Really. Wow.
```

Including Hidden Data

Want to send certain data items to the server script that processes a form but don't want the user to see them? Use the input type="hidden" attribute. This attribute has no effect on the display at all; it just adds any name and value you specify to the form results when they are submitted.

You might use this attribute to tell a script where to email the form results. For example, the following might indicate that the results should be mailed to me@mysite.com:

```
<input type="hidden" name="mail_to" value="me@mysite.com" />
```

For this attribute to have any effect, someone must create a script or program to read this line and do something about it. My ISP's form script uses this hidden value to determine where to email the form data.

Most scripts require at least one or two hidden input elements. Consult the person who wrote or provided you with the script for details.

Check Boxes

NEW TERM The simplest input type is a *check box*, which appears as a small square the user can select or deselect by clicking. You must give each check box a name. If you want a check box to be checked by default when the form comes up, include the checked attribute. For example, the following would make two check boxes:

```
<input type="checkbox" name="baby" checked /> Baby Grand Piano
<input type="checkbox" name="mini" /> Mini Piano Stool
```

The one labeled Baby Grand Piano would be checked. (The user would have to click it to turn it off if he didn't want a piano.) The one marked Mini Piano Stool would be unchecked to begin with, so the user would have to click it to turn it on.

When the form is submitted, selected check boxes appear in the form result:

```
baby=on
```

Blank (*deselected*) check boxes do not appear in the form output at all.

8

The new XHTML and XML standards will require all attributes to have an equal sign followed by a value. Therefore, to make your pages 100 percent XHTML compatible, you may eventually need to start using `checked="checked"` instead of just `checked`.

Right now, however, I recommend using `checked` without the `="checked"` to avoid confusing some older Web browsers.

Speaking of XHTML, the standard also includes several new form input elements to give you greater control over how form data is entered and processed. This is certainly something to look forward to, but as yet no current Web browsers recognize those new input elements.

You can use more than one check box with the same name, but different values, as in the following code:

```
<input type="checkbox" name="pet" value="dog"> dog
<input type="checkbox" name="pet" value="cat"> cat
<input type="checkbox" name="pet" value="iguana"> iguana
```

If the user checks both cat and iguana, the submission result includes the following:

```
pet=cat
pet=iguana
```

Radio Buttons

NEW TERM *Radio buttons*, where only one choice can be selected at a time, are almost as simple to implement as check boxes. Just use `type="radio"` and give each of the options its own `input` tag, but use the same `name` for all of the radio buttons in a group:

```
<input type="radio" name="card" value="v" checked /> Visa
<input type="radio" name="card" value="m" /> MasterCard
```

The `value` can be any name or code you choose. If you include the `checked` attribute, that button is selected by default. (No more than one radio button with the same `name` can be checked.)

If the user selects MasterCard from the preceding radio button set, the following is included in the form submission to the server script:

```
card=m
```

If the user doesn't change the default `checked` selection, `card=v` is sent instead.

Selection Lists

NEW TERM Both *scrolling lists* and *pull-down pick lists* are created with the `<select>` tag. You use this tag together with the `<option>` tag:

```
<select name="extras" size="3" multiple>
<option selected> Electric windows</option>
<option> AM/FM Radio</option>
<option> Turbocharger</option>
</select>
```

No HTML tags other than `<option>` and `</option>` should appear between the `<select>` and `</select>` tags.

Unlike the text input type, the `size` attribute here determines how many items show at once on the selection list. If `size="2"` were used in the preceding code, only the first two options would be visible, and a scrollbar would appear next to the list so the user could scroll down to see the third option.

Including the `multiple` attribute allows users to select more than one option at a time, and the `selected` attribute makes an option selected by default. The actual text that accompanies selected options is returned when the form is submitted. If the user selected Electric windows and Turbocharger, for instance, the form results would include the following lines:

```
extras=Electric windows
extras=Turbocharger
```

(As I cautioned you earlier with regard to the `checked` attribute, the new XHTML standard will eventually require you to use `multiple="multiple"` and `selected="selected"`. For now you should continue to use just `multiple` and `selected` for maximum compatibility with current browsers.)

If you leave out the `size` attribute or specify `size="1"`, the list will create a pull-down pick list. Pick lists cannot allow multiple choices; they are logically equivalent to a group of radio buttons. For example, another way to choose between credit card types follows:

```
<select name="card">
<option> Visa</option>
<option> MasterCard</option>
</select>
```

Text Areas

8

The `<input type="text">` attribute mentioned earlier only allows the user to enter a single line of text. When you want to allow multiple lines of text in a single input item, use the `<textarea>` and `</textarea>` tags instead. Any text you include between these two tags is displayed as the default entry. Here's an example:

```
<textarea name="comments" rows="4" cols="20">
Please send more information.
</textarea>
```

As you probably guessed, the `rows` and `cols` attributes control the number of rows and columns of text that fit in the input box. Text area boxes do have a scrollbar, however, so the user can enter more text than fits in the display area.

 Some older browsers do not support the placement of default text within the text area. In these browsers, the text may appear outside the text input box.

Submit!

Every form must include a button that submits the form data to the server. You can put any label you like on this button with the `value` attribute:

```
<input type="submit" value="Place My Order Now!" />
```

A gray button will be sized to fit the label you put in the `value` attribute. When the user clicks it, all data items on the form are sent to the email address or program script specified in the `form action` attribute.

You can also include a button that clears all entries on the form so users can start over if they change their minds or make mistakes. Use the following:

```
<input type="reset" value="Clear This Form and Start Over" />
```

Creating a Custom Submit Button

You can combine forms with all the HTML bells and whistles you learn about in this book, including backgrounds, graphics, text colors, tables, and frames. When you do so, however, the standard Submit and Reset buttons may start looking a little bland.

Fortunately, there is an easy way to substitute your own graphics for those buttons. Type the following to use an image of your choice for a Submit button:

```
<input type="image" src="button.gif" />
```

The image named button.gif will appear on the page, and the form will be submitted whenever someone clicks that image. You can also include any attributes normally used with the <img /> tag, such as border or align. (Hour 10, "Putting Graphics on a Web Page," introduces the <img /> tag.)

The exact pixel coordinates where the mouse clicked an image button are sent along with the form data. For example, if someone entered bigjoe@chicago.net in the form in Figure 8.6, the resulting form data might look like the following:

Anotherone=bigjoe@chicago.net

&x=75

&y=36

Normally you should ignore the x and y coordinates, but some server scripts use them to turn the button into an imagemap.

Figures 8.5 and 8.6 show a very simple form that uses a customized submit button. (You'll see how to make graphics like the signup.gif button in Hour 9, "Creating Your Own Web Page Graphics.")

FIGURE 8.5

The <input /> *tag on this page uses a custom graphical submit button.*

```
<html><head><title>FREE!</title></head>
<body>
<h1>Free Electronic Junk Mail!</h1>
To start receiving junk e-mail from us daily*, enter your
e-mail address below and click on the <i>SignUP!</i> button.
<form method="POST" action="/htbin/generic">
<input type="text" name="anotherone" size="25" />
<input type="image" src="signup.gif" border="0" align="top" />
</form>
*<small>By clicking the above button, you also agree to the
terms of our Marketing Agreement, which is available upon
request at our offices in Bangkok, Thailand. A fee may be
charged for removal from our list if you elect at a later
date not to receive additional sales literature.</small>
</body></html>
```

FIGURE 8.6

Forms don't need to be complex to be effective. (They might need to be a little less blunt, though.)

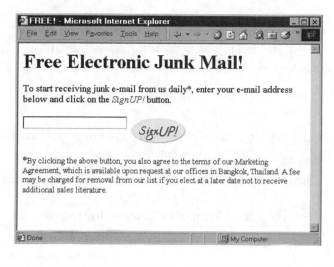

8

You can make a button that cancels the form and proceeds to another page (ignoring all information the user has entered so far) simply by linking to that other page. Here is an example:

```
<a href="nodice.htm">Click here to cancel.</a>
```

There is no specific form type for a graphical reset button, but you can achieve the same effect by putting an image link to the current page, like this:

```
<a href="thispage.htm"><img src="cancel.gif" /></a>
```

(Don't worry if you don't really understand the last line yet. You'll learn all about the `<img />` tag in Hour 10.)

The most common mistake many companies make when putting a first order form on the Internet is the same all too often made on paper order forms: leaving out a key piece of information. To avoid yourself the embarrassment of an incomplete order form, visit the 24-Hour HTML Café site at `http://24hourHTMLcafe.com/hour8/`.

Click the "Sample Form" link to bring up a sample order form. This is just your basic, run-of-the-mill product order form with credit card information, name, address, and so forth. Use it as a starting template and then add your own products, graphics, and unique information. Don't forget to change the `<form action>` to your own server script address!

Summary

This hour demonstrated how to create HTML forms, which allow your Web pages readers to enter specific information and send it back to you via email.

You also found that you can set up a script or program to process form data. Your ISP or server software vendor can help you do this.

You will learn how to make an order form add its own totals automatically in Hour 19, "Web Page Scripting for Non-Programmers."

Table 8.1 summarizes the HTML tags and attributes covered in this hour.

TABLE 8.1 HTML Tags and Attributes Covered in Hour 8

Tag	Attribute	Function
`<form>...</form>`		Indicates an input form.
	`action="..."`	The address of the script to process this form input.
	`method="..."`	How the form input will be sent to the server. Normally set to post, rather than get.
`<input />`		An input element for a form.
	`type="..."`	The type for this input widget. Possible values are checkbox, hidden, radio, reset, submit, text, and image.
	`name="..."`	The name of this item, as passed to the script.
	`value="..."`	The default value for a text or hidden item; for a check box or radio button, the value to be submitted with the form; for reset or submit buttons, the label for the button itself.
	`src="..."`	The source file for an image.
	`checked`	For check boxes and radio buttons, indicates that this item is checked.
	`size="..."`	The width, in characters, of a text input region.
	`maxlength="..."`	The maximum number of characters that can be entered into a text region.
	`align="..."`	For images in forms, determines how the text and image will align (same as with the `<img />` tag; see Hour 10).

Tag	Attribute	Function
`<textarea>...</textarea>`		Indicates a multiline text entry form element. Default text can be included.
	`name="..."`	The name to be passed to the script.
	`rows="..."`	The number of rows this text area displays.
	`cols="..."`	The number of columns (characters) this text area displays.
`<select>...</select>`		Creates a menu or scrolling list of possible items.
	`name="..."`	The name that is passed to the script.
	`size="..."`	The number of elements to display. If size is indicated, the selection becomes a scrolling list. If no size is given, the selection is a pull-down pick list menu.
	`multiple`	Allows multiple selections from the list.
`<option>...</option>`		Indicates a possible item within a <select> element.
	`selected`	With this attribute included, the option will be selected by default in the list.
	`value="..."`	The value to submit if this option is selected when the form is submitted.

Q&A

Q I've heard that it's dangerous to send credit card numbers over the Internet. Can't thieves intercept form data on its way to me?

A It is possible to intercept form data (and any Web pages or email) as it travels through the Internet. If you ask for credit card numbers or other sensitive information on your forms, you should ask the company who runs your Web server about "secure" forms processing. There are several reliable technologies for eliminating the risk of high-tech eavesdroppers, but it may cost you quite a bit to implement the security measures.

To put the amount of risk in perspective, remember that it is much more difficult to intercept information traveling through the Internet than it is to look over someone's shoulder in a restaurant or retail store.

Q **I'm not set up to take credit cards or electronic payments. How do I make an order form for people to print out on paper and mail to me with a check?**

A Any form can be printed out. Just leave off the Submit button if you don't want any email submissions; instead, instruct people to fill out the form and select File, Print. Remember to include a link to some other page so they can return to the rest of your Web site after printing the form—and don't forget to tell them where they should send the check!

Q **Can I put forms on a CD-ROM, or do they have to be on the Internet?**

A You can put a form anywhere you can put a Web page. If it's on a disk or CD-ROM instead of a Web server, it can be filled out by people whether they are connected to the Internet or not. Of course, they must be connected to the Internet (or your local intranet) when they click the Submit button, or the information won't get to you.

Q **I've seen sites on the Internet that use pick-lists to link between multiple pages, kind of like a navigation menu. How do they do that?**

A All things are possible if you have a professional programmer to write custom scripts for you. Even if you don't, you can find some sample prewritten scripts for this sort of thing on the Internet (search under *CGI Scripts* in any major search engine, such as www.yahoo.com). Even after you locate a prewritten script, however, you may still need some assistance installing it and getting it to work properly on your Web server.

Workshop

Quiz

1. What do you need to get from the people who administer your Web server computer before you can put a form on the Internet?

2. Write the HTML to create a "guestbook" form that asks someone for his or her name, sex, age, and email address. Assume that you have a form-processing script set up at /cgi/generic and that you need to include the following hidden input element to tell the script where to send the form results:

   ```
   <input type="hidden" name="mailto" value="you@yoursite.com" />
   ```

3. If you had created an image named sign-in.gif, how would you use it as the Submit button for the guestbook in question 2?

8

Answers

1. The Internet address of a script or program that is set up specifically to process form data.

2.
```
<html><head><title>My Guestbook</title></head>
<body>
<h1>My Guestbook: Please Sign In</h1>
<form method="post" action="/cgi/generic">
<input type="hidden" name="mailto" value="you@yoursite.com" />
Your name: <input type="text" name="name" size="20" /><p>
Your sex:
<input type="radio" name="sex" value="male" /> male
<input type="radio" name="sex" value="female" /> female<p>
Your age: <input type="text" name="age" size="4" /><p>
Your e-mail address:
<input type="text" name="email" size="30" /><p>
<input type="submit" value="sign in" />
<input type="reset" value="erase" />
</form>
</body></html>
```

3. Replace

```
<input type="submit" value="Sign In" />
```

with

```
<input type="image" src="sign-in.gif" />
```

Exercise

- Create a form using all of the different types of input elements and selection lists to make sure you understand how each of them works.

PART III

Web Page Graphics

Hour

HOUR 9

Creating Your Own Web Page Graphics

You don't have to be an artist to put high-impact graphics and creative type on your Web pages. You don't need to spend hundreds or thousands of dollars on software, either. This hour tells you how to create the images you need to make visually exciting Web pages. Although the example figures in this chapter use a popular Windows graphics program (Paint Shop Pro 6 from JASC Software), you can easily follow along with any major Windows or Macintosh graphics application.

This hour is only concerned with creating the actual graphics files, so it doesn't actually discuss any HTML tags at all. In Hour 10, "Putting Graphics on a Web Page," you'll see how to integrate your graphics with your HTML pages.

One of the best ways to save time creating the graphics and media files is, of course, to avoid creating them altogether. Any graphic or media clip you see on any site is instantly reusable as soon as the copyright holder grants (or sells) you the right to copy it.

Grabbing a graphic from any Web page is as simple as right-clicking it (or holding down the button on a Macintosh mouse) and selecting Save Image As in Netscape Navigator or Save Picture As in Microsoft Explorer. Extracting a background image from a page is just as easy: Right-click it and select Save Background As.

Choosing Graphics Software

You can use almost any computer graphics program to create graphics images for your Web pages, from the simple paint program that comes free with your computer's operating system to an expensive professional program such as Adobe Photoshop. If you have a digital camera or scanner attached to your computer, it probably came with some graphics software capable of creating Web page graphics.

If you already have some software you think might be good for creating Web graphics, try using it to do everything described in this chapter. If it can't do some of the tasks covered here, it probably won't be a good tool for Web graphics.

To Do

One excellent and inexpensive program that does provide everything you're likely to need is Paint Shop Pro from JASC, Inc. If you are using a Windows computer, I highly recommend that you download a free, fully functional evaluation copy of Paint Shop Pro 6 before reading the rest of this chapter. (Macintosh users should download BME from http://www.softlogik.com instead, because Paint Shop Pro is currently available for Windows only.)

1. Start your Web browser and go to http://www.jasc.com/.

2. Click the Downloads link and choose Paint Shop Pro.

3. Click the download site nearest you; the file will transfer to your hard drive. You are asked to confirm where you want to put the file on your hard drive—be sure to remember which folder it goes into!

4. Once the download transfer is complete, use Windows Explorer to find the file you downloaded and double-click it to install Paint Shop Pro.

The Paint Shop Pro software you can get online is a fully functional share-ware evaluation copy. If you agree with me that it's essential for working with Web page images, please be prompt about sending the $99 registra-tion fee to the program's creators at JASC Software. (The address is in the online help in the software.) I'm confident that you're not going to find any other graphics software even close to the power and usability of Paint Shop Pro for anywhere near $99. (In fact, I have—and know how to use—all the leading super-expensive commercial graphics programs from Photoshop on down, and Paint Shop Pro is the best by far for day-to-day work with Web graphics.)

9

Almost all the graphics you see in this book were created with Paint Shop Pro, and this chapter uses Paint Shop Pro to illustrate several key Web graphics techniques you'll need to know. Of course, there are so many ways to produce images with Paint Shop Pro I can't even begin to explain them all. If you'd like a quick but complete tutorial on using Paint Shop Pro to make high-impact Web page graphics, I recommend *Sams Teach Yourself Paint Shop Pro in 24 Hours*. You can order this book from JASC when you reg-ister the software or at any computer bookstore.

Graphics Basics

Two forces are always at odds when you post graphics and multimedia on the Internet. Your eyes and ears want everything to be as detailed and accurate as possible, but your clock and wallet want files to be as small as possible. Intricate, colorful graphics mean big file sizes, which can take a long time to transfer even over a fast connection.

How do you maximize the quality of your presentation while minimizing file size? To make these choices, you need to understand how color and resolution work together to create a subjective sense of quality.

NEW TERM The *resolution* of an image is the number of individual dots, or *pixels* (the indi-vidual dots that make up a digital image), that make up an image. Large, high-resolution images generally take longer to transfer and display than small, low-resolution images. Resolution is usually written as the width times the height; a 300×200 image, for example, is 300 dots wide and 200 dots high.

NEW TERM You might be surprised to find that resolution isn't the most significant factor determining an image file's storage size (and transfer time). This is because images used on Web pages are always stored and transferred in *compressed* form. *Image compression* is the mathematical manipulation that images are put through to squeeze out repetitive patterns. The mathematics of image compression is complex, but the basic idea is that repeating patterns or large areas of the same color can be squeezed out when the image is stored on a disk. This makes the image file much smaller and allows it to be transferred faster over the Internet. The Web browser program can then restore the original appearance of the image when the image is displayed.

In the rest of this chapter, you'll learn exactly how to create graphics with big visual impact and small file sizes. The techniques you'll use to accomplish this depend on the contents and purpose of each image. There are as many uses for Web page graphics as there are Web pages, but four types of graphics are by far the most common:

- Photos of people, products, or places
- Graphical banners and logos
- Snazzy-looking buttons or icons to link between pages
- Background textures or wallpaper to go behind pages

The last of these is covered in Hour 11, "Custom Backgrounds and Colors," but you can learn to create the other three kinds of graphics right now.

Preparing Photographic Images

To put photos on your Web pages, you need some kind of scanner or digital camera. You'll often need to use the custom software that comes with your scanner or camera to save pictures on your hard drive. Note, however, that you can control any scanner that is compatible with the TWAIN interface standard directly from Paint Shop Pro and most other graphics programs—see the software documentation for details.

> If you don't have a scanner or digital camera, any Kodak film-developing store can transfer photos from 35mm film to a CD-ROM for a modest fee. You can then use Paint Shop Pro to open and modify the Kodak Photo-CD files. Some large photo developers other than Kodak offer similar digitizing services.

Once you have the pictures, you can use Paint Shop Pro (or another similar graphics program) to get them ready for the Web.

You want Web page graphics to be as compact as possible, so you'll usually need to crop or reduce the size of your digital photos. Follow these steps to crop a picture in Paint Shop Pro:

1. Click the rectangular selection tool on the tools palette. (The tools palette is shown on the left in Figure 9.1. You can drag it wherever you want it, so it may be in a different place on your screen.)

2. Click the top-left corner of the part of the image you want to keep, and hold down the left mouse button while you drag down to the lower-right corner.

3. Select Image, Crop to Selection (see Figure 9.1).

9

FIGURE 9.1

Use the rectangular selection tool to crop images as tightly as possible.

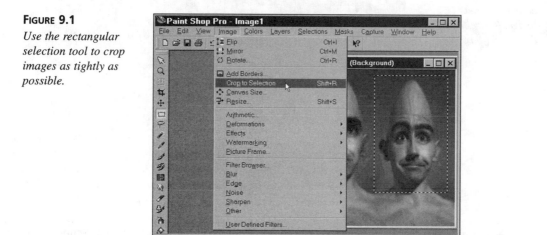

Even after cropping, your image may be larger than it needs to be for a Web page. Generally, a complex photograph should be no more than 300×300 pixels, and a simpler photo can look fine at 100×50 or so.

> Notice that in Paint Shop Pro the resolution of the current image is shown at the bottom-right corner of the window. The image may look larger or smaller than it really is because Paint Shop Pro automatically adjusts the image to fit in the window while you're working on it. (The current magnification ratio is shown just above each image, in the title bar.) To see the image at the size it will appear on a Web page, select View, Normal Viewing (1:1).

To change an image's resolution, and therefore its apparent size, use the Image, Resize command. (Notice that in some software, including earlier versions of Paint Shop Pro, this option is called Resample.) You'll get the Resize dialog box shown in Figure 9.2.

You'll almost always want Smart Size, Resize All Layers, and Maintain Aspect Ratio Of selected. When you enter in pixels or a percentage of the original the width you'd like the image to be, the height will be calculated automatically to keep the image from squishing out of shape.

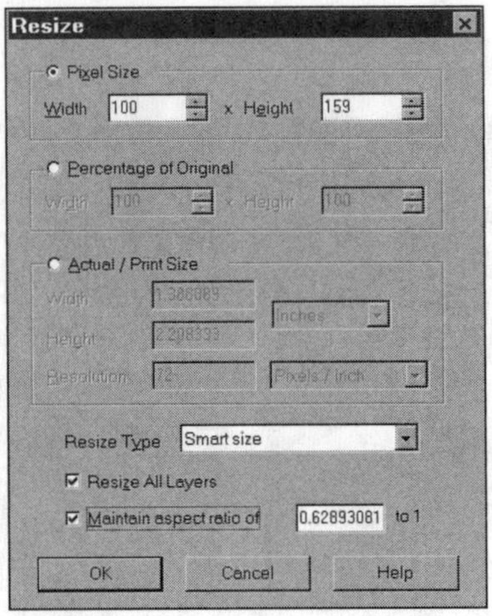

FIGURE 9.2

To change the size of an image, select Image, Resize to get this dialog box.

Many photographs will require some color correction to look their best on a computer screen. Like most photo editing programs, Paint Shop Pro offers many options for adjusting an image's brightness, contrast, and color balance.

Most of these options are pretty intuitive, but the most important and powerful one may be unfamiliar if you're not an old graphics pro. Whenever an image appears too dark or too light, select Colors, Adjust, Gamma Correction. For most images, this works better than Colors, Adjust, Brightness/Contrast, because it doesn't wash out bright or dark areas.

As shown in Figure 9.3, you can move the sliders in the Gamma Correction dialog box to adjust the correction factor until the image looks about right. (Numbers above 1 make the image lighter, and numbers between 1 and 0 make the image darker.) If the color in the image seems a little off, try deselecting the Link check box, which allows you to move the Red, Green, and Blue sliders separately and to adjust the color balance.

Most of the other image editing tools in Paint Shop Pro offer small preview windows like the one in Figure 9.3, so a little playful experimentation is the best way to find out what each of them does.

FIGURE 9.3

Gamma correction is the best way to fix images that are too dark or too light.

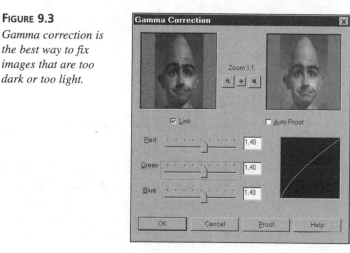

Controlling JPEG Compression

Photographic images look best when saved in the JPEG file format. When you're finished adjusting the size and appearance of your photo, select File, Save As and choose the JPEG-JFIF Compliant file type with Standard Encoding, as shown in Figure 9.4.

Figure 9.4 also shows the dialog box you'll see when you click the Options button on the Save As dialog box. You can control the compression ratio for saving JPEG files by adjusting the Compression Factor setting between 1 percent (high quality, large file size) and 99 percent (low quality, small file size).

FIGURE 9.4

Paint Shop Pro allows you to trade reduced file size for image quality when saving JPEG images.

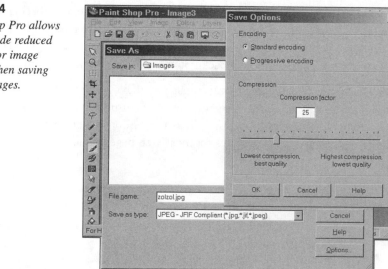

You may want to experiment a bit to see how various JPEG compression levels affect the quality of your images, but 25 percent compression is generally a good compromise between speed and quality for most photographic images.

Creating Banners and Buttons

Graphics that you create from scratch, such as banners and buttons, involve considerations different than photographs.

The first decision you need to make when you produce a banner or button is how big it should be. Almost everyone accessing the Web now (or in the foreseeable future) has a computer with one of three screen sizes. The most common resolution for palm-sized computers and televisions is 640×480 pixels. The resolution of most laptop computers today is 800×600 pixels, and 1,024×768 pixels is the preferred resolution of most new desktop computers and future laptops. You should generally plan your graphics so that they will always fit in the smallest of these screens, with room to spare for scrollbars and margins.

This means that full-sized banners and title graphics should be no more than 600 pixels wide. Photos and large artwork should be from 100 to 300 pixels in each dimension, and smaller buttons and icons should be 20 to 100 pixels tall and wide.

Figure 9.5 shows the dialog box you get when you select File, New to start a new image. You should always begin with 16.7 million colors (24-bit) as the image type. You can always change its size later with Image, Crop or Image, Enlarge Canvas; don't worry if you aren't sure exactly how big it needs to be.

For the background color, you should usually choose white to match the background that most Web browsers use for Web pages. (You'll see how to change a page's background color in Hour 11.) When you know you'll be making a page with a background other than white, you can choose a different background color, as shown in Figure 9.5.

When you enter the width and height of the image in pixels and click OK, you are faced with a blank canvas—an intimidating sight if you're as art-phobic as most of us! Fortunately, computer graphics programs such as Paint Shop Pro make it amazingly easy to produce professional-looking graphics for most Web page applications.

FIGURE 9.5

You need to decide on the approximate size of an image before you start working on it.

New Image	☒
Image Dimensions	

Width 300
Height 100   Pixels
Resolution 72   Pixels / inch

Image Characteristics

Background color   Background Color
Image type   16.7 Million Colors (24 Bit)

Memory Required: 87.9 KBytes

OK   Cancel   Help

9

Often, you will want to incorporate some fancy lettering into your Web page graphics. For example, you might want to put a title banner at the top of your page that uses a decorative font with a drop-shadow or other special effects. To accomplish this in Paint Shop Pro, perform the following steps:

1. Choose the color you want the lettering to be from the color palette on the right edge of the Paint Shop Pro window. (Press the letter C to make the color palette appear if you don't see it.)

2. Click the A tool on the toolbar, and then click anywhere on the image. The Add Text dialog box shown in Figure 9.6 appears.

3. Choose a font and point size for the lettering, and make sure Floating and Antialias are selected under Create As. (This smoothes the edges of the text.) Click OK.

4. Click anywhere in the image, and then grab and drag the text with the mouse to position it where you want it (usually in the center of the image).

The list of fonts you see when you use the text tool will almost certainly be different than those shown in Figure 9.6. You will see only the fonts previously installed on your computer.

When you first put the text onto the image, it shimmers with a moving dotted outline. This means that it is selected and that any special effects you choose from the menu will apply to the shape of the letters you just made. For example, you might select Image, Effects, Chisel to add a chiseled outline around the text. Figure 9.7 shows the dialog box that would appear.

FIGURE 9.6
Use Paint Shop Pro's text tool to create elegant lettering in a graphics image.

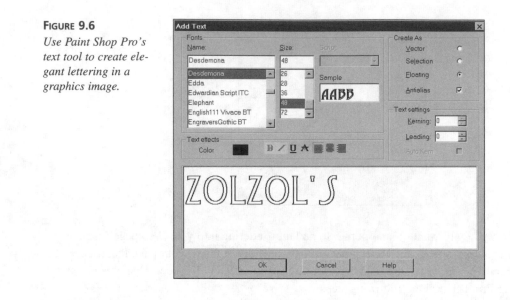

Notice that you can adjust the chisel effect and see the results in a small preview window before you actually apply them to the image. This makes it very easy to learn what various effects do simply by experimenting with them. Using only the text tool and the four choices on the Image, Effects submenu (Buttonize, Chisel, Cutout, and Drop Shadow), you can create quite a variety of useful and attractive Web graphics.

FIGURE 9.7
Like most menu choices in Paint Shop Pro, the Image, Effects, Chisel command gives you an easy-to-use preview.

You may also want to deform, blur, sharpen, or otherwise play around with your text after you've applied an effect to it. To do so, simply select Image, Deformations, Deformation Browser (to warp the shape of the letters) or Image, Filter Browser (to apply an image-processing filter). You get a dialog box like the one shown in Figure 9.8, which lets you pick from a list of effects and preview each one.

In Figure 9.8, I chose the Edge Enhance filter from the Filter Browser, which adds a sparkly effect to the chiseled lettering. You can have a lot of fun playing around with all the different options in the filter and deformation browsers!

FIGURE 9.8

Select Image, Filter Browser to play with all the image-processing filters available, and then choose the one you want.

9

Reducing the Number of Colors

One of the most effective ways to reduce the download time for an image is to reduce the number of colors. This can drastically reduce the visual quality of some photographic images, but works great for most banners, buttons, and other icons.

In Paint Shop Pro, you can do this by selecting Colors, Decrease Color Depth. (Most other graphics programs have a similar option.) Choose 16 Colors (4-bit) when your image has very few colors in it. If the image has lots of colors (or the image doesn't look good when you try 16 Colors), select Colors, Decrease Color Depth, 256 Colors (8-bit) instead. The software will automatically find the best palette of 16 or 256 colors for approximating the full range of colors in the image.

Even if you only use two or three colors in an image, you should still select Colors, Reduce Color Depth, 16 Colors before you save it. If you don't, the image file will waste some space "leaving room for" lots of colors—even though very few are actually in use.

When you reduce the number of colors in an image, you will see a dialog box with several choices (see Figure 9.9). For Web page images, you will almost always want to choose Optimized Octree and Nearest Color. Leave all the options on the right side of the dialog box unchecked; they will seldom improve the quality of an image noticeably.

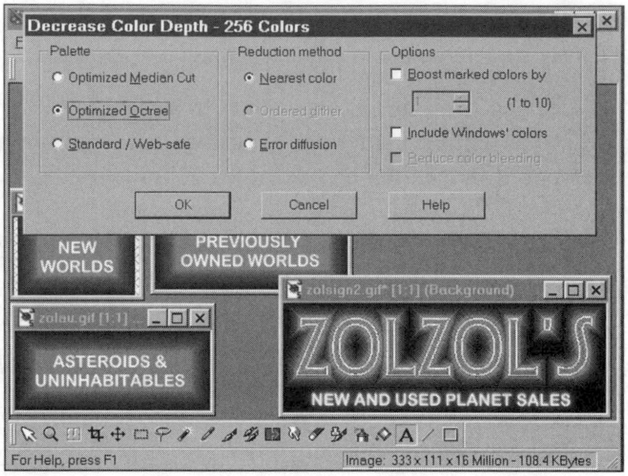

FIGURE 9.9

Reducing the number of colors in an image can significantly decrease file size without dramatically changing the appearance of the image.

Dithering (also called *error diffusion* in Paint Shop Pro) means using random dots or patterns to intermix palette colors. This can make images look better in some cases, but should usually be avoided for Web page graphics. Why? It substantially increases the information complexity of an image, and that almost always results in much larger file sizes and slower downloads. Listen to your Great Uncle Oliver and "Don't dither!"

There is a special file format for images with a limited number of colors; it's called the Graphics Interchange Format (GIF). To save a GIF image in Paint Shop Pro, select File, Save As and choose CompuServe Graphics Interchange (*.gif) as the image type.

Interlaced GIFs and Progressive JPEGs

Both the GIF and JPEG image file formats offer a nifty feature that makes images appear faster than they otherwise could. An image can be stored in such a way that a "rough draft" of the image appears quickly, and the details are filled in as the download finishes. This has a profound psychological effect, because it gives people something to look at instead of drumming their fingers, waiting for a large image to pour slowly onto the screen.

A file stored with this feature is called an *interlaced GIF* or *progressive JPEG*. Despite the different names, the visual results are similar.

NEW TERM An *interlaced GIF* file is an image that appears blocky at first, and then more and more detailed as it finishes downloading. Similarly, a *progressive JPEG* file appears blurry at first and then gradually comes into focus.

Most graphics programs that can handle GIF files enable you to choose whether to save them interlaced or noninterlaced. In Paint Shop Pro, for example, you can choose Version 89a and Interlaced by clicking the Options button in the Save As dialog box just before you save a GIF file (see Figure 9.10).

9

FIGURE 9.10

Paint Shop Pro lets you save interlaced GIF images, which appear to display faster when loading.

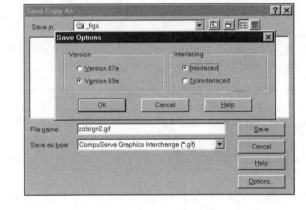

To save a progressive JPEG file, select Save As (or Save Copy As), choose the JPG-JPEG-JFIF Compliant image type, click the Options button, and select Progressive Encoding. The progressive JPEG standard is quite new and is only supported by Netscape Navigator version 2 or later and Microsoft Internet Explorer version 3 or later.

Browsers that don't support progressive JPEG will not display the file as if it were just a regular JPEG—they will display either nothing at all or a message saying the file isn't recognizable. Interlaced GIFs, on the other hand, appear correctly even in older browsers that don't support two-stage display.

 Image files smaller than about 3KB will usually load so fast that nobody will ever see the interlacing or progressive display anyway. In fact, very small images may actually load more slowly when interlaced. Save these tricks for larger images.

Summary

In this hour you learned the basics of preparing graphics for use on Web pages. You saw how to download and use the popular graphics program Paint Shop Pro when working with photos, banners, buttons, and other Web page images (although the techniques you learned will work with many other graphics programs as well). You also found out how to decide among the various graphics file formats used for Web page graphics, and how to make images that appear in stages, for the illusion of speed.

Q&A

Q **Shouldn't I just hire a graphics artist to design my pages instead of learning all this stuff?**

A If you have plenty of money and need a visually impressive site—or if you think that ugly building with chartreuse trim that people are always complaining about actually looks pretty nice—hiring some professional help might not be a bad idea. Remember, however, that you probably know what you want better than anyone else does, which often counts more than artistic skills in producing a good Web page.

Q **I've produced graphics for printing on paper. Is making Web page graphics much different?**

A Yes. In fact, many of the rules for print graphics are reversed on the Web. Web page graphics have to be low-resolution, while print graphics should be as high-resolution as possible. White washes out black on computer screens, while black bleeds into white on paper. Also, someone may stop a Web page when only half the graphics are done. Try to avoid falling into old habits if you've done a lot of print graphics design.

Workshop

Quiz

1. Suppose you have a scanned picture of a horse that you need to put on a Web page. How big should you make it, and in what file format should you save it?

2. Your company logo is a black letter Z with a red circle behind it. What size should you draw or scan it, and in what file format should you save it for use on your Web page?

3. Should you save a 100×50 pixel button graphic as an interlaced GIF file?

Answers

1. Depending on how important the image is to your page, as small as 100×40 pixels or as large as 300×120 pixels. The JPEG format, with about 50 percent compression, would be best.

2. About 100×100 pixels is generally good for a logo, but a simple graphic like that will compress very well; you could make it up to 300×300 pixels if you want. Save it as a 16-color GIF file.

3. No. A small file like that will load just as fast or faster without interlacing.

Exercises

- If you have an archive of company (or personal) photos, look through it to find a few that might enhance your Web site. Scan them (or send them out to be scanned) so that you'll have a library of graphics all ready to draw from as you produce more pages in the future.

- Before you start designing graphics for an important business site, try spicing up your own personal home page. This will give you a chance to learn Paint Shop Pro (or your other graphics software) so you'll look like you know what you're doing when you tackle it at work.

9

HOUR 10

Putting Graphics on a Web Page

In Hour 9, "Creating Your Own Web Page Graphics," you started making some digital images for your Web pages. This hour shows you how easy it is to put those graphics on your pages with HTML.

To Do

You should get two or three images ready now so you can try putting them on your own pages as you follow along with this hour.

If you have some image files already saved in the GIF or JPEG format (the filenames will end in .gif or .jpg), use those. Otherwise, you can just grab some graphics I've put on the Internet for you to practice with. Here's how:

1. Enter the following address into your Web browser:

   http://24hourHTMLcafe.com/hour10/images.htm

   You should see a page with four images of hats and stars at the bottom.

2. Click Sample Images. You should see a magic hat and some stars.

▼   3. Save each of the graphics to your computer's hard drive by right-clicking each
       image (or holding down the mouse button if you use a Macintosh computer), and
       then selecting Save Image As from the pop-up menu.

       Put the graphics on your hard drive in whichever folder you use for creating Web
       pages.

    4. As you read this chapter, use these image files to practice putting images on your
       pages. (It's also fine to use any graphics you created while reading the previous
▲   chapter.)

At the *24-Hour HTML Café*, you'll find live links to many graphics and multimedia hotlists and hot sites, where you can find ready-to-use graphics. To
access these links, go to http://24hourHTMLcafe.com/hotsites.htm.

The familiar Web search engines and directories such as yahoo.com,
hotbot.com, and infoseek.com can become a gold mine of graphics images
just by leading you to sites related to your own theme. They can also help
you discover the oodles of sites specifically dedicated to providing free and
cheap access to reusable media collections.

Placing an Image on a Web Page

To put an image on a Web page, first move the image file into the same directory folder
as the HTML text file. Insert the following HTML tag at the point in the text where you
want the image to appear. Use the name of your image file instead of *myimage.gif*:

```
<img src="myimage.gif" />
```

Figure 10.1, for example, inserts several images at the top and bottom of the page.
Whenever a Web browser displays the HTML file in Figure 10.1, it will automatically
retrieve and display the image files as shown in Figure 10.2.

If you guessed that img stands for *image*, you're right; src stands for *source*, which is a
reference to the location of the image file. (As discussed in Hour 1, "Understanding
HTML and XML," a Web page image is always stored in a separate file from the text,
even though it appears to be part of the same page.)

Just as with the <a href> tag (covered in Hour 3, "Linking to Other Web Pages"),
you can specify any complete Internet address as the <img src>. Alternatively, you can
specify just the filename if an image will be located in the same directory folder as the
HTML file. You may also use relative addresses such as photos/birdy.jpg or
../smiley.gif.

FIGURE 10.1

Use the <img /> tag to place graphics images on a Web page.

```
<html>
<head><title>ZOLZOL's New &amp; Used Planets</title></head>
<body>
<img src="zolzol2.jpg" alt="Friendly Fen" />
<img src="zolsign2.gif" alt="ZOLZOL New and Used Planets" />
<img src="zolzol1.jpg" alt="Honest Han" />
<h1><img src="zolmodel.gif" alt="HomeStar 12" />
The HomeStar Model 12</h1>
<h3><i>Manufactured Home Planets for Today's Lifeforms</i></h3>
<p>Tired of sinking endless time and resources into the same
old run-down ecosystem? Maybe it's time to think about the
<b>modern solution</b> to all your environmental problems! Why
spend a fortune on another filthy, volcano-stained planet
riddled with unsightly hurricanes and lightning storms, when
you can own a <b>factory new</b> manufactured planet for a
fraction of the price? We custom-build each HomeStar Model 12
to your race's specifications, with your choice of sky and
ground colors, synthetic Sim-Veg landscaping, and odor-free
Quick-Gro hydroponic agricultural systems. Call ZOLZOL's for a
<b>free quotation</b> today!</p>
<p><small>(Orbital installation may incur additional fees, and
may require local zoning permits.)</small></p>
<div align="center">
<a href="zolzol.htm"><img src="zolhome.gif" border="0"
alt="ZOLZOL Home Page" /><br />
Click here for more bargains!</a></div>
</body></html>
```

10

FIGURE 10.2

When a Web browser displays the HTML page in Figure 10.1, it adds the images named zolzol2.jpg, zolsign.gif, zolzol1.jpg, zolmodel.gif, *and* zolzol.gif.

Theoretically, you can include an image from any Internet Web page within your own pages. For example, you could include a picture of my family by putting the following on your Web page:

`<img src="http://netletter.com/dicko/olivers.gif" />`

The image would be retrieved from my server computer whenever your page was displayed.

You could do this, but you shouldn't! Not only is it bad manners (it often costs people money whenever you pull something from their server computer), it can also make your pages display more slowly. You also have no way of controlling whether the image has been changed or deleted. If someone gives you permission to republish an image from one of his pages, always transfer a copy of that image to your computer and use a local file reference such as `<img src="olivers.gif" />`.

Labeling an Image

Each `<img />` tag in Figure 10.1 includes a short text message, such as `alt="Friendly Fen"`. The `alt` stands for *alternate text* because this message will appear in place of the image in older Web browsers that don't display graphics, or for those users who choose to turn off automatic image downloading in their Web browser preferences.

People who are using the latest Web browser software will see the message you put in the `alt` attribute, too. Because graphics files sometimes take a while to transfer over the Internet, most Web browsers show the text on a page first with the `alt` messages in place of the graphics (as shown in Figure 10.3).

Even after the graphics replace the `alt` messages, the `alt` message appears in a little box whenever the mouse pointer passes over an image. In Figure 10.2, for example, the mouse arrow is over the photo of Han Zol, and the `alt` message `Honest Han` is showing. The `alt` message also helps anyone who is visually impaired (or is using a voice-based telephone interface to read the Web page).

You should generally include a suitable `alt` attribute in every `<img />` tag on your Web pages, keeping in mind the variety of situations where people might see that message. A very brief description of the image is usually best, but Web page authors sometimes put short advertising messages or subtle humor in their `alt` messages. For small or unimportant images, it's fine to omit the `alt` message altogether.

FIGURE 10.3

People will see the alt *messages while they wait for the graphics to appear.*

Images That Are Links

You can make any image into a clickable link to another page with the same `<a href>` tag used to make text links. Figures 10.1 and 10.2 show an example; clicking the big button at the bottom of the page (or the words `Click here for more bargains!`) retrieves the page named `zolzol.htm`.

Normally, Web browsers draw a colored rectangle around the edge of each image link. Like text links, the rectangle usually appears blue to people who haven't visited the link recently, and purple to people who have. Since you seldom, if ever, want this unsightly line around your beautiful buttons, you should always include `border="0"` in any `<img />` tag within a link. (You learn more about the `border` attribute in Hour 13, "Page Design and Layout.")

Hour 11, "Custom Backgrounds and Colors," explains how to change the link colors. All the same rules and possibilities discussed in Hour 3, and Hour 7, "Email Links and Links Within a Page," apply to image links exactly as they do for text links. (You can link to another part of the same page with `<a href="#name">` and `<a name="name">`, for example.)

Horizontal Image Alignment

As discussed in Hour 5, "Text Alignment and Lists," you can use
`<div align="center">`, `<div align="right">`, and `<div align="left">` to align part of
a page to the center, right margin, or left margin. These tags affect both text and images.

For example, the last `<img />` tag in Figure 10.1 occurs between the `<div align=
"center">` tag and the closing `</div>` tag. You can see in Figure 10.2 that this causes
the image (as well as the text below it) to be centered on the page. Like text, images
are normally lined up with the left margin unless a `<div align="center">` or
`<div align="right">` tag indicates that they should be centered or right-justified.

As the first three images in Figures 10.4 and 10.5 demonstrate, you can also use
`<div align="center">` to center more than one image at a time. Since there are no
`<br />` or `<p>` tags between them, the three images all appear on one line and the entire
line is centered horizontally in the browser window.

FIGURE 10.4

*This page contains
examples of both
horizontal and vertical
image alignment, as
well as automatic
wrapping of text
around images.*

```
<html>
<head><title>ZOLZOL's New &amp; Used Planets</title></head>
<body>
<div align="center">
<img src="zolzol2.jpg" />
<img src="zolsign2.gif" align="top" />
<img src="zolzol1.jpg" /></div>
<h1><img src="zolsol3.gif" align="middle" /> Sol III</h1>
<h3><i>A real water planet at a desert planet price!</i></h3>
<p>This baby has its <b>original ecosystem</b> still installed,
and comes pre-populated by a technologically-savvy <b>ideal
slave species</b>! <i>PLUS:</i> <b>atmospheric oxygen</b>,
plenty of hydrocarbons, <b>H<sub>2</sub>O by the gigaton</b>,
and a wide range of metals, all pre-mined and ready for
off-planet shipment asan <b>immediate source of income</b> for
you and your families! So pack up the kids, hop in the
battlecruiser, and move onto this barely-used world today! Did
we mention the huge, close moon?
<img src="zolmoon.gif" align="absmiddle" />
<b>What a space base!</b> Don't let this once-in-a-millenium
opportunity pass you buy: <b> call ZOLZOL's</b> to place your
bid for Sol III* <b>right now!</b></p>
<p><img src="zolsol2.gif" align="left" />
<img src="zolsol4.gif" align="right" />
(And don't forget to bid on Sol III's sister planets, Sol II
and Sol IV! With a little investment in these great
fixer-uppers, you could have the <b>three-planet home of your
dreams</b> for one low price. <b>Call NOW!</b>)</p>
<br clear="all" /><hr />
<p><small><b>*Disclaimer:</b> One or more races on this planet
may possess chemical and/or nuclear weapons. All sales are
final. Invasion and enslavement of native species is the sole
responsibility of the customer and ZolZol's makes no
warrantees, expressed or implied. ZolZol believes this planet
to be in inhabititable condition, but some environmental
degradation is normal for speciated worlds.</small></p>
<div align="center">
<a href="zolzol.htm"><img src="zolhome.gif" border="0" /></a>
<a href="zolnew.htm"><img src="zolnew.gif" border="0" /></a>
<a href="zoljunk.htm"><img src="zoljunk.gif" border="0" /></a>
</div>
</body></html>
```

FIGURE 10.5

The HTML page listed in Figure 10.4, as it appears in a Web browser.

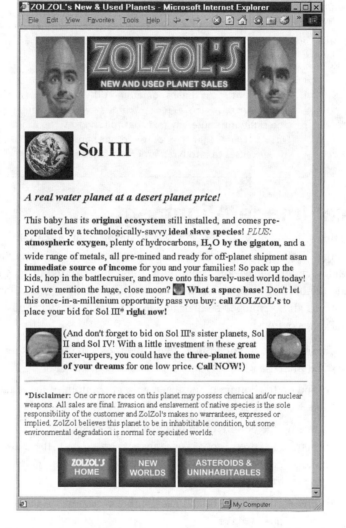

You can also make text wrap around images, as the paragraph around the pictures of Mars and Venus in the lower-middle part of Figure 10.5 does. You do this by including an `align` attribute within the `<img />` tag itself, as shown in the fifth and sixth `<img />` tags in Figure 10.4.

`<img align="left" />` aligns the image to the left and causes text to wrap around the right side of it. As you'd expect, `<img align="right" />` aligns the image to the right and causes text to wrap around the left side of it.

You can't use <img align="center" /> because text won't wrap around a centered image. You must use <div align="center"> if you want an image to be centered on the page, as I did with the top image in Figures 10.4 and 10.5.

 Notice that align means something different in an <img /> tag than it does in a <div> tag. <img align="right" /> will align an image to the right and cause any text that follows to wrap around the image. <div align="right" />, on the other hand, just controls the alignment and never causes text to wrap around images.

Vertical Image Alignment

Sometimes, you may want to insert a small image right in the middle of a line of text; or you might like to put a single line of text next to an image as a caption. In either case, it would be handy to have some control over how the text and images line up vertically. Should the bottom of the image line up with the bottom of the letters, or should the text and images all be arranged so their middles line up? You can choose between these and several other options:

- To line up the top of an image with the top of the tallest image or letter on the same line, use <img align="top" />.
- To line up the bottom of an image with the bottom of the text, use <img align="bottom" />.
- To line up the bottom of an image with the bottom of the lowest image or letter on the same line, use <img align="absbottom" />. (If there are some larger images on the same line, align="absbottom" might place an image lower than align="bottom".)
- To line up the middle of an image with the baseline of the text, use <img align="middle" />.
- To line up the middle of an image with the overall vertical center of everything on the line, use <img align="absmiddle" />. This might be higher or lower than align="middle", depending on the size and alignment of other images on the same line.

Three of these options are illustrated in Figures 10.4 and 10.5. The ZOLZOL's logo is aligned with the top of the photos on either side of it by using align="top"; the picture of the water planet uses align="middle" to line up the baseline of the words Sol III with the center of the Earth; and the little image of the moon is lined up in the exact center of the text around it using align="absmiddle".

If you don't include any `align` attribute in an `<img />` tag, the image will line up with the bottom of any text next to it. That means you never actually have to type in `align="bottom"` because it does the same thing.

In fact, you probably won't use any of the vertical alignment settings much; the vast majority of Web page images use either `align="left"`, `align="right"`, or no `align` attribute at all. Don't worry about memor-izing all these options—you can always refer to this book if you ever do need them.

Figures 10.6 and 10.7 show a few more examples of using horizontal and vertical alignment tags.

FIGURE 10.6

You can control the vertical alignment of images with the align *attribute.*

```
<html>
<head><title>ZOLZOL's New &amp; Used Planets</title></head>
<body background="zolstars.jpg" text="white">
<div align="center">
<img src="zolzol2.jpg" align="left" alt="Friendly Fen" />
<img src="zolzol1.jpg" align="right" alt="Honest Han" />
<img src="zolsign2.gif" alt="ZOLZOL New and Used \Planets" />
<p><i>"Make us an offer, we'll make you a deal!"</i>
<br clear="all" />
<img src="zolfen.gif" align="left" />
<img src="zolhan.gif" align="right" />
<br clear="all" /></p>
</div>
<p>ZOLZOL's: the <b>best planets</b> at the <b>best prices</b>
in the galaxy! And have we got a zee-binger for you <b>right
now</b>! This <b>special exclusive</b> is a nine-planet system
out on a quiet spiral arm by a pretty little star the locals
call <i> Sol</i>. (Not <i>Zol</i>, ha ha! That's us!) So
<b>escape the chaos</b> of galactic downtown! Buy these
peaceful, out-of-the-way planets as a complete
<b>ready-to-invade</b> star system, or if you're short on cash
just pick the rock you like the best! Click below to see
<b>what a find</b> and <b>what a bargain</b> this system really
is! (But click quick, these premium spheres are sure to <b>sell
fast!</b>)</p>
<div align="center">
<a href="zolused.htm"><img src="zolused.gif" border="0"
alt="Previously Owned Worlds" /></a>
<a href="zolnew.htm"><img src="zolnew.gif" border="0"
alt="New Worlds" /></a>
<a href="zoljunk.htm"><img src="zoljunk.gif" border="0"
alt="Asteroids and Uninhabitables" /></a></div>
</body></html>
```

You may notice that Figure 10.7 has a custom background instead of the standard white background. You'll learn all about this sort of thing in Hour 11, but you can probably figure out the basic idea of how it's done just by looking at the `<body>` tag in Figure 10.6.

FIGURE 10.7

The top, middle, and bottom of each line depends on the size of the text and images on that line. Notice that the words "Friendly Fen" Zol and "Honest Han" Zol are actually two small image files, not text.

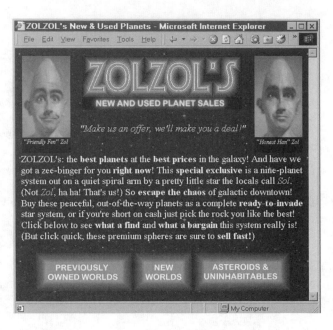

To Do

To Do

Try adding some images to your Web pages now, and experiment with all the different values of align. To get you started, here's a quick review of how to add the magic hat image to any Web page. (See the "To Do" section at the beginning of this hour for help downloading the magic hat image.)

- Copy the magic.gif image file to the same directory folder as the HTML file.
- With a text editor, add <img src="magic.gif" /> where you want the image to appear in the text.
- If you want the image to be centered, put <div align="center"> before the <img /> tag and </div> after it. To wrap text around the image instead, add align="right" or align="left" to the <img /> tag.

  If you have time for a little more experimentation, try combining multiple images of various sizes (such as the stars and the magic hats) with various vertical alignment settings.

Summary

This hour has shown you how to use the <img /> tag to place graphics images on your Web pages. You learned to include a short text message to appear in place of the image as it loads and to appear whenever someone moves the mouse pointer over the image. You also learned to control the horizontal and vertical alignment of each image and how to make text wrap around the left or right of an image.

Finally, you learned how to make images into "buttons" that link to other pages by using the same <a> tag introduced in Hour 3. You also got a sneak preview of the kind of custom page backgrounds you'll learn to use in Hour 11.

Table 10.1 summarizes the attributes of the <img /> tag covered in this hour.

TABLE 10.1 HTML Tag and Attributes Covered in Hour 10

Tag	Attribute	Function
<img />		Places an image file within the page.
	src="..."	The address or filename of the image.
	alt="..."	A text message that can be displayed in place of the image.
	align="..."	Determines the alignment of the given image. If left or right, the image is aligned to the left or right column, and all following text flows beside that image. All other values, such as top, middle, bottom, absmiddle, or absbottom, determine the vertical alignment of this image with other items in the same line.

Q&A

Q I found a nice image on a Web page on the Internet. Can I just use Save Image As to save a copy and then put the image on my Web pages?

A It's easy to do that, but unfortunately it's also illegal in most countries. You should first get written permission from the original creator of the image. Most Web pages include the author's email address, which makes it a simple matter to ask for permission—a lot simpler than going to court!

Q How long a message can I put after alt= in an <img /> tag?

A Theoretically, as long as you want. For practicality, you should keep the message short enough so that it will fit in less space than the image itself. For big images, 10 words may be fine. For small images, a single word is better.

Q I used the <img /> tag just like you said, but all I get is a little box with an X or some shapes in it when I view the page. What's wrong?

A The broken image icon you're seeing can mean one of two things: Either the Web browser couldn't find the image file, or the image isn't saved in a format the browser can understand. To solve either one of these problems, open the image file by using Paint Shop Pro (or your favorite graphics software), select Save As, and be sure to save the file in either the GIF or JPEG format. Also make sure you save it in the same folder as the Web page that contains the `<img />` tag referring to it and that the filename on the disk precisely matches the filename you put in the `<img />` tag (including capitalization).

Q How do I control both the horizontal and vertical alignment of an image at once?

A The short answer is that you can't. For example, if you type `<img align="right" align="middle" src="myimage.gif">`, the `align="middle"` will be ignored.

There are ways around this limitation, however. In Part IV, "Web Page Design," you will discover several techniques for positioning text and images exactly where you want them in both horizontal and vertical directions.

Q Why do the examples in this book put a slash at the end of every `<img>` tag? None of the Web pages I see on the Internet do that.

A As discussed in Hour 2 (yes, I know that was a long time ago), the new XML and XTHML standards will require any tag that doesn't have a closing tag to include a slash at the end. Though it may be unlikely that anyone will ever write software that fails to accept the traditional `<img>` tag without the slash, I use `<img />` just to be on the safe side. (Remember, people once thought it was unlikely that four-digit date codes would ever be necessary in the software they were writing....)

Workshop

Quiz

1. How would you insert an image file named `elephant.jpg` at the very top of a Web page?

2. How would you make the word `Elephant` appear whenever the actual `elephant.jpg` image couldn't be displayed by a Web browser?

3. Write the HTML to make the `elephant.jpg` image appear on the right side of the page, with a big headline reading `"Elephants of the World Unite!"` on the left side of the page next to it.

4. Write the HTML to make a tiny image of a mouse (named `mouse.jpg`) appear between the words `"Wee sleekit, cow'rin,"` and the words `"tim'rous beastie"`.

5. Suppose you have a large picture of a standing elephant named `elephant.jpg`. Now make a small image named `fly.jpg` appear to the left of the elephant's head and `mouse.jpg` appear next to the elephant's right foot.

Answers

1. Copy the image file into the same directory folder as the HTML text file, and type `<img src="elephant.jpg" />` immediately after the `<body>` tag in the HTML text file.

2. Use the following HTML:

   ```
   <img src="elephant.jpg" alt="elephant" />
   ```

3. ```
   <img src="elephant.jpg" align="right" />
   <h1>Elephants of the World Unite!</h1>
   ```

4. ```
   Wee sleekit, cow'rin,<img src="mouse.jpg" />tim'rous beastie
   ```

5. ```
   <img src="fly.jpg" align="top" />
   <img src="elephant.jpg" />
   <img src="mouse.jpg" />
   ```

Exercise

- Try using any small image as a "bullet" to make lists with more flair. If you also want the list to be indented, use the `<dl>` definition list and `<dd>` for each item (instead of `<ul>` and `<li>`, which would give the standard boring bullets). Here's a quick example, using the `star.gif` file from my sample images page:

  ```
  <dl><dd><img src="star.gif">A murder of crows
  <dd><img src="star.gif">A rafter of turkeys
  <dd><img src="star.gif">A muster of peacocks</dl>
  ```

10
  ```

Hour **11**

Custom Backgrounds and Colors

Nearly every example Web page in Hours 1 through 10 has a white background and black text. In this hour, you'll find out how to make pages with background and text colors of your choosing. You'll also discover how to make your own custom background graphics and how to let the background show through parts of any image you put on your Web pages.

The World Wide Web Consortium—the group that created the HTML 4 standard—recommends that you control the colors on your Web pages using style sheets instead of the regular HTML tags discussed in this hour.

In Hour 16 you'll learn all about using style sheets and why they are officially recommended. However, style sheets only work in Netscape Navigator 4 or later and Microsoft Internet Explorer 4 or later. If you want anyone using a different Web browser (or an earlier version) to be able to see your color choices, you should still use the tags and attributes discussed in this hour.

> This hour also explains how to make transparent images and background tiles—techniques that will come in handy whether or not you are using style sheets.

To Do

The black-and-white figures printed in this book obviously don't convey colors very accurately, so you may want to view the example pages online. You can also try the colors on your own Web pages as you read about how to make them.

> To find all the examples from this hour online, go to
> `http://24hourHTMLcafe.com/hour11/`.

Background and Text Colors

To specify blue as the background color for a page, put `bgcolor="blue"` inside the `<body>` tag. Of course, you can use many colors other than blue. You can choose from the 16 standard Windows colors: black, white, red, green, blue, yellow, magenta, cyan, purple, gray, lime, maroon, navy, olive, silver, and teal. (You can call magenta by the name *fuchsia* and cyan by the name *aqua* if you want to feel more artsy and less geeky.)

You can also specify colors for text and links in the `<body>` tag. For example, in Figure 11.1 you'll notice the following `<body>` tag:

```
<body bgcolor="teal" text="fuchsia" link="yellow" vlink="lime" alink="red">
```

As you probably guessed, `text="fuchsia"` makes the text fuchsia (which is the same as magenta). There are three separate attributes for link colors:

- `link="yellow"` makes links that haven't been visited recently yellow.
- `vlink="lime"` makes recently visited links lime green.
- `alink="red"` makes links briefly blink red when someone clicks them.

> Here's a neat trick: If you make the `vlink` color the same as the `bgcolor` color, links to pages that a visitor has already seen will become invisible. This can make your page seem "smart"—offering people only links to places they haven't been. (Note, however, that it may also annoy anybody who wants to return to a page he's already seen!)

Figures 11.1 and 11.2 illustrate how color can be used in combination with links. Because I used pure, beautiful teal as the background color in the graphics images, they blend right into the background of the Web page. (I didn't need to use *transparent* images, which you'll learn about later in this hour.)

FIGURE 11.1

You can specify colors for the background, text, and links in the <body> tag of any Web page.

```
<html><head><title>The Teal and the Fuchsia</title></head>
<body bgcolor="teal" text="fuchsia"
 link="yellow" vlink="lime" alink="red">
<img src="c.gif" align="right" />
<h1><a href="index.htm">CREDLEY HIGH SCHOOL</a></h1>
<h2>"The Old Teal and Fuchsia"</h2>
<div align="center">
<i><b>Oh, hail! Hail! Sing Credley!<br />
Our colors jump and shout!<br />
Deep teal like ocean's highest waves,<br />
Fuchsia like blossoms bursting out!</b></i>
<p><i><b><img src="cheer.gif" align="left" />
As Credley conquers every team<br />
So do our brilliant colors peal<br />
From mountain tops &amp; florist shops<br />
Sweet sacred fuchsia, holy teal!</b></i></p>
<p><i><b>Our men are tough as vinyl siding<br />
Our women, strong as plastic socks<br />
Our colors tell our story truly<br />
We may be ugly, but we rock!</b></i></p>
</div></body></html>
```

11

FIGURE 11.2

On a color screen, this ever-so-attractive page has a teal background, fuchsia body text, and yellow link text, as specified in Figure 11.1.

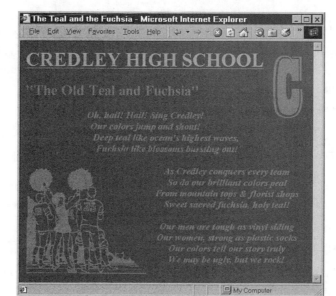

Creating Custom Colors

If the 16 named colors don't include the exact hue you're after, you can mix your own custom colors by specifying how much red, green, and blue light should be mixed into each color.

The format is #rrggbb where rr, gg, and bb are two-digit hexadecimal values for the red, green, and blue components of the color. If you're not familiar with hexadecimal numbers, don't sweat it. Just remember that ff is the maximum and 00 is the minimum, and use one of the following codes for each component:

- ff means full brightness
- cc means 80 percent brightness
- 99 means 60 percent brightness
- 66 means 40 percent brightness
- 33 means 20 percent brightness
- 00 means none of this color component

For example, bright red is #ff0000, dark green is #003300, bluish-purple is #660099, and medium-gray is #999999. To make a page with a red background, dark green text, and bluish-purple links that turn white when you click them and gray when you've visited them, the HTML would look like the following:

```
<body bgcolor="#ff0000" text="#003300" link="#660099" alink="#ffffff"
vlink="#999999">
```

Though the colors you specify in the <body> tag apply to all text on the page, you can also use either color names or hexadecimal color codes to change the color of a particular word or section of text by using the <font> tag. This is discussed in Hour 6, "Text Formatting and Font Control."

> For a very handy chart showing the 216 most commonly used hexadecimal color codes, along with the colors they create, go to http://24hourHTMLcafe.com/colors.
>
> You can then choose any of the standard 16 text colors to see how each of them looks over every color in the table.

Keep in mind that even though you can specify millions of different colors, some computers are set to display only the 16 named colors. Other computers only reliably display the 216 colors in the color code reference mentioned in the previous tip. All others will be approximated by dithered patterns, which can make text look messy and difficult to read.

Also, you should be aware that different computer monitors may display colors in very different hues. I recently designed a page with a beautiful blue background for a company I work for, only to find out later that the president of the company saw it on his computer as a lovely purple background! Neutral, earth-tone colors such as medium gray, tan, and ivory can lead to even more unpredictable results on many computer monitors, and may even seem to change color on one monitor depending on lighting conditions in the room and the time of day.

The moral of the story: Stick to the named colors and don't waste time mucking with hexadecimal color codes, unless you have precise control over your intended audience's computer displays—and to be safe, do test your page on different monitors if possible.

> You can set the color of an individual link to a different color than the rest by putting a `<font>` tag with a `color` attribute *after* the `<a href>`. (Also include a `</font>` tag before the `</a>` tag.) For example, the following would make a green link:
>
> Visit the `<a href="thumb.htm"><font color="green">`Green Thumb page`</font></a>` to become a better gardener.
>
> However, older versions of some browsers (including Microsoft Internet Explorer 3) will always display all links with the colors set in the `<body>` tag. Very old browsers may completely ignore some or all of your color specifications.

11

Background Image Tiles

Background tiles let you specify an image to be used as a wallpaper pattern behind all text and graphics in a document. You put the image filename after `background=` in the `<body>` tag at the beginning of your page:

```
<body background="image.jpg">
```

Like other Web graphics, background tiles must be in either the GIF or JPEG file format, and you can create them by using Paint Shop Pro or any other graphics software. For example, the `tile.gif` file referred to by the `<body>` tag in Figure 11.3 is an image of one small tile. As you can see in Figure 11.4, most Web browsers will repeat the image behind any text and images on the page, like floor tile.

FIGURE **11.3**

You can specify a background image to tile behind a page in the background *attribute of the* <body> *tag.*

```
<html><head><title>Motawi Tileworks</title></head>
<body background="tile.gif">
<img src="mtworks.gif" />
<p><img src="motawis.gif" align="left" />
Karim and Nawal Motawi (brother and sister) welcome you to <a
href="http://www.motawi.com">Motawi Tileworks</a>, an art tile
studio specializing in the Arts &amp; Crafts style. We create
low-relief and polychrome tiles as accents and as art pieces,
as well as many varieties of flat tiles, architectural borders,
trims, and custom pieces.</p>
<div align="center">
<h2><a href="http://www.motawi.com">www.motawi.com</a></h2>
33 North Staebler, Suite 2, Ann Arbor, MI 48103<br />
tel: (734) 213-0017 fax: (734) 213-2569
</div></body></html>
```

FIGURE **11.4**

The tile.gif *file (specified in Figure 11.3 and shown in Figure 11.5) is automatically repeated to cover the entire page.*

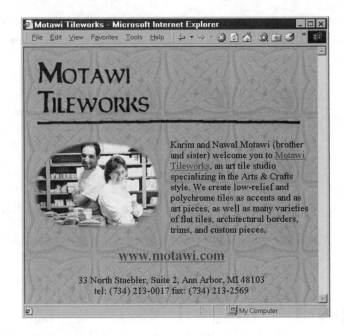

Tiled background images should be implemented with great care to avoid distracting from the main content of the page itself. The text in Figure 11.4, for example, would be very difficult to read if I hadn't made it all bold-face—and may still be hard to decipher on some computer monitors. Many pages on the Web are almost impossible to read due to overdone backgrounds.

Before you include your company logo or baby pictures as wallpaper behind your Web pages, stop and think. If you had an important message to send someone on a piece of paper, would you write it over the top of the letterhead logo or on the blank part of the page? Backgrounds should be like fine papers: attractive, yet unobtrusive.

Transparent Images

You will see how to make your own background tiles later in this hour, but first a word about how to let the background show through parts of your foreground graphics.

Web page images are always rectangular. However, the astute observer of Figure 11.4 (that's you) will notice that the background tiles show through portions of the images, and therefore the title and picture don't look rectangular at all. You'll often want to use partially transparent images to make graphics look good over any background color or background image tile.

Figure 11.5 shows the images from Figure 11.4, as they looked in Paint Shop Pro when I created them. (Figure 11.5 also shows the single tile used for the background in Figure 11.4.)

FIGURE **11.5**

When I saved two of these images in Paint Shop Pro, I made the background color transparent. (The third image, at the top left, is the background tile.)

11

To make part of an image transparent, the image must have 256 or fewer colors, and you must save it in the GIF file format. (JPEG images can't be made transparent.) Most graphics programs that support the GIF format allow you to specify one color to be transparent.

To Do

Follow these steps to save a transparent GIF in Paint Shop Pro:

1. Select Colors, Decrease Color Depth, 256 Colors (8-bit) or Colors, Decrease Color Depth, 16 Colors (4-bit), and check the Optimized Octree and Nearest Color boxes. (This is recommended in Hour 9, "Creating Your Own Web Page Graphics.")

▼   2. Choose the eyedropper tool and right-click the color you want to make transparent.

3. Select Colors, View Palette Transparency. If any part of the image is already set to be transparent, you will see a gray checkered pattern in that part now.

4. Select Colors, Set Palette Transparency.

5. You should see the dialog box shown in Figure 11.6. Choose Set the Transparency Value to the Current Background Color, and then click OK.

6. The transparent parts of the image turn to a gray checkerboard pattern. (If you hadn't already selected View Palette Transparency in step 3, you would need to click the Proof button shown in Figure 11.6 to see the transparency effect.)

7. You can use any of the painting tools to touch up parts of the image where there is too little or too much of the transparent background color.

▲   8. When everything looks right, select File, Save As (or File, Save Copy As) and choose CompuServe Graphics Interchange (*.gif) as the file type.

FIGURE 11.6

This dialog box appears when you select Colors, Set Palette Transparency. You will usually want the middle option.

If you select Colors, View Palette Transparency (or when you click the Proof button as shown in Figure 11.6), Paint Shop Pro shows transparent regions of an image with a gray checkerboard pattern. You can change the grid size and colors used under File, Preferences, General Program Preferences, Transparency.

In early versions of Paint Shop Pro, and in some other software, transparency control is implemented very differently. In Paint Shop Pro 3.11 and 4, for example, you would find transparency settings under Options in the Save As dialog box when saving a GIF file.

Creating Your Own Backgrounds

Any GIF or JPEG image can be used as a background tile. Pages look best, however, when the top edge of a background tile matches seamlessly with the bottom edge, and the left edge matches with the right.

If you're clever and have some time to spend on it, you can turn any image into a seamless tile by meticulously cutting and pasting, while touching up the edges. Paint Shop Pro provides a much easier way to automatically make any texture into a seamless tile: Simply use the rectangular selection tool to choose the area you want to make into a tile, and then choose Selections, Convert to Seamless Pattern. Paint Shop Pro crops the image and uses a sophisticated automatic procedure to overlay and blur together opposite sides of the image.

In Figure 11.7 I did this with part of an image of the planet Jupiter, taken from a NASA image archive. The resulting tile—shown as the background of a Web page in Figure 11.8—tiles seamlessly, but has the tone and texture of the eye of Jove himself.

You'll find similar features in other graphics programs, including Photoshop (use Filter, Other, Offset with Wrap Turned On), Kai's Power Tools, and the Macintosh programs Mordant and Tilery.

11

FIGURE 11.7

Paint Shop Pro can automatically take any region of an image and turn it into a background pattern that can be easily made into tiles.

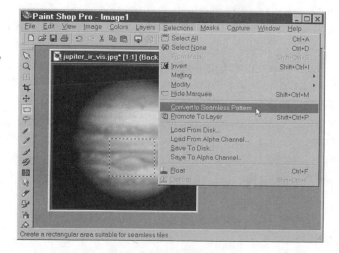

FIGURE **11.8**

*These are the results of
using an area of the
image in Figure 11.7
as a background image
for a Web page.*

The "Convert to Seamless Pattern" command
on the Selections menu in Paint Shop Pro was
used to create the background of this page
from a NASA image of the planet Jupiter.

To Do

Here are some tips for making your own background tiles with Paint Shop Pro:

- If you have a scanner or digital camera, try using some textures from around the house or office, such as the top of a wooden desk, leaves of houseplants, or clothing.

- Using the Image, Blur, Blur More filter on an image (as I did with the Jupiter picture in Figures 11.7 and 11.8) before you turn it into a seamless tile will help it look better as a background. Using Colors, Adjust, Brightness and Contrast is usually also necessary to keep the background subtle in color variation.

- When you select an area to be turned into a tile, try to choose part of the image that is fairly uniform in brightness from side to side. Otherwise, the tile may not look seamless even after you use Convert to Seamless Pattern.

- You must also use an image big enough so that you can leave at least the width and height of the tile on either side of your selection. If you don't, when you select Convert to Seamless Pattern you'll get a message saying Your selection is too close to the edge to complete this operation.

- You can also make some almost-automatic textures with the paper texture feature in the paintbrush style palette in Paint Shop Pro. You can make great paper textures, too, by selecting Image, Noise, Add followed by Image, Blur, Blur and Colors, Colorize.

If you just cannot seem to get the pattern you want, there are hundreds of sites on the Internet that offer public domain background images that are free or inexpensive and professionally designed. A good starting place is the Background Underground Lounge at the *24-Hour HTML Café* `http://24hourHTMLcafe.com/bgu/`.

This page presents several flashy backgrounds (tone them down with Colors, Adjust before using them on your pages) and links to hundreds more.

If you happen to see a background image on someone else's page that you wish you could use on your own page, it is a simple matter to right-click the background and select Save Background As to save a copy of it. Be careful, though, to ask the person who created the image for permission before you use it.

Summary

In this hour you learned how to set the background and text colors for a Web page. You also found out how to make a tiled background image appear behind a Web page, how to make foreground images partially transparent so the background shows through, and how to create seamless image tiles for use as backgrounds.

Table 11.1 summarizes the attributes of the <body> tag discussed in this hour.

TABLE 11.1   The <body> Tag and Attributes Covered in Hour 11

Tag	Attribute	Function
<body>...</body>		Encloses the body (text and tags) of the HTML document
	background="..."	The name or address of the image to tile on the page background
	bgcolor="..."	The color of the page background
	text="..."	The color of the page's text
	link="..."	The color of unfollowed links
	alink="..."	The color of activated links
	vlink="..."	The color of followed links

11

Q&A

Q Doesn't Netscape Navigator let people choose their own background and text color preferences?

A Yes, and so does Microsoft Internet Explorer. Both programs allow users to override the colors you, as a Web page author, specify. Some may see your white-on-blue page as green-on-white or their own favorite colors instead, but very few people use this option. The colors specified in the <body> tag will usually be seen.

Q I've heard that there are 231 "browser-safe colors" that I should use on Web pages, and that I shouldn't use any other colors. Is that true?

A Here's the real story: There are 231 colors that will appear less "fuzzy" to people who operate their computers in a 256-color video mode. (The other 25 colors are used for menus and stuff like that.) Some Web page authors try to stick to those colors. However, true-color or high-color computer displays are increasingly common, and they show all colors with equal clarity. On the other hand, lots of people still use a 16-color video mode, which makes most of the 231 "magic" colors look fuzzy too. I recommend sticking to the 16 named colors for text and using whatever colors you want for graphics.

Q My background image looks okay in my graphics editing program, but has weird white or colored gaps or dots in it when it comes up behind a Web page. Why?

A There are two possibilities: If the background image you're using is a GIF file, it probably has transparency turned on, which makes one of the colors in the image turn white (or whatever color you specified in the body bgcolor attribute). The solution is to open the file with your graphics program and turn off the transparency. (In Paint Shop Pro, select Colors, Set Palette Transparency, and pick No transparency.) Re-save the file.

If a JPEG or non-transparent GIF image looks spotty when you put it on a Web page, it may just be the Web browser's dithering. That's the method the software uses to try to show more colors than your system is set up to display at once by mixing colored dots together side-by-side. There's not much you can do about it, although you'll find hints for minimizing the problem in Hour 9, "Creating Your Own Web Page Graphics."

Workshop

Quiz

1. How would you give a Web page a black background and make all text, including links, bright green?

2. How would you make an image file named `texture.jpg` appear as a repeating tile behind the text and images on a Web page with white text and red links that turn blue after being followed?

3. If `elephant.jpg` is a JPEG image of an elephant standing in front of a solid white backdrop, how do you make the backdrop transparent so only the elephant shows on a Web page?

4. Which menu choice in Paint Shop Pro automatically creates a background tile from part of any image?

Answers

1. Put the following at the beginning of the Web page:

```
<body bgcolor="black"
text="lime" link="lime" vlink="lime" alink="black">
```

The following would do exactly the same thing:

```
<body bgcolor="#000000"
text="#00ff00" link="#00ff00" vlink="#00ff00" alink="#000000">
```

2.
```
<body background="texture.jpg"
text="white" link="red" vlink="blue" alink="black">
```

3. Open the image in Paint Shop Pro and then use Colors, Decrease Color Depth, 256 Colors to pick the best 256 colors for the image. Right-click the white area, select Colors, Set Palette Transparency; elect to make the background color transparent. Touch up any off-white spots that didn't become transparent and then use File, Save As to save it in the GIF 89a format.

4. Selections, Convert to Seamless Pattern. See the Paint Shop Pro documentation if you need a little more help using it than this hour provides.

11

Exercises

- Try getting creative with some background tiles that don't use Convert to Seamless Pattern. You'll discover some sneaky tricks for making background tiles that don't look like background tiles in Hour 13, "Page Design and Layout," but I bet you can figure out some interesting ones on your own right now. (Hint: What if you made a background tile 2,000 pixels wide and 10 pixels tall?)

- If you have some photos of objects for a Web-based catalog, consider taking the time to paint a transparent color carefully around the edges of them. (Sometimes the magic wand tool can help automate this process.) You can also use Paint Shop Pro's Image, Effects, Drop Shadow feature to add a slight shadow behind or beneath each object, so they appear to stand out from the background.

Hour 12

Creating Animated Graphics

There are several ways to add movement to a Web page, and most of them are covered in the two more advanced chapters of this book: Hour 20, "Setting Pages in Motion with Dynamic HTML," and Hour 17, "Embedding Multimedia in Web Pages." However, you can actually add animation to standard GIF images, and it's so easy to do that the technique doesn't even qualify as "advanced."

GIF animations are a great way to make simple animated icons and add a little motion to spice up any Web page. They also transfer much faster than most video or multimedia files. In this chapter you'll learn how to create GIF animations and how to optimize them for the fastest possible display.

Software for Making Web Page Animations

The latest version of Paint Shop Pro from JASC includes a module called Animation Shop, which is designed especially for creating Web page GIF animations. There are a few other GIF animation programs available, including both freeware and advanced commercial software packages. Animation Shop offers the best mix of great features, ease of use, and low price.

(For Macintosh users, I recommend GifBuilder, which is available free at `http://www.shareware.com`. Another good GIF animation program for the Macintosh is Gif.g1F.giF at `http://www.cafe.net/peda/ggg/`.)

As mentioned in Hour 9, "Creating Your Own Web Page Graphics," you can download a free evaluation copy of Paint Shop Pro 6, which includes Animation Shop 6, from `www.jasc.com`. If you haven't already, I recommend that you download and install it now so you can try your hand at building an animation or two as you read this chapter.

Creating the Pictures You Want to Animate

The first step in creating a GIF animation is to create a series of images to be displayed one after the other. Each of these images is called a *frame*. (By the way, this use of the word *frame* has nothing whatsoever to do with the *frames* you learn about in Hour 21, "Multipage Layout with Frames.") You can use any graphics software you like to make the images, although Paint Shop Pro is an obvious choice if you plan on using Animation Shop to put the animation together.

Figure 12.1 shows three pictures I drew with Paint Shop Pro. In each picture, the icon of the man and the "NO" symbol around him are exactly identical, but the flames and smoke on his body are slightly different. When these three images are put together into an animation, the flames seem to flicker.

Notice that the images in Figure 12.1 are transparent—the checkerboard background isn't part of the picture, it's how Paint Shop Pro indicates transparency. The animation made from them will therefore be transparent, too, and will look great over any light-colored Web page background. (See Hour 11, "Custom Backgrounds and Colors," for more on making transparent GIF images.)

FIGURE 12.1

Use Paint Shop Pro or any other graphics program to produce the individual frames of your animation.

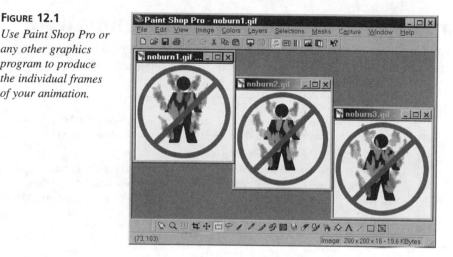

If you know how to use Paint Shop Pro's (or any other advanced graphics software) Layers feature, you'll find that creating animation frames is easier because you can easily turn parts of a picture on and off to make variations or move layers to simulate motion. For example, I actually created one image with separate transparent layers for the man, the "NO" symbol, and the flame and smoke variations. I then used Edit, Copy Merged and Edit, Paste, As New Image to make the three individual images in Figure 12.1, with different opacity settings for each layer.

Don't fret, however, if all that layer manipulation is a bit beyond you at the moment. You can easily make very effective animations by copying an ordinary one-layer image and painting on some variations, or moving some parts of it around to make the next frame.

When you have your animation's individual frames ready, use Colors, Decrease Color Depth to limit them to 256 or 16 colors, and then save each of them as a separate GIF file. (Refer to Hour 9 for more detailed instructions if you need a refresher on creating and saving GIF files.)

To Do

If you would like to work with the same three animation frames I use for the first example in this chapter, you'll find them at the sites:

```
http://24hourHTMLcafe.com/hour12/noburn1.gif
http://24hourHTMLcafe.com/hour12/noburn2.gif
http://24hourHTMLcafe.com/hour12/noburn3.gif
```

Assembling the Pictures into an Animation

Once you have the individual GIF files saved, select File, Run Animation Shop from within Paint Shop Pro to start putting them together into a single animation file.

> The fastest way to create a simple GIF animation with Animation Shop is to select File, Animation Wizard. This starts an "interview" that leads you through all the steps discussed next.
>
> In this hour, however, I show you how to create animations "by hand," without using the Animation Wizard. This will give you a head start when you want to use the advanced animation tricks discussed toward the end of the hour.

The basic idea here couldn't be simpler: You just need to tell Animation Shop which pictures to show and in what order. There are also a couple of other picky details you need to specify: how long to show each picture before moving on to the next one and how many times to repeat the whole sequence. Follow this step-by-step procedure to assemble an animation:

1. Select File, Open (in Animation Shop, not in Paint Shop Pro). Select the image file that you want to be the first frame of the animation. It will appear as shown in Figure 12.2. Notice that the transparency is preserved, as indicated by the gray checkerboard pattern showing through.

FIGURE 12.2

This is a single-frame GIF image as it first appears when opened in Animation Shop.

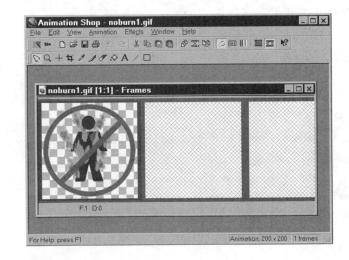

2. Select Animation, Insert Frames, From File to get the dialog box shown in Figure 12.3. Click the Add File button and choose the image you want to appear second in the animation. Click Add File again to add the third frame, and so forth, until the list contains all the images you made for this animation. Click OK.

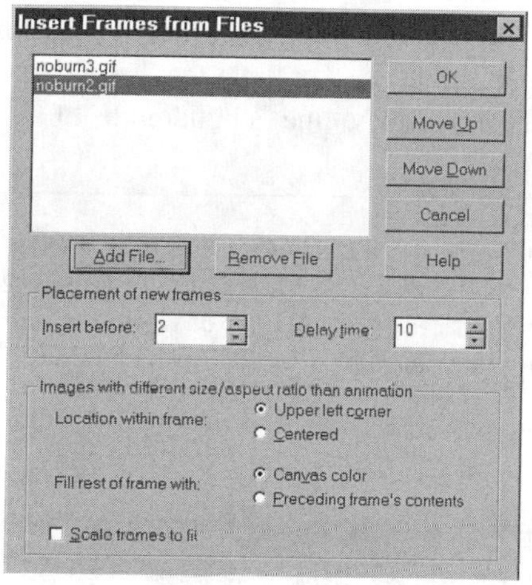

FIGURE 12.3

Selecting Edit, Insert Frames, From File gives you this dialog box. The Add File button lets you choose an image to add to the animation.

3. You should now see all the frames laid out next to each other like a filmstrip (see Figure 12.4). You can use the scrollbar to move forward and back through the filmstrip if all the frames aren't visible at once. If you'd like to see a preview of the animation, select View, Animation. If any frames are in the wrong order, simply grab and drag them into the proper positions with the mouse.

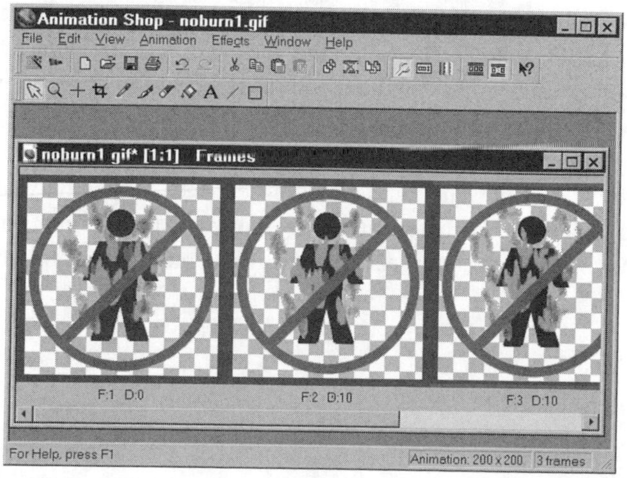

12

FIGURE 12.4

Animation Shop displays all of an animation's frames side-by-side, like a filmstrip.

If you don't tell it any different, Animation Shop normally puts a tenth of a second between each frame of the animation. That was actually about right for my little burning-man icon. However, you will often want to control the length of time each individual frame is displayed before the next one replaces it.

4. To set the timing for a frame, click it; the border around it will turn blue and red. Select Edit, Frame Properties; alternatively, you can right-click the frame and pick Properties from the pop-up menu. You'll get the dialog box shown in Figure 12.5, where you can specify the display time in hundredths of a second.

> Notice that there is also a Delay Time setting in Figure 12.3. This allows you to adjust the timing of all the frames at once, when you first put the anima-tion together. This can save you a lot of work if all or most of your frames will have the same delay; it saves you from having to change their frame properties one by one.

FIGURE 12.5

Right-click a frame and choose Properties to set the amount of time that frame should be displayed.

Frame Properties

| Display Time | Comments |

Display time (in 1/100th sec): 10

OK   Cancel   Help

5. One final detail, and your animation will be done! Select Edit, Animation Properties (alternately, right-click the gray area below the filmstrip and pick Properties from the pop-up menu) to get the Animation Properties dialog box shown in Figure 12.6. I want my flames to flicker as long as someone is viewing my animation, so I chose Repeat the Animation Indefinitely. In some cases, how-ever, you may want your animation sequence to play only once (or some other number of times) before stopping to display the last frame as a still image. In that case, you'd select the second choice and enter the number of repetitions.

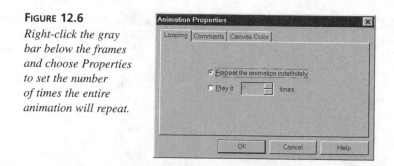

FIGURE 12.6

Right-click the gray bar below the frames and choose Properties to set the number of times the entire animation will repeat.

6. Your animation is complete. Select File, Save As to save it. You are presented with a control like the one shown in Figure 12.7, which allows you to choose a balance between good image quality and small file size.

The long list of optimizations may seem bewildering—and all the choices you'd have to make if you clicked the Customize button is even more mind-boggling. Fortunately, Animation Shop usually does an excellent job of choosing the most appropriate optimizations for you based on the slider setting. Move the slider up for better image quality, down for smaller file size.

How do you decide where it goes? Animation Shop helps there, too. Pick a setting and click Next. After some chugging and crunching, you'll see a report like the one shown in Figure 12.8. This makes it much easier for you to decide how big too big is; return to adjust the slider by clicking Back. When the file size seems acceptable, click Finish.

FIGURE 12.7

When you save a GIF animation, Animation Shop automatically figures out which optimizations will work best.

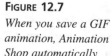

12

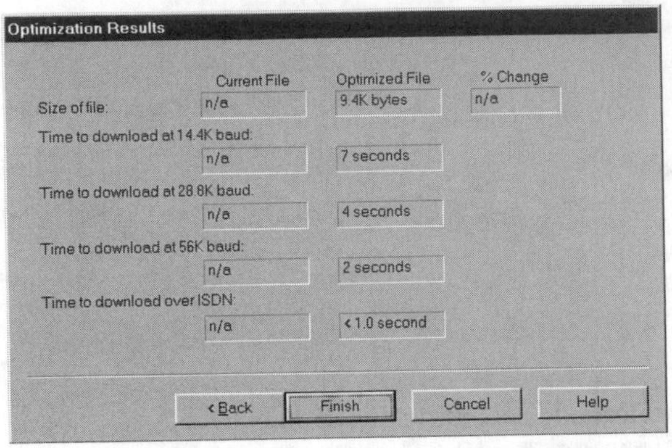

FIGURE 12.8

When you set the slider in Figure 12.7 and click Next, this report helps you decide whether you found the right balance.

Putting a GIF Animation onto a Web Page

In Hour 10, "Putting Graphics on a Web Page," you learned to use the `<img />` tag to make GIF images appear on your Web pages. To put a GIF animation on a Web page, you use exactly the same tag in exactly the same way. For example, suppose I gave my animated anti-flaming icon the name `noburn.gif` when I saved it in Animation Shop. The HTML that puts it on a Web page follows:

```
<img src="noburn.gif" />
```

Just as with any other graphic, you can include `alt=` if you want a text message to be associated with the image. You can also include the `align` attribute to line up the animation with other graphics or text next to it, or to wrap text to the left or right of the animation. All the `<img />` tag attributes discussed in Hour 10 also work with GIF animations.

Figure 12.9 is a simple HTML page incorporating `noburn.gif` along with a few other animations and still images. Figure 12.10 doesn't move because this book is made out of boring old paper, but if you view the file on your computer you'll see the flames fly. (Go to `http://24hourHTMLcafe.com` and click "An Animated Warning.")

FIGURE 12.9

Some of the .gif files specified in the `<img />` tags are still images and some are animations. The HTML is exactly the same, either way.

```
<html><head><title>NO SMOKING OR FLAMING</title></head>
<body>
<div align="center">
<img src="noburn.gif" alt="Defense de Combustion" /><br />
<img src="rgt.gif" /><img src="no.gif" /><img src="lft.gif" />
<br /><img src="awarn.gif" /><br />
The Webmaster General has determined that spontaneous
combustion may be hazardous to your health and the health of
those around you.<br /> Please refrain from smoking or flaming
while visiting this Web site.
</div></body></html>
```

Figure 12.10

Viewed online, this page contains a burning icon, a scrolling marquee, and an animated special-effect title.

Generating Transitions and Text Effects

Animation Shop (like some other GIF animation programs) can do much more than just collect multiple GIF images into a single animation file. It can also generate some impressive special effects and even create scrolling text banners all by itself. There's not room in this book to explain in detail how to use these features, but they're easy enough that you can probably pick it up on your own with a little help from the Animation Shop online help system.

Just to get you started, Figures 12.11 and 12.12 show how I made the two bottom animations shown in Figure 12.10. One uses the Effects, Image Transitions feature to dissolve between a picture of the word ATTENTION and a picture of the word WARNING. (I made these two pictures in Paint Shop Pro ahead of time.) The other uses Effects, Text Transitions to scroll the words NO SPONTANEOUS COMBUSTION PLEASE smoothly across a white background. This didn't require any images at all, since the text transition effects generate their own pictures of the text as they do their magic.

Once you get started with Web page animation, it's hard not to get carried away. I couldn't resist adding a flashing neon sign to the *24-Hour HTML Café*. In the examples page for this hour (http://24hourHTMLcafe.com/hour10/), you'll also find links to several other animations that you are welcome to reuse for your own pages. (The book that turns its own pages is especially popular.)

12

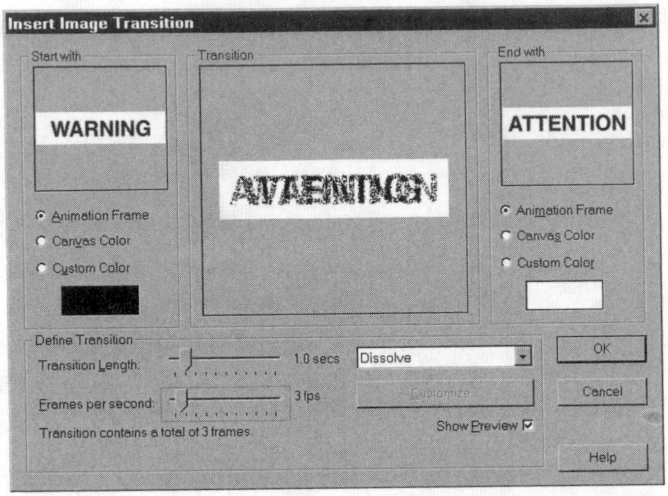

FIGURE 12.11

Use Effects, Image Transitions to generate fades, wipes, dissolves, and other automatic transitions between images.

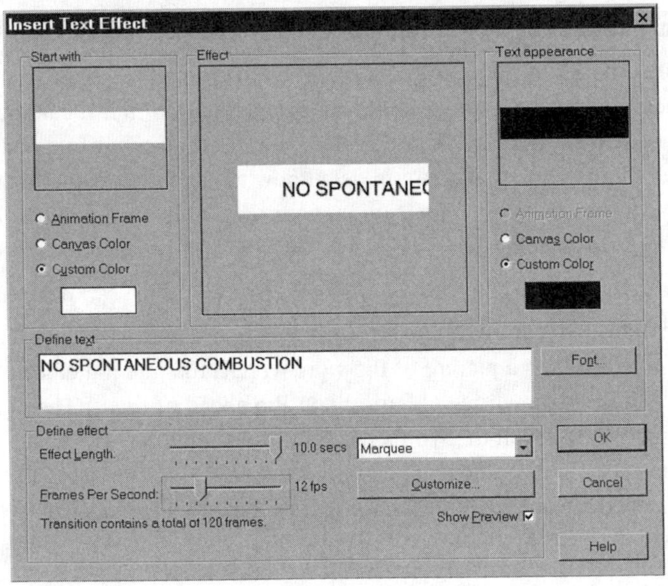

FIGURE 12.12

Use Effects, Text Transitions to generate moving text and special-effect text over a frame or a set of frames.

Summary

This hour introduced you to animated GIF images, which are the easiest and quickest way to add some action to your Web pages. You found out how to use Animation Shop 6, the animation module that puts together GIF animations for Paint Shop Pro 6. You also saw how to control how many times an animation repeats and the timing of each frame in an animation, as well as how to make animations partially transparent.

GIF animations can be placed on Web pages via the same `<img />` tag as ordinary, unmoving images. All the `<img />` attributes and options discussed in Hour 10 also work with animated images.

Like some other graphics programs, Animation Shop can generate some or all frames of an animation using a variety of special effects and automatic transitions.

Q&A

Q I've seen quite a few animations on the Web that show a three-dimensional object rotating. Can I make those with Animation Shop?

A Yes, but you'll also need some kind of 3D modeling and rendering software to create the individual frames.

You may have also seen interactive, three-dimensional virtual reality scenes and objects embedded in Web pages. Those are something completely different than GIF animations, made with a special language called the Virtual Reality Modeling Language, or VRML. For more information on VRML, refer to `http://www.sgi.com/vrml/`.

Q I've seen moving marquee-type signs on Web pages. Are those GIF animations?

A Sometimes they are and sometimes they aren't. There are several ways to make text move across an area on a Web page. One of the easiest is to use Animation Shop, which can make fancy marquees from a simple string of text that you type. See the Animation Shop online help for details.

Note that GIF animations are only one way to make marquees. They are Java applets or ActiveX controls (see Hour 18, "Interactive Pages with Applets and ActiveX"). Some versions of Microsoft Internet Explorer even support a special `<marquee>` tag, but this tag is now obsolete.

Q I have a Windows AVI video clip. Can I turn it into a GIF animation?

A Yes. Simply open the AVI file with Animation Shop 6 to convert it to a GIF animation. (You are given the option to reduce the number of frames; it's usually a good idea to sample every third frame or so to keep the file size down to reasonable proportions.)

You can also embed AVI files directly into Web pages, as discussed in Hour 17.

12

Workshop

Quiz

1. If you want your logo to bounce up and down on your Web page, how would you do it?

2. How would you make a quarter-of-a-second pause between each frame of the animation?

3. How would you modify a GIF animation that repeats infinitely to instead play only three times before stopping?

Answers

1. Use Paint Shop Pro or another graphics program to make a few images of the logo at various heights (perhaps squishing when it reaches a line at the bottom). Then assemble those images using Animation Shop, and save them as a multi-image GIF animation file named `bounce.gif`. You can then place that animation on a Web page using the `<img src="bounce.gif" />` tag, just as you would any GIF image.

2. When you build the animation in Animation Shop, enter `25` as the time delay (in centiseconds).

3. Open the animation in Animation Shop; select Edit, Animation Properties; choose Play It; and enter the number `3`.

Exercises

- Animation Shop can make slide shows of dissimilar images by automatically generating transition effects, such as fading between pictures. It can also automatically add a number of special effects to still or moving text. If you take a little time to explore the advanced features of this program, I'm sure you'll find it time well spent.

- Don't forget that the free copy of Paint Shop Pro and Animation Shop you can download from `www.jasc.com` is an evaluation copy only. If you like it (and who wouldn't!?), be sure to send JASC, Inc., its well-earned registration fee to purchase the software.

PART IV

Web Page Design

Hour

Hour 13

Page Design and Layout

You've learned in earlier hours how to create Web pages with text and images on them. This hour goes a step further by showing you some HTML tricks to control the spaces *between* your text and images. These tricks are essential for making your pages attractive and easy to read. This hour provides practical advice that helps you design attractive and highly readable pages, even if you're not a professional graphics designer.

This hour also teaches you how to ensure that your Web pages will appear as quickly as possible when people try to read them. This is essential for making a good impression with your pages, especially for people who will be accessing them through Internet modem connections.

When it comes to designing and laying out your pages, you might think that a graphical Web page layout tool such as Microsoft FrontPage or Netscape Composer would be more intuitive and powerful than editing the HTML by hand, as you'll be doing in this hour.

It's true that designing your pages with an interactive graphical tool can be more intuitive, and I recommend that you have a good graphical tool like FrontPage 2000 available for that purpose.

However, you'll still be very glad to know the HTML you learn in this hour when it comes time to fine-tune all those little spacing problems that graphical tools tend to leave you with. This hour also covers page design techniques that are essential both when writing HTML by hand and when using a graphical tool.

You'll also find this hour very helpful for fixing the messy mistakes that some graphical layout programs (especially Adobe PageMill and Netscape Composer) can introduce into your Web pages when you try to rearrange or resize images.

To Do

The techniques covered in this hour are intended to help you make the pages you've already created better and faster. Select some of the most important and impressive pages that you've made to date, and see if you can make them look even better.

- Choose pages with some graphics on them. Almost all tricks in this hour involve images.
- If you have a page you think might especially benefit from a creative layout or unique background, start with that one.
- You may have some text and images that you haven't gotten around to putting on a Web page yet. If so, this hour can help make those new pages your best yet.
- Copy the pages you select into their own directory folder, and play with new design possibilities for them as you read through this hour.

Web Page Design

So far, this book has focused on the exact mechanics of Web page creation. Before getting into the nitty-gritty of spacing and layout tricks, you should take a moment now to step back and think about the overall visual design of your Web pages. Now that you know basic HTML, you need to learn how to apply it wisely.

Every aspect of a Web page should reflect the goals that led you to create the page in the first place. Not only should the text and graphics themselves communicate your message, but the way you fit those elements together can make an enormous impact on the reader's perceptions of you and your company.

Table 13.1 is checklist to help you think about the key design elements of a Web page. You should aim for most of your pages to meet the recommendations in this table, although some individual pages will undoubtedly need to "break the rules."

Table 13.1   Key Elements of Web Page Design

Things to Consider	Suggested Guidelines
Text content	Between 100 and 500 words per page
Text breaks	A headline, rule, or image every 40 to 100 words (except in long articles or stories)
Page length	Two to four screens (at 640×480 resolution)
File size	No more than 50KB per page, including images; animated GIFs can be up to 100KB per page
Speed	First screen of text and key images appear in less than 3 seconds over a 28.8Kbps modem
Colors	Two to four thematic colors dominant
Fonts	No more than three fonts (in graphics and text)
Blank space	Background should show on at least 50 percent of page
Contrast	No color in background should be close to text color
Tone and style	All text and graphics consistent in mood and theme
Overall impact	Page as a whole should appear balanced and attractive

Most of the tips in Table 13.1 are common to any page design, on paper or electronic. Some, however, are particularly tricky to control on Web pages.

The next section of this hour presents some HTML commands for handling the blank space and overall visual impact of your pages. This hour then wraps up with some techniques for meeting the speed requirements of today's Web, even when you use relatively large images.

Image Spacing and Borders

Figures 13.1 through 13.3 show the HTML text, images, and final appearance of a well-designed Web page. It meets all the criteria outlined in Table 13.1.

13

When you look at Figure 13.2, remember that Paint Shop Pro uses cross-hatching to indicate that a window is bigger than the image it contains, and a checkerboard pattern to indicate which regions of an image are transparent. For example, spacer.gif is actually a very small, entirely transparent square.

FIGURE 13.1

This page uses several techniques for adding blank space between images and text.

```
<html><head><title>The Varieties of Proboscis</title></head>
<body background="wainscot.gif"
 text="green" link="maroon" vlink="green" alink="white">
<div align="center">
 <img src="vofp.gif" align="top" width="400" height="100" />
 <img src="bosc.gif" align="top" width="125" height="135" />
 <br /><img src="spacer.gif" width="20" height="20" /><br />
</div>
<h2><a href="point.htm">
<img src="point.gif" align="left" width="120" height="120"
border="3" hspace="20" vspace="5" />The Needle</a></h2>
Being perhaps the most refined and coveted variety, this
proboscis is favoured by accountants, lawyers, librarians, and
all persons of great intellect and bile.<br clear="left" />
<img src="spacer.gif" width="20" height="20" /><br />
<h2 align="right"><a href="arch.htm">
<img src="arch.gif" align="right" width="140" height="100"
border="3" hspace="20" vspace="5" />The Arch</a></h2>
An original inspiration for both Roman and Gothic archetectural
motifs, this well-loved proboscis boasts an extensive history
in the fine arts.<br clear="right" />
<img src="spacer.gif" width="20" height="20" /><br />
<h2><a href="bulb.htm">
<img src="bulb.gif" align="left" width="140" height="100"
border="3" hspace="20" vspace="5" />The Bulb</a></h2>
A long-standing favourite of politicians and food service
professionals, this is the traditional proboscis of good cheer
and prolific oration.<br clear="left" />
<img src="spacer.gif" width="20" height="20" /><br />
<h2 align="right"><a href="hook.htm">
<img src="hook.gif" align="right" width="120" height="120"
border="3" hspace="20" vspace="5" />The Hook</a></h2>
This most visible and respected proboscis type commands prompt
attention and high regard in both religous and secular
circles.<br clear="right" />
<img src="spacer.gif" width="20" height="20" />
<div align="center">
 <img src="flourish.gif" width="136" height="30" />
 <p><a href="index.htm"><i>Return to the
 European Anatomy HomePage.</i></a></p>
</div></body></html>
```

Notice the generous amount of space between images and paragraphs in Figure 13.3. Web browsers tend to crowd everything together, but you can easily add space three different ways:

- Use small, totally transparent images to leave room between other things. The spacer.gif file (shown in Figure 13.2 and referred to in Figure 13.1) creates 20 pixels of blank space between each of the main parts of this page.

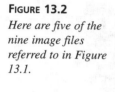

Figure 13.2

Here are five of the nine image files referred to in Figure 13.1.

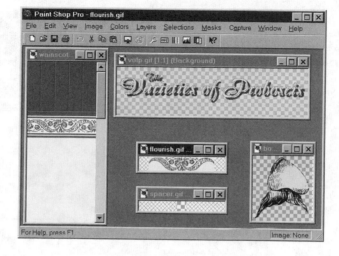

- When you wrap text around an image by using `<img align="right" />` or `<img align="left" />`, you can skip past the bottom of that image at any time with `<br clear="right" />` or `<br clear="left" />`. If you have images on both the right and left, you can type `<br clear="all" />` to go past both of them.

- You can add extra space on the left and right sides of any image with `hspace`. To add space on the top and bottom sides, use `vspace`. For example, each image in Figure 13.3 has 20 pixels of blank space to the left and right of it, and 5 pixels above and below it. This is because each `<img />` tag in Figure 13.1 includes the attributes `hspace="20" vspace="5"`.

You'll read about the `width` and `height` attributes of the `<img />` tag later in this hour, in the "Specifying Image Width and Height" section.

The `<img />` tags in Figure 13.1 also include a `border="3"` attribute, which enlarges the rectangular border around the images. The border is normally one pixel thick for any image inside an `<a>` link, but `border="3"` makes it three pixels thick.

The most popular use of the `border` attribute is making the image border disappear completely by typing `border="0"`. This is especially handy with transparent images, which often look funny with a rectangle around them.

The color of the border will be the same as the color of any text links. In this page, images that link to pages someone hasn't visited yet will have maroon borders. Images that link to a recently visited page will have green borders.

13

FIGURE 13.3

Thanks to generous spacing and a carefully premeditated layout, the HTML in Figure 13.1 looks great as a Web page.

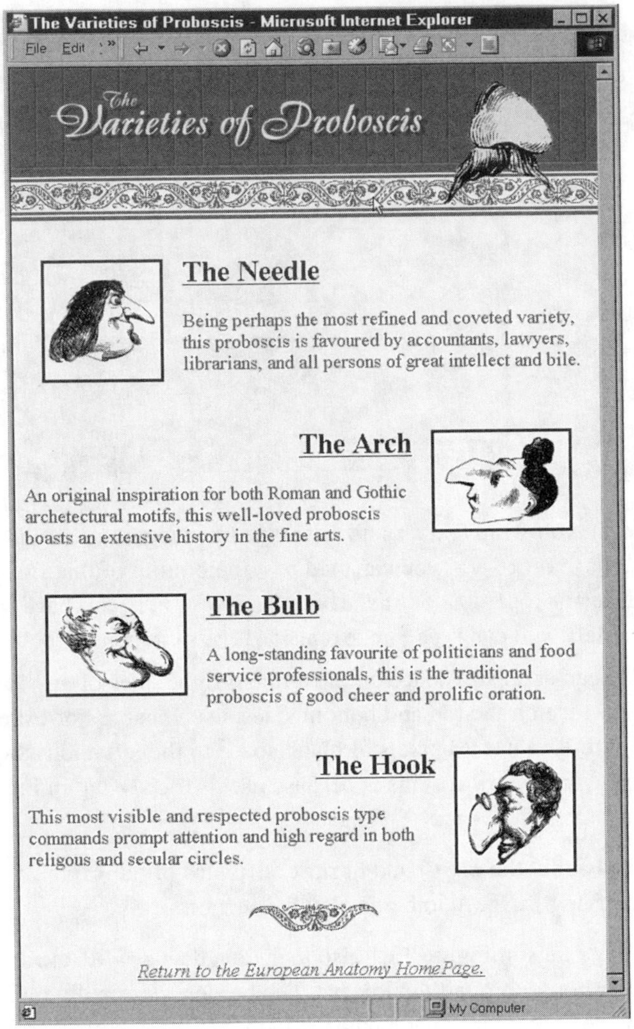

The Varieties of Proboscis - Microsoft Internet Explorer

File   Edit

The Varieties of Proboscis

The Needle

Being perhaps the most refined and coveted variety, this proboscis is favoured by accountants, lawyers, librarians, and all persons of great intellect and bile.

The Arch

An original inspiration for both Roman and Gothic archetectural motifs, this well-loved proboscis boasts an extensive history in the fine arts.

The Bulb

A long-standing favourite of politicians and food service professionals, this is the traditional proboscis of good cheer and prolific oration.

The Hook

This most visible and respected proboscis type commands prompt attention and high regard in both religous and secular circles.

Return to the European Anatomy HomePage.

My Computer

If you include a `border` attribute in an `<img />` that isn't between `<a>` and `</a>` link tags, all versions of Netscape Navigator and Microsoft Internet Explorer version 4 or 5 will draw the border by using the regular body text color. However, earlier versions of Microsoft Internet Explorer will never draw a border around an image that isn't a link, even if you include a `border` attribute.

The Old Background Banner Trick

One of the most prominent tricks employed in Figure 13.3 is the use of a 1,000-pixel-high background image (named `wainscot.gif`). Because the entire page is unlikely to be more than 1,000 pixels high, the background only appears to repeat in the horizontal direction. Since the bottom part of the image is all the same color, it looks like the background is only a banner at the top of the page.

Unlike a foreground image used as a banner, however, this wainscoting will automatically size itself to go from "wall to wall" of any sized window. It takes up less space on a disk and transfers over the Internet faster because only one repetition of the pattern needs to be stored.

If you use this trick to make background banners on your own Web pages, you should make them at least 2,000 pixels high. The page shown in Figure 13.3 can actually become longer than 1,000 pixels when someone uses a very large font size, in which case the wainscoting shows up again at the very bottom or middle of the page.

"Hang on," you say, "143×1,000 is 143,000 pixels! Won't that make an enormous image file and take forever to download?" The answer is no; large areas of uniform color take up virtually no space at all when compressed in the GIF file format. (`wainscot.gif` is only a 3KB file.)

By using a very wide background that repeats vertically, you can easily make a repeating banner that runs down the left side of a page, too. If you don't want text to obscure the banner, put a very large, totally transparent image at the beginning of the HTML page with `<img align="left" />`.

Figures 13.4 through 13.6 show the HTML and graphics that implement a left-side banner, as well as the resulting Web page.

Note that I right-justified the other graphics, both for aesthetic reasons and so that I could avoid using `<br clear="left" />`, which would skip all the way to the bottom of the left-justified banner graphic.

13

If you use a left-aligned transparent banner, be sure to add enough blank space around the actual foreground image to fill the area on the page you want to cover. The "Varieties of Proboscis" title graphic in Figures 13.5 and 13.6, for example, is 170×1,200 pixels.

Because almost nobody views Web pages in a window larger than 1600×1,200 pixels, vertically tiled background banners can safely be 2,000 pixels wide.

FIGURE 13.4

With a few strategic changes, you could put the top banner in Figure 13.3 to the left side.

```
<html><head><title>The Varieties of Proboscis</title></head>
<body background="wainsco2.gif"
 text="green" link="maroon" vlink="green" alink="white">
<img src="vofp2.gif" align="left" width="170" height="1200"/>
<img src="spacer.gif" width="20" height="20" /><br />
<h2><a href="point.htm">
<img src="point.gif" align="right" width="120" height="120"
border="3" hspace="20" vspace="5" />The Needle</a></h2>
Being perhaps the most refined and coveted variety, this
proboscis favoured by accountants, lawyers, librarians, and
all persons of great intellect and bile. <br clear="right" />
<img src="spacer.gif" width="20" height="20" /><br />
<h2 align="right"><a href="arch.htm">
<img src="arch.gif" align="right" width="140" height="100"
border="3" hspace="20" vspace="5" />The Arch</a></h2>
An original inspiration for both Roman and Gothic archetectural
motifs, this well-loved proboscis boasts an extensive history
in the fine arts.<br clear="right" />
<img src="spacer.gif" width="20" height="20" /><br />
<h2><a href="bulb.htm">
<img src="bulb.gif" align="right" width="140" height="100"
border="3" hspace="20" vspace="5" />The Bulb</a></h2>
A long-standing favourite of politicians and food service
professionals, this is the traditional proboscis of good cheer
and prolific oration.<br clear="right" />
<img src="spacer.gif" width="20" height="20" /><br />
<h2 align="right"><a href="hook.htm">
<img src="hook.gif" align="right" width="120" height="120"
border="3" hspace="20" vspace="5" />The Hook</a></h2>
This most visible and respected proboscis type commands prompt
attention and high regard in both religous and secular
circles.<br clear="right" />
<img src="spacer.gif" width="20" height="20" />
<div align="center">
 <img src="flourish.gif" width="136" height="30" />
 <p><a href="index.htm"><i>Return to the
European Anatomy Home Page.</i></a></p>
</div></body></html>
```

FIGURE 13.5

FIGURE 13.5

The rotated graphics for a left-side banner. (Notice how I changed the direction of the light source and shadowing, too.)

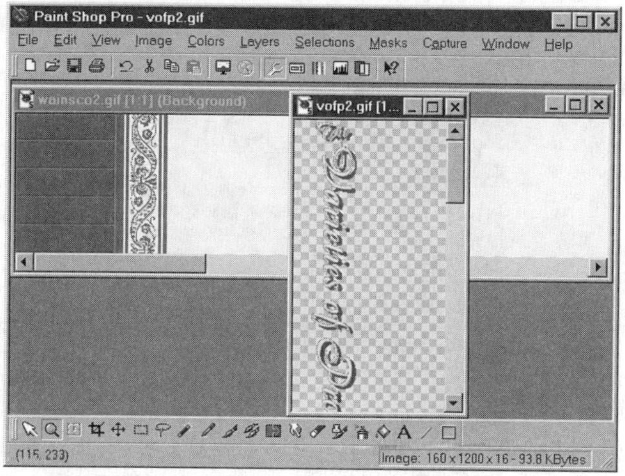

You'll sometimes choose to push the limits of HTML layout. The home page of the *24-Hour HTML Café* (`http://24hourHTMLcafe.com`) does exactly that—combining several tricks from this and other hours into a flexible layout that adjusts itself to the size of the browser window gracefully.

If you view the page in a small enough window (fewer than about 600 pixels wide), you'll notice that the images start crawling all over each other in ways God obviously never intended them to try. I could have solved this problem with tables (see Hour 15) or other advanced tricks, but I went for simplicity at the risk of annoying the very few people who look at the Web through extremely small windows.

13

FIGURE **13.6**

The HTML from Figure 13.4 and the banner from Figure 13.5 appear like this in Microsoft Internet Explorer.

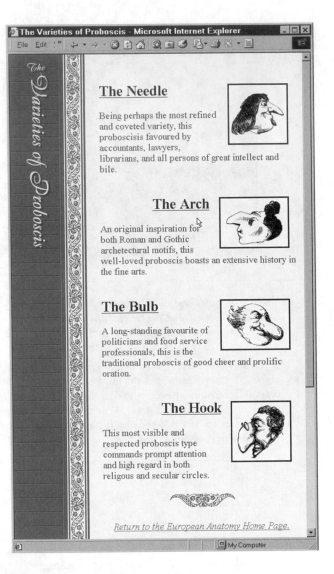

Specifying Image Width and Height

Because text moves over the Internet much faster than do graphics, most Web browsers will display the text on a page before the images. This gives people something to read while they're waiting to see the pictures, which makes the whole page seem faster.

You can make sure that everything on your page appears as quickly as possible and in the right places by explicitly stating each image's width and height. That way, a Web browser can leave the right amount of space for that image as it lays out the page and return for the actual image file later.

For each image on your page, use Paint Shop Pro or another graphics program to find out the exact width and height in pixels. (In Paint Shop Pro, this information appears at the bottom-right corner of the main window when you move the mouse over any part of an image.) Then include those dimensions in the <img /> tag, like this:

```
<img src="myimage.gif" width="200" height="100" />
```

The width and height specified for an image don't have to match the image's actual width and height. The Web browser program will try to squish or stretch the image to whatever size you specify.

This usually makes images look very ugly, but there is one excellent use for it: You can save a very small, totally transparent image and use it as any size "spacer" by specifying the width and height of the blank region you want to create on your page.

Summary

This hour provided some guidelines for designing attractive, highly readable Web pages. It also explained how to create and control blank space on your pages, as well as how to put borders around images. You saw how to use backgrounds to create banners across the top or left edge of a page and how to make sure people always have text to look at while waiting for the images on your page.

Table 13.2 summarizes the tags and attributes discussed in this chapter.

TABLE 13.2   HTML Tags and Attributes Covered in Hour 13

Tag	Attribute	Function
<img />		Inserts an inline image into the document.
	src="..."	The address of the image.
	align="..."	Determines the alignment of the given image (see Hour 10, "Putting Graphics on a Web Page").
	vspace="..."	The space between the image and the text above or below it.
	hspace="..."	The space between the image and the text to its left or right.

continues

13

TABLE 13.2 continued

Tag/Attribute		Function
	width="..."	The width, in pixels, of the image. If width is not the actual width, the image is scaled to fit.
	height="..."	The width, in pixels, of the image. If height is not the actual height, the image is scaled to fit.
	border="..."	Draws a border of the specified value in pixels to be drawn around the image. In case the images are also links, border changes the size of the default link border.
 		A line break.
	clear="..."	Causes the text to stop flowing around any images. Possible values are right, left, all.

Q&A

Q **I'd like to know exactly how wide the margins of a page are so I can line up my background and foreground images the way I want.**

A Unfortunately, different browsers (and even the same browser on different types of computers) leave different amounts of space along the top and left side of a page, so you can't precisely line up foreground graphics with background images. Generally, you can expect the top and left margins to be 8 to 12 pixels.

The good news is that you'll learn an elegant and precise way to control margin width in Hour 16, "Using Style Sheets."

Q **I used a graphical layout program to design my pages, and when I put the pages online my images look blotchy and seem to take forever to show up. What can I do?**

A Here's what might be going on: When you place and resize an image in some graphical Web page layout programs (such as Adobe PageMill), the program simply changes the width and height attributes without actually resizing the image file itself. This usually makes the images look kind of crinkly, and can mean that what looks like a little 100×100-pixel image on the page may actually be a huge 2,000×2,000-pixel monster that takes half an hour to download.

Here's how you can fix it: Open the image in Paint Shop Pro (or your favorite image editing software) and resize the image there to that specified in the width and height attributes of the corresponding <img /> tag.

Q **I've seen pages on the Web with multiple columns of text, wide margins, and other types of nice layouts you didn't discuss. How were those pages made?**

A Probably with the HTML table tags, which are discussed in Hour 15, "Advanced Layout with Tables," or with style sheets, discussed in Hour 16.

Workshop

Quiz

1. How would you wrap text around the right side of an image, leaving 40 pixels of space between the image and the text?

2. How could you insert exactly 80 pixels of blank space between two paragraphs of text?

3. If you have a circular button that links to another page, how do you prevent a rectangle from appearing around it?

4. What four attributes should you always include in every `<img />` tag as a matter of habit?

Answers

1. ```
   <img src="myimage.gif" hspace=40 vspace=40 align="left" />
   Text goes here.
   ```

2. Create a small image that is all one color and save it as `nothing.gif` with that color transparent. Then put the following tag between the two paragraphs of text:
   ```
   <img src="nothing.gif" width=1 height=80 />
   ```

3. Use the `border="0"` attribute, like the following:
   ```
   <a href="another_page.htm"><img src="circle.gif" border="0" /></a>
   ```

4. `src`, `alt`, `width`, and `height`. An example:
   ```
   <img src="fred.jpg" alt="fat fred" width="300" height="100">
   ```

Exercises

- Try creating a page with the wildest layout you can manage with the HTML tags you've learned so far. If you're resourceful, you should be able to create a staggered diagonal line of images or place short sentences of text almost anywhere on the page.

- Make a very large background—so big that people will see only one "tile" and you don't have to worry about it being seamless. Most Web browsers will display all foreground content (in front of the `bgcolor` you specify in the `<body>` tag) while the background image loads. Go ahead and play around with the creative possibilities that large backdrops open up.

13
   ```

HOUR 14

Graphical Links and Imagemaps

If you've read Hour 10, "Putting Graphics on a Web Page," you know
how to make an image link to another document. (If you don't quite recall
how to do it right now, it looks like this: `<a href="gohere.htm">`
`<img src="image.gif" /></a>`.)

You can also divide an image into regions that link to different documents,
depending on where someone clicks. This is called an *imagemap*, and any
image can be made into an imagemap. A Web site with medical information
might show an image of the human body and bring up different pages of
advice for each body part. A map of the world could allow people to click
any country for regional information. Many people use imagemaps to create
a "navigation bar" that integrates icons for each page on their Web site into
one cohesive imagemap.

Netscape Navigator and Microsoft Internet Explorer allow you to choose
between two different methods for implementing imagemaps. Nowadays, all
your imagemaps should be done using the latest method, which is called a

client-side imagemap. You may also want to make them work the old-fashioned server-side way for users of older browser programs. I explain both kinds of imagemaps in this hour.

NEW TERM An *imagemap* is an image on a Web page that leads to two or more different links, depending on which part of the image is clicked. Modern Web browsers use *client-side imagemaps*, but you can also create *server-side imagemaps* for compatibility with old browsers.

How and Why to Avoid Using Imagemaps

The first thing I must say about imagemaps is that you probably won't need—or want—to use them! It's almost always easier, more efficient, and more reliable to use several ordinary images, placed right next to one another, with a separate link for each image.

For example, imagine that you wanted to make a Web page that looks like the one in Figure 14.1, with each of the glowing words leading to a different link. The obvious approach is to use a single imagemap for the entire central graphic. You'll see how to do that later this hour.

However, the better solution is to cut the graphic into pieces by using Paint Shop Pro (or any other graphics program) and make each piece a separate image on the Web page. This way, the page is compatible with all versions of all Web browsers without requiring any server scripting or advanced HTML. Figure 14.2 shows how to cut the picture so that each link area is a separate image. Figure 14.3 shows the HTML that creates the page in Figure 14.1, using the images in Figure 14.2.

Notice that I was very careful not to put any spaces or line breaks in the bottom two `<img />` tags in Figure 14.3. A space or line break between `<img />` tags creates a small space between the images on the page, and the illusion of everything fitting together into one big image would be totally destroyed.

For the same reason, it's important not to put several images whose widths add up to more than about 580 pixels on a single line. The result might look good on your 800×600 screen, but someone looking at the page in a 640×480 window would see the images broken onto separate lines.

FIGURE 14.1

You can create this page using ordinary `<img />` tags and `<a href>` links. Imagemaps aren't necessary.

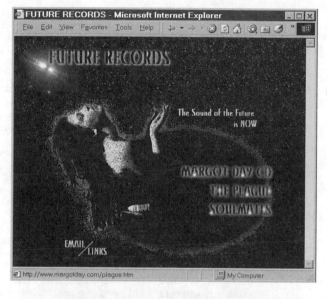

FIGURE 14.2

To avoid using imagemaps, you need to cut the image on the left into the seven images on the right. (Cut and paste using the rectangular selection tool.)

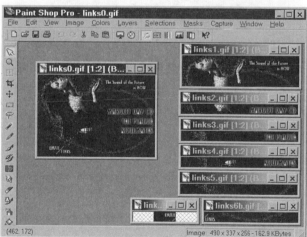

When *would* you want to use an imagemap, then? Only when the parts of an image you want to link are so numerous or oddly arranged that it would be a big hassle to chop the image into smaller images.

That does happen from time to time, so it's a good idea to know how to create imagemaps when you truly need to. The rest of this hour shows you how.

14

FIGURE 14.3

*Using the images in
Figure 14.3 is one way
to implement the page
in Figure 14.1. (The
big image in Figure
14.3,* links0.gif, *isn't
used.)*

```
<html><head><title>FUTURE RECORDS</title></head>
<body bgcolor="#000008" background="fade2.gif"
  text="F0F0F0" link="F000FF" vlink="8000F0" alink="8080FF">
<img src="future2.gif" width="320" height="108"
  alt="FUTURE RECORDS" />
<div align="center">
<img src="links1.gif" width="490" height="127"
  alt="The Sound of the Future is NOW" /><br />
<a href="http://www.margotday.com/margotcd.htm"><img
  src="links2.gif" width="490" height="40" border="0"
  alt="MARGOT DAY CD" /></a><br />
<a href="http://www.margotday.com/plague.htm"><img
  src="links3.gif" width="490" height="40" border="0"
  alt="THE PLAGUE" /></a><br />
<a href="http://www.margotday.com/soulmate.htm"><img
  src="links4.gif" width="490" height="40" border="0"
  alt="SOULMATES" /></a><br />
<img src="links5.gif" width="490" height="40" /><br />
<a href="mailto:margot@together.net"><img
  src="links6a.gif" width="93" height="40" border="0"
  alt="EMAIL" /></a><a
href="http://www.margotday.com/links.htm"><img
  src="links6b.gif" width="397" height="40" border="0"
  alt="LINKS"/></a></div>
</body></html>
```

Mapping Regions Within an Image

To make any type of imagemap, you need to figure out the numerical pixel coordinates
of each region within the image that you want to turn into a clickable link. An easy way
to do this is to open the image with Paint Shop Pro and watch the coordinates at the
bottom of the screen as you use the rectangle selection tool to select a rectangular region
of the image (see Figure 14.4). When the mouse button is down, the coordinates at the
bottom of the screen show both the top-left and bottom-right corners of the rectangle.
When the mouse button isn't down, only the x,y position of the mouse is shown.

You could use the whole image in Figure 14.4 as an imagemap, linking to seven Web
pages about the various literary genres. To do so, you would first need to decide which
region of the image should be linked to each Web page. You can use rectangles, circles,
and irregular polygons as regions. Figure 14.5 shows an example of how you might
divide the image into these shapes.

Graphical Web page editors such as Microsoft FrontPage 2000 allow you to paint *hotspots* onto an imagemap (see Figure 14.5) interactively and they generate the necessary HTML for you. This is one situation where a graphical editor is very handy to have around.

There are also programs available that let you highlight a rectangle with your mouse and automatically spew out imagemap coordinates into a file for you to cut-and-paste into your HTML, but they are rather cumbersome to use. If you don't have access to FrontPage or another good graphical Web page editor, you can easily locate the pixel coordinates in Paint Shop Pro or your favorite general-purpose graphics program.

FIGURE 14.4

Paint Shop Pro can easily give the coordinates for imagemap regions without mucking about with special image-mapping utilities.

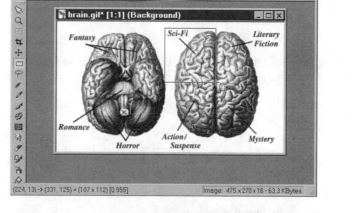

FIGURE 14.5

Microsoft FrontPage 2000 lets you draw clickable hotspot links onto your imagemaps with your mouse.

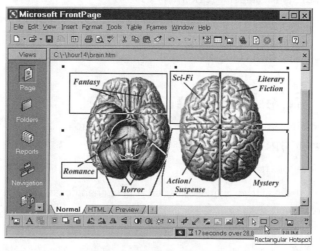

14

To create the imagemap, first jot down the pixel coordinates of the top-left and bottom-right corners of each rectangular region shown in Figure 14.5. You also need to locate and record the center point and radius of the circle, as well as the coordinates of each corner of the irregularly shaped regions. (If you want to follow along with this by using an image of your own, just write the coordinates on a piece of paper for now. You'll see exactly how to put them into an HTML file momentarily.)

These coordinates are as follows:

- Fantasy (region 1): A rectangle from 15,15 to 220,100.
- Romance (region 2): A rectangle from 0,200 to 75,235 and a circle centered at 140,150 with radius 40.
- Horror (region 3): An irregular polygon with corners at the following eight points: (70,175), (90,155), (125,195), (160,195), (190,160), (220,185), (185,270), and (110,270).
- Sci-Fi (region 4): A rectangle from 225,10 to 330,120.
- Literary Fiction (region 5): A rectangle from 330,10 to 475,120.
- Action/Suspense (region 6): An irregular polygon with corners at the following five points: (230,130), (330,130), (330,270), (210,270), and (210,230).
- Mystery (region 7): A rectangle from 330,130 to 475,270.

To Do

▼ To Do

You'll better remember how to make imagemaps if you get an image of your own and turn it into an imagemap as you read the following explanation.

- For starters, it's easiest to choose a fairly large image that is visually divided into roughly rectangular regions.
- If you don't have a suitable image handy, use Paint Shop Pro (or your favorite graphics program) to make one. One easy and useful idea is to put a word or an icon for each of your important pages together into a button bar or signpost.

▲

Client-Side Imagemaps

Once you have the coordinates written down, you're ready to create an HTML imagemap. Type the following just after the <body> tag in your Web page:

```
<map name="brainmap">
```

(You can use whatever name you want if brainmap doesn't describe the image you're using very well.)

Now you need to type an `<area />` tag for each region of the image. Figure 14.6 shows how you would define the eight regions of the brain image.

FIGURE 14.6

The `<map>` and `<area />` tags define the regions of an imagemap.

```
<html><head><title>Best Seller Brain</title></head>
<body>
<map name="brainmap">
<area shape="rect" coords="15,15,220,100" href="fantasy.htm" />
<area shape="rect" coords="0,200,75,235" href="romance.htm" />
<area shape="circle" coords="140,150,40" href="romance.htm" />
<area shape="poly" coords="70,175, 90,135, 125,195, 160,195,
190,160, 220,185, 185,270, 110,270" href="horror.htm" />
<area shape="rect" coords="225,10,330,120" href="scifi.htm" />
<area shape="rect" coords="330,10,475,120" href="litfi.htm" />
<area shape="poly" coords="230,130, 330,130, 330,270, 210,270,
210,230" href="action.htm" />
<area shape="rect" coords="330,130,475,270"
 href="mystery.htm" />
</map>
<div align="center">
<h1>The Best Seller Brain</h1>
<img src="brain.gif" usemap="#brainmap" border="0" />
<p><i>"Only a person with a Best Seller mind
can write Best Sellers."</i></p></div>
<div align="right">-Aldous Huxley</div>
</body></html>
```

Each `<area />` tag in Figure 14.3 has three attributes:

- shape indicates whether the region is a rectangle (`shape="rect"`), a circle (`shape="circle"`), or an irregular polygon (`shape="poly"`).

- coords gives the exact pixel coordinates for the region. For rectangles, give the x,y coordinates of the top-left corner followed by the x,y coordinates of the bottom-right corner. For circles, give the x,y center point followed by the radius in pixels. For polygons, list the x,y coordinates of all the corners, in connect-the-dots order.

- href specifies the page to which the region links. You can use any address or file name that you would use in an ordinary `<a href>` link tag.

After the `<area />` tags, you are done defining the imagemap; insert a closing `</map>` tag.

To place the actual imagemap on the page, you use an ordinary `<img />` tag and add a usemap attribute:

```
<img src="brain.gif" usemap="#brainmap">
```

Use the name you put in the `<map>` tag (and don't forget the # symbol). It is best to include width and height attributes for any image on a Web page.

14

It is also possible to put the map definition in a separate file by including that file's name in the usemap attribute, like the following:

```
<img src="thisthat.gif" usemap="maps.htm#thisthat">
```

For instance, if you used an imagemap on every page in your Web site, you could just put the <map> and <area> tags for it on one page instead of repeating it on every page it appears.

Figure 14.7 shows the imagemap in action. Notice that Microsoft Internet Explorer displays the link address for whatever region the mouse is moving over at the bottom of the window, just as it does for "normal" links. If someone clicked where the mouse cursor (the little hand) is shown in Figure 14.7, the page named fantasy.htm would come up.

FIGURE 14.7

The imagemap defined in Figure 14.6 appears like this on the Web page.

Mouse over imagemap link

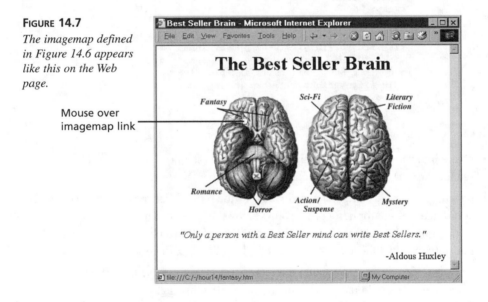

You may want to include text links at the bottom of your imagemap that lead to the same pages the map itself links to. This allows people who have older Web browsers—or who don't want to wait for the image to finish loading—to access those pages.

For an example—and a little tongue-in-cheek history lesson thrown into the bargain—click "The Immortal Presidents" at http://24hourHTMLcafe.com/hour14/.

Server-Side Imagemaps

The old-fashioned way to create an imagemap is to let the server computer where the Web page resides do all the work. Most Web authors don't bother with server-side imagemaps anymore because it's easier and just as effective to provide text links for people using older browsers. There are still an awful lot of people out there using pre-1995 Web browsers, and it isn't that difficult to make your imagemaps work for them. You can read the following explanation of what's involved and decide for yourself whether it's worth your time to provide server-side imagemaps.

When the user clicks an image that has been mapped this way, the browser program just sends the mouse's x,y coordinates to a special script on the server. Usually, this script is located in some subdirectory of `cgi-bin` on the server, and the HTML to implement the imagemap is just a normal anchor link.

```
<a href="/cgi-bin/imagemap/thisthat"><img src="thisthat.gif" ismap /></a>
```

Simple—but when you install a Web page including such a link, you need to tell the imagemap script which parts of the image should be associated with which link addresses. This is normally done in a *map file*. Each line in the map file is simply the word `rect` followed by an URL and two sets of x,y coordinates representing the top-left corner and the bottom-right corner of a region of the image. Some server scripts also support non-rectangular regions with the word `poly` and `circle` (or `round`).

The first line in a map file begins with the word `default`, followed by the URL that should be used if the user happens to click outside any rectangular region defined by a `rect` line. A map file named `thisthat.map` might look like the following:

```
default /top/this.htm
rect /top/this.htm 0,0,102,99
rect /top/that.htm 103,0,205,99
```

The final step in setting up a server-side imagemap is telling the imagemap script which map file to use for which image. You do this by adding a line to a system file named `imagemap.conf`. This file will already exist and includes entries for every imagemap defined on the server. You simply add a line with the name used in the `href` attribute of the `<a>` tag, a colon, and then the actual location and name of the associated map file. For example, the previous reference is `href="/cgi-bin/imagemap/thisthat"`, and the preceding map file is named `thisthat.map`. If this map file were in a directory named `/mapfiles`, the line in `imagemap.conf` would read like this:

```
thisthat : /mapfiles/thisthat.map
```

14

All this isn't nearly as difficult as it may sound if you've never set up an imagemap, but it can be a hassle—especially if your pages reside on somebody else's server and you don't have the rights to modify system files such as `imagemap.conf` yourself. What's worse, server-side imagemaps don't work at all on Web pages located on your hard drive, a CD-ROM, or most local networks.

There are also some variations in the exact syntax for imagemap implementation; they depend on the software installed on your server. If you move your pages to a different server, the imagemaps may not work anymore. Yuck.

Fortunately, the latest versions of all the major browsers support the client-side imagemaps discussed earlier in this hour, where the association of links with specific regions in an image is handled by the browser itself instead of a server script. This means that you can include imagemaps in your HTML files without imposing an additional burden on your ISP's server, and you can be more certain that they will be processed correctly and dependably.

Combined Client/Server Imagemaps

There is a way for you to provide client-side imagemaps that automatically switch to server-side imagemaps if the user's browser doesn't support client-side maps. With a single line of code, you can allow an imagemap to be interpreted either by the end user's software or by the server by including the `ismap` attribute in the `<img />` tag, and then including both a `usemap=` attribute and `cgi-bin/imagemap` reference.

```
<map "#thisthat">
<area shape="rect" coords="0,0,102,99" href="this.htm" />
<area shape="rect" coords="103,0,205,99" href="that.htm" /></map>
<a href="/cgi-bin/imagemap/thisthat">
<img src="thisthat.gif" usemap="#thisthat" ismap /></a>
```

Here, as with any unrecognized tag, browsers that don't support client-side imagemaps will simply ignore the `<usemap>` and `<ismap>` tags and treat the preceding code like an old-fashioned server-side imagemap.

Since the new XML and XHTML standards don't technically allow attributes without values, you may have to use `ismap="ismap"` in the future instead of just plain `ismap`.

As it stands today, all current-version Web browsers treat `ismap` and `ismap="ismap"` exactly the same.

Summary

This hour explained how to create imagemaps—links that lead to more than one place, depending on where you click an image—as well as why and how to avoid using them whenever possible. You saw how to define rectangular and circular link regions within an image, as well as irregularly shaped polygonal regions. You also learned to provide an alternate link for people using older browsers that don't support the current imagemap standard. Finally, you got a quick run-down on providing server-side imagemaps on most types of Web servers—just in case you want to provide the best possible experience for users of outdated browsers.

Table 14.1 is a summary of the tags and attributes covered in this hour.

TABLE 14.1 HTML Tags and Attributes Covered in Hour 14

Tag	Attribute	Function
`<img />`		Inserts an image into the document.
	`ismap`	This image is a clickable imagemap.
	`src="..."`	The image's URL.
	`usemap="..."`	The name of an imagemap specification for client-side image mapping. Used with `<MAP>` and `<AREA>`.
`<map>...</map>`		A client-side imagemap, referenced by `<img usemap="..." />`. Includes one or more `<area>` tags.
`<area />`		Defines a clickable link within a client-side `imagemap`.
	`shape="..."`	The shape of the clickable area. Currently, `rect`, `poly`, and `circle` (or `round`) are the valid options.
	`coords="..."`	The left, top, right, and bottom coordinates of the clickable region within an image.
	`href="..."`	The URL that should be loaded when the area is clicked.

Q&A

Q I'd like to know exactly which browsers support client-side imagemaps and which support server-side imagemaps.

A All browsers that display graphics support server-side imagemaps. All versions of Netscape Navigator and Microsoft Internet Explorer with version numbers 2 or higher also support client-side imagemaps. Any other Web browser produced after 1995 probably supports client-side imagemaps, too.

14

Q My imagemaps with polygonal and circular regions don't seem to work right in Netscape 2. Why?

A Netscape Navigator version 2 and Microsoft Internet Explorer version 2 only support rectangular regions in client-side imagemaps. Only people using version 3 or later of these browsers will be able to click non-rectangular regions.

Q I don't have Paint Shop Pro and my graphics software doesn't tell me x,y coordinates. How do I figure out the coordinates for my imagemaps?

A Here's a sneaky way to do it using Netscape Navigator. Put the image on a page with the ismap attribute and an <a> tag around it, like the following:

```
<a href="nowhere"><img src="myimage.gif" ismap /></a>
```

When you view that page with Navigator, move the mouse over the image. You will see the coordinates in the message box at the bottom of the window.

Workshop

Quiz

1. You have a 200×200-pixel image named quarters.gif for your Web page. When viewers click the top-left quarter of the image, you want them to get a page named toplft.htm. When they click the top-right quarter, they should get toprgt.htm. Clicking the bottom left should bring up btmlft.htm, and the bottom right should lead to btmrgt.htm. Write the HTML to implement this as a client-side imagemap.

2. If you want people using older browsers that don't support client-side imagemaps to get a page named oldies.htm when they click any part of the imagemap, how do you modify the HTML you wrote for question 1?

3. How could you implement the effect described in question 1 without using imagemaps at all?

Answers

```
1. <map name="quartersmap">
   <area shape="rect" coords="0,0,99,99" href="toplft.htm" />
   <area shape="rect" coords="100,0,199,99" href="toprgt.htm" />
   <area shape="rect" coords="0,100,99,199" href="btmlft.htm" />
   <area shape="rect" coords="100,100,199,199" href="btmrgt.htm" />
   </map>
   <img src="quarters.gif" width="200" height="200"
   usemap="#quartersmap" />
```

2. Replace the `<img />` tag above with:

```
<a href="oldies.htm">
<img src="quarters.gif width="200" height="200" ismap
usemap="#quartersmap" /></a>
```

3. Use a graphics program such as Paint Shop Pro to chop the image into four quarters and save them as separate images named `toplft.gif`, `toprgt.gif`, `btmlft.gif`, and `btmrgt.gif`. Then write this:

```
<a href="toplft.htm"><img src="toplft.gif"
width="100" height="100" border="0" /></a>
<a href="toprgt.htm"><img src="toprgt.gif"
width="100" height="100" border="0" /></a> <br />
<a href="btmlft.htm"><img src="btmlft.gif"
width="100" height="100" border="0" /></a>
<a href="btmrgt.htm"><img src="btmrgt.gif"
width="100" height="100" border="0" /></a>
```

(Be careful to break the lines of the HTML *inside* the tags as shown in this code, to avoid introducing any spaces between the images.)

Exercises

- If you have some pages containing short lists of links, see if you can cook up an interesting imagemap to use instead.

- Imagemaps are usually more engaging and attractive than a row of repetitive-looking icons or buttons. Can you come up with a visual metaphor related to your site that would make it easier—and maybe more fun—for people to navigate through your pages? (Thinking along these lines is a good preparation for the issues you'll be tackling in Part VI, "Building a Web Site," by the way.)

14

Hour 15

Advanced Layout with Tables

One of the most powerful tools for creative Web page design is the *table*, which allows you to arrange text and graphics into multiple columns and rows. This hour shows you how to build HTML tables and how to control the spacing, layout, and appearance of the tables you create.

NEW TERM A *table* is an orderly arrangement of text and/or graphics into vertical *columns* and horizontal *rows*.

To Do

As you read this hour, think about how arranging text into tables could benefit your Web pages. The following are some specific ideas to keep in mind:

- Of course, the most obvious application of tables is to organize tabular information, such as a multicolumn list of names and numbers.

- If you want more complex relationships between text and graphics than the `<img align="left" />` or `<img align="right" />` can provide, tables can do it.

▼   • Tables can be used to draw borders around text or around several graphics images.

         • Whenever you need multiple columns of text, tables are the answer.

For each of your pages that meets one of these criteria, try adding a table modeled after
the examples in this hour. The "Exercises" section at the end of this hour offers a couple

▲   of detailed suggestions along these lines as well.

Creating a Simple Table

To make tables, you have to start with a `<table>` tag. Of course, you end your tables
with the `</table>` tag. If you want the table to have a border, use a `border` attribute to
specify the width of the border in pixels. A border size of `0` (or leaving the `border`
attribute out entirely) will make the border invisible, which is often handy when you are
using a table as a page layout tool.

With the `<table>` tag in place, the next thing you need is the `<tr>` tag. `<tr>` creates a
table row, which contains one or more cells of information before the closing `</tr>`. To
create these individual cells, you use the `<td>` tag. `<td>` stands for table data; you place
the table information between the `<td>` and `</td>` tags.

> **NEW TERM**   A *cell* is a rectangular region that can contain any text, images, and HTML tags.
> Each row in a table is made up of at least one cell.

There is one more basic tag involved in building tables: The `<th>` tag works exactly like
a `<td>` tag, except `<th>` indicates that the cell is part of the heading of the table. Some
Web browsers render `<th>` and `<td>` cells exactly the same, but Netscape Navigator and
Microsoft Internet Explorer (version 4 or greater) both display the text in `<th>` cells as
centered and boldface.

You can create as many cells as you want, but each row in a table should have the same
number of columns as the other rows. The example in Figures 15.1 and 15.2 shows a
simple table using only these four tags.

> As you know, HTML ignores extra spaces between words and tags. However,
> you might find your HTML tables easier to read (and less prone to time-
> wasting errors) if you use spaces to indent `<td>` tags, as I did in Figure 15.1.

FIGURE 15.1

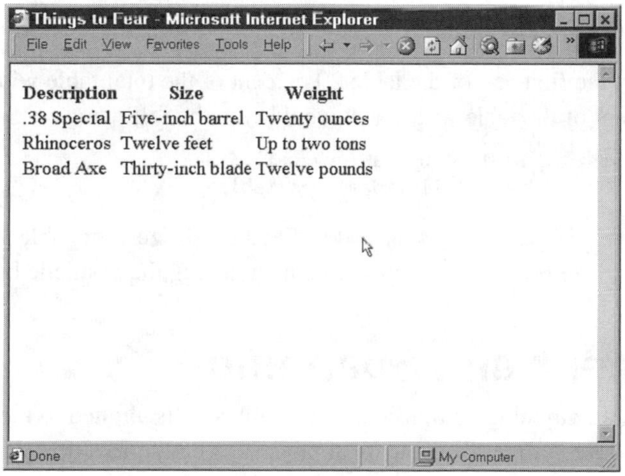

The <table>, <tr>, and <td> tags are all you need to create simple tables. The <th> tag can also be used to specify a heading.

```
<html><head><title>Things to Fear</title></head>
<body>
<table>
<tr><th>Description</th>
    <th>Size</th>
    <th>Weight</th></tr>
<tr><td>.38 Special</td>
    <td>Five-inch barrel</td>
    <td>Twenty ounces</td></tr>
<tr><td>Rhinoceros</td>
    <td>Twelve feet</td>
    <td>Up to two tons</td></tr>
<tr><td>Broad Axe</td>
    <td>Thirty-inch blade</td>
    <td>Twelve pounds</td></tr>
</table>
</body></html>
```

FIGURE 15.2

The HTML in Figure 15.1 creates a table with four rows and three columns.

You can place virtually any other HTML element into a table cell. However, tags used in one cell don't carry over to other cells, and tags from outside the table don't apply within the table. For example, if you wrote the following, the word there would be neither boldface nor italic because neither the <b> tag outside the table nor the <i> tag from the previous cell affects it:

```
<b>
<table><tr>
 <td><i>hello</td>
 <td>there</td>
</tr></table>
</b>
```

To make both the words hello and there boldface, you would need to type this:

```
<table><tr>
 <td><b>hello</b></td>
 <td><b>there</b></td>
</tr></table>
```

Table Size

Ordinarily, the size of a table and its individual cells automatically expand to fit the data you place into it. However, you can choose to control the exact size of the entire table by putting width and/or height attributes in the <table> tag. You can also control the size of each cell by putting width and height attributes in the individual <td> tags. The width and height can be specified as either pixels or percentages. For example, the following HTML makes a table 500 pixels wide and 400 pixels high:

```
<table width="500" height="400">
```

To make the first cell of the table 20 percent of the total table width and the second cell 80 percent of the table width, you would type the following:

```
<table><tr><td width="20%">skinny cell</td>
<td width="80%">fat cell</td></tr></table>
```

When you use percentages instead of fixed pixel sizes, the table will resize automatically to fit any size browser window, while maintaining the aesthetic balance you're after.

Alignment and Spanning

By default, anything you place inside a table cell is aligned to the left and vertically centered. You can align the contents of table cells both horizontally and vertically with the align and valign attributes.

You can apply these attributes to any <tr>, <td>, or <th> tag. Alignment attributes assigned to a <tr> tag apply to all cells in that row. Depending on the size of your table, you can save yourself a considerable amount of time and effort by applying these attributes at the <tr> level and not in each individual <td> or <th> tag. The HTML code in Figure 15.3 uses valign="top" to bring the text to the top of each cell. Figure 15.4 shows the result.

At the top of Figure 15.4, a single cell spans two columns. This is accomplished with the colspan="2" attribute in the <th> tag for that cell. As you might guess, you can also use the rowspan attribute to create a cell that spans more than one row.

FIGURE 15.3

You can use alignment, cell spacing, borders, and background colors to bring clarity and elegance to your tables.

```html
<html><head><title>Things to Fear</title></head>
<body>
<table border="2" cellpadding="8" cellspacing="3">
<tr bgcolor="silver">
  <th colspan="2">Description</th>
  <th>Size</th><th>Weight</th><th>Speed</th></tr>
<tr valign="top">
  <td><img src="handgun.gif" /></td>
  <td><h2>.38 Special</h2></td>
  <td>Five-inch barrel.</td>
  <td>Twenty ounces.</td>
  <td>Six rounds in four seconds.</td></tr>
<tr valign="top">
  <td><img src="rhino.gif" /></td>
  <td><h2>Rhinoceros</h2></td>
  <td>Twelve feet, horn to tail.</td>
  <td>Up to two tons.</td>
  <td>Thirty-five miles per hour in bursts.</td></tr>
<tr valign="top">
  <td><img src="axeman.gif" /></td>
  <td><h2>Broad Axe</h2></td>
  <td>Thirty-inch blade.</td>
  <td>Twelve pounds.</td>
  <td>Sixty miles per hour on impact.</td></tr>
</table>
</body></html>
```

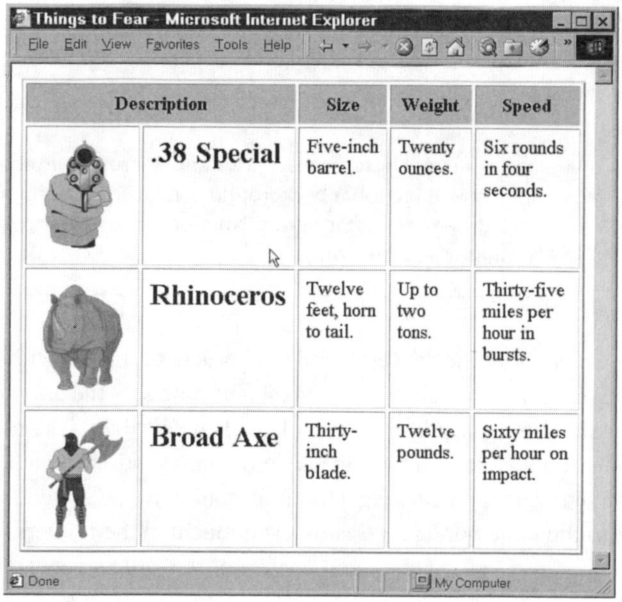

15

FIGURE 15.4

The colspan *attribute in Figure 15.3 allows the top-left cell to span multiple columns.*

Keeping the structure of rows and columns organized in your mind can be the most difficult part of creating tables with cells that span multiple columns or rows. The tiniest error can often throw the whole thing into disarray. You'll save yourself time and frustration by sketching your tables out on graph paper before you start writing the HTML to implement them.

You can also use an interactive Web page layout program to arrange the rows and columns in your table. This can make table design much easier, as long as you choose a program (such as Microsoft FrontPage 2000) that creates well-formatted HTML that you can edit by hand when you choose.

Be especially wary of early versions of Netscape Composer (and most other similar programs, including FrontPage 98), which were so full of bugs that laying out complex tables with them was a frustrating and often futile exercise.

Backgrounds and Spacing

There are a few tricks in Figures 15.3 and 15.4 that I haven't mentioned yet. You can give an entire table—and each individual row or cell in a table—its own background, distinct from any background you might use on the Web page itself. You do this by placing a bgcolor or background attribute in the <table>, <tr>, <td>, or <th> tag exactly as you would in the <body> tag (see Hour 11, "Custom Backgrounds and Colors"). To give an entire table a yellow background, for example, you would use
<table bgcolor="yellow"> or the equivalent <table bgcolor="#ffff00">.

Only users of Netscape Navigator and Microsoft Internet Explorer version 3 or later will see table background colors. Table background images are supported by Microsoft Internet Explorer versions 3 and 4 and Netscape Navigator version 4 only.

You can also control the space around the borders of a table with the cellpadding and cellspacing attributes. The cellspacing attribute sets the amount of space (in pixels) between table borders and between table cells themselves. The cellpadding attribute sets the amount of space around the edges of information in the cells. Setting the cellpadding value to 0 causes all the information in the table to align as closely as possible to the table borders, possibly even touching the borders. cellpadding and cellspacing give you good overall control of the table's appearance.

15

You saw the effect of background color and spacing attributes in Figures 15.3 and 15.4.

NEW TERM You can place an entire table within a table cell, and that separate table can possess any and all the qualities of any table you might want to create. In other words, you can *nest* tables inside one another.

Nested tables open a vast universe of possibilities for creative Web page layout. For example, if you wanted a column of text to appear to the left of a table, you could create a two-column table with the text in one column and the subtable in the other column, like the following:

```
<table>
<tr><td>To the right, you see all our telephone numbers.</td>
<td>
  <table border="1">
  <tr><td>voice<td>802-888-2828</td></tr>
  <tr><td>fax   <td>802-888-6634</td></tr>
  <tr><td>data  <td>802-888-3009</td></tr>
  </table>
</table>
</table>
```

Notice that the inner table has borders, but the outer table does not.

Before you get too excited about the preceding tip, you should know that Netscape Navigator 4 contains a bug that often prevents nested tables from displaying properly. There are an awful lot of people using Navigator 4, so it's a good idea to avoid putting tables within tables even though most other browsers (including Navigator 3 and 5) handle nested tables just fine.

Creative Page Layout with Tables

The boring, conventional way to use tables is for tabular arrangements of text and numbers. The real fun begins when you make the borders of your tables invisible and use them as guides for arranging graphics and columns of text any way you please. For an example, take a look at Figures 15.5 and 15.6.

While I worked on building this table, I left the borders visible so I could make sure everything was placed the way I wanted. Then, before incorporating this table into the final Web page, I removed the border="1" attribute from the <table> tag to make the lines invisible.

FIGURE **15.5**

Use tables whenever you want multiple columns of text or wide margins.

```
<html><head><title>Mathew Eber, D.D.E.</title></head>
<body><div align="center">
<table cellspacing="10"><tr valign="top">
<td><img src="handgun.gif" /><br />Five-inch barrel. Twenty
ounces. Six rounds in four seconds.</td>
<td><img src="rhino.gif" /><br />Twelve feet, horn to tail. Up
to two tons. Thirty-five miles per hour.</td>
<td><img src="axeman.gif" /><br />Thirty-inch blade. Twelve
pounds. Sixty miles per hour on impact.</td>
<td><img src="dentist.gif" /><br /><b>Two-millimeter bit. Under
an ounce. Fifty revolutions per second.</b></td>
</tr></table>
<table width="400"><tr><td align="center">
<h1>Visit the Dentist.</h1>
<h2>It's Really Not So Bad.</h2>
<p>Getting yourself to go to the dentist shouldn't be like
pulling teeth. Modern oral care is relatively painless and
inexpensive, compared to some of the alternatives. So make an
appointment today.</p>
<p><b>1-800-PAINLESS</b><br />
<i>Dr. Mathew Eber, D.D.E.</i></p>
</td></tr></table>
</div></body></html>
```

FIGURE **15.6**

HTML tables give you greater flexibility and control when laying out your Web pages.

I used two different tables in Figures 15.5 and 15.6. The top one allowed me to arrange the images and text into four columns. The bottom one let me confine the text to the middle 400 pixels of the screen, essentially giving me extra-wide margins. Remember both of these applications—you'll probably find uses for them often!

> For an example of how you can use tables for creative layout, click "LOOK: The Site of the '90s" at http://24hourHTMLcafe.com/hour15/.
>
> Your real-world site will probably be a bit more tame than the LOOK site—but some of you will start getting even crazier ideas....

Summary

In this hour you learned to arrange text and images into organized arrangements or rows and columns, called tables. You learned the three basic tags for creating tables and many optional attributes for controlling the alignment, spacing, and appearance of tables. You also saw that tables can be used together and nested within one another for an even wider variety of layout options.

Table 15.1 summarizes the tags and attributes covered in this hour.

TABLE 15.1 HTML Tags and Attributes Covered in Hour 15

Tag	Attribute	Function
`<table>...</table>`		Creates a table that can contain any number of rows (`<tr>` tags).
	`border="..."`	Indicates the width in pixels of the table borders. (`border="0"`, or omitting the `border` attribute, makes borders invisible.)
	`cellspacing="..."`	The amount of space between the cells in the table.
	`cellpadding="..."`	The amount of space between the edges of the cell and its contents.
	`width="..."`	The width of the table on the page, in either exact pixel values or as a percentage of page width.
	`bgcolor="..."`	Background color of all cells in the table that do not contain their own `background` or `bgcolor` attribute.

continues

Tag	Attribute	Function
	background="..."	Background image to tile within all cells in the table that do not contain their own background or bgcolor attribute (Microsoft Internet Explorer 3 or later only).
`<tr>...</tr>`		Defines a table row, containing one or more cells (`<td>` tags).
	align="..."	The horizontal alignment of the contents of the cells within this row. Possible values are left, right, and center.
	valign="..."	The vertical alignment of the contents of the cells within this row. Possible values are top, middle, and bottom.
	bgcolor="..."	Background color of all cells in the row that do not contain their own background or bgcolor attributes.
	background="..."	Background image to tile within all cells in the row that do not contain their own background or bgcolor attributes.
`<td>...</td>`		Defines a table data cell.
	align="..."	The horizontal alignment of the contents of the cell. Possible values are left, right, and center.
	valign="..."	The vertical alignment of the contents of the cell. Possible values are top, middle, and bottom.
	rowspan="..."	The number of rows this cell will span.
	colspan="..."	The number of columns this cell will span.
	width="..."	The width of this column of cells, in exact pixel values or as a percentage of the table width.
	bgcolor="..."	Background color of the cell.
	background="..."	Background image to tile within the cell.
`<th>...</th>`		Defines a table heading cell. (Takes all the same attributes as `<td>`.)

Q&A

Q **I made a big table and when I load the page, nothing appears for a long time. Why the wait?**

A Because the Web browser has to figure out the size of everything in the table before it can display any part of it, complex tables can take a while to appear on the screen. You can speed things up a bit by always including width and height tags for every graphics image within a table. Using width attributes in the <table> and <td> tags also helps.

Q **I've noticed that a lot of pages on the Web have tables in which one cell changes while others stay the same. How do they do that?**

A Those sites are using *frames*, not tables. Frames are similar to tables except that each frame contains a separate HTML page and can be updated independently of the others. The new *floating frames* can actually be put inside a table, so they can look just like a regular table even though the HTML that creates them is quite different. You'll find out how to make frames in Hour 21, "Multi-Page Layout with Frames."

Q **I read in another book that there is a table <caption> tag, but you didn't mention it in this book. Why not?**

A The <caption> tag is hardly ever used, and considering how much you're learning at once here, I didn't think you needed an extra tag to memorize! Since you asked, however, all the <caption> does is center some text over the top of the table. You can easily do the same thing with the <div align="center"> tag you're already familiar with, but the idea behind <caption> is that some highly intelligent future software might associate it with the table in some profound and meaningful way, thus facilitating communication with higher life-forms and saving humanity from cosmic obscurity and almost-certain destruction. Obviously, this doesn't matter to your short-term quarterly profits, so you can safely pretend the <caption> tag doesn't exist.

Q **Weren't there some new table tags in HTML 4? And isn't this a book about HTML 4?**

A The HTML 4 standard introduced several new table tags not discussed in this book. The primary practical uses of these extensions are to prepare the ground for some advanced features that no Web browser yet offers, such as tables with their own scrollbars and more reliable reading of tables for visually impaired users. If either of these things is of direct concern to you, you can find out about the new tags at the www.w3c.org Web site. The new tags do not directly affect how tables are displayed in any existing Web browser.

Don't worry—the new tags do not and will not make any of the table tags covered in this hour obsolete. They will all continue to work just as they do now.

Workshop

Quiz

1. You want a Web page with two columns of text side by side. How do you create it?

2. You think the columns you created for question 1 look too close together. How do you add 30 pixels of space between them?

3. Write the HTML to create the table shown in the following figure:

Answers

1. With the following table:

   ```
   <table><tr><td align="top">
   ...First column of text goes here...
   </td><td align="top">
   ...Second column of text goes here...
   </td></tr></table>
   ```

2. Add `cellspacing=30` to the `<table>` tag. (Alternatively, you could use `cell-padding=15` to add 15 pixels of space inside the edge of each column.)

3. ```
   <table border="5">
   <tr>
    <td rowspan="3">A</td>
    <td colspan="3">B</td>
   </tr>
   <tr>
    <td>E</td>
    <td>F</td>
    <td rowspan="2">C</td>
   </tr>
   <tr>
    <td colspan="2">D</td>
   </tr>
   </table>
   ```
   ```

Exercises

- You can use a simple one-celled table with a border to draw a rectangle around any section of text on a Web page. By nesting that single-cell table in another two-column table, you can put a "sidebar" of text to the left or right side of your Web page. Outlined sections of text and sidebars are very common on printed paper pages, so you'll probably find uses for them on your Web pages, too.

- Do you have any pages where different visitors might be interested in different information? Use a table to present two or three columns of text, each with its own heading (and perhaps its own graphic). That way, something of interest to everyone will be visible at the top of the page when it first appears.

15

HOUR 16

Using Style Sheets

Style sheets are without a doubt the Next Big Thing in the fast-paced world of the Web. The concept is simple: You create a single style sheet document that specifies the fonts, colors, backgrounds, and other characteristics that establish a unique look. You then link every page that should have that look to the style sheet, instead of specifying all those style elements repeatedly in each separate document. When you decide to change your official corporate typeface or color scheme, you can modify all your Web pages at once just by changing one or two style sheets.

NEW TERM A *style sheet* is a single page of formatting instructions that can control the appearance of many HTML pages at once.

If style sheets accomplished this and nothing else, they'd save millions of dollars worth of Webmasters' time and become an integral part of most Web publishing projects. But they aim to do this and much more as well. The HTML style sheet standard enables you to set a great number of formatting characteristics that were never malleable before with any amount of effort. These include exacting typeface controls, letter and line spacing, margins and page borders, and expanded support for non-European languages and characters. They also enable sizes and other measurements to be specified in familiar units such as inches, millimeters, points, and picas. You can also use style sheets to precisely position graphics and text anywhere on a Web page.

In short, style sheets bring the sophistication level of paper-oriented publishing to the Web. And they do so—you'll pardon the expression—with style.

 If you have three or more Web pages that share (or should share) similar formatting and fonts, you may want to create a style sheet for them as you read this hour.

A Basic Style Sheet

Despite their intimidating power, style sheets can be very simple to create. Consider the documents in Figures 16.1 and 16.2. These documents share several properties that could be put into a common style sheet.

- They use the Book Antiqua font for body text and Prose Antique for headings.
- They use an image named parchmnt.jpg as a background tile.
- All text is maroon colored (on a color screen, not in this book!).
- They have wide margins and indented body text.
- There is lots of vertical space between lines of text.
- The footnotes are centered and in small print.

Some of these properties, such as text color, background tile, and centered small print, are easy to achieve with ordinary HTML tags. Others, such as line spacing and wide margins, are beyond the scope of standard HTML. All of them can now be achieved easily with style sheets.

Figure 16.3 shows how an HTML style sheet that specified these properties would look.

The first thing you'll undoubtedly notice about this style sheet is that it doesn't look anything like normal HTML. Style sheet specifications are really a separate language.

FIGURE 16.1

This page uses a style sheet to fine-tune the appearance and spacing of the text and background.

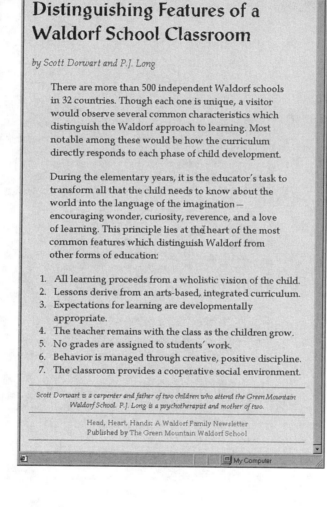

16

FIGURE 16.2

This page uses the same style sheet as the one in Figure 16.1.

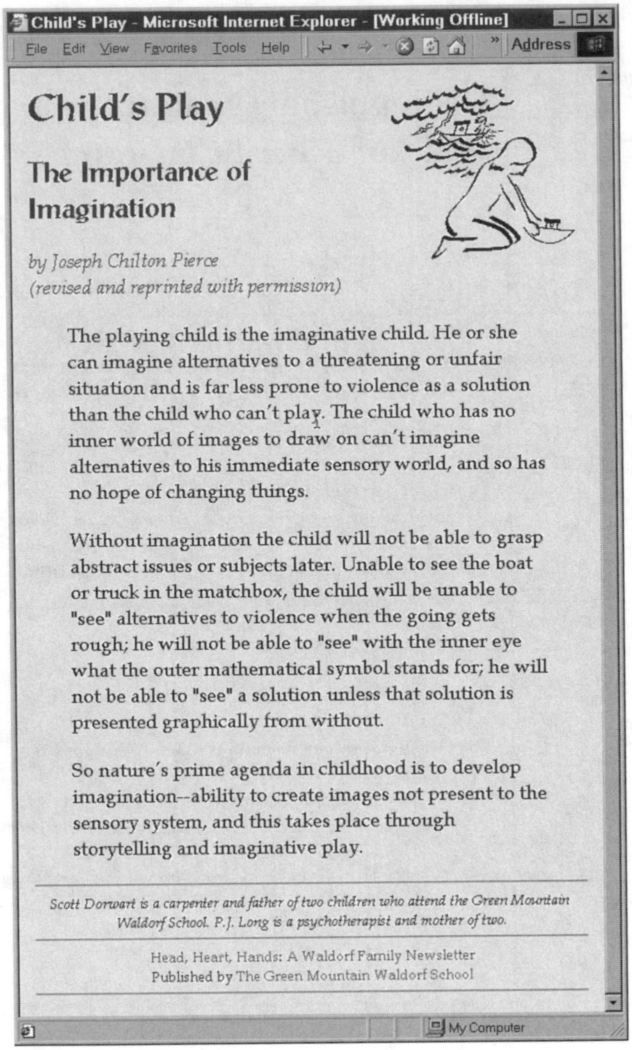

Child's Play - Microsoft Internet Explorer - [Working Offline]

File Edit View Favorites Tools Help   ↩ ▾ → ⊗ ▣ ⌂   » Address

Child's Play

The Importance of Imagination

by Joseph Chilton Pierce
(revised and reprinted with permission)

The playing child is the imaginative child. He or she can imagine alternatives to a threatening or unfair situation and is far less prone to violence as a solution than the child who can't play. The child who has no inner world of images to draw on can't imagine alternatives to his immediate sensory world, and so has no hope of changing things.

Without imagination the child will not be able to grasp abstract issues or subjects later. Unable to see the boat or truck in the matchbox, the child will be unable to "see" alternatives to violence when the going gets rough; he will not be able to "see" with the inner eye what the outer mathematical symbol stands for; he will not be able to "see" a solution unless that solution is presented graphically from without.

So nature's prime agenda in childhood is to develop imagination—ability to create images not present to the sensory system, and this takes place through storytelling and imaginative play.

Scott Dorwart is a carpenter and father of two children who attend the Green Mountain Waldorf School. P.J. Long is a psychotherapist and mother of two.

Head, Heart, Hands: A Waldorf Family Newsletter
Published by The Green Mountain Waldorf School

My Computer

FIGURE 16.3

A single style sheet can specify the properties of any number of pages. Figures 16.1 and 16.2 both use this style sheet.

```
/* Make all body text maroon-colored 12-point Book Antiqua
    with 16-point vertical spacing between lines of text
    and 10-point margins. Use parchmnt.gif as the background.
*/
body {font-size: 12pt;
      font-family: "Book Antiqua";
      color: maroon;
      background: url(parchmnt.gif);
      line-height: 16pt;
      margin-left: 10pt;
      margin-right: 10pt;}

/* Indent paragraphs */
p {margin-left: 24pt;
   margin-right: 24pt;}

/* Make headings Prose Antique bold with generous line spacing.
    If user doesn't have Prose Antique, use Lucida Handwriting.
*/
h1 {font: 24pt ProseAntique, Lucida Handwriting;
    font-weight: bold;
    line-height: 30pt;}

h2 {font: 18pt ProseAntique, Lucida Handwriting;
    font-weight: bold;
    line-height: 22pt;}

/* Don't underline links, and make all links red.
    Make links flash black when activated.
*/
a {text-decoration: none;}
a:link {color: red;}
a:visited {color: red;}
a:active {color: black;}

/* Format footnotes as 9-point Book Antiqua, and center them.
*/
div.footnote {font-size: 9pt;
              line-height: 12pt;
              text-align: center}
```

Of course, there are some familiar HTML tags in there. As you might guess, body, p, h1, h2, a, and div in the style sheet refer to the corresponding tags in the HTML documents to which the style sheet will be applied. In curly braces after each tag name are the specifications for how all text within that tag should appear.

In this case, all body text that isn't within some other tag should be rendered at a size of 12 points, in the Book Antiqua font if possible, and with the color maroon and 16 points between lines. The page should have 10-point margins, and the background should be the image found at the relative URL parchmnt.jpg.

Any paragraph starting with a <p> tag will be indented an additional 24 points.

Any text within <h1> or <h2> tags should be rendered in boldface ProseAntique at a size of 24 points and 18 points, respectively. If a user doesn't have a font named ProseAntique installed, the Lucida Handwriting font will be used instead.

NEW TERM The pt after each measurement in Figure 16.3 means *points* (there are 72 points in an inch). If you prefer, you can specify any style sheet measurement in inches (in), centimeters (cm), pixels (px), or widths-of-a-letter-m, which are called ems (em).

> The "point sizes" used in the HTML <font> tag are not the same as the point sizes specified in style sheets. <font size="3"> corresponds to approximately 12-point text, <font size="1"> is about 6-point text, and <font size="7"> (the maximum size for the font tag) is about 24-point text. You can specify font sizes as large as you like with style sheets, although most display devices and printers will not correctly handle fonts over 200 points.

To link this style sheet to the HTML documents, you include a <link /> tag in the <head> section of each document. Figure 16.4 is the HTML for the page in Figure 16.1. It contains the following <link /> tag:

```
<link rel="stylesheet" type="text/css" href="hhh.css" />
```

This assumes the style sheet was saved under the name hhh.css in the same directory folder as the HTML document. Netscape Navigator 4 and Internet Explorer 4 and later will then give the body and heading text the properties specified in the style sheet, without the need for any <font> tags or <body background> attribute in the document itself.

FIGURE 16.4

When viewed in Netscape Navigator or Microsoft Internet Explorer (version 4.0 or later), this page looks like Figure 16.1. In older browsers that don't support style sheets, it looks like Figure 16.5.

```html
<html><head><title>Features of a Waldorf Classroom</title>
<link rel="STYLESHEET" type="text/css" href="hhh.css" /></head>
<body>
<h1>Distinguishing Features of a Waldorf School Classroom</h1>
<i>by Scott Dorwart and P.J. Long</i>
<p>There are more than 500 independent Waldorf schools in 32
countries. Though each one is unique, a visitor would observe
several common characteristics which distinguish the Waldorf
approach to learning. Most notable among these would be how the
curriculum directly responds to each phase of child
development.</p>
<p>During the elementary years, it is the educator&rsquo;s task
to transform all that the child needs to know about the world
into the language of the imagination&mdash;encouraging wonder,
curiosity, reverence, and a love of learning. This principle
lies at the heart of the most common features which distinguish
Waldorf from other forms of education:</p>
<ol>
<li>All learning proceeds from a wholistic vision of the
child.</li>
<li>Lessons derive from an arts-based, integrated
curriculum.</li>
<li>Expectations for learning are developmentally
appropriate.</li>
<li>The teacher remains with the class as the children
grow.</li>
<li>No grades are assigned to students&rsquo; work.</li>
<li>Behavior is managed through creative, positive
discipline.</li>
<li>The classroom provides a cooperative social
environment.</li>
</ol>
<div class="footnote"><hr />
<i>Scott Dorwart is a carpenter and father of two children who
attend the Green Mountain Waldorf School. P.J. Long is a
psychotherapist and mother of two.</i><hr />
<a href="http://www.sover.net/~gmws/hhh.htm">Head, Heart,
Hands: A Waldorf Family Newsletter</a><br />Published by
<a href="http://www.sover.net/~gmws/">The Green
Mountain Waldorf School</a><hr />
</div>
</body></html>
```

In most Web browsers, you can see the commands in a style sheet by opening the .css file and choosing Notepad or another text editor as the helper
application to view the file. (To determine the name of the .css file, look at
the HTML source of any document that links to it.)

Unfortunately, Netscape Navigator 4 refuses to let you view style sheet files.
There's not even an easy way to download them to your hard drive with
Navigator 4 and view them with another application. If you want to have a
peek at other people's style sheets that you find on the Internet, you'll need
to use a Web browser other than Navigator 4.

CSS1 Versus CSS2

NEW TERM There are actually two different languages to choose from when you make a style
sheet. The one I recommend you use is called *cascading style sheets, level 1*
(CSS1), since it is compatible with both Netscape Navigator 4 (or later) and Microsoft
Internet Explorer 4 (or later). The new CSS2 standard is only partially implemented in
the current crop of browsers, and neither Netscape nor Microsoft is currently claiming
that its next version will fully support CSS2. They do already support some parts of
CSS2, such as the capability to precisely position text and graphics on the page (discussed under "Specifying Inline Styles" later in this hour).

You'll find a complete reference guide to both the CSS1 and CSS2 style sheet languages
at www.w3c.org. The rest of this hour explains how to put the information from those reference documents to use in a way that is compatible with the current generation of Web
browsers.

If you are a JavaScript programmer and the only browser you need to support is
Netscape Navigator, you may prefer the *JavaScript Style Sheets* language instead. It has
all the same capabilities as CSS1, but uses a slightly different syntax. See the Netscape
Developer's Edge Online Web site (http://developer.netscape.com/) for a reference
guide to that language.

Older Web Browsers

Style sheetsare only supported by Netscape Navigator version 4 or later and Microsoft
Internet Explorer version 3 or later. Older browsers, as well as many HTML viewers
built into word processors or other business software applications, simply ignore the
<link /> tag and display the page without any special formatting. Figure 16.5, for
example, shows how the HTML from Figure 16.4 looks in Netscape Navigator 3.

FIGURE **16.5**

The HTML from Figure 16.4, viewed in Netscape Navigator 3. This is the same page as shown in Figure 16.1, even though it looks different.

Distinguishing Features of a Waldorf School Classroom

by Scott Dorwart and P.J. Long

There are more than 500 independent Waldorf schools in 32 countries. Though each one is unique, a visitor would observe several common characteristics which distinguish the Waldorf approach to learning. Most notable among these would be how the curriculum directly responds to each phase of child development.

During the elementary years, it is the educator's task to transform all that the child needs to know about the world into the language of the imagination—encouraging wonder, curiosity, reverence, and a love of learning. This principle lies at the heart of the most common features which distinguish Waldorf from other forms of education:

1. All learning proceeds from a wholistic vision of the child.
2. Lessons derive from an arts-based, integrated curriculum.
3. Expectations for learning are developmentally appropriate.
4. The teacher remains with the class as the children grow.
5. No grades are assigned to students' work.
6. Behavior is managed through creative, positive discipline.
7. The classroom provides a cooperative social environment.

Scott Dorwart is a carpenter and father of two children who attend the Green Mountain Waldorf School. P.J. Long is a psychotherapist and mother of two.

Head, Heart, Hands: A Waldorf Family Newsletter
Published by The Green Mountain Waldorf School

16

You should always test your style sheet–enhanced pages without the style sheet to make sure they still look acceptable. Use an older browser, or just temporarily change the name of the style sheet so the browser can't find it.

There is also a special "problem case" you should be aware of: Microsoft implemented rudimentary style sheet support in Internet Explorer version 3. Since this was done before the official style sheet specification had been released, and didn't try to support the full specification anyway, the results can sometimes be quite different than what you would see with a more modern browser. Specifically, the spacing of items is often strange and the background specified in a style sheet will not appear.

It's not a bad idea to test your pages with Internet Explorer 3 if you think a significant amount of your intended audience is still using that browser (and if you can find a copy of it yourself to test with). There isn't much more you can do about it, except encourage your pages' readers to upgrade quickly to either the latest version of Microsoft Internet Explorer or Netscape Navigator.

Style Properties

The following list explains everything that you can reliably do with style sheets if you want to stay compatible with Microsoft Internet Explorer 3 or later and Netscape Navigator 4 or later. The CSS1 standard includes a number of additional formatting options, some of which are supported by version 5 browsers. I didn't include those here since a great many people today are still using version 4 browsers, but you can find the complete CSS1 specification online at www.w3c.org.

- `font:` Lets you set many font properties at once. You can specify a list of font names separated by commas; if the first is not available, the next is tried, and so on. You can also include the words `bold` and/or `italic` and a font size. Each of these font properties can be specified separately with `font-family:`, `font-size:`, `font-weight: bold`, and `font-style: italic` if you prefer.

- `line-height:` Also known in the publishing world as *leading*. This sets the height of each line of text, usually in points.

- `color:` Sets the text color, using the standard color names or hexadecimal color codes (see Hour 11, "Custom Backgrounds and Colors").

- `text-decoration:` Useful for turning link underlining off—simply set text decoration to `none`. The values of `underline`, `italic`, and `line-through` are also supported.

- `text-align:` Aligns text to the `left`, `right`, or `center` (just like the `<div align>` HTML attribute). The CSS1 standard allows a value of `justify` for text aligned to both the left and right margins, but current version browsers do not display full-justified text reliably.

- `text-indent:` Indents beyond the left margin by a specified amount. You can say how far to indent in units (`px`, `in`, `cm`, `mm`, `pt`, `pc`), or you can specify a percentage of the page width (such as `20%`).

- `margin:` Sets the left and right margins to the same value, which can be in measurement units or a percentage of the page width. Use `margin-left:` and `margin-right:` if you want to set the left and right margins independently, and `margin-top:` to set the top margin.

- `background:` Places a color or image behind text, either with a color or an `url(address)` where *address* points to a background image tile. Note that this can be assigned not only to the `<body>` tag, but to any tag or span of text to "highlight" an area on a page. (Also note that it doesn't always work quite right in Microsoft Internet Explorer 3, although it generally works fine in version 4 browsers.)

Since the <a> tag can be used for two fundamentally different purposes (depending on whether it contains a name attribute or an href attribute— see Hours 3 and 7), the style sheet standard gives you a way to say "only <a> tags that are links." In fact, you can even say "only visited links" or "only active links," too.

For example, the style sheet in Figure 16.3 contains the following, which makes both visited and unvisited links red while making active links black:

```
a:link {color: red;}
a:visited {color: red;}
a:active {color: black;}
```

16

Style Classes

This is a "teach yourself" book, so you don't have to go to a single class to learn how to give your pages great style, although you do need to learn what a style class is. Whenever you want some of the text on your pages to look different than the other text, you can create what amounts to a custom-built HTML tag. Each type of specially formatted text you define is called a style class.

NEW TERM   A *style class* is a custom set of formatting specifications that can be applied to any passage of text in a Web page.

For example, suppose you wanted two different kinds of <h1> headings in your documents. You would create a style class for each one by putting the following text in the style sheet.

```
h1.silly {font: 36pt Comic Sans;}
h1.serious {font: 36pt Arial;}
```

To choose between the two style classes in an HTML page, you would use the class attribute, as follows:

```
<h1 class="silly">Marvin's Munchies Inc.</h1>
Text about Marvin's Muchies goes here.
<h1 class="serious">MMI Investor Information</h1>
Text for business investors goes here.
```

The words Marvin's Munchies Inc. would appear in 36-point Comic Sans to people whose browsers support style sheets (assuming you included a <link /> to the style sheet at the top of the Web page and assuming he or she has the Comic Sans font installed). The words MMI Investor Information would appear in the 36-point Arial font.

What if you want to create a style class that could be applied to any text, rather than just headings or some other particular tag? You can associate a style class with the `<div>` tag (which, as you may recall from Hour 5, "Text Alignment and Lists," can enclose any text but doesn't do anything except what its `align` or other attributes indicate).

You can essentially create your own custom HTML tag by using `div.` followed by any style class name you make up and any style specifications you choose. That tag can control any number of font, spacing, and margin settings all at once. Wherever you want to apply your custom tag in a page, use a `<div>` tag with the `class=` attribute followed by the class name you created.

For example, the style sheet in Figure 16.3 includes the following style class specification:

```
div.footnote {font-size: 9pt;
              line-height: 12pt;
              text-align: center;}
```

This style class is applied in Figure 16.4 with the following tag:

```
<div class="footnote">
```

Everything between that tag and the accompanying `</div>` tag in Figure 16.1 appears in 9-point centered text with 12-point vertical line spacing. The same style class was also used on the footnote in Figure 16.2.

Specifying Inline Styles

In some situations, you might want to specify styles that will be used in only one Web page. You can then enclose a style sheet between `<style>` and `</style>` tags and include it in the beginning of an HTML document, between the `</head>` and `<body>` tags. No `<link />` tag is needed, and you cannot refer to that style sheet from any other page (unless you copy it into the beginning of that document, too).

If you want to specify a style for only a small part of a page, you can go one step further and put a `style` attribute within a `<p>`, `<div>`, or `<span>` tag.

> `<span>` and `</span>` are *dummy* tags that do nothing in and of themselves except specify a range of text to apply any `style` attributes that you add. The only difference between `<div>` and `<span>` is that `<div>` forces a line break, while `<span>` doesn't. Therefore, you should use `<span>` to modify the style of any portion of text shorter than a paragraph.

Here's how a sample `style` attribute might look:

```
<p style="color: green">This text is green, but
<span style="color: red"> this text is red.</span>
Back to green again, but...</p>
<p>...now the green is over, and we're back to the default color for
this page.</p>
```

Although the effect of this example could be achieved as easily with the `<font color>` tag (see Hour 6, "Text Formatting and Font Control"), many style specifications have no corresponding HTML tag. Generally, you should avoid inline styles except when there is no way to do what you're after in HTML and you feel that using an external style sheet would be too cumbersome.

16

In all the Web browsers released so far, style sheet formatting tends to work more reliably when a `<link />` to a separate style sheet is used instead of inline `style` attributes. The most important example of this is the `margin:` property, which both Netscape Navigator 4 and Microsoft Internet Explorer 4 seem to have trouble interpreting properly as an inline `style`.

To give the pages at the *24-Hour HTML Café* a consistent look and feel, I created a style sheet that is linked to every page in the site. For your edification and convenience, I copied that style sheet text into an HTML page, which you can access from `http://24hourHTMLcafe.com/hour16`.

Here's a little trick to notice in the `htmlcafe.css` style sheet: I gave the `<p>` tag a style with a left margin of 40 pixels. This means that every `<p>` tag in the *24-Hour HTML Café* pages doesn't just start a new paragraph, but also indents the text 40 pixels. Whenever I don't want indentation, I can leave out the `<p>` and `</p>` tags before and after a paragraph or place `<p></p>` before the paragraph to skip a line without indenting.

Positioning and Layers

Here's the bad news: Neither the official HTML 4 standard nor the official cascading style sheets, level 1 (CSS1) standard gives you any direct way to control the exact position of the images and text on your Web pages. The closest thing you can do is adjust the margins of your page. For example, the following HTML would position the first image on the page exactly 50 pixels to the left and 40 pixels down from the top-left corner of the browser window. It would then indent the text exactly 60 pixels from the left edge of the browser window.

```
<body>
<span style="margin-left: 50px; margin-top: 40px">
<img src="pretty.gif" /></span>
<span style="margin-left: 60px;">
This is a pretty picture.</span>
```

A lot of Web page designers have prayed to the HTML gods for the power to be more direct about where they want an image to be. Overlapping layers of images and text are high on a lot of wish lists, too. Unfortunately, there is no officially sanctioned way to say, "Put this image at pixel position 100,50 and this text at 200,52."

The good news is that the new cascading style sheets, level 2 (CSS2) standard includes positioning, and both Netscape Navigator and Microsoft Internet Explorer already started conforming to part of that standard as of version 4. It's a simple, elegant extension to the CSS1 style sheet standard, so you'll find it quite easy to use.

 Netscape has also created its own unique way of handling positioning and layering: a non-standard tag called <layer>. I don't cover that tag here because it isn't likely to be accepted as a standard. The style-based positioning technique achieves the same results in a way that's more likely to be compatible with non-Netscape browsers.

The following line of HTML shows how to position an image with the top-left corner exactly 50 pixels from the left and 40 pixels down from the top edge of the browser window. Although I use a <span> tag here, you can include a similar style attribute in almost any HTML tag to position some text precisely where you want it.

```
<span style="position: absolute; left: 50px; top: 40px">
<img src="pretty.gif" /></span>
```

 If you leave out the position: absolute part, measurements will be relative to wherever the text or image would normally appear on the page, rather than relative to the top-left corner of the browser window.

Along with `left:` and `top:` positioning, you can also optionally include `width:` and `height:` for text blocks.

Figure 16.6 is a simple HTML document with style-based positioning included. You can see the resulting Web page, as displayed by Microsoft Internet Explorer 5, in Figure 16.7. The page would look exactly the same in Microsoft Internet Explorer 4 and Netscape Navigator version 4 or later.

Notice that elements are drawn onto the page in the order that they occur in the HTML document. For example, the white streak appears to be layered on top of the logo, but is underneath the body text, because of the order they were drawn.

16

FIGURE 16.6

This HTML page uses inline styles to precisely position images and text.

```
<html><head><title>Refractal Design Inc.</title></head>
<body text="yellow" background="gradcom4.jpg">
<span style="position: absolute; left: 390px; top: 40px">
<img src="spianim.gif" height="140" width="140" /></span>
<span style="position: absolute; left: 16px; top: 110px;">
<img src="streak.gif" height="260" width="444" /></span>
<div style="position: absolute; left: 300px; top: 60px;">
<h2>Refractal</h2></div>
<div style="position: absolute; left: 510px; top: 120px;">
<h2>Design</h2></div>
<div style="position: absolute; left: 55px; top: 130px; width:
340px;">Refractal Design Inc. produces heirloom quality limited
edition fine jewelry, jewelry accessories, and other related
items. We are both a design house and a manufacturing
facility.</div>
</body></html>
```

FIGURE 16.7

Microsoft Internet Explorer 5 displays the HTML from Figure 16.6.

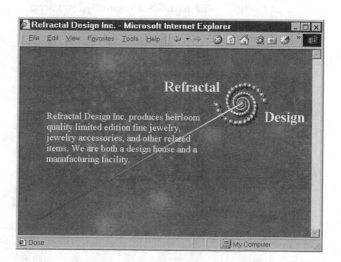

According to the proposed standard, `style` specifications can go in any tag you like. For example, assume the following:

```
<div style="position: absolute; left: 300px; top: 60px;">
<h2>Refractal</h2></div>
```

It does exactly the same thing this code does:

```
<h2 style="position: absolute; left: 300px; top:
60px;">Refractal</h2>
```

These two approaches are indeed equivalent in Netscape Navigator 4. However, putting the positioning information in the `<h2>` tag doesn't work in Microsoft Internet Explorer 4. This was corrected in version 5 of Internet Explorer, but for maximum compatibility you should always use `<span>` or `<div>` tags for positioning.

Although exact positioning control is a great idea, always remember that anyone using Netscape Navigator version 3 or earlier, Microsoft Internet Explorer version 3 or earlier, or almost any other Web browser will not see any of your fancy positioning. The HTML from Figure 16.6, for example, looks like Figure 16.8 when displayed in Netscape Navigator 3.

Also remember that changes in font or window size can easily destroy the appearance of your carefully positioned elements. As with all style sheet stuff, I strongly recommend that you use style-based positioning for fine tuning only—at least until most of your intended audience has moved up to at least version 4 browsers.

FIGURE 16.8

The HTML from Figure 16.6 doesn't look very artistic in Netscape Navigator 3 because none of the positioning shows up.

Summary

In this hour you learned that a style sheet can control the appearance of many HTML pages at once. It can also give you extremely precise control over typography, spacing, and the positioning of HTML elements. You also learned that by adding a `style` attribute to almost any HTML tag, you can control the style of any part of an HTML page without referring to a separate style sheet document.

Table 16.1 summarizes the tags discussed in this hour. Refer to the CSS1 and CSS2 style sheet standards at www.w3c.org for details on what options can be included after the `<style>` tag or the `style` attribute.

16

TABLE 16.1   HTML Tags and Attributes Covered in Hour 16

Tag	Attribute	Function
`<style>...</style>`		Allows an internal style sheet to be included within a document. Used between `<head>` and `</head>`.
`<link />`		Links to an external style sheet (or other document type). Used in the `<head>` section of the document.
	`href="..."`	The address of the style sheet.
	`type="..."`	The Internet content type. (Always `"text/css"` for a style sheet.)
	`rel="..."`	The link type. (Always `"stylesheet"` for style sheets.)
`<span>...</span>`		Does nothing at all, except provide a place to put `style` or other attributes. (Similar to `<div>...</div>`, but does not cause a line break.)
	`style="..."`	Includes inline style specifications. (Can be used in `<span>`, `<div>`, `<body>`, and most other HTML tags.)

Q&A

Q How do I use positioning and layers to make text and graphics fly around the page? Isn't that what they call dynamic HTML?

A *Dynamic HTML* is a general term (used mostly for marketing purposes) meaning anything that makes Web pages move. You'll learn more about that in Hour 19, "Web Page Scripting for Non-Programmers," and Hour 20, "Setting Pages in Motion with Dynamic HTML."

In a nutshell, scripting lets you use a simple programming language called JavaScript to modify any HTML or style sheet information (including positioning) on-the-fly in response to the mouse movements and clicks of people who visit your pages.

Q Say I link a style sheet to my page that says all text should be blue, but there's a `<span style="font-color: red">` tag in the page somewhere. Will that text come out blue or red?

A Red. Local inline styles always take precedence over external style sheets. Any style specifications you put between `<style>` and `</style>` tags at the top of a page will also take precedence over external style sheets (but not over inline styles later in the same page).

Q Can I link more than one style sheet to a single page?

A Sure. For example, you might have a sheet for font stuff and another one for margins and spacing—just include a `<link />` for each one.

Workshop

Quiz

1. Create a style sheet to specify half-inch margins, 30-point blue Arial headings, and all other text in double-spaced 10-point blue Times Roman (or the default browser font).

2. If you saved the style sheet you made for question 1 as `corporat.css`, how would you apply it to a Web page named `intro.htm`?

3. Write the HTML that makes Netscape Navigator 4 or Microsoft Internet Explorer 4 display the words `What would you like to`, starting exactly at the top-left corner of the browser window, and `THROW TODAY?` in large type exactly 80 pixels down and 20 pixels to the left of the corner.

Answers

```
1. body {font: 10pt blue;
   line-height: 20pt;
   margin-left: 0.5in;
   margin-right: 0.5in;
   margin-top: 0.5in;
   margin-bottom: 0.5in}
   h1 {font: 30pt blue Arial}
```

2. Put the following tag between the `<head>` and `</head>` tags of the `intro.htm` document:

```
<link rel="stylesheet" type="text/css" href="corporat.css" />
```

3.
```
<span style="position: absolute; left: 0px; top: 0px">
What would you like to</span>
<h1 style="position: absolute; left: 80px; top: 20px">
THROW TODAY?</H1>
```

Exercises

- Develop a standard style sheet for your Web site and link it into all your pages. (Use inline styles for pages that need to deviate from it.) If you work for a corporation, chances are it has developed font and style specifications for printed materials. Get a copy of those specifications and follow them for company Web pages, too.

- Be sure to explore the official style sheet specs at www.w3c.org

16

PART V

Dynamic Web Pages

Hour

Hour 17

Embedding Multimedia in Web Pages

Multimedia is a popular buzzword for sound, motion video, and interactive animation. This hour shows you how to include multimedia in your Web pages.

The first thing you should be aware of is that computer multimedia is still in its youth, and Internet multimedia is barely in its infancy. The infant technology's rapid pace of growth creates three obstacles for anyone who wants to include audiovisual material in a Web page:

- There are many incompatible multimedia file formats from which to choose, and none has yet emerged as a clear industry standard.

- Most people do not have Internet connections fast enough to receive high-quality audiovisual data without a long wait.

- Each new Web browser version that comes out uses different HTML tags to include multimedia in Web pages.

The moral of the story: Whatever you do today to implement a multimedia Web site, plan on changing it before too long.

The good news is that you can sidestep all three of these obstacles to some extent today, and they are all likely to become even easier to overcome in the near future. This hour shows you how to put multimedia on your Web pages for maximum compatibility with the Web browser versions that most people are now using. It also introduces you to the new standard way that Web page multimedia will be handled in the future.

> The Microsoft ActiveX controls and Java applets discussed in Hour 18, "Interactive Pages with Applets and ActiveX," can be used with many of the same types of media files discussed in this hour. Be sure to read Hour 18 before you make any final decisions about how you will incorporate multimedia into your Web site.

To Do

Before you see how to place multimedia on your Web pages in any way, you need to have some multimedia content to start with.

Creating multimedia of any kind is a challenging and complicated task. If you're planning to create your own content from scratch, you'll need far more than this book to become the next crackerjack multimedia developer. Once you have some content, however, this hour will show you how to place your new creations into your Web pages.

For those of us who are artistically challenged, a number of alternative ways to obtain useful multimedia assets are available. Aside from the obvious (such as hiring an artist), here are a few suggestions:

1. The Web itself is chock-full of useful content of all media types, and stock media clearinghouses of all shapes and sizes now exist online. See the hotlist at the *24-Hour HTML Café*—`http://24hourhtmlcafe.com/hotsites.htm#multimedia`—for links to some of the best stock media sources on the Web.

2. Don't feel like spending any money? Much of the material on the Internet is free. Of course, it's still a good idea to double-check with the author or current owner of the content; you don't want to be sued for copyright infringement. In addition, various offices of the U.S. government generate content which, by law, belongs to all Americans. (Any NASA footage found online, for instance, is free for your use.)

3. Many search engines (altavista.com, hotbot.com, etc.) have specific search capabilities for finding multimedia files. As long as you are careful about copyright issues, this can be an easy way to find multimedia related to a specific topic.

▼

4. Check out the online forums and Usenet newsgroups that cater to the interests of videographers. As clearly as possible, describe your site and what you want to do with it. Chances are you'll find a few up-and-coming artists who'd be more than happy to let thousands of people peruse their work online.

▲

Putting Multimedia on a Web Page

The following sections show you how to add some audio and video to a Web page in three ways:

1. The "old way" for maximum compatibility with all Web browsers

2. The "today way" that's best for Netscape Navigator 2, 3, 4, and 5 and Microsoft Internet Explorer 3, 4, and 5

3. The "new way" that doesn't work well with any existing Web browser, but will be the official standard technique for the future

In the ActiveX section of Hour 18, you'll discover an alternative approach to embedding multimedia that works especially well with Microsoft Internet Explorer.

17

I use Windows AVI video and MIDI sound files in this hour's sample pages. For better compatibility with non-Windows computers, you could use Apple's QuickTime audio/video, the RealAudio/RealVideo, the popular MP3 sound format, or any other media format supported by today's Web browsers. The procedures shown in this hour for incorporating the files into your Web pages are the same, no matter which file format you choose.

Multimedia the Old-Fashioned Way

The simplest and most reliable option for incorporating a video or audio file into your Web site is to simply link it in with `<a href>`, exactly as you would link to another HTML file. (See Hour 3, "Linking to Other Web Pages," for coverage of the `<a>` tag.)

For example, the following line could be used to offer an AVI video of a Maine lobster:

```
<a href="lobstah.avi">Play the lobster video.</a>
```

When the user clicks the words `Play the lobster video`, the `lobstah.avi` video file is transferred to her computer. Whichever helper application or plug-in she has installed automatically starts as soon as the file has finished downloading. If no AVI-compatible helper or plug-in can be found, the Web browser offers her a chance to download the appropriate plug-in or save the video on the hard drive for later viewing.

In case you're unfamiliar with *helper applications* (*helper apps* for short), they are the external programs that a Web browser calls on to display any type of file it can't handle on its own. (Generally, the helper application associated with a file type in Windows is called on whenever a Web browser can't display that type of file.) *Plug-ins* are a special sort of helper applications that are specifically designed for tight integration with Netscape Navigator.

Embedding Sound in a Web Page

Over the past few years, Microsoft and Netscape have offered various conflicting solutions to the problem of how to put multimedia on a Web page. Some of these, such as Microsoft's proprietary extensions to the `<img>` tag, are now completely obsolete.

One non-standard tag has endured, however; Netscape's `<embed />` tag is now actually more compatible with both Netscape and Microsoft browsers than the official HTML 4 `<object>` tag, which was supposed to replace it.

The `<embed />` tag enables you to place any type of file directly into your Web page. For the media to appear on the Web page, however, every user must have a plug-in or OLE-compatible helper application that recognizes the incoming data type and knows what to do with it. The media players that come bundled with Internet Explorer and Netscape Navigator can handle most common media types, including WAV, AU, MPEG, MID, EPS, VRML, and many more. Many other plug-ins are also available from other companies to handle almost any type of media file.

Netscape maintains a Web page that lists all registered plug-ins and plug-in developers. To check out the current assortment, head to `http://home.netscape.com/plugins/`. You can see which plug-ins are installed in your Netscape browser by entering **about:plugins** in the Location bar (where you would normally type an Internet address).

The Plug-ins Development Kit, available for free from Netscape, allows developers to create new plug-ins for their own products and data types. For more information, see Netscape's Web site at `http://home.netscape.com/`.

The following line of HTML would embed a sound clip named `hello.wav` and display the playback controls at the current position on the page, as long as visitors to the page have a WAV-compatible plug-in or helper app.

```
<embed src="hello.wav" />
```

Notice that, like the `<img>` tag, `<embed />` requires a `src` attribute to indicate the address of the embedded media file. Also like `<img>`, the `<embed />` tag can take `align`, `width`, and `height` attributes. The `src`, `width`, `height`, and `align` attributes are interpreted by the browser just as they would be for a still image. However, the actual display of the data is handled by whichever plug-in or helper application each user may have installed. In the case of sound files, the sound is played and some controls are usually displayed. Which controls actually appear depend on which plug-in or helper application each individual user has installed, so you, as a Web page author, can't know ahead of time exactly what someone will see.

Thc `<embed />` tag also enables you to set any number of optional parameters, which are specific to the plug-in or player program. For instance, the page in Figure 17.1 includes the following:

```
<embed src="atune.mid" width="1" height="1"
 autostart="true" loop="true" hidden="true" />
```

This causes the music file `atune.mid` to play whenever the page is displayed. As you can see in Figure 17.2, this has no visual effect on the page whatsoever. (Since this book doesn't have any speakers, you can't hear the auditory effect unless you pull the page up online at `http://24hourHTMLcafe.com/hour17/`.)

FIGURE 17.1

The `<embed />` tag embeds multimedia files directly into a Web page in Netscape Navigator and Microsoft Internet Explorer.

```
<html><head><title>Music</title></head>
<body background="wiggles.jpg">
<a href="nosound.htm">
<img src="shutup.gif" border=0 align="right" alt="Stop music" />
</A>
<table width=500>
<tr><td><img src="piano.gif" width=200 height=172 /></td></tr>
<tr><td><b>Roaming through the jungle of 'oohs' and 'ahs,'
searching for a more agreeable noise, I live a life of
primitivity with the mind of a child and an unquenchable
thirst for sharps and flats.</b>
&#151;Duke Ellington, <i>Music Is My Mistress</i>
</td></tr></table>
<embed src="atune.mid" width=1 height=1
 autostart="true" loop="true" hidden="true" />
<noembed>
  <a href="atune.mid">Click here to hear.</a>
</noembed>
</body></html>
```

Figure 17.2

If you were looking at this page (from Figure 17.1) on a computer with a sound card and speakers, you would hear the atune.mid *file playing.*

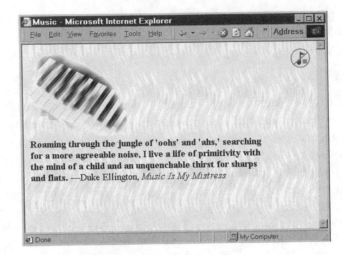

autostart, loop, and hidden are not standard attributes of the <embed /> tag, so the browser simply hands them over to the plug-in program to interpret. autostart="true", loop="true", and hidden="true" are specific to the LiveAudio plug-in that comes built-in to Netscape Navigator 3 and 4. (They tell it to automatically play the sound as soon as it loads, to play it over again each time it finishes, and not to display any controls on the Web page.) If a user has a different AVI plug-in, or no plug-in at all for handling MIDI (Musical Instrument Digital Interface) files, these attributes will do nothing at all. Refer to the Web pages of each plug-in developer for information on the commands that its plug-in will accept as attributes in the <embed /> tag.

If a suitable plug-in can't be found for an <embed /> tag, the Windows 95/98 versions of both Netscape Navigator and Microsoft Internet Explorer may embed an OLE-compliant application (such as the Media Player application that comes with Windows) to play the media file. Therefore, the sound will play successfully in both Netscape Navigator and Microsoft Internet Explorer.

Whenever you set up a Web page to play a sound automatically, it's a good idea to give people some way to turn the sound off. (There's nothing more annoying than surfing the Web with your favorite CD on and hitting a musical Web page that can't be turned off!) The easiest way to turn off a sound is to simply link to a page with no sounds embedded in it. For example, clicking the shutup.gif icon in the upper-right corner of Figure 17.2 loads a silent but otherwise identical page.

Embedding Video in a Web Page

The HTML page in Figure 17.3 demonstrates the use of <embed /> with a video clip in the Windows AVI (Audio-Video Interleave) format. The <embed /> tag in Figure 17.3 also includes the autostart and loop attributes, which tell Netscape's LiveVideo plug-in to start playing the video when the page loads and to repeat it as long as the page is being displayed. Figure 17.4 shows the resulting page as viewed with Netscape Navigator 4.

FIGURE 17.3

You can embed a video into a Web page with the same <embed /> tag used to embed sound.

```
<html><head><title>Fractal Video Clip</title></head>
<body>
  <embed src="3dtetra2.avi" autostart="true" loop="true"
   width="160" height="120" vspace="10" hspace="20"
   align="left" />
 <noembed>
   <a href="3dtetra2.avi">
     <img src="3dtetra.jpg" border="0" align="left"
      width="160" height="120" vspace="10" hspace="20" />
   </a>
 </noembed>
<h2>A Spinning 3-D Fractal</h2>
If the video clip to the left doesn't start on its own,
click on it to make it play. Once it starts, you can
right-click on it and choose Pause to make it stop.
</body></html>
```

17

FIGURE 17.4

This is the page in Figure 17.3 as seen in Netscape Navigator 4. If this page were a computer screen, the fractal would be spinning and a soundtrack would be playing.

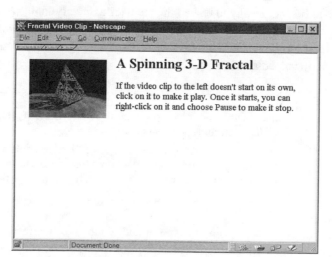

Microsoft Internet Explorer will recognize the <embed /> tag and try to find an OLE-compliant Windows application to display the media file. In the case of AVI video, the Windows Media Player application will usually be embedded into the Web page, as shown in Figure 17.5.

Notice that the size of the video is reduced to make room for the Media Player controls. This isn't ideal, since it makes the video appear differently in Internet Explorer than it does in Netscape Navigator. In the next section of this hour you learn how to remedy this problem.

FIGURE 17.5

This is the page in Figure 17.3 as seen in Microsoft Internet Explorer 5. The Windows Media Player is automatically embedded in the Web page.

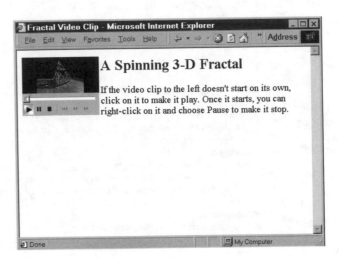

When Navigator and Explorer encounter an `<embed />` tag, they basically try their hardest to find some way to embed the media file directly in the Web page. As a Web page author, you can't predict what plug-in or helper application will be selected, but you can at least try to put some instructions on the Web page telling your audience from where to download a suitable player.

Embedded helper apps only work in Windows 95, 98, NT, or 2000. They will not function for Macintosh or UNIX users.

Also, you should not confuse this use of Windows object linking and embedding (OLE) with the ActiveX controls discussed in the next section—even though they do rely on the same underlying OLE technology.

You can use `<embed />` with any type of audio, video, or interactive multimedia files as long as your audience has the correct player software installed.

Unfortunately, you as a Web page author have no control over or knowledge of which file types and applications people who visit your pages will have configured on their computers, or even how many visitors will be using a Microsoft Windows operating system. So the exotic uses of <embed /> are probably best left to corporate intranets or other situations where the page publisher has some control over the intended audience's computer setup.

Trying to Please Everybody

Because Netscape knew that not all Web browsers would support its non-standard <embed /> tag, it provided an easy way to include alternate content for other browsers. Immediately following an <embed /> tag, you can specify any amount of HTML code for other browsers, between the <noembed> and </noembed> tags. For example, Figure 17.3 contains the following code:

```
<embed src="3dtetra2.avi" autostart="true" loop="true"
  width=160 height=120 vspace=10 hspace=20 align="left" />
  <noembed>
    <a href="3dtetra2.avi">
      <img src="3dtetra.jpg" border=0
        width=160 height=120 vspace=10 hspace=20 align="left" />
    </a>
  </noembed>
```

Here's how this will work in various browsers:

1. Netscape Navigator 3, 4, or 5 sees only the <embed /> tag and ignores everything between <noembed> and </noembed>. (If the Netscape LiveMedia plug-in is installed, it interprets autoplay and loop as discussed earlier.)

2. In Netscape Navigator 2, if no AVI-compatible plug-in is installed, users may see an unsightly puzzle-piece icon and a message saying plug-in not loaded. If they click the Get the Plug-In button, they are taken to a page on Netscape Corporation's Web site that explains how to get and install plug-ins and helper apps.

3. Microsoft Internet Explorer 3, 4, or 5 looks in the Windows file type registry for a player for the <embed /> tag. It usually finds mplayer.exe, the Windows Media Player, and embeds it into the Web page.

4. Microsoft Internet Explorer 2, like most other older browsers, sees only the <a> and <img> tags. It displays the 3dtetra.jpg image, so that users with an AVI-compatible helper application can click the image to play the 3dtetra2.avi video clip in a separate window.

5. Netscape Navigator version 1.2 is actually a special problem case because it recognizes the <embed /> tag, but not the <noembed> tag. It displays both the image specified in img src and an embedded OLE display or, more often, a broken image icon resulting from a failed attempt to display the <embed /> tag. Clicking the 3dtetra.jpg image still launches an AVI helper application if one is available.

17

To thicken the plot, some people who already have the software they need to view your embed media files may see a message announcing boldly, `warning: there is a possible security hazard here`. This message really means that the user has a helper application available on his system that can display the media file, and Netscape Navigator 2 or higher is about to run it. The alarmist tone of the message is very unfortunate because the likelihood of having any security risk is actually no greater than any other time a helper application is invoked or a page is displayed.

Some novice users are sure to become convinced that they must click Cancel or risk having the monitor blow up, but what you really want them to do is click Continue, so they can watch a totally harmless video clip. Unfortunately, there's really nothing you can do as a Web page author to control whether this message appears. Most people with current browser versions won't see it. However, you should still be aware of what some users may see so you can intelligently choose if and when to use the `<embed />` tag, and what sort of caveats to offer along with your embedded media.

Multimedia the New Way

Netscape's `<embed />` tag has come under fire for a number of reasons, both technical and political. Officially, it has already been made obsolete by a new tag called `<object>`, which has the blessing of Netscape, Microsoft, and the official World Wide Web Consortium (W3C) standards-setting committee. The `<object>` tag will do everything Netscape wants the `<embed />` tag to do, plus a lot more.

Unfortunately, the 4 versions of Microsoft Internet Explorer and Netscape Navigator interpret the `<object>` tag somewhat unreliably, because they were released before the official standard for the tag was approved. The fact that most people are still using earlier browser versions has also slowed widespread use of the `<object>` tag. Alas, support of `<object>` in Microsoft Internet Explorer 5 isn't any better, nor does it look likely that the next update of Netscape Navigator will support the standard fully.

You can read more about the `<object>` tag, including an example of its current use, under "ActiveX Controls" in Hour 18.

Another beacon of hope has appeared on the Web multimedia horizon as well. The W3C has officially sanctioned SMIL 1, the Synchronized Multimedia Integration Language. When Web browsers start conforming to this new standard, you will have a reliable way to synchronize multiple sound, video, and animation sources on your Web pages. (Assuming, that is, that your intended audience has high-speed network connections capable of delivering multiple media streams by then.) You can dream of the possibilities as you read about SMIL at the `www.w3.org` Web site and experience an early implementation of SMIL in the Real Player G2 at `www.real.com`.

In this hour you have struggled with a turgid tangle of incompatible HTML extensions and media formats. And if you, the Web page author, find it a bit confusing (as I assure you that I sometimes do), just think how confusing it might be to your audience when your Web page video encounters an uncooperative browser.

My bottom-line advice is this: For now, avoid embedded multimedia if you possibly can. Most people would rather have a good old-fashioned clickable link to the multimedia file. `<a href="hotvideo.avi">hot video (avi for-mat, 240k)</a>` allows people to play the video if and when they want to, or download it and play it from their hard drive. If you have software that can convert between AVI and QuickTime, offer links to the same video in both formats to accommodate both Windows and Macintosh users. (Offer both WAV and AU formats if it's a sound clip.)

To experience both the new and old-fashioned approaches to Web page multimedia yourself, kick back, grab an appropriate beverage, and tune your browser to `http://24hourHTMLcafe.com/hour17`.

17

Summary

In this hour you've seen how to embed video and sound into a Web page. But remember that the `<embed />` tag (and its successor, the `<object>` tag) can be used to include a vast array of media types besides just AVI and MIDI files. Some of these media types are alternative audio and video formats that aim to achieve greater compression, quality, or compatibility than the Windows standard formats. Others, such as Shockwave and QuickTime VR, add a variety of interactive features that old-fashioned audiovisual media types lack. Table 17.1 summarizes the tags discussed in this hour.

TABLE 17.1 HTML Tags and Attributes Covered in Hour 17

Tag	Attribute	Function
`<embed />`		Embeds a file to be read or displayed by a Netscape plug-in application.
	`src="..."`	The URL of the file to embed.
	`width="..."`	The width of the embedded object in pixels.
	`height="..."`	The height of the embedded object in pixels.
	`align="..."`	Determines the alignment of the media window. Values are the same as for the `<img>` tag.
	`vspace="..."`	The space between the media and the text above or below it.

continues

TABLE 17.1   continued

Tag	Attribute	Function
	hspace="..."	The space between the media and the text to its left or right.
	border="..."	Draws a border of the specified size in pixels around the media.
<noembed>...</noembed>		Alternate text or images to be shown to users who do not have a plug-in installed or are using browsers that don't recognize the <embed /> tag.
<object>...</object>		Inserts images, videos, Java applets, ActiveX controls, or other objects into a document. (See Hour 18 for attributes of the <object> tag.)

In addition to the <embed /> attributes listed in Table 17.1, you can designate applet-specific attributes to be interpreted by the plug-in that displays the embedded object.

Q&A

Q I hear a lot about "streaming" video and audio. What does that mean?   A
In the past, video and audio files took minutes and sometimes hours to retrieve through most modems, which severely limited the inclusion of video and audio on Web pages. The goal that everyone is moving toward is streaming video or audio, which will play while the data is being received. This is to say that you will not have to completely download the clip before you can start to watch it.

Streaming playback is now widely supported through Microsoft Internet Explorer's built-in features and Netscape Navigator plug-ins, as well as the popular RealPlayer from www.real.com. The examples in this hour use Windows AVI and WAV audio files to demonstrate both streaming and the old-fashioned download-and-play methods of delivering audiovisual media.

Q How do I choose among audiovisual file formats such as QuickTime, Windows AVI/WAV, RealVideo/RealAudio, and MPEG? Is there any significant difference among them?

A QuickTime is the most popular video format among Macintosh users, although QuickTime players are available for Windows 3.1 and Windows 95 as well. Similarly, AVI and WAV are the video and audio formats of choice for Windows users, but you can get AVI and WAV players for the Macintosh. However, all these are almost certain to be eclipsed by MPEG as the online audio and video standard of choice within the next couple of years. MPEG-1 video is best for Internet transmission because it is far more compact than MPEG-2. MPEG-3 is already gaining ground as the high-fidelity audio standard of choice. Unfortunately, relatively few people have MPEG-compatible players installed now.

How do you choose? If most of your audience uses Windows, pick AVI or WAV. If your audience includes a significant number of Macintosh users, pick QuickTime or at least offer it as an alternative. If cross-platform compatibility is essential, consider the RealVideo or RealAudio format—although only those who download special software from www.real.com will be able to see that format. In any case, plan to switch to MPEG eventually.

Workshop

Quiz

1. What's the simplest way to let the widest possible audience see a video on your Web site?

2. Write the HTML to embed a video file named myvideo.avi into a Web page so that both Netscape Navigator and Microsoft Internet Explorer users will be able to see it, and users of other browsers will see an image linking to it.

3. What tag will soon replace <embed /> and work with future versions of all major Web browsers?

Answers

1. Just link to it:

   ```
   <a href="myvideo.avi">my video</a>
   ```

2. Use the following HTML:

   ```
   <embed src="myvideo.avi" />
   <noembed>
   <a href="myvideo.avi"><img src="theimage.gif"></a>
   </noembed>
   ```

3. `<object>`

Exercises

- If you include multimedia elements that require special players, you might need a special page to help people understand and set up what they need to make the most of your site. A link to that page should be prominently located near the top of your home page, steering newcomers aside just long enough to give them a clue.

- The techniques and tags covered in this hour for embedding media also work with Virtual Reality Modeling Language (VRML) files. To find out how you can use VRML to put interactive three-dimensional scenes and objects in your Web pages, check out the VRML home page at `http://home.netscape.com/eng/live3d/ howto/vrml_primer_index.html`.

Interactive Pages with Applets and ActiveX

Congratulations. You HTML under your belt, and you're ready to graduate from the school of Web publishing and enter the real world of Web development. The World Wide Web of the past was simply a way to present information, and browsing wasn't too different from sitting in a lecture hall, watching a blackboard, or staring at an overhead projector screen. Today's Web surfer, however, is looking for interactive, animated sites that change with each viewer and each viewing.

To achieve that level of interactivity, this hour introduces a number of ways you can go beyond passive text and graphics into the dynamic world of modern Web site development.

It would take a book many times the length of this one to teach you all the scripting and programming languages that can be used to create interactive programs for the Web. However, you can easily learn the HTML to incorporate prewritten programs into your Web pages.

To Do

Reading this hour will give you enough information to decide what types of programs or scripts might be best for your Web site. If you decide to take the leap into actually using some (or even creating your own) programs on your pages, you should look to the following resources:

- You'll find a list of online sources for prewritten scripts and reusable program components in the Advanced Developer Resources section of the *24-Hour HTML Café* hotlist page at http://24hourHTMLcafe.com/hotsites.htm.

- If you want to write your own interactive programming for Web pages, I recommend *Dynamic Web Publishing Unleashed* or *Sams Teach Yourself JavaScript 1.3 in 24 Hours*. You'll also find some online tutorials in the *24-Hour HTML Café* hotlist.

The Old Way

Until very recently, there were only two ways to enhance the functionality of a Web browser. You could write and place programs on the Web server computer to manipulate documents as they were sent out, or you could write and install programs on the user's computer to manipulate or display documents as they were received.

You can still do both of these things, and they may still be the most powerful and flexible means of enhancing Web pages. Unfortunately, both involve a high level of expertise in traditional programming languages (such as C++) and knowledge of Internet transfer protocols and operating system architecture. If you're not fortunate enough to already be an experienced UNIX or Windows programmer, as well as something of a Net guru, you're not going to start cranking out cool Web applications tomorrow (or the next day, or the next).

On the server side, simplified scripting languages like Perl can flatten the learning curve quite a bit. Many people who don't consider themselves real programmers can hack out a Common Gateway Interface (CGI) script to process Web forms or feed animations to a Web page without too many false starts. With visual programming tools such as Visual Basic, you can learn to produce a respectable client-side helper application fairly quickly as well.

There is an easier way, and because this hour is intended to take you on the fast track to Web development, I have to recommend that you avoid the old ways until you run into something that you just can't accomplish any other way.

Before dashing into the inside lane, I do need to tell you about one way to enhance the Web that is not easier than server programming. It is, however, even more powerful when used well. Netscape Navigator plug-ins are custom applications designed especially to extend Netscape's capabilities.

You're probably familiar with some of the more popular plug-ins, such as Shockwave and Acrobat. Because these programs are usually written in C++ and have direct access to both the client computer's operating system and Netscape's data stream, developing plug-ins is not for the faint of heart or inexperienced. Still, if you can call yourself a programmer without blushing, you may find it well worth the effort. All in all, writing and debugging a plug-in is still considerably less daunting than developing a full-blown business application.

Internet Programming for the Rest of Us

Suppose you just want your Web order form to add totals automatically when customers check off which products they want. This is not rocket science; implementing it shouldn't be either. You don't want to learn UNIX or C++ or the Windows 95 Applications Programming Interface. You don't want to compile and install half a dozen extra files on your Web server, or ask the user to download your handy-dandy calculator application. You just want to add some numbers; or maybe you just want to change a graphic depending on the user's preferences, or the day of the week, or whatever; or maybe you want to tell a random joke every time somebody logs on to your home page. Until now, there really was no simple way to do these simple things.

Scripting languages such as JavaScript (which you learn about in Hour 19, "Web Page Scripting for Non-Programmers") give you a way. Okay, so it's still programming—but it's the kind of programming you can learn in an afternoon, or in an hour if you've fooled around with BASIC or Excel macros before. It's programming for the rest of us. Scripts go directly into your Web pages' HTML, wherever you want something intelligent to happen.

Strong Java

JavaScript and its competitors do have drawbacks and limitations. Scripting would be too slow for any high-volume data or image-processing work, and complex applications of any kind are poorly suited for direct inclusion in the text of an HTML document. After all, there are only so many lines of code you want to wade through to see the HTML itself.

18

When you outgrow JavaScript, does that mean you'll need to return to server-side scripting or applications programming? No. JavaScript is just the baby sister of a more robust
and powerful language called Java. Like JavaScript, Java is especially designed for the
Web. Also like JavaScript scripts, Java programs install and run automatically whenever a
Web page is loaded. However, unlike JavaScript, Java programs are compiled into a more
compact and efficient form (called *bytecodes*) and stored in a file separate from the Web
pages that may call them.

Java also includes a complete graphics drawing library, security features, strong type
checking, and other professional-level programming amenities that serious developers
need. The biggest limiting factor with Java mini-applications (called *applets*) is that they
must be small enough that downloading them doesn't delay the display of a Web page an
intolerable amount of time. Fortunately, Java applets are extremely compact in their compiled form and are often considerably smaller than the images on a typical Web page.

A Java program will work equally well on both Windows and Macintosh computers. Best
of all, Java's syntax is nearly identical to JavaScript's, so you can cut your teeth on
JavaScript and easily move to Java when you need or want to.

You'll find many ready-to-use Java applets on the Web, and Figure 18.1 shows how to
include them in a Web page. The two <applet> tags in Figure 18.1 insert two separate
Java applets named Bounce.class and RnbText.class. (These class files must be placed
in the same directory as the Web page.) The Bounce applet makes a graphical icon hop
up and down, and the RnbText applet below it makes some text wiggle like a wave while
rainbow colors flow through it. Figure 18.2 is a snapshot of these animated effects.

FIGURE 18.1

*Java applets are
prewritten programs
that you place on your
Web page with the
<applet> tag.*

```
<html><head><title>Oh Happy Day</title></head>
<body><div align="center">
<applet code="Bounce.class" width="500" height="300">
No Java? How sad.
</applet>
<applet code="RnbText.class" width="500" height="50">
<param name="text" value="B E H A P P Y , L IK E M E !!!" />
</applet>
</div></body></html>
```

According to both the HTML 4 and XTHML 1 standards, the <applet> tag is
officially obsolete. The <object> tag that replaces it is discussed at the end of
this hour. However, many people still use earlier versions of Web browsers that
require the <applet> tag, and the current versions of both Netscape Navigator
and Microsoft Internet Explorer still support <applet>. You should continue to
use <applet> until all of your intended audience switches to HTML 4–compatible browsers—which isn't likely to happen for quite some time.

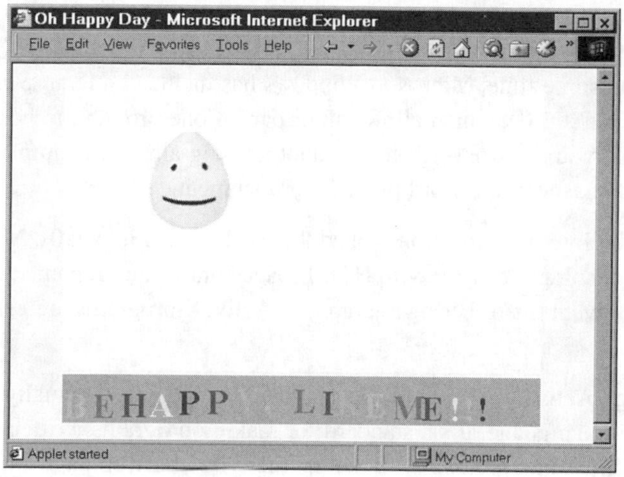

FIGURE 18.2

The <applet> *tags in Figure 18.1 insert programs for drawing a bouncing happy face and some wiggly, colorfully animated text.*

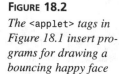

The width and height attributes in the <applet> tag do just what you'd expect them to—specify the dimensions of the region on the Web page that will contain the applet's output. The <param /> tag supplies any information that a specific applet needs in order to do its thing. name identifies what information you're supplying to the applet, and value is the information itself. In this example, the RnbText applet is designed to display some text, so you have to tell it what text to display. The Bounce applet doesn't require any <param /> tag because it was designed to do just one thing, with no optional settings.

Every applet requires different settings for the name and value attributes, and most applets require more than one <param /> tag to set all their options. Whoever created the applet will tell you (usually in some kind of readme.txt or other documentation file) what name attributes you need to include and what sort of information to put in the value attributes for each name.

> You can use the same applet more than once on the page. This is quite efficient because the applet only needs to be downloaded once; the Web browser then automatically creates two copies. For example, you could use RnbText to display two different lines of animated, rainbow-colored text on a page.

18

ActiveX Controls

For quite some time, Microsoft Windows has included a feature called *object linking and embedding* (OLE), which allows all or part of one program to be embedded in a document that you are working on with another program. For example, you can use OLE to put a spreadsheet in a word processing document.

When the Internet explosion rocked the world in the mid-'90s, Microsoft adapted its OLE technology to work with HTML pages online and renamed it ActiveX. Everybody likes to invent his or her own jargon, so ActiveX programs are called *controls* rather than *applets*.

Although ActiveX is touted as Java's main competitor, it actually isn't a specific programming language. It's a standard for making programs written in any language conform to the same protocols, so that neither you, the Web page author, nor the people who view your pages need to be aware of the language in which the control was written. It just works, whether the programmer used Visual Basic, VBScript (a simplified version of Visual Basic), C++, or even Java.

It's not surprising that support for the Microsoft ActiveX protocol is built into Microsoft Internet Explorer (versions 3 and later). For users of Netscape Navigator to be able to see ActiveX controls, they need to download and install the ScriptActive plug-in from Ncompass Labs (`http://www.ncompasslabs.com`).

ActiveX controls will only work on Windows and Macintosh computers. Also, ActiveX controls must be separately compiled for each different operating system so you can't easily create a single control that works for both Macintosh and Windows users.

Because ActiveX is the newest of the technologies discussed in this hour, you must use the new `<object>` tag to insert it into a page.

As Figure 18.3 shows, an ActiveX `<object>` tag looks rather bizarre.

The bizarre part is the `classid` attribute, which must include a unique identifier for the specific ActiveX control you are including. If you use an automated program, such as Microsoft's ActiveX Control Pad, to create your ActiveX pages, it will figure out this magic number for you. Otherwise, you need to consult the documentation that came with the ActiveX control to find the correct `classid`.

FIGURE 18.3

The <object> tag on this page embeds an ActiveX control.

```html
<html><head><title>Label Control</title></head>
<body>
<object id="labelA"
  classid="clsid:99B42120-6EC7-11CF-A6C7-00AA00A47DD2"
  type="application/x-oleobject"
  width="240" height="240" align="left">
<param name="Angle" value="30" />
<param name="Alignment" value="4" />
<param name="BackStyle" value="0" />
<param name="Caption" value="Wowza!" />
<param name="FontName" value="Arial" />
<param name="FontSize" value="36" />
<param name="ForeColor" value="#9900FF" />
</object>
<p>With the ActiveX Label Control, you can draw text of any
size, in any color, at any angle, without waiting for great big
graphics files to download.</p>
<p>Best of all, the Label Control is already installed on your
computer if you have Microsoft Internet Explorer version 4.0.
(Internet Explorer 5.0 will download the control automatically
upon demand.)</p>
</body></html>
```

As if the long string of gibberish in classid weren't enough, the id attribute must include another unique identifier, but this time you get to make it up. You can use any label you want for id, as long as you don't use the same label for another ActiveX control in the same document. (id is used for identifying the control in any scripts you might add to the page.)

18

If you are something of a whiz with Windows, you can use regedit.exe to look in the Windows class registry for the clsid in hkey_classes_root. If the previous sentence makes no sense to you, you need to rely on the person who wrote the ActiveX control (or an automated Web page authoring tool) to tell you the correct classid.

The <param /> tags work the same with <object> as they do with the <applet> tag, discussed earlier in this hour: They provide settings and options specific to the particular ActiveX control you are placing on the Web page, with name identifying the type of information and value giving the information itself. In the example from Figure 18.3, <param /> tags are used to specify the alignment, orientation, font, and color of some text to be displayed by the Label control. This is one of many ActiveX controls built into Microsoft Internet Explorer 4 and documented at the Microsoft Developer Network Web site at www.microsoft.com. (Internet Explorer 5 automatically downloads the control from the Microsoft Web site upon demand.)

Notice that nothing in the HTML itself gives any clue as to what the ActiveX control on that page actually looks like or does. Only when you view the page, shown in Figure 18.4, do you see that it is a nifty little program that displays rotated text.

FIGURE 18.4

The ActiveX control on this page is a program for displaying fancy text, although you wouldn't know it by looking at the HTML in Figure 18.3.

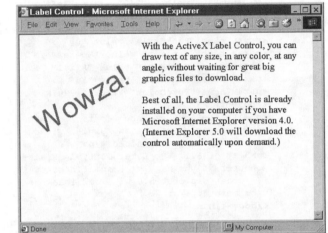

Using ActiveX to Embed a Video

ActiveX controls can do anything a programmer can cook up, but there is one specific ActiveX control included with Microsoft Internet Explorer that you should definitely know how to use. The ActiveMovie control is the Microsoft equivalent of Netscape's LiveVideo plug-in. Using ActiveMovie is currently the most reliable way to play a video in Microsoft Internet Explorer without displaying the clunky controls you get when the Windows Media player is embedded in a Web page.

Figure 18.5 shows the classid and <param /> options you need to know to use the ActiveMovie control. (The parameters are pretty self-explanatory, as long as you know that "1" means yes/on and "0" means no/off.) Take a look at Figure 18.6. This ActiveX object creates exactly the same effect in Microsoft Internet Explorer 4 and 5 as the <embed /> example from Hour 17 creates for Netscape Navigator 4.

Notice that I included the Netscape <embed /> tag between the <object> and </object> tags in Figure 18.5. If an <object> tag is successful in embedding the object it refers to (in this case, the ActiveMovie control), it will ignore all the HTML up to its closing </object> tag (except any <param /> tags). However, if the requested object can't be found or displayed for any reason, the rest of the HTML in front of the closing </object> tag is not ignored. In this case, that means that if the <object> tag doesn't work (probably because someone isn't using Microsoft Internet Explorer as his or her browser), the <embed /> tag will be called on instead. Therefore, the page will work nicely in both Microsoft Internet Explorer and Netscape Navigator.

FIGURE 18.5

You can use the ActiveMovie *control to play a video with the* <object> *tag shown here.*

```
<html><head><title>Fractal Video Clip</title></head>
<body>
<object id="ActiveMovie1"
 classid="CLSID:05589FA1-C356-11CE-BF01-00AA0055595A"
 width="160" height="120" vspace="10" hspace="20" align="left">
<param name="ShowDisplay" valus="0" />
<param name="ShowControls" value="0" />
<param name="AutoStart" value="1" />
<param name="PlayCount" value="10" />
<param name="FileName" value="3dtetra2.avi" />
  <embed src="3dtetra2.avi" autostart="true" loop="true"
   width="160" height="120" vspace="10" hspace="20"
   align="left" />
  <noembed>
    <a href="3dtetra2.avi">
      <img src="3dtetra.jpg" border="0" align="left"
       width="160" height="120" vspace="10" hspace="20" />
    </a>
  </noembed>
</object>
<h2>A Spinning 3-D Fractal</h2>
If the video clip to the left doesn't start on its own,
click on it to make it play. Once it starts, you can
right-click on it and choose Pause to make it stop.
</body></html>
```

18

FIGURE 18.6

The page listed in Figure 18.5 looks the same in both Netscape Navigator and Microsoft Internet Explorer.

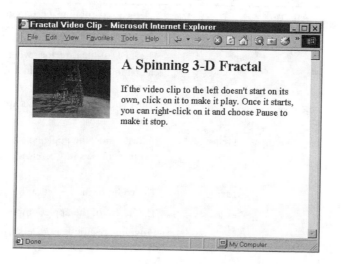

As a last resort, an image linked to the video is included between <noembed> and </noembed> tags. This won't be seen by any recent version of Microsoft Internet Explorer or Netscape Navigator; it's just there for other Web browsers that don't support either ActiveX or embedded multimedia.

Summary

This hour has given you a brief outline of the three types of interactive programming that are easiest to add to your Web site: JavaScript, Java applets, and ActiveX controls. It also discussed the difference between these technologies and more traditional server-side scripting and Netscape plug-ins.

You didn't get enough technical stuff in this short hour to write your own programs and scripts, but you did learn the basic HTML to insert prewritten ones into your Web pages. You also saw how to use an ActiveX control to embed video in a page and how to combine that with what you learned in Hour 17 for maximum compatibility.

In Hour 19 you learn to write some of your own simple JavaScripts to perform some of the easiest—and most useful—tasks for which scripting is commonly used.

Table 18.1 summarizes the tags covered in this hour.

TABLE 18.1   HTML Tags and Attributes Covered in Hour 18

Tag	Attribute	Function
<applet>...<applet>		Inserts a self-running Java applet.
	class="..."	The name of the applet.
	src="..."	The URL of the directory where the compiled applet can be found (should end in a /, as in "http://mysite/myapplets/"). Do not include the actual applet name, which is specified with the class attribute.
	align="..."	Indicates how the applet should be aligned with any text that follows it. Current values are top, middle, and bottom.
	width="..."	The width of the applet output area in pixels.
	height="..."	The height of the applet output area in pixels.
<param />		Program-specific parameters. (Always occurs within <applet> or <object> tags.)

Tag	Attribute	Function
	name="..."	The type of information being given to the applet or ActiveX control.
	value="..."	The actual information to be given to the applet or ActiveX control.
<object>...<object>		Inserts images, videos, Java applets, or ActiveX OLE controls into a document.
	classid="..."	The address of a Java applet or identification code for an ActiveX program.
	id="..."	Gives an identifying name for a Microsoft ActiveX program (Microsoft only).
	data="..."	Can be used in some situations to tell an applet or program where to find some data that it needs.
	type="..."	Can indicate the type of data referred to by a data attribute.
	standby="..."	Lets you specify a text message to be displayed while an applet or program object is being loaded and initialized.

In addition to the standard <applet> attributes in Table 18.1, you can specify applet-specific attributes to be interpreted by the Java applet itself.

18

Q&A

Q What exactly is the difference between "scripting" and "programming" anyway?

A Usually, the word *scripting* is used for programming in relatively simple computer languages that are integrated directly into an application (or into HTML pages). However, the line between scripting and "real programming" is pretty fuzzy.

Q I've used Visual Basic before, and I heard I could use it in Web pages. Is that true?

A Yes, but only if you want to limit the audience for your pages to users of Microsoft Internet Explorer version 3 or later. So far the rest of the world is sticking to JavaScript. Visit the Microsoft Web site (http://www.microsoft.com) for details about the differences between VBScript and Visual Basic.

Q **I've heard about ActiveX scripting and ActiveX documents. How are these different from ActiveX controls?**

A In Microsoft-speak, *ActiveX scripting* means VBScript or JavaScript linking to a page as an ActiveX control. *ActiveX documents* are HTML pages that use an ActiveX control to view a word-processing document or spreadsheet within a Web page. (Career tip: If you want a job at Microsoft, consider listing your first name as "ActiveX" on the application form. They like that.)

Q **Most of the Java applets I find on the Internet have two files, one ending with `.java` and one ending with `.class`. Which one do I put on my Web page, and what do I do with the other one?**

A Put the file ending with `.class` on your Web page with the `<applet>` tag. The `.java` file is the actual Java source code, provided in case you are a Java programmer and want to change it. You don't need the `.java` file to use the applet.

Workshop

Quiz

1. Suppose you found a cool Java game on the Internet and the documentation with it says it's free for anyone to use. It says you need to give the applet two parameters: The "speed" should be between 1 and 100, and the "skill" should be between 1 and 5. The applet itself is named `roadkill.class`. Write the HTML to display it in a 400×200-pixel area in the middle of a Web page.

2. The ActiveX `Label` control displays some text in any orientation you choose. Write the HTML to insert the ActiveX control in a Web page, given the following information:

    The class ID is:

    ```
    clsid:{99b42120-6ec7-11cf-a6c7-00aa00a47dd2}
    ```

    Confine the display area to 300×300 pixels.

    Specify the following parameter values:

    Caption: `"New and Exciting!"`

    Angle: `45`

    FontName: `Arial Black`

    FontSize: `18`

Answers

1.
```
<applet code="roadkill.class" width=400 height=200>
<param name="speed" value=50 />
<param name="skill" value=2 />
</applet>
```

2.
```
<object classid="clsid:99b42120-6ec7-11cf-a6c7-00aa00a47dd2"
id="label" width=300 height=300>
<param name="caption" value="new and exciting!" />
<param name="angle" value="45" />
<param name="fontname" value="arial black" />
<param name="fontsize" value="18" />
</object>
```

Exercise

- You'll find many more reusable applets and controls by visiting
http://24hourhtmlcafe.com/hotlist.htm#developer and checking out the
developer resources links. If you find one that actually adds enough value to your
site from the visitor's perspective to be worth the install-and-initialize waiting time,
try incorporating it into your pages.

18

Hour 19

Web Page Scripting for Non-Programmers

Scripting is a polite word for *computer programming*, and that's obviously an enormous topic you're not going to learn much about in a one-hour lesson. Still, there are some awfully handy things you can do in a snap with scripting—and things you can't do any other way. So with a spirit of bold optimism, this hour aims to help you teach yourself just enough Web page scripting to make your pages stand out from the "non-de-script" crowd.

Specifically, you'll learn in this hour how to make the images (or multimedia objects) on your Web pages change in response to mouse movements or mouse clicks, as well as how to automatically add up totals on an order form. Using the JavaScript language, you can do these tasks in a way that is compatible with version 3 or later of both Netscape Navigator and Microsoft Internet Explorer. Other Web browsers won't respond to your scripting, but will properly display the pages.

You'll learn some additional JavaScript tricks in Hour 20, "Setting Pages in Motion with Dynamic HTML." If the ease and power of the few JavaScript commands you learn in these two hours whet your appetite for more (as I think it will), I encourage you to turn to a book such as *Sams Teach Yourself JavaScript 1.3 in 24 Hours*.

Interactive Highlighting

If you've used any graphical CD-ROM software application, you have probably seen buttons that light up or change when your mouse passes over them. This looks cool and gives you some visual feedback before you click something, which research shows can reduce confusion and errors.

You can add the same sort of visual feedback to the links on your Web pages, too. The first step toward achieving that effect is to create the graphics for both the dark and the lit icons. Figure 19.1 shows some pumpkin faces I created in Paint Shop Pro. I made two copies of each pumpkin: one darkened and one illuminated as if it had a candle inside.

FIGURE 19.1

Four graphics images, each with a highlighted version to replace it when the mouse points to it.

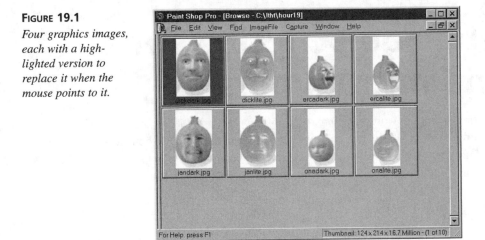

To Do

Do you have any pages that would look flashier or be easier to understand if the navigation icons or other images changed when the mouse passed over them? If so, try creating some highlighted versions of the images, and try modifying your own page as you read the following few paragraphs. Here are a few ideas to get you started:

- Use Paint Shop Pro's text tool to make graphical titles that change color when the mouse points to them.

▼
- Use the Image, Effects, Buttonize command in Paint Shop Pro with various background colors to make buttons that light up just before they're pressed.
- Use the techniques you learned in Hour 12, "Creating Animated Graphics," to make icons that rotate, wiggle, or blink when the mouse passes over them. (You can use a regular, unanimated GIF for the image to present when the mouse isn't pointing to the icon.)
- If you have a list of choices, put a blank (totally transparent) image in front of each choice and make an arrow or bullet icon appear in front of the item to which the mouse is pointing.

▲

Here's how the HTML for a graphical link would look before any scripting is added. This should all look easy and familiar to you. (If it doesn't, review Hour 10, "Putting Graphics on a Web Page," and Hour 13, "Page Design and Layout.")

```
<a href="erica.htm"><img src="ercadark.jpg"
 width=98 height=214 border=0 alt="erica" /></a>
```

The first thing you need to do is give this particular <img> tag its own name. You'll use this name to refer to this specific spot on the page when you want to change which image is displayed in that spot. We'll name this spot erica by putting a name attribute in the <img> tag:

```
<a href="erica.htm"><img name="erica" src="ercadark.jpg"
 width=98 height=214 border=0 alt="erica" /></a>
```

Now for the magic part: You can add JavaScript commands to any link on a Web page by including two special attributes called OnMouseOver and OnMouseOut. With OnMouseOver, you tell the Web browser what to do when the mouse passes over any text or images within that link. With OnMouseOut, you indicate what to do when the mouse moves out of the link area.

In this case, you want the image to change to ercalite.jpg when the mouse passes over the corresponding link and change back to ercadark.jpg when the mouse moves away.

Here's what that looks like in HTML and JavaScript:

```
<a href="erica.htm" OnMouseOver="erica.src='ercalite.jpg'"
OnMouseOut="erica.src='ercadark.jpg'"><img name="erica"
src="ercadark.jpg" width=98 height=214 border=0 alt="erica" /></a>
```

Notice that you need to enclose the name of the image file in single quotation marks (apostrophes), but the whole JavaScript command gets enclosed by double quotation marks (inch marks).

When you do this on your Web pages, just follow my example closely, substituting your own image names and graphics files.

19

Figure 19.2 shows the complete HTML for a Web page using the pumpkin images as links. You can see how the pumpkins light up when the mouse passes over them in Figures 19.3 and 19.4, or online at `http://24hourHTMLcafe.com/hour19`.

FIGURE 19.2

This is the JavaScript-enhanced HTML for the page shown in Figures 19.3 and 19.4.

```html
<html><head><title>The Olivers</title></head>
<body><div align="center">
<h1>The Oliver Family</h1>
<a href="erica.htm" OnMouseOver="erica.src='ercalite.jpg'"
                    OnMouseOut="erica.src='ercadark.jpg'"
><img name="erica" id="erica" src="ercadark.jpg"
  width="98" height="214" border="0" alt="Erica" /></a
><a href="dick.htm" OnMouseOver="dick.src='dicklite.jpg'"
                    OnMouseOut="dick.src='dickdark.jpg'"
><img name="dick" src="dickdark.jpg"
  width="124" height="214" border="0" alt="Dick" /></a
><a href="jan.htm" OnMouseOver="jan.src='janlite.jpg'"
                    OnMouseOut="jan.src='jandark.jpg'"
><img name="jan" src="jandark.jpg"
  width="136" height="214" border="0" alt="Jan" /></a
><a href="ona.htm" OnMouseOver="ona.src='onalite.jpg'"
                    OnMouseOut="ona.src='onadark.jpg'"
><img name="ona" src="onadark.jpg"
  width="100" height="214" border="0" alt="Ona" /></a>
<p>Click on a family member to find out all about us.</p>
</div></body></html>
```

FIGURE 19.3

When the mouse passes over the pumpkin with my daughter's face, it lights up and her name (from the alt *attribute) appears.*

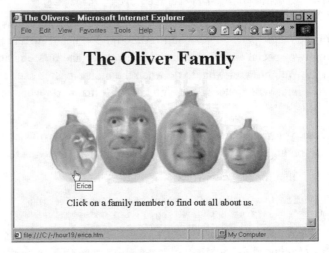

FIGURE 19.4

When you move the mouse to my pumpkin, my face lights up instead of Erica's.

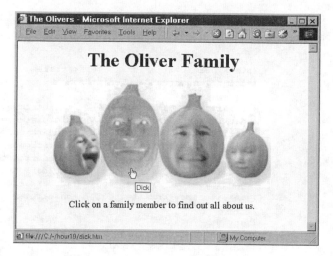

You will usually want the image that the mouse is passing over to light up or change, but you aren't limited to doing it that way. For example, if you wanted all the pumpkins to light up whenever the mouse moved over one of them, you could put the following JavaScript in each <a> tag:

```
<a href="erica.htm" OnMouseOver="erica.src='ercalite.jpg';
dick.src='dicklite.jpg'; jan.src='janlite.jpg'; ona.src='onalite.jpg'"
OnMouseOut="erica.src='ercadark.jpg'";
dick.src='dickdark.jpg'; jan.src='jandark.jpg'; ona.src='onadark.jpg'">
```

As you can see, modifying multiple images is as simple as putting a semicolon (;) after the first JavaScript command and following it with another command. You can put as many commands as you need in the same OnMouseOver (or OnMouseOut) attribute, as long as you separate them with semicolons.

19

Preloading Images for Speed

The code in Figure 19.2 works flawlessly with both Microsoft Internet Explorer and Netscape Navigator (versions 3 and later of both browsers). There is only one minor problem: The lit images won't be downloaded from your Web site until someone actually moves the mouse over the image. This can cause a significant delay before the high-lighted image appears, possibly lowering the all-important Gee Whiz Factor (GWF).

You can avoid this annoyance by including some JavaScript telling the browser to pre-load the images as soon as possible when the page is displayed. That way, by the time the slow human reader gets around to passing his or her mouse over the link, those images will usually be ready to pop onto the screen. This makes the animations seem to

appear without any download delay, giving the page a snappy feel and pumping the
GWF back up to truly nerdly levels. Figure 19.5 shows how it's done.

FIGURE 19.5

This page looks and acts exactly like the page in Figure 19.2, except that all the "lite" images are pre-loaded for enhanced responsiveness.

```
<html><head><title>The Olivers</title>
<script language="JavaScript">
<!--
  ercalite=new Image(98,214);    ercadark=new Image(98,214);
  dicklite=new Image(124,214);   dickdark=new Image(124,214);
  janlite=new Image(136,214);    jandark=new Image(136,214);
  onalite=new Image(100,214);    onadark=new Image(100,214);
  ercalite.src="ercalite.jpg";   ercadark.src="ercadark.jpg";
  dicklite.src="dicklite.jpg";   dickdark.src="dickdark.jpg";
  janlite.src="janlite.jpg";     jandark.src="jandark.jpg";
  onalite.src="onalite.jpg";     onadark.src="onadark.jpg";
//-->
</script></head>
<body><div align="center">
<h1>The Oliver Family</h1>
<a href="erica.htm" OnMouseOver="erica.src='ercalite.jpg'"
                    OnMouseOut="erica.src='ercadark.jpg'"
><img name="erica" id="erica" src="ercadark.jpg"
  width="98" height="214" border="0" alt="Erica" /></a
><a href="dick.htm" OnMouseOver="dick.src='dicklite.jpg'"
                    OnMouseOut="dick.src='dickdark.jpg'"
><img name="dick" src="dickdark.jpg"
  width="124" height="214" border="0" alt="Dick" /></a
><a href="jan.htm" OnMouseOver="jan.src='janlite.jpg'"
                    OnMouseOut="jan.src='jandark.jpg'"
><img name="jan" src="jandark.jpg"
  width="136" height="214" border="0" alt="Jan" /></a
><a href="ona.htm" OnMouseOver="ona.src='onalite.jpg'"
                    OnMouseOut="ona.src='onadark.jpg'"
><img name="ona" src="onadark.jpg"
  width="100" height="214" border="0" alt="Ona" /></a>
<p>Click on a family member to find out all about us.</p>
</div></body></html>
```

There are a couple of things worthy of note in Figure 19.5. The most important is the
`<script>` tag. This is used whenever you need some JavaScript that doesn't go in an
attribute of some other tag. You can put `<script>` tags anywhere in the `<head>` or `<body>`
section of a document. (The forms example later in this hour talks more about that.)

The `<!--` and `//-->` tags just inside the `<script>` and `</script>` tags are actually comment tags, which have the effect of hiding the script from older browsers that otherwise
might become confused and try to display the code as text on the page. You should
always put each of these comment tags on a line by itself, as I did in Figure 19.5.

I won't go too deep into an explanation of the JavaScript in Figure 19.5 because that would get us into a course on computer programming. You don't need to understand exactly how this works in order to copy it into your own pages, using your own image names and graphics files. When you do try this on your pages, don't overlook the fact that I had to use the names from the JavaScript definitions at the top of the page instead of the actual graphics filenames. For example, the OnMouseOver attribute of the name="erica" image now looks like this:

```
OnMouseOver="erica.src=ercalite.src"
```

instead of this:

```
OnMouseOver="erica.src='ercalite.jpg'"
```

You can also use the OnMouseOver and OnMouseOut attributes with imagemaps (which are covered in Hour 14, "Graphical Links and Imagemaps"). For an example of a large interactive imagemap, using no fewer than 24 separate images, move your mouse cursor around the pocket watch at the completed *24-Hour HTML Café* site at http://24hourHTMLcafe.com.

Peeking at the source code shows you exactly how to incorporate JavaScript commands into an imagemap. (It also reveals that the clock is actually five separate images—four imagemaps and the changing image in the center. They don't call me "Tricky Dicky" for nuthin'.)

Also, don't forget that you can use animated GIFs with JavaScripts, too! For an example, check out the "Predictions and Fictions" link at http://24hourHTMLcafe.com/hour19.

19

Adding Up an Order Form

One of the most common uses of scripting is making an order form that adds its own totals based on what items the customer selects. Figure 19.6 is an example that you can copy to create self-totaling forms yourself.

Although the code in Figure 19.6 is unrealistically simple for any real company's order form (most companies would like at least the address and phone number of the person placing the order), it is a completely functional JavaScript-enhanced Web page. Figure 19.7 demonstrates what the form would look like after a user entered the number 3 in the first box and the number 1 in the third box of the Qty column. The numbers in the Totals column are computed automatically.

FIGURE **19.6**

This simple order form uses JavaScript to automatically compute totals.

```html
<html><head><title>Parts</title>
<script language="JavaScript">
<!--
  function CalculateTotals() {
    f=document.orderform;
    f.total1.value=parseInt(f.qty1.value)*50;
    f.total2.value=parseInt(f.qty2.value)*295;
    f.total3.value=parseInt(f.qty3.value)*395;
    f.total4.value=parseInt(f.qty4.value)*750;
    f.grandtotal.value=parseInt(f.total1.value)
                      +parseInt(f.total2.value)
                      +parseInt(f.total3.value)
                      +parseInt(f.total4.value);}
//-->
</script></head>
<body>
<h1>Parts Order Form</h1>
<p>Indicate how many of each part you wish to order in the
"Qty" column. The total amount of your order will be calculated
automatically. When you are ready to submit your order, click
on the <b>Make Purchase</b> button.</p>
<form name="orderform" method="post" action="/htbin/generic">
<table border="3"><tr>
<th>Qty</th><th>Part #</th><th>Description</th>
<th>Price</th><th>Total</th></tr>
<tr><td>
<input name="qty1" size="3" OnBlur="CalculateTotals()" /></td>
<td>25791</td><td>Chromated Flywheel Knob</td>
<td align="right">$50</td>
<td><input name="total1" size="7"
     OnFocus="document.orderform.qty2.select();
              document.orderform.qty2.focus();" /></td></tr>
<tr><td>
<input name="qty2" size="3" OnBlur="CalculateTotals()" /></td>
<td>17557</td><td>Perambulatory Dramograph</td>
<td align="right">$295</td>
<td><input name="total2" size="7"
     OnFocus="document.orderform.qty3.select();
              document.orderform.qty3.focus();" /></td></tr>
<tr><td>
<input name="qty3" size="3" OnBlur="CalculateTotals()" /></td>
<td>98754</td><td>Triple-Extruded Colorizer</td>
<td align="right">$395</td>
<td><input name="total3" size="7"
     OnFocus="document.orderform.qty4.select();
              document.orderform.qty4.focus();" /></td></tr>
<tr><td>
<input name="qty4" size="3" OnBlur="CalculateTotals()" /></td>
<td>47594</td><td>Rediculation Kit (Complete)</td>
<td align="right">$750</td>
<td><input name="total4" size="7"
     OnFocus="document.orderform.qty1.select();
              document.orderform.qty1.focus();" /></td></tr>
<tr><td></td><td></td><td></td>
<td align="right"><b>GRAND TOTAL:</b></td>
<td><input name="grandtotal" size="7"
     OnFocus="document.orderform.qty1.select();
              document.orderform.qty1.focus();" /></td></tr>
</table>
<br /><input type="submit" value="Make Purchase" />
</form>
<script language="JavaScript">
<!--
  f=document.orderform;
  f.qty1.value=0; f.qty2.value=0;
  f.qty3.value=0; f.qty4.value=0;
  f.total1.value=0; f.total2.value=0;
  f.total3.value=0; f.total4.value=0;
  f.grandtotal.value=0;
//-->
</script>
</body></html>
```

FIGURE 19.7

The JavaScript in Figure 19.6 produces this form. Here, the customer has entered some desired quantities and the form has figured out the total cost.

Parts Order Form

Indicate how many of each part you wish to order in the "Qty" column. The total amount of your order will be calculated automatically. When you are ready to submit your order, click on the **Make Purchase** button.

Qty	Part #	Description	Price	Total
3	25791	Chromated Flywheel Knob	$50	150
0	17557	Perambulatory Dramograph	$295	0
1	98754	Triple-Extruded Colorizer	$395	395
0	47594	Rediculation Kit (Complete)	$750	0
			GRAND TOTAL:	545

    Make Purchase

Most programmers could probably customize and expand the page in Figure 19.6 quite a bit without knowing anything whatsoever about JavaScript. What's more, this page works on any server and any JavaScript-enabled browser on any operating system.

Even if you don't do programming at all, you can easily adapt the code in Figure 19.6 to your own uses. The following list highlights the key elements of this JavaScript that you'll need to understand.

> If you're not already familiar with HTML forms, you should review Hour 8, "Creating HTML Forms," before you try to understand or modify this example.

19

- As in the earlier example, I started by giving a name to all the parts of the page I would need to modify. Using the name attribute, I named the `<form>` itself `"orderform"`. I also gave each input element in the form a name, such as `"qty1"`, `"qty2"`, `"total1"`, `"total2"`, and so on.

- The HTML page itself is always named `"document"`, so I refer to the form as `"document.orderform"`. The first input item on that form is `"document.orderform.qty1"`, the `"grandtotal"` input item is `"document.orderform.grandtotal"`, and so forth. You'll notice that I put `f=document.orderform` at the beginning of each `<script>`. This just saved me some typing, since I could then use the letter f from then on instead of typing out `document.orderform` as part of every name.

- The function near the top of the page, which I chose to name ComputeTotals(), is the part of the script that actually carries out the computations. This function is pretty straightforward: It multiplies the quantities the user entered by the prices to get the totals, then adds the totals to make a grand total. The only tricky thing here is all that parseInt() business. You have to use parseInt() to indicate that something is a number whenever you want to do computations. (This isn't necessary in most other programming languages. JavaScript is a little weird that way.) If you want to allow numbers that aren't integers, such as 12.5 or 13.333, use parseFloat() instead of parseInt().

- The <script> at the bottom of the page just sets all the input elements to 0 when the page first appears. This has to be done after the form itself is defined on the page with the <form> and </form> tags.

- The real action happens in the <input> tags. Just as the earlier example in this hour uses OnMouseOver to respond to a mouse movement, this example responds to OnFocus and OnBlur. The OnFocus stuff happens when the user first clicks in (or tabs to) an input box to enter data. The OnBlur commands are triggered when the user is done entering data in a box and moves on to the next one.

- Take a look at the <input> tags named qty1, qty2, qty3, and qty4. In each of these, you'll see OnBlur="CalculateTotals()", which simply does all the math in the CalculateTotals function in the top <script> every time the user enters a number in the Qty column. (JavaScript takes care of displaying the totals and grand total automatically, so you don't see any explicit command to "print" these numbers.)

- Now look at all the other <input> tags. Each contains two commands, similar to the following:

```
OnFocus="document.orderform.qty2.focus();
         document.orderform.qty2.select()"
```

This causes the cursor to skip to the next input box so that the user doesn't get a chance to modify the totals. It also causes whatever data is in that next input box to be selected, so whatever the user types will replace the old data instead of being tacked onto the end of it.

Whew! That may seem like a lot to figure out, especially if you've never done any programming before! With a little experimentation and a few careful readings of this explanation, you should be able to put together a simple automatic order form of your own without any further knowledge of JavaScript.

Time for a confession: There's a form-input tag I didn't tell you about in Hour 8, "Creating HTML Forms." The `<button>` tag creates a button—sort of like `<input type="submit">`, except that a `<button>` button doesn't actually do anything—not until you tell it what to do with some JavaScript, that is. If a programmable button sounds like something you'd like to use on your forms, hop on over to the JavaScript Button example at `http://24hourHTMLcafe.com/hour19` to see one in action, and check out the HTML that makes it work.

The Wide World of JavaScript

You've learned enough in this hour to have a head start on JavaScript and to add some snazzy interaction to your Web pages. You've probably also gotten the idea that there's a lot more you can do, and it isn't as hard as you may have thought.

You may also find some scripts online that can be incorporated into a Web page of your own with little or no modification. (Check out the JavaScript-related links at `http://24hourHTMLcafe.com/hotsites.htm#developer` for good places to find scripts.)

When you find scripts you'd like to reuse or experiment with, use Figure 19.6 as a guide for placing the JavaScript elements where they should go; generally, functions go in the `<head>` area, preceded by `<script language="javascript">` and followed by `</script>`. The parts of the script that actually carry out the actions when the page is loaded go in the `<body>` part of the page, but still need to be set aside with the `<script>` tag. Sections of script that respond to specific form entries go in the `<a>` or `<input>` tags, with special attributes such as `OnMouseOver` or `OnBlur`.

You can also put JavaScript into a separate file by putting the name of that file in a `src` attribute within the `<script>` tag, like the following:

```
<script language="javascript" src="bingo.htm"></script>
```

This is especially handy when you are using a script that someone else wrote and you don't want it cluttering up your HTML. Some parts of the script, such as JavaScript attributes of form `<input>` tags, may still have to go in your HTML document.

19

Netscape and Microsoft have slightly different—and often incompatible—implementations of JavaScript (Microsoft officially calls its JScript, and its browser also supports a completely different scripting language called VBScript). The Web sites at http://home.netscape.com and http://www.microsoft.com are the best places to find out about the exact differences. Many simple scripts, including all those in this book, will work the same in both browsers.

Summary

In this hour you've seen how to use scripting to make the images on your Web pages respond to mouse movements. You've also seen how similar JavaScript commands can be used to change multiple images at once and to perform automatic calculations on form data. These tasks don't require much in the way of programming skills, although they may inspire you to learn the JavaScript language to give your pages more complex interactive features.

Q&A

Q Are there other, "secret," attributes besides OnMouseOver, OnMouseOut, OnBlur, and OnFocus that I can use just as easily? And can I put them anyplace other than in an <a> or <input> tag?

A Yes and yes. Each HTML tag has an associated set of JavaScript attributes, which are called *events*. For example, OnClick can be used within the <a> tag and some forms tags to specify a command to be followed when someone clicks that link or form element. Refer to Appendix C, "Complete HTML 4 Quick Reference," for a complete listing of the events you can use in each tag.

Q Doesn't Microsoft use a different scripting language for Internet Explorer?

A Yes, Microsoft recommends using a scripting language based on Visual Basic called VBScript, but Microsoft Internet Explorer version 3 or later also supports JavaScript. Many commands work slightly differently in the Microsoft implementation of JavaScript than they do in Netscape Navigator, however. Fortunately, the simple commands covered in this hour work exactly the same in both browsers so you can use them with confidence.

Q I tried using the tricks from this hour with images that were arranged in a table, but it didn't always work. Why?

A There's a bug in Netscape Navigator 3 that causes problems when you dynamically change images in a table. The trouble was corrected in Netscape Navigator 4 and was never an issue with Microsoft Internet Explorer. Because some people still use Navigator 3, it's safer to avoid changing any image within a table using JavaScript.

Workshop

Quiz

1. Say you've made a picture of a button and named it `button.gif`. You also made a simple GIF animation of the button flashing green and white and named it `flashing.gif`. Write the HTML and JavaScript to make the button flash whenever someone moves the mouse pointer over it, and link to a page named `gohere.htm` when someone clicks the button.

2. How would you modify what you wrote for question 1 so that the button starts flashing when someone moves the mouse over it, and keeps flashing even if he or she moves the mouse away?

3. Write the HTML for a form that automatically calculates a total order cost, based on the number of widgets the user wants and a price of $25 per widget.

Answers

1.
```
<a href="gohere.htm"
OnMouseOver="flasher.src='flashing.gif';
OnMouseOut="flasher.src='button.gif'">
<img name="flasher" src="button.gif" border=0 /></a>
```

2.
```
<a href="gohere.htm"
OnMouseOver="flasher.src='flashing.gif'">
<img name="flasher" src="button.gif" border=0 /></a>
```

3.
```
<html><head><title>widget order form</title>
<script language="javascript">
<!--
function CalculateTotal() {
document.orderform.total.value=
parseInt(document.orderform.qty.value)*25}
//-->
</script></head><body>
<form name="orderform" method="post"
action="/htbin/generic">
Please send me
```

19

```
<input name="qty" size=3 onblur="CalculateTotal()">
widgets at $25 each = TOTAL:
<input name="total" size=5>
<input type="submit" value="Order Now">
</form>
<script language="javascript">
<!--
document.orderform.qty.value=0;
document.orderform.total.value=0;
//-->
</script>
</body></html>
```

Exercise

- Hey, what are you waiting for? Now that you're an HTML expert, get yourself a copy of the new *Sams Teach Yourself JavaScript 1.3 in 24 Hours* and take the next quantum leap in Web publishing!

Hour **20**

Setting Pages in Motion with Dynamic HTML

As we all know, a word must be spelled with all capital letters and no vowels in order to qualify as genuine computer jargon. The latest unpronounceable buzzword along this line is *DHTML*, which stands for *Dynamic HTML*. Like all the best tech-talk, this term means quite a few things, depending on whom you ask.

Everyone agrees that Dynamic HTML brings a new level of power and excitement to Web pages. Everyone also agrees that it has something to do with scripting, animation, and interactivity. Unfortunately, nobody yet agrees exactly how you get to have all this fun. Microsoft, Netscape, and the World Wide Web Consortium (the folks who set the standards) still disagree about the details of what you can do with Dynamic HTML and how you should go about doing it. Creating Dynamic HTML pages therefore currently requires a certain amount of fortitude, cleverness, and perhaps foolhardiness.

Since I am obviously well endowed with all of these attributes, in this hour I will bravely lead you into the wilds of Dynamic HTML. Don't expect to become a DHTML guru in the next 60 minutes, but you can count on coming away with some reusable scripts to animate the contents of your Web pages in ways you couldn't before. You will also emerge with the know-how necessary to put these scripts to work and to modify them for your own purposes.

To Do

Since the example for this hour involves interactive animation, it's easier to see how everything works if you have the actual page on your computer, instead of just the static pictures in this book. I therefore recommend that you download the example files from the *24-Hour HTML Café* before you continue reading. Here's how:

- If you don't already own version 4 or later of Netscape Navigator (for Windows PCs or the Macintosh) or version 4 or later of Microsoft Internet Explorer (for Windows only), go to Netscape at `http://home.netscape.com` or Microsoft at `http://www.microsoft.com/ie/` and follow the instructions for downloading and installing the latest browser version.

- Start your Web browser and go to the *24-Hour HTML Café* at `http://24hourHTMLcafe.com/hour20`.

- Under The XYZ Files example, you will see a list of seven filenames. Use the right mouse button (or hold down the button if you're using a Macintosh) to click each of these, choosing Save Link As from the pop-up menu each time. Save all seven files in the same folder on your hard drive.

  (The files are `xyfiles.htm`, `slide.js`, `nodhtml.htm`, `xfolder.gif`, `yfolder.gif`, `zfolder.gif`, and `empty.gif`. The last of these GIF images is invisible, so don't worry if you try to look at it after saving and don't see anything. You also may not see anything if you try to view `slide.js` with a Web browser.)

  Once you have those seven files on your hard drive, you can use your favorite text editor and Web browser to look at them (and, if you're bold, modify them to work with your own graphics and text) as you read the rest of this hour.

Learning How to Fly

For the first part of this hour, your noble quest will be to make some text "fly in" from the edge of a page when that page first comes up in the browser window. Just to make the quest more worthy of pursuit, you'd better make the text slide diagonally, instead of left to right. Naturally, what you really want (and shall no doubt soon gain) is a general-purpose script that you can use to slide any text or graphics any way you want.

While you're at it, why not go wild and ask for a script that can slip things underneath the edge of other things, or slide one layer of text and graphics behind or in front of any number of other layers?

Figures 20.1 and 20.2 are snapshots of a Dynamic HTML Web page with flying text. This is the xyzfiles.htm document you were just instructed to download from the *24-Hour HTML Café*, so you may want to look at it on your computer screen now. See how the text glides in from behind the file folders as soon as you pull up the page? Pretty cool, huh?

FIGURE 20.1

Dynamic HTML lets you animate overlapping layers of text and graphics. This text is emerging from behind some images.

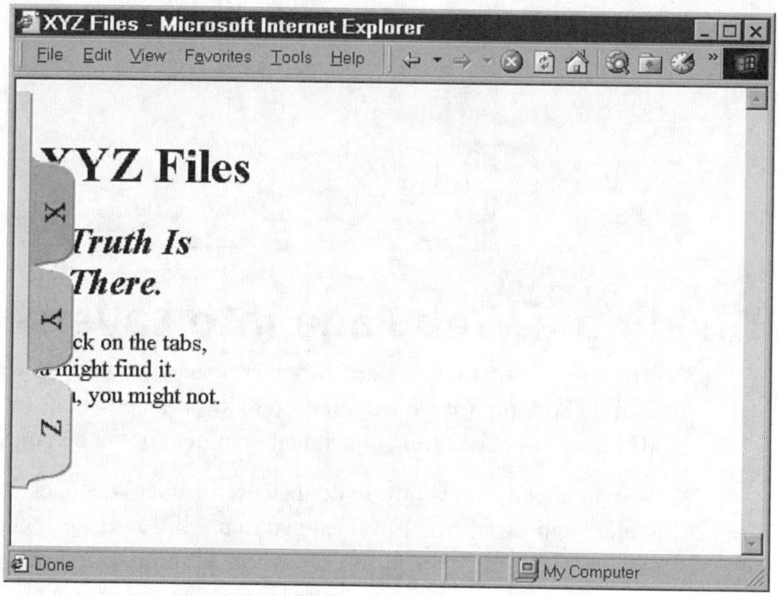

To achieve the effect shown in Figures 20.1 and 20.2, your HTML and JavaScript code needs to do all of the following:

1. Check to make sure that the user's Web browser can handle Dynamic HTML and provide some alternative content if it can't.

2. Define and name the layer containing the text; hide it out of sight beyond the edge of the page.

3. Define and name the layers that contain the file tab images. (Each tab is actually assigned its own layer because later in this hour they are all animated separately.)

4. Animate the text layer sliding onto the page.

Figure 20.3 shows the HTML that does all these things. The following sections explain how each of these four tasks is accomplished.

20

FIGURE 20.2

The text that was moving in Figure 20.1 has settled into place and stopped.

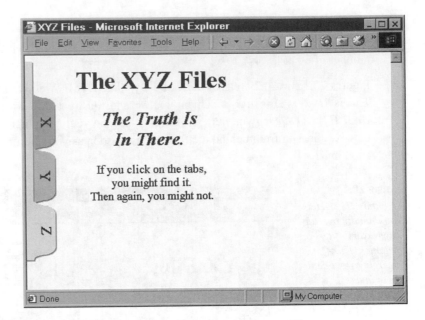

Dividing a Web Page into Layers

Shortly, you'll learn how to detect whether a page is being viewed with a DHTML-compatible Web browser. First you need to know an essential secret of all Dynamic HTML: how to define layers of text and graphics so you can move them around.

Wait—you already know how to do that! Remember way back in Hour 5, "Text Alignment and Lists," when you learned to use `<div align="center">` to center a bunch of text and graphics on the page? The whole purpose of the `<div>` and `</div>` tags is to define a region of the page (also called a *division* or *layer*) so you can then do something with that whole region at once.

As you found out in Hour 16, "Using Style Sheets," centering the contents of a `<div>` region is only one of many possibilities for playing with it. You could also turn all the text in the region red with `<div style="color: red">`, or put a red background behind the region with `<div style="background-color: red">`, or even pick up the whole region and move it to the top-left corner of the browser window with `<div style="position: absolute; left: 0px; top: 0px">`.

Now you're about to learn how to do all these things dynamically, in response to user-initiated events such as mouse movements or link clicks. Of course, you'll need a name for each `<div>` region you want to order around. In some older versions of JavaScript, you would use the familiar `name` attribute for this purpose, but for reasons beyond my ken, a new attribute called `id` is now used instead.

FIGURE 20.3

This is the HTML for the page in Figures 20.1 and 20.2. The JavaScript that does the animation is in a separate file (see Figure 20.6), named slide.js.

```html
<html><head><title>XYZ Files</title>
<script src="slide.js" language="javascript"></script>
</head>

<!-- Check for DHTML compatibility and if it's okay,
     then fly in the headings and body text -->
<body OnLoad="if (checkDHTML()) {
layername=makeName('intro');
yhop=-2; ygoal=20; xhop=10; xgoal=80; slide() }">

<!-- Tell users of non-JavaScript browsers to go away,
     but hide the message from DHTML-compatible browsers -->
<div style="position: absolute;
            left: -250px; top: 10px; width: 250">
<p>Your browser can't cope with this DHTML page.</p>
<a href="nodhtml.htm">Click here for a regular HTML page.</a>
</div>

<!-- Get the headings and body text ready to fly in -->
<div id="intro" style="text-align: center; z-index: 0;
 position: absolute; left: -260px; top: 88px; width: 260px">
<h1>The XYZ Files</h1>
<h2><i>The Truth Is<br />In There.</i></h2>
If you click on the tabs,<br />you might find it.<br />
Then again, you might not.</div>

<!-- Give each file folder image its own layer -->
<div id="layer1" style="position: absolute;
 left: -250px; top: 10px; width: 300; z-index: 1">
<img src="xfolder.gif" width="300" height="330" /></div>
<div id="layer2" style="position: absolute;
 left: -250px; top: 10px; width: 300; z-index: 2">
<img src="yfolder.gif" width="300" height="330" /></div>
<div id="layer3" style="position: absolute;
 left: -250px; top: 10px; width: 300; z-index: 3">
<img src="zfolder.gif" width="300" height="330" /></div>
```

All text between <!-- and --> tags in Figure 20.3 (or any other HTML page) is completely ignored by the Web browser. These comments are just reminders the Web page author has written to himself (that's me) and anyone else who might need some hints to understand how the page works (that's you).

20

For example, the following code from Figure 20.3 defines a layer named `"intro"`:

```
<div id="intro" style="text-align: center; z-index: 0;
 position: absolute; left: -260px; top: 88px; width: 260px">
<h1>The XYZ Files</h1>
<h2><i>The Truth Is<br />In There.</i></h2>
If you click on the tabs,<br />you might find it.<br />
Then again, you might not.</div>
```

The `style` attribute positions this layer 88 pixels down from the top edge of the browser window, and negative 260 pixels from the left edge. *Negative* means to the left, so in other words you won't actually be able to see this layer (until you move it) because it's completely outside the viewing window, off to the left side. The `style` attribute also specifies the width of the layer as 260 pixels and indicates that the text should be centered in that 260-pixel–wide region.

Each of the last three `<div>` tags in Figure 20.3 contains a single `<img />` tag, placing a 300×330-pixel image of a file folder on the page. If you look carefully at the `style` attributes for these `<div>` tags, you'll notice that each layer is positioned 250 pixels outside the left edge of the browser window, so that only the rightmost 50 pixels of the image are visible in Figures 20.1 and 20.2. The rest is hidden beyond the edge of the viewing window and will not be revealed until later this hour when I show you how to interactively animate the file folder images.

You'll also notice that all three of these `<div>` layers are placed in exactly the same spot, right on top of one another. The only reason you can see the bottom two folder tabs is that the images covering them are partially transparent GIFs, allowing parts of the image and background beneath to show through.

With all these semi-transparent layers piled on top of one another, you need some way to determine which layer appears in front, which one is in the back, and the stacking order of those layers in between. You can do this by including `z-index:` followed by a number in the `style` attribute of each layer. Higher numbered layers appear in front of lower numbered layers. In Figure 20.3, the `"intro"` layer gets a `z-index` of 0 (the very bottom layer), and the X, Y, and Z file tabs get `z-index`es of 1, 2, and 3, respectively. Figure 20.1 clearly shows the result of this stacking order. (If you gave the `"intro"` layer a `z-index` of 4 or higher, the text would appear in front of the file tabs instead of behind them.)

Offering Alternate Content in Plain HTML

There's one more `<div>` layer in Figure 20.3 that I haven't mentioned yet. The code for it looks like the following:

```
<div style="position: absolute;
  left: -250px; top: 10px; width: 250">
Your browser can't cope with this DHTML page.<p>
<a href="nodhtml.htm">Click here for a regular HTML page.</a>
<p></div>
```

Like the "intro" layer mentioned earlier, this layer is nothing more than a little text positioned completely out of view beyond the edge of the browser window. The point here is that older browsers that don't support style sheet positioning won't know enough to hide this layer; those browsers' users will see the text telling them how lame their browser is and offering a link to an alternative page—presumably one that doesn't use any Dynamic HTML jugglery.

Figure 20.4 shows what the page from Figures 20.1 to 20.3 looks like when viewed with the Opera browser, which doesn't support style sheets or JavaScript. The style and id attributes of the <div> tags have no effect at all in Opera, so the contents of all the layers are displayed one after the other down the page.

FIGURE 20.4

When the page in Figures 20.1 to 20.3 is viewed in Opera 3.21, a link to an alternate page appears.

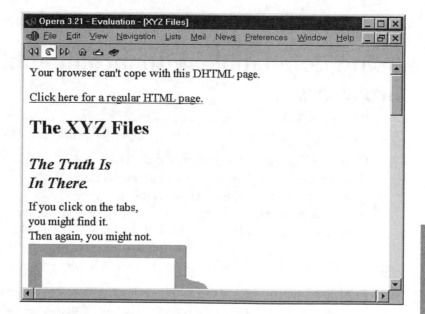

When a user follows the "Click here for a regular HTML page" link in Figure 20.4, she gets the nodhtml.htm document shown in Figure 20.5. You can make any page you want and name it nodhtml.htm (or change the "nodhtml.htm" reference to the page of your choice). Instead of telling the user that her browser isn't advanced enough for your state-of-the-art pages, you might choose instead to simply present equivalent content without the fancy DHTML animation.

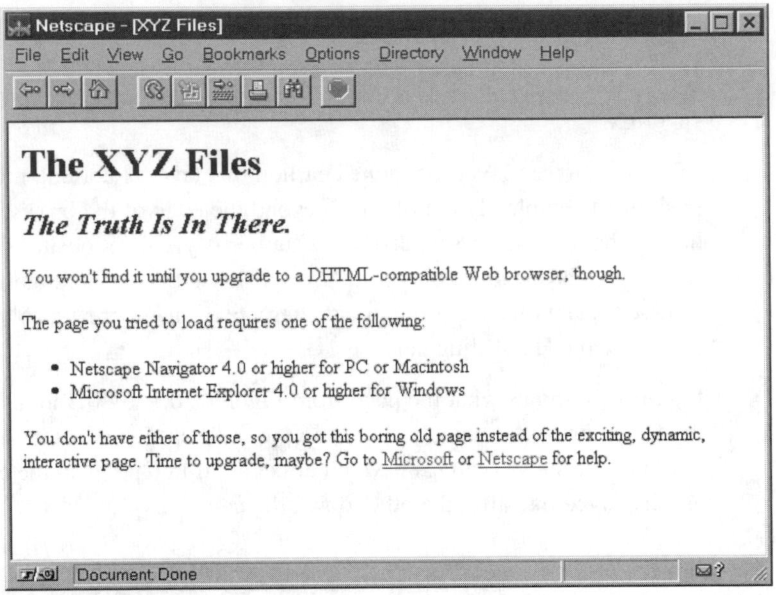

FIGURE 20.5

*Clicking the link in
Figure 20.4 takes the
user to a plain-vanilla
HTML page, with no
DHTML enhance-
ments.*

Being Compatible with Incompatible Browsers

With all the layers in place, and users of under-powered browsers properly warned, the only thing left to do is write a little JavaScript to slide the `"intro"` layer onto the page.

Unfortunately, that's not quite true. There are still some ugly browser-compatibility issues to resolve first. You've seen how to offer some level of compatibility with browsers that support neither style sheet positioning nor JavaScript. If you want a page that works out in the real world, you also need to be ready for Web browsers that understand older versions of JavaScript but still can't handle advanced stuff like layer animation. If you don't detect and divert those browsers, anyone using those browsers to view your DHTML pages may see all sorts of strange behavior and error messages.

To make matters worse, the two most popular Web browsers use incompatible scripting languages. For some simple applications, like those presented in Hour 19, "Web Page Scripting for Non-Programmers," Netscape Navigator and Microsoft Internet Explorer are compatible enough to write simple scripts that work in both browsers; when you try to do more interesting things, such as moving overlapping layers of text and graphics around, Netscape's JavaScript and Microsoft's JScript are just not talking the same language.

None of this would be a big deal if you were creating Web pages for a corporate intranet where all employees always used exactly the same software. (Such corporations do exist, I'm told, although I'm not sure I believe it.) Most of us, however, want our pages to look good to anyone who pulls them off the Internet, no matter what Web browser they are using. At the very least, we'd like our fancy interactive bells and whistles to work with the latest browsers from Netscape and Microsoft, and perhaps gracefully offer a less exciting page to users of any other Web browser.

Time for the bad news: Achieving this level of compatibility is a huge headache. The good news is that I already got the headache for you, had a beer, got over it, and wrote the necessary scripts so you don't have to. I won't even try to teach you enough to understand how I did it, but if you take a look at Figure 20.6, I will tell you what the JavaScript does and why.

> As mentioned in Hour 19, you can either type a script directly into a Web page, between the `<script>` and `</script>` tags, or you can put the script in a separate file and indicate the filename with a `src` attribute in the `<script>` tag. The Web page in Figure 20.3 uses the latter approach to include the `slide.js` script listed in Figure 20.6. This allows you to use the same script in as many Web pages as you want without having to maintain multiple copies of the script itself.

> Any line starting with `//` is ignored by the JavaScript interpreter, the same way anything between `<!--` and `-->` tags is ignored by HTML browsers. The lines starting with `//` in Figure 20.6 are just comments by the Web page author, reminding anyone who reads the code what each function does.

As you may remember from Hour 19, a *function* is a piece of JavaScript code that can be called on to do a specific task. The first function in Figure 20.6 checks to see if a Web page is being viewed with a DHTML-compatible Web browser. In order to qualify as DHTML-compatible (according to me on this particular Thursday, anyway), a browser must understand some version of JavaScript advanced enough to group text and graphics into layers and dynamically position those layers anywhere on a Web page. The following are the only browsers that meet these criteria:

- Netscape Navigator 4 or later for Windows or Macintosh (but not UNIX)
- Microsoft Internet Explorer 4 or later for Windows (but not Macintosh or UNIX)

20

FIGURE 20.6

You can link this `slide.js` *JavaScript file to your own pages to give them instant cross-browser Dynamic HTML compatibility.*

```javascript
// Define all variables and set the default delay to 5ms
var layername, xgoal, ygoal, xhop, yhop, delay=5;

// Check to see if the browser is DHTML-compatible
function checkDHTML() {
  if ((parseInt(navigator.appVersion)>=4) &&
     ((navigator.appName!="Netscape" &&
       navigator.appVersion.indexOf("X11") == -1) ||
      (navigator.appName!="Microsoft Internet Explorer" &&
       navigator.appVersion.indexOf("Macintosh") == -1)))
    { return 1 }
  else
    { document.location="nodhtml.htm"; return 0 }
}

// Construct a valid reference to a layer
// in either Netscape JavaScript or Microsoft JScript
function makeName(layerID) {
  if (navigator.appName=="Netscape")
    { refname = eval("document." + layerID) }
  else
    { refname = eval("document.all." + layerID + ".style") }
  return refname
}

// Slide over xhop,yhop pixels every delay milliseconds
// until the layer reaches xgoal and ygoal
function slide() {
  if ((parseInt(layername.left) != xgoal) ||
     (parseInt(layername.top) != ygoal))
    { layername.left = parseInt(layername.left) + xhop;
      layername.top = parseInt(layername.top) + yhop;
      window.setTimeout("slide()", delay) }
}
```

You'll see how to use the checkDHTML function on your Web pages momentarily, but first you should know what it does when it detects an incompatible browser. The following line of JavaScript deals with this eventuality:

```javascript
{ document.location="nodhtml.htm"; return 0 }
```

This takes the user to the nodthtml.htm page in Figure 20.5, while sending a signal to the original page to let it know that it shouldn't try to perform any DHTML tricks.

The next function in Figure 20.6, makeName, is pure black magic. To understand the need for it, you have to realize exactly how Microsoft and Netscape's implementations of JavaScript differ when it comes to handling layers.

To change the position of a layer (for example, the layer named `"intro"`), you need some way to say "the top of the layer named intro" and "the left side of the layer named intro" in JavaScript—and that's where the trouble starts. To move the layer down so its top edge is 200 pixels from the top edge of the browser window, you need a different command in Netscape Navigator than in Microsoft Internet Explorer. The Netscape way follows:

```
document.intro.top = 200
```

This is the Microsoft way to say the same thing:

```
document.all.intro.style = 200
```

This clearly makes it a pain in the proverbial Back button to write a script that works with both browsers.

Now for the black magic. If you give the `makeName` function in Figure 20.1 the name `"intro"`, it gives you either `"document.intro"` or `"document.all.intro.style"`, depending on which browser you are using. If you use this result to refer to a layer, it works nicely for Netscapians and Microsofters alike. You will soon see exactly how this works in practice because you're finally ready to see how Dynamic HTML layer animation is accomplished.

Moving a Layer Around with JavaScript

The only two sections of code in Figures 20.3 and 20.6 I haven't explained yet in this hour are the `<body>` tag in Figure 20.3 and the `slide` function in Figure 20.6. Together, they create the effect seen in Figures 20.1 and 20.2: the text layer flying onto the page. The `<body>` tag looks like this:

```
<body OnLoad="if (checkDHTML()) {
 layername=makeName('intro');
 yhop=-2; ygoal=20; xhop=10; xgoal=80; slide() }">
```

Any JavaScript commands you put after OnLoad= in the `<body>` tag are carried out as soon as the Web page is displayed. (OnLoad is also triggered every time the user hits the Reload button in Netscape Navigator or the Refresh button in Microsoft Internet Explorer.)

What does the JavaScript in this OnLoad attribute do? First, it starts the `checkDHTML` function. If this function detects a DHTML-compatible browser, the following steps are carried out:

1. The `makeName` function is given the layer ID `"intro"` so that it can construct the appropriate Netscape or Microsoft version of the layer name. The result is saved as `layername`.

20

2. The numbers -2, 20, 10, and 80 are put into storage boxes (or, if you speak math, *variables*) named yhop, ygoal, xhop, and xgoal. The point is to tell the slide function where you want the layer moved to and how fast to move it (more on that shortly).

3. The slide function is called on to "fly in" the layer.

Here's the slide function from Figure 20.6:

```
function slide() {
  if ((parseInt(layername.left) != xgoal) ¦¦
     (parseInt(layername.top) != ygoal))
   { layername.left = parseInt(layername.left) + xhop;
     layername.top = parseInt(layername.top) + yhop;
     window.setTimeout("slide()", delay) }
}
```

I can't teach enough JavaScript in this hour for you to be able to write your own functions like this, but you can probably get the general gist of how this function works. First, it determines whether the layer referred to by layername is already at the location specified by xgoal and ygoal. If the layer isn't there yet, it moves the layer xhop pixels horizontally and yhop pixels vertically. It then waits for a short time and goes back to the beginning of the function. It keeps on hopping until it reaches the goal.

If xhop is a negative number, the layer will hop to the left instead of to the right. Likewise, the layer will move up instead of down if yhop is negative. The bigger the values of xhop and yhop, the faster the layer will get where it's going. You can also control the length of the pause between hops by changing the value of delay. For example, adding delay=100; to the OnLoad commands just before the slide() would cause a 100-millisecond (1/10th of a second) delay between each step in the layer movement.

In the example page from Figure 20.3, the <div style> attribute initially places the "intro" layer at the x,y pixel location (-260,88). In the <body OnLoad> attribute, xgoal and ygoal are set to (80,20), while xhop and yhop are set to (10,-2). The slide moves the layer from (-260,88) to each of the following positions, one after the other, until it finally reaches (80,20):

```
(-250,86)    (-240,84) (-230,82) (-220,80) ... etc.
```

I had to be very careful when I chose the values for xhop and yhop because they must reach the xgoal and ygoal in exactly the same number of steps. If I had used (9,-3) instead of (10,-2), the layer would never land on the spot (80,20) and would therefore never stop moving! When you use the slide function for your own animations, be sure to grab a calculator and make sure the two sides of the following equation come out to the same number (using the initial x,y position of the layer for xstart and ystart):

```
(xgoal - xstart) / xhop = (ygoal - ystart) / yhop
```

I could have added some JavaScript to the slide function to check this automatically, but the whole point is that Dynamic HTML functions can be pretty simple and still get the job done.

If you've programmed in other languages, it may seem strange that there aren't any explicit commands in Figure 20.6 to draw anything on the screen. JavaScript takes care of updating the display automatically as soon as you change the position settings for anything on the Web page.

Interactive Layer Animation

The rest of this hour demonstrates another application of the slide function and shows you how Dynamic HTML can respond to user-initiated events. The goal this time is to modify the XYZ Files example page so that the user can click any of the three file tabs to "pull out" the hidden part of that graphic.

Figures 20.7 and 20.8 show an example: The user clicks the file tab marked X, and that image slides to the right. If the user clicked the tab again, it would slide back into its original location. You could achieve this interactive animation by adding the Dynamic HTML code in Figure 20.9 to the end of the page presented earlier (in Figure 20.3).

FIGURE 20.7

You can make layers respond to the user's actions. Here, the image of the X file slides out in response to a mouse click.

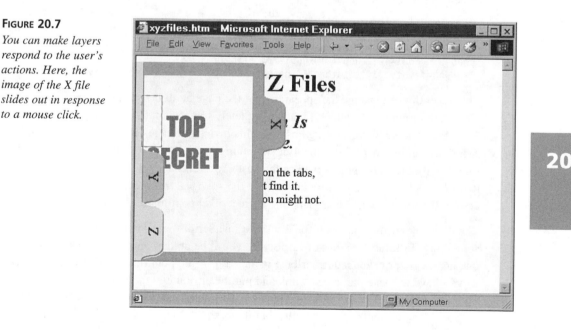

20

FIGURE 20.8

Notice here and in Figure 20.7 that the moving image stays in front of the text but behind the other two images as it slides.

The first `<div>` layer defined in Figure 20.9 enables the file tab marked X to display the behavior you see in Figures 20.7 and 20.8 (and which you can see on your computer screen by clicking the X tab).

```
<div style="position: absolute;
 left: 10px; top: 65px; z-index: 4">
<a href="#" OnClick="layername=makeName('layer1');
 yhop=0; ygoal=10; xhop=40; xgoal=70; slide()">
<img src="empty.gif" width="35" height="85" border="0" /></a></div>
```

This layer doesn't change the appearance of the page at all because it contains only a single image (`empty.gif`), which I made completely transparent before saving it in Paint Shop Pro. The `<div style>` tag positions this invisible image directly over the tab of the X file image, in order to give the user something to click. (It took some trial and error to find exactly the right spot, as well as the best `width` and `height` for the image. To make it easier, I left out the `border=0` attribute of the `<img />` tag, making a visible border around the image, until I had found the correct pixel coordinates for it.)

The `OnClick` attribute lets you specify some JavaScript to respond when the mouse clicks something. In future versions of JavaScript, you'll be able to put an `OnClick`, `OnMouseOver`, or `OnMouseOut` attribute in an `<img />` tag, but for now that doesn't work, so you have to make the image a link and put the attribute in the `<a>` tag. In this case, I didn't want the link to actually go anywhere, so I just used `href="#"` to make a link to the top of the current page (a bit silly, but it works).

FIGURE 20.9

Adding this to the end of the page in Figure 20.3 enables the interactive behavior shown in Figures 20.7 and 20.8.

```
<!-- Use invisible image links to nowhere as triggers
     to pull out and put away the file folders -->
<div style="position: absolute;
 left: 10px; top: 65px; z-index: 4">
<a href="#" OnClick="layername=makeName('layer1');
 yhop=0; ygoal=10; xhop=40; xgoal=70; slide()">
<img src="empty.gif" width="35" height="85" border="0" /></a>
</div>
<div style="position: absolute;
 left: 330px; top: 65px; z-index: 5">
<a href="#" OnClick="layername=makeName('layer1');
 yhop=0; ygoal=10; xhop=-40; xgoal=-250; slide()">
<img src="empty.gif" width="35" height="85" border="0" /></a>
</div>
<div style="position: absolute;
 left: 10px; top: 155px; z-index: 6">
<a href="#" OnClick="layername=makeName('layer2');
 yhop=0; ygoal=10; xhop=40; xgoal=70; slide()">
<img src="empty.gif" width="35" height="85" border="0" /></a>
</div>
<div style="position: absolute;
 left: 330px; top: 155px; z-index: 7">
<a href="#" OnClick="layername=makeName('layer2');
 yhop=0; ygoal=10; xhop=-40; xgoal=-250; slide()">
<img src="empty.gif" width="35" height="85" border="0" /></a>
</div>
<div style="position: absolute;
 left: 10px; top: 245px; z-index: 8">
<a href="#" OnClick="layername=makeName('layer3');
 yhop=0; ygoal=10; xhop=40; xgoal=70; slide()">
<img src="empty.gif" width="35" height="85" border="0" /></a>
</div>
<div style="position: absolute;
 left: 330px; top: 245px; z-index: 9">
<a href="#" OnClick="layername=makeName('layer3');
 yhop=0; ygoal=10; xhop=-40; xgoal=-250; slide()">
<img src= "empty.gif" width="35" height="85" border="0" /></a>
</div>
</body></html>
```

20

You can also use OnClick and other events in the <area> tag of an imagemap (see Hour 14, "Graphical Links and Imagemaps"), which might have been a more elegant way of achieving the result I was after in this example.

Don't forget that you can initiate JavaScript events, including Dynamic HTML animations, in response to form input, too (see Hour 19).

The JavaScript commands in the `<a OnClick>` attribute are very similar to those you saw earlier in the `<body OnLoad>` attribute. The `makeName` function is used to make a valid layer name; `xgoal` and `ygoal` are then set to the destination of the layer, while `xhop` and `yhop` are set to the size of each hop on the way there. (Notice that `yhop` is `0` and `ygoal` is the same as the initial `top:` setting, since the image only moves horizontally.) Finally, `slide` is called on to do the actual animation.

The second `<div>` layer in Figure 20.9 is almost the same, but is located 320 pixels further to the right. The `xgoal` is also 320 pixels further to the left, and `xhop` is `-40` instead of `40`. This gives the user a place to click to put away the file folder image after it has been pulled out.

The remaining four `<div>` layers provide exactly the same interactive behavior for the file tabs marked Y and Z.

Summary

This was undoubtedly the most challenging hour in the book. Don't be surprised or discouraged if you need to read through it more than once and experiment with the example page to begin successfully adapting the Dynamic HTML code to your own purposes.

If you have any experience with computer programming, you probably gleaned enough from this hour and the previous one to start writing your own JavaScript enhancements to your pages. Even if you have never written a line of computer-language code before in your life, you can still copy the code in the book and use it on your own pages.

In this hour, you've seen how to combine HTML, style sheets, and JavaScript to animate independent layers of text and graphics. You learned how to initiate an animation when a page first loads, or in response to a mouse click on any region of the page.

Of course, all this is only the tip of the Dynamic HTML iceberg. Current scripting languages allow you to modify any of the content or formatting of your pages on-the-fly, in response to a wide variety of events. Future versions of JavaScript are likely to make it much easier to do so in a way that is fully compatible with all major Web browsers. The promising future of Dynamic HTML is discussed in Hour 24, "Planning for the Future of HTML."

Q&A

Q Isn't there some way to make layers without using the `style` attribute?

A Only in Netscape Navigator versions 3 and 4. Netscape invented its own `<layer>` tag, which is unlikely to ever become part of the HTML standard or to be supported by other browsers. For more information on this tag, visit `http://developer.netscape.com`.

Q In Hour 16 you stressed the concept of keeping style specifications in a separate document, but in this hour you put all the style stuff right in with the HTML. Aren't you being hypocritical?

A Sort of. It is often a good idea to keep styles in a separate document, and you can combine true style sheets and Dynamic HTML. For example, I could have made a style sheet that included a style like the following:

```
div.peekaboo {position: absolute; left: -250px; top: 10px; width: 300;}
```

I could then have applied that style to each of the three file tab layers with `<div class="peekaboo">`. Doing so, however, would probably have just made the page harder to understand and maintain. When you are working with JavaScript and style-based positioning, I usually find it easier and more efficient to use inline styles than to use separate style sheets.

Q I'm a professional programmer, and I think it was inelegant of you to employ global variables instead of parameter passing in your implementation of the recursive function `slide()`. Furthermore...

A. Was that a question? I didn't think so. Get over it, okay?

Workshop

Quiz

1. Modify the following Web page so that the Balzout Skydiving heading and `fall.gif` image drop into place together from above the top edge of the browser window. (Use the `slide.js` script presented in this hour.)

```
<html><head><title>Take a Dive</title>
</head><body>
<img src="diver.gif" align="left" width="100" height="200" />
<h1>Balzout Skydiving</h1>
Join Richard Balzout for a free chute-packing lesson
on June 15th at the Sewerside Memorial Airfield.
</body></html>
```

20

2. Now modify the page from Question 1 so that clicking the `fall.gif` image makes it leap back out of sight.

Answers

1. The following is one possibility. You could change the speed of the fall by adjusting the value of yhop. (This quiz answer is included in the online examples at `http://24hourHTMLcafe.com/hour20`, by the way.)

```
<html><head><title>Take a Dive</title>
<script src="slide.js" language="javascript">
</script></head><body>
<body OnLoad="if (checkDHTML()) {
 layername=makeName('ComeOnDown');
 yhop=5; ygoal=10; xhop=0; xgoal=10; slide() }">
<div id="ComeOnDown"
 style="position: absolute; left: 10px; top: -210px;">
<img src="diver.gif" align="left" width="100" height="200" />
<h1>Balzout Skydiving</h1></div>
<div style="position: absolute; left: 10px; top: 220px;">
Join Richard Balzout for a free chute-packing lesson
on June 15th at the Sewerside Memorial Airfield.</div>
</body></html>
```

2. Replace the `<img />` tag with the following:

```
<a href="#" OnClick="layername=makeName('ComeOnDown');
 yhop=-10; ygoal=-210; xhop=0; xgoal=10; slide()">
<img src="diver.gif" align="left"
 width="100" height="200" border="0" /></a>
```

Exercise

- Try combining the techniques you learned in this hour with the JavaScript examples in Hour 19. For example, you might create a graphical meter by moving an image up and down on the page in response to a number entered in a form input box. The possibilities are endless, so grab your imagination and get creative!

PART VI

Building a Web Site

Hour

Hour 21

Multipage Layout with Frames

One major limitation of HTML in the old days was that you could see only one page at a time. *Frames* overcome this limitation by dividing the browser window into multiple HTML documents.

Frames are like tables (covered in Hour 15, "Advanced Layout with Tables") in that they allow you to arrange text and graphics into rows and columns. Unlike a table cell, any frame can contain links that change the contents of other frames (or itself). For example, one frame could display an unchanging index page while another frame could change based on which links the reader clicks.

Frames are only supported by Netscape Navigator version 2 or later and Microsoft Internet Explorer version 3 or later. However, you'll see how to provide alternative content for other browsers that don't display frames.

To Do

▼ To Do

Frames are basically a way of arranging and presenting several Web pages at once. You'll be able to learn the material in this hour faster if you have a few related Web pages all ready before you continue.

- If you have an index page or table of contents for your Web site, copy it to a separate directory folder so you can experiment with it without changing the original. Copy a few of the pages that the index links to as well.

- As you read this hour, try modifying the sample frames I present to incorporate your own Web pages.

▲

What Are Frames?

At first glance, Figure 21.1 may look like an ordinary Web page, but it is actually two separate HTML pages, both displayed in the same Netscape Navigator window. Each of these pages is displayed in its own *frame*, separated by a horizontal bar.

NEW TERM   A *frame* is a rectangular region within the browser window that displays a Web page, alongside other pages in other frames.

The main advantage of using frames becomes apparent when a reader clicks one of the links in the top frame of Figure 21.1. The top frame will not change at all in this example, but a new page will be loaded and displayed in the bottom frame, as in Figure 21.2.

Creating a Frameset Document

How did I make the sites in Figures 21.1 and 21.2? First, I created the contents of each frame as an ordinary HTML page. These pages (listed in Figure 21.4) don't contain any tags you haven't already seen in other hours.

To put them all together, I used a special kind of page called a frameset document.

A *frameset document* actually has no content. It only tells the browser which other pages to load and how to arrange them in the browser window. Figure 21.3 shows the frameset document for the Entropy Almanac site in Figures 21.1 and 21.2.

FIGURE 21.1

Frames allow more than one Web page to be displayed at once.

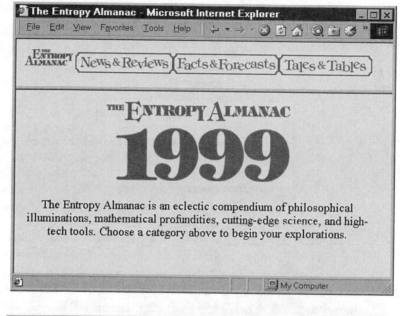

FIGURE 21.2

Clicking Facts & Forecasts in Figure 21.1 brings up a new bottom page, but leaves the top frame the same.

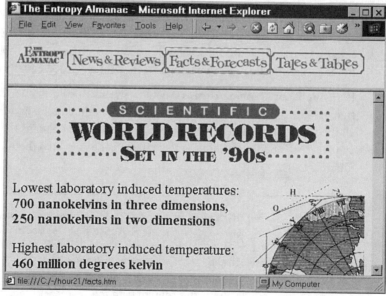

NEW TERM   A *frameset document* is an HTML page that instructs the Web browser to split its window into multiple frames and specifies which Web page should be displayed in each frame.

21

FIGURE 21.3

*If you load this frame-
set document in
Netscape Navigator,
you see the site shown
in Figure 21.1.*

```
<html><head><title>The Entropy Almanac</title></head>
<frameset rows="80,*">
  <frame src="banner.htm" name="top" />
  <frame src="greeting.htm" name="main" />
</frameset>
<noframes>
 <body>
 <h1>The Entropy Almanac</h1>
 Your browser does not support frames.
 Please <a href="noframes.htm">click here</a> for
 the frameless version of this Web site.
 </body>
</noframes>
</html>
```

In Figure 21.3, there is a <frameset> tag instead of a <body> tag. No tags that would
normally be contained in a <body> tag can be within the <frameset> tag. The
<frameset> tag in Figure 21.3 includes a rows attribute, meaning that the frames should
be arranged on top of each other like the horizontal rows of a table. If you want your
frames to be side-by-side, use a cols attribute instead of rows.

You must specify the sizes of the rows or cols, either as precise pixel values or as percentages of the total size of the browser window. You can also use an asterisk (*) to indicate that a frame should fill whatever space is available in the window. If more than one
frame has an * value, the remaining space will be divided equally between them.

In Figure 21.3, <frameset rows="80,*"> means to split the window vertically into two
frames. The top frame will be exactly 80 pixels tall, and the bottom frame will take up
all the remaining space in the window. The top frame contains the document
banner.htm, and the bottom frame contains greeting.htm (both of which are listed in
Figure 21.4).

After the framesets in Figure 21.3, I included a complete Web page between
the <body> and </body> tags. Notice that this doesn't appear at all in Figure
21.1 or 21.2. All Web browsers that support frames will ignore anything
between the <noframes> and </noframes> tags.

Because some browsers still do not support frames, it is probably wise to
include alternative content with the <noframes> tag. If nothing else, just
include a note recommending that people get either Microsoft or Netscape's
browser to see the frames.

Some Web page publishers actually produce two versions of their site—one
with frames, one without. You can save yourself that hassle by simply
including links between all the pages that will appear in your primary frame.

Because you can't predict the size of the window in which someone will view your Web page, it is often convenient to use percentages rather than exact pixel values to dictate the size of the rows and columns. For example, to make a left frame 20 percent of the width of the browser window with a right frame taking up the remaining 80 percent, you would type the following:

```
<frameset cols="20%,80%">
```

An exception to this rule is when you want a frame to contain graphics of a certain size; then you would specify that size in pixels and add a few pixels for the margins and frame borders. This is the case in Figure 21.3, where the images in the top frame are each 42 pixels tall. I allowed 38 extra pixels for margins and borders, making the entire frame 80 pixels tall.

Whenever you specify any frame size in pixels, there must also be at least one frame in the same frameset with a variable (*) width so that the document can be displayed in a window of any size.

The <frame /> Tag

Within the <frameset> and </frameset> tags, you should have a <frame /> tag indicating which HTML document to display in each frame. (If you have fewer <frame /> tags than the number of frames defined in the <frameset> tag, any remaining frames will be left blank.)

Include a src attribute in each <frame> tag with the address of the Web page to load in that frame. (You can put the address of an image file instead of a Web page if you just want a frame with a single image in it.)

You can include any HTML page you want to in a frame. For smaller frames, however, it's a good idea to create documents specifically for the frames with the reduced display area for each frame in mind. The top frame in Figure 21.1, for instance, is listed first in Figure 21.4. It is much shorter than most Web pages because it was designed specifically to fit in a frame less than 80 pixels tall.

You may notice that the <a> and <img /> tags in the banner.htm document in Figure 21.4 are arranged a bit strangely. Since I didn't want any space between the graphics, I had to make sure there were no spaces or line breaks between any of the tags. Therefore, I had to put all the line breaks inside the tags, between attributes. This makes the HTML a bit harder to read, but keeps the images right next to each other on the page.

21

FIGURE 21.4

These two Web pages were designed specifically to fit in frames shown in Figure 21.1. The bottom document in Figure 21.2 is not listed here.

The banner.htm document:

```
<html><head><title>The Entropy Almanac</title></head>
<body background="back.gif">
  <a href="greeting.htm" target="main"
 ><img src="eatiny.gif" border= "0" align="left"
/></a><a href="news.htm" target="main"
 ><img src="news.gif" border="0"
/></a><a href="facts.htm" target="main"
 ><img src="facts.gif" border="0"
/></a><a href="tales.htm" target="main"
 ><img src="tales.gif" border="0" /></a>
</body></html>
```

The greeting.htm document:

```
<html><head><title>The Entropy Almanac</title></head>
<body background="back.gif">
<div align="center">
<img src="easmall.gif" /><br /><img src="1999.gif" />
<p>The Entropy Almanac is an eclectic compendium of
philosophical illuminations, mathematical profundities,
cutting-edge science, and high-tech tools. Choose a
category above to begin your explorations.</p>
</div></body></html>
```

Linking Between Frames and Windows

The real fun begins when you give a frame a name with the name attribute in the
<frame /> tag. You can then make any link on the page change the contents of that
frame by using the target attribute in an <a> tag. For example, Figure 21.3 includes
the following tag:

```
<frame src="greeting.htm" name="main">
```

This displays the greeting.htm page in that frame when the page loads and names the
frame "main".

In the top frame, listed in Figure 21.4, you will see the following link:

```
<a href="facts.htm" target="main"><img src="facts.gif" border=0 /></a>
```

When the user clicks this link, facts.htm is displayed in the frame named main (the
lower frame). To accomplish this sort of interactivity before the invention of frames, you
would have had to use complex programming or scripting languages. Now you can do it
with a simple link!

If the `target="main"` attribute hadn't been included, the `facts.htm` page would have been displayed in the current (top) frame instead.

To save space, I haven't listed the `facts.htm` page in a figure; it's just a regular Web page with no special frame-related features. You can see what the top of it looks like in Figure 21.2, and you can see this whole frameset online at `http://24hourHTMLcafe.com/hour21`.

> Want to open a page into a new window? Get rid of a frameset and go back to displaying a regular single-frame document? Just use one of the following special names with the `target` attribute. (Example: `<a href="popup.htm" target="_blank">Click here to open the popup.htm document in a new window.</a>`)
>
> - `_blank` loads the link into a new, unnamed window.
> - `_top` loads the link into the entire browser window. Use this when you want to get rid of all frames or replace the entire window with a whole new set of frames.
> - `_parent` loads the link over the parent frame if the current frame is nested within other frames. (This name does the same thing as `top` unless the frames are nested more than one level deep.)
> - `_self` loads the link into the current frame, replacing the document now being displayed in this frame. (You'll probably never use this because you can achieve the same thing by simply leaving out the `target` attribute altogether.)
>
> All other names beginning with an underscore (_) will be ignored.

Nested Frames

By nesting one `<frameset>` within another, you can create rather complex frame layouts. For example, the document shown in Figure 21.5 and listed in Figure 21.6 has a total of nine frames. A `cols` frameset is used to split each row of the `rows` frameset into three pieces.

Figure 21.7 lists the HTML for all nine of the separate Web pages shown in Figure 21.5. The corners and side frames contain blank HTML documents, showing nothing more than specially designed background tiles. The top frame is a permanent title graphic, and the bottom frame is a navigation bar similar to the one shown in the previous example. The net effect is to surround the middle frame within a sort of "picture frame" border. Figure 21.8 shows thumbnails of all the background tiles and other graphics incorporated into the pages.

21

FIGURE 21.5

This window contains nine frames, some of which are nothing more than blank pages with custom background tiles.

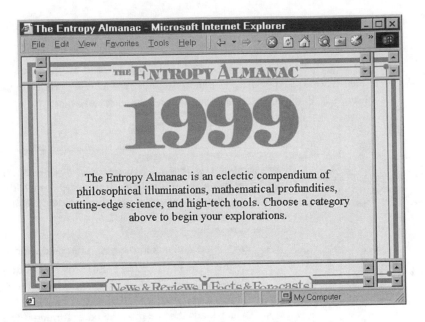

FIGURE 21.6

To create Figure 21.5, I used three horizontal <frameset>s within a vertical <frameset>.

```html
<html><head><title>The Entropy Almanac</title></head>
<frameset rows="43,*,43">
  <frameset cols="43,*,43">
    <frame src="ctoplft.htm" name="toplft" />
    <frame src="bordtop.htm" name="top" />
    <frame src="ctoprgt.htm" name="toprgt" />
  </frameset>
  <frameset cols="43,*,43">
    <frame src="bordlft.htm" name="left" />
    <frame src="main.htm" name="main" />
    <frame src="bordrgt.htm" name="right" />
  </frameset>
  <frameset cols="43,*,43">
    <frame src="cbtmlft.htm" name="btmlft" />
    <frame src="bordbtm.htm" name="btm" />
    <frame src="cbtmrgt.htm" name="btmrgt" />
  </frameset>
</frameset>
</html>
```

FIGURE 21.7

These are the nine separate HTML documents shown in Figure 21.5 and referred to in Figure 21.6.

The ctoplft.htm document:
```
<html><body background="ctoplft.gif"></body></html>
```

The bordtop.htm document:
```
<HTML><HEAD><TITLE>The Entropy Almanac</TITLE></HEAD>
<BODY BACKGROUND="bordtop.gif">
<DIV ALIGN="center">
<A HREF="main.htm" TARGET="main">
<IMG SRC="easmall.gif" BORDER=0></A>
</DIV></BODY></HTML>
```

The ctoprgt.htm document:
```
<html><body background="ctoprgt.gif"></body></html>
```

The bordlft.htm document:
```
<html><body background="bordlft.gif"></body></html>
```

The main.htm document:
```
<HTML><HEAD><TITLE>The Entropy Almanac</TITLE></HEAD>
<BODY BACKGROUND="back.gif">
<DIV ALIGN="center"><IMG SRC="1999.gif"><P>
The Entropy Almanac is an eclectic compendium of
philosophical illuminations, mathematical profundities,
cutting-edge science, and high-tech tools.<P>
Choose a category below to begin your explorations.
</DIV></BODY></HTML>
```

The bordrgt.htm document:
```
<HTML><BODY BACKGROUND="bordrgt.gif"></BODY></HTML>
```

The cbtmlft.htm document:
```
<HTML><BODY BACKGROUND="cbtmlft.gif"></BODY></HTML>
```

The bordbtm.htm document:
```
<HTML><HEAD><TITLE>The Entropy Almanac</TITLE></HEAD>
<BODY BACKGROUND="bordbtm.gif"><DIV ALIGN="center">
<A HREF="news.htm" TARGET="main">
<IMG SRC="news.gif" BORDER=0></A>
<A HREF="facts.htm" TARGET="main">
<IMG SRC="facts.gif" BORDER=0></A>
<A HREF="tales.htm" TARGET="main">
<IMG SRC="tales.gif" BORDER=0></A>
</DIV></BODY></HTML>
```

The cbtmrgt.htm document:
```
<HTML><BODY BACKGROUND="cbtmrgt.gif"></BODY></HTML>
```

21

Figure 21.8

To create the border effect in Figures 21.5 and 21.10, I designed several custom background tiles and matching title graphics.

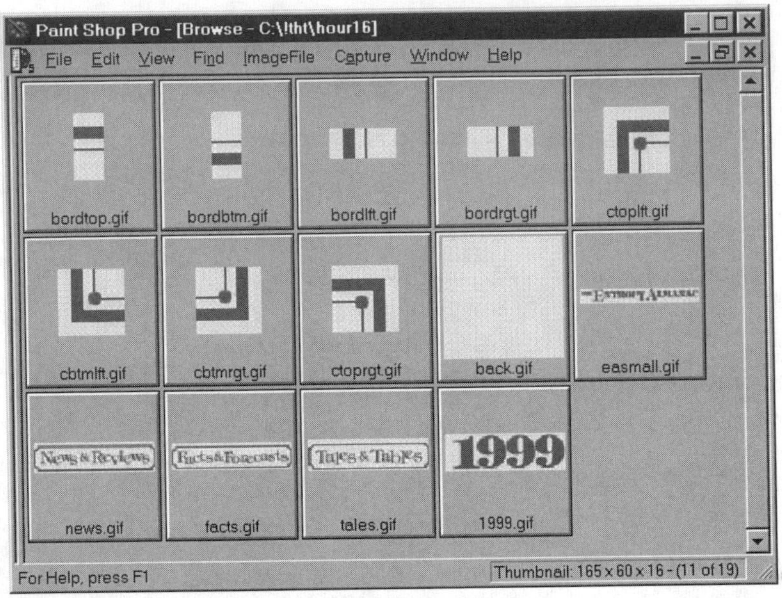

Margins, Borders, and Scrolling

The problem with the nine-frame arrangement in Figure 21.5 is that it looks ugly and stupid. We can fix that.

The ugly parts are the gray dividers between the frames, which completely ruin the effect of surrounding the center frame with nicely designed graphics. There also isn't enough room in the top and bottom frames to display the graphics without scrollbars. Fortunately, there are HTML commands to get rid of the frame dividers, make more space in small frames by reducing the size of the margins, and force frames not to have scrollbars.

Before you read about these HTML magic tricks, take a look at the dramatic results they can achieve. Figure 21.10 is a nine-frame window displaying the same Web pages shown in Figure 21.5. Obviously, Figure 21.10 looks much nicer! In Figure 21.9, you can see the anti-ugliness medication I gave to the frameset code from Figure 21.6.

FIGURE 21.9

Like Figure 21.5, this is actually nine separate Web pages being displayed in nine frames.

```html
<html><head><title>The Entropy Almanac</title></head>
<frameset rows="43,*,43" border="0">
  <frameset cols="43,*,43" border="0">
    <frame src="ctoplft.htm" name="toplft"
     scrolling="no" frameborder="0" />
    <frame src="bordtop.htm" name="top"
     scrolling="no" frameborder="0" marginheight="1" />
    <frame src="ctoprgt.htm" name="toprgt"
     scrolling="no" frameborder="0" />
  </frameset>
  <frameset cols="43,*,43" border="0">
    <frame src="bordlft.htm" name="left"
     scrolling="no" frameborder="0" />
    <frame src="main.htm" name="main" frameborder="0" />
    <frame src="bordrgt.htm" name="right"
     scrolling="no" frameborder="0" />
  </frameset>
  <frameset cols="43,*,43" border="0">
    <frame src="cbtmlft.htm" name="btmlft"
     scrolling="no" frameborder="0" />
    <frame src="bordbtm.htm" name="btm"
     scrolling="no" frameborder="0" marginheight="1" />
    <frame src="cbtmrgt.htm" name="btmrgt"
     scrolling="no" frameborder="0" />
  </frameset>
</frameset>
</html>
```

FIGURE 21.10

This is the frameset document shown in Figure 21.9. By adding some attributes to the <frame /> tags, I was able to make the frames look much nicer.

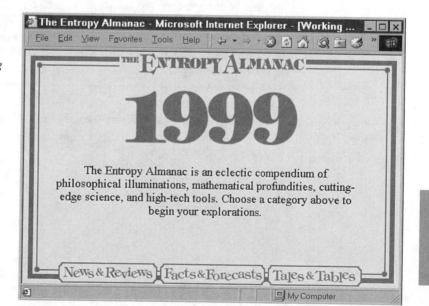

21

In addition to the name attribute, the <frame /> tag can take the following special frame-related attributes:

- marginwidth   Left and right margins of the frame (in pixels).
- marginheight   Top and bottom margins of the frame (in pixels).
- scrolling   Display scrollbar for the frame? ("yes" or "no")
- frameborder   Display dividers between this frame and adjacent frames? (1 means yes, 0 means no)
- noresize   Don't allow this frame to be resized by the user.

marginwidth and marginheight are pretty self-explanatory, but each of the other attributes is discussed in detail in the next few paragraphs.

Normally, any frame that isn't big enough to hold all of its contents will have its own scrollbar(s). The top and bottom frames in Figure 21.5 are examples. If you don't want a particular frame to ever display scrollbars, you can put scrolling="no" in the frame tag. Conversely, scrolling="yes" forces both horizontal and vertical scrollbars to appear, whether they are needed or not.

> When graphics just fit within a small frame, Netscape Navigator and Microsoft Internet Explorer often display scrollbars that only scroll a few pixels down and have no real purpose. Rather than make the frame bigger (and take up valuable window real estate with empty margin space), you will often want to just turn off the scrollbars with scrolling="no".
>
> The only situation I can think of where you might want to use scrolling="yes" is if some graphics won't line up right unless you can count on the scrollbars always being there. Chances are, you'll probably never need scrolling="yes".

People viewing your frames can ordinarily resize them by grabbing the frame border with the mouse and dragging it around. If you don't want anyone messing with the size of a frame, put noresize in the <frame /> tag.

Both Microsoft Internet Explorer and Netscape Navigator allow you to control the size of the frame borders or eliminate the borders altogether. This makes a frame document look just like a regular Web page, with no ugly lines breaking it up.

Unfortunately, you need to use three different sets of HTML tags for maximum compatibility:

- For Microsoft Internet Explorer 3, you can make the borders disappear by including `frameborders="no"` in the `<frameset>` tag.

- For Netscape Navigator and Microsoft Internet Explorer 4, use `border="0"` in the `<frameset>` tag to eliminate borders, or `border=` followed by a number of pixels to change the size of the frame borders.

- If you want borderless frames to show up in all recent versions of both popular browsers, type `frameborders="no" border="0"` in your `<frameset>` tag.

Guess what? The official HTML 4 standard actually specifies yet another method for eliminating frame borders. To be compatible with that standard, you need to put a `frameborder="0"` attribute in every single `<frame />` tag—not just in the `<frameset>` tags. This doesn't have any effect in any existing browser, but it's a good idea to include it now to avoid future compatibility problems.

The frameset document in Figure 21.10 uses all these methods, just to be thorough. I recommend you do the same.

When used together with custom graphics, borderless frames can allow you to create sites that are easier to navigate and more pleasant to visit. For example, when someone visits the site in Figure 21.10 and clicks one of the navigation choices in the bottom frame, the page he chose comes up in the middle frame quickly because the title graphic, navigation buttons, and border graphics all remain in place. The frames also automatically adapt to changes in the size of the browser window, so the nice "picture frame" effect looks just as good at 1,024×768 resolution as it does at 640×480.

Figure 21.11 shows the result of clicking the "Facts & Forecasts" link in Figure 21.10. Note that the middle frame gets its own scrollbar whenever the contents are too big to fit in the frame.

21

FIGURE 21.11

*Clicking a link at the
bottom of Figure 21.10
brings up a new page
in the middle frame,
without redrawing any
of the other frames.*

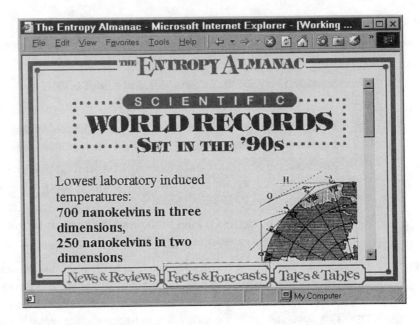

The official HTML 4 standard includes an `<iframe>` tag for embedding a
frame into an HTML page. For example, the following displays the page
`mybio.htm` in a 200×200-pixel region, underneath the heading Short Bios. If
the document `mybio.htm` didn't fit in that small region, it would have its
own little scrollbar(s) next to it.

```
<html><head><title>bios</title></head><body>
<h1>Short Bios</h1>
<iframe name="bioframe" src="mybio.htm" width="200" height="200">
</iframe><p>
<a href="yourbio.htm" target="bioframe" >Your Bio</a><p>
<a href="mybio.htm" target="bioframe">My Bio</a>
</body></html>
```

Clicking the "Your Bio" link would replace the contents of the 200×200-pixel
region with `yourbio.htm`. Clicking "My Bio" would put `mybio.htm` back into
that region.

Unfortunately, the only browser that currently understands the `<iframe>` tag
is Microsoft Internet Explorer. The tag is ignored by Netscape Navigator and
all other current Web browsers, so it isn't of much practical use today unless
all your intended audience uses Internet Explorer version 3 or later. Other
browsers should support it in the future. (You can view an `<iframe>` example
online at `http://24hourHTMLcafe.com/hour21` if you have Microsoft Internet
Explorer.)

Summary

In this hour you learned how to display more than one page at a time by splitting the Web browser window into *frames*. You learned to use a *frameset document* to define the size and arrangement of the frames, as well as which Web page or image will be loaded into each frame. You saw how to create links that change the contents of any frame you choose, while leaving the other frames unchanged. You also discovered several optional settings that control the appearance of resizable borders and scrollbars in frames. Finally, you saw how to nest framesets to create complex frame layouts.

Table 21.1 summarizes the tags and attributes covered in this hour.

TABLE 21.1 HTML Tags and Attributes Covered in Hour 21

Tag	Attribute	Function
`<frameset>...</frameset>`		Divides the main window into a set of frames that can each display a separate document.
	`rows="..."`	Splits the window or frameset vertically into a number of rows specified by a number (such as 7), a percentage of the total window width (such as 25%), or an asterisk (*) indicating that a frame should take up all the remaining space or divide the space evenly between frames (if multiple * frames are specified).
	`cols="..."`	Works similar to rows, except that the window or frameset is split horizontally into columns.
	`framespacing="..."`	Space between frames, in pixels (Microsoft Internet Explorer 3 only).
	`frameborder="..."`	Specifies whether to display a border for the frames. Options are yes and no (Microsoft Internet Explorer 3 only).
	`border="..."`	Size of the frame borders in pixels (Netscape Navigator only).
`<frame />`		Defines a single frame within a `<frameset>`.
	`src="..."`	The URL of the document to be displayed in this frame.

continues

21

TABLE 21.1   continued

Tag	Attribute	Function
	name="..."	A name to be used for targeting this frame with the target attribute in `<a href>` links.
`<marginwidth>`		The amount of space (in pixels) to leave to the left and right side of a document within a frame.
`<marginheight>`		The amount of space (in pixels) to leave above and below a document within a frame.
	scrolling="..."	Determines whether a frame has scroll-bars. Possible values are yes, no, and auto.
	noresize	Prevents the user from resizing this frame (and possibly adjacent frames) with the mouse.
`<noframes>...</noframes>`		Provides an alternative document body in `<frameset>` documents for browsers that do not support frames (usually encloses `<body>...</body>`).
`<iframe>...</iframe>`		Creates an inline frame. Currently only works in Microsoft Internet Explorer version 3 or later.
		(`<iframe>` accepts all the same attributes as does `<frame />`.)

Q&A

Q **Can I display other people's Web pages from the Internet in one frame, and my own pages in another frame at the same time? What if those sites use frames, too?**

A You can load any document from anywhere on the Internet (or an intranet) into a frame. If the document is a frameset, its frames are sized to fit within the existing frame into which you load it.

For example, you could put a hotlist of your favorite links in one frame and have the pages that those links refer to appear in a separate frame. This makes it easy to provide links to other sites without risking that someone will get lost and never come back to your own site. Note, however, that if any link within that site has `target="_top"`, it will replace all your frames.

You should also be aware that framing somebody else's pages so that they appear to be part of your own site may get you in legal trouble. Several major lawsuits are pending on this exact issue, so be sure to get explicit written permission from anyone whose pages you plan to put within one of your frames (just as you would if you were putting images or text from his site on your own pages).

Q Do I need to put a `<title>` in all my frames? If I do, which title will be displayed at the top of the window?

A The title of the frameset document is the only one that will be displayed. `<head>` and `<title>` tags are not required in framed documents, but it's a good idea to give all your pages titles just in case somebody opens one by itself outside any frame.

Workshop

Quiz

1. Write the HTML to list the names Mickey, Minnie, and Donald in a frame taking up the left 25 percent of the browser window. Make it so that clicking each name brings up a corresponding Web page in the right 75 percent of the browser window.

2. Write a frameset document to make the frame layout pictured here:

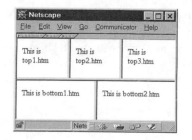

Answers

1. You need five separate HTML documents. The first document is the frameset:

```
<html><head><title>Our Friends</title></head>
<frameset cols="25%,75%">
<frame src="index.htm" />
<frame src="mickey.htm" name="mainframe" />
</frameset>
</html>
```

21

Next, you need the index.htm document for the left frame:

```
<html><head><title>Our Friends Index</title></head>
<body>
Pick a friend:<p>
<a href="mickey.htm" target="mainframe">Mickey</a><p>
<a href="minnie.htm" target="mainframe">Minnie</a><p>
<a href="donald.htm" target="mainframe">Donald</a><p>
</body></html>
```

Finally, you need the three HTML pages named mickey.htm, minnie.htm, and donald.htm. They contain the information about each friend.

2.
```
<html><head><title>Nested Frames</title></head>
<frameset rows="*,*">
 <frameset cols="*,*,*">
  <frame src="top1.htm" />
  <frame src="top2.htm" />
  <frame src="top3.htm" />
 </frameset>
 <frameset cols="*,*">
  <frame src="bottom1.htm" />
  <frame src="bottom2.htm" />
 </frameset>
</frameset>
</html>
```

Exercise

- For now, try your hand at creating a couple of documents using frames. In Hour 23, "Helping People Find Your Web Pages," though, you discover how to make a page that loads another page automatically after a specified time interval. When you combine that trick with frames, you can create all sorts of interesting animated layout effects.

HOUR 22

Organizing and Managing a Web Site

The first 21 hours of this book led you through the design and creation of your own Web pages and the graphics to put on those pages. Now it's time to stop thinking about individual Web pages and start thinking about your Web site as a whole.

This hour shows you how to organize and present multiple Web pages, so that people will be able to navigate among them without confusion. You also read about ways to make your Web site memorable enough to visit again and again.

Because Web sites can be (and usually should be) updated frequently, creating pages that can be easily maintained is essential. This hour shows you how to add comments and other documentation to your pages so that you—or anyone else on your staff—can understand and modify your pages.

To Do

To Do

By this point in the book, you should have enough HTML knowledge to produce most of your Web site. You have probably made a number of pages already, and perhaps even published them online.

As you read this hour, think about how your pages are organized now and how you can improve that organization. Don't be surprised if you decide to do a "redesign" that involves changing almost all of your pages—the results are likely to be well worth the effort!

If you have been using a simple text editor such as Windows Notepad or Macintosh SimpleText to create your HTML pages, this is an excellent time to consider trying out an interactive Web site management software package such as Microsoft FrontPage 2000, Macromedia DreamWeaver, or NetObjects Fusion. Aside from helping you write HTML quickly, these programs offer time-saving ways to modify and keep track of many pages at once.

On the other side of the coin, these programs cost quite a bit of money and are not at all necessary for managing a small- to medium-sized Web site. Unless you plan to have at least 50 Web pages on your site, or unless you were planning to buy Microsoft Office 2000 anyway (in which case you'll get FrontPage 2000 in the bargain), you may save the most time and money by using the simple text editor and file transfer software you already know how to use.

When One Page Is Enough

Building and organizing an attractive and effective Web site doesn't always need to be a complex task. In some cases, you can effectively present a great deal of useful information on a single page, without a lot of flashy graphics. In fact, there are several advantages to a single-page site:

- All the information on the site downloads as quickly as possible.
- The whole site can be printed out on paper with a single print command, even if it is several paper pages long.
- Visitors can easily save the site on their hard drive for future reference, especially if it uses a minimum of graphics.
- Links between different parts of the same page usually respond more quickly than links to other pages.

Figure 22.1 shows the first part of a Web page that serves its intended audience better as a single lengthy page than it would as a multi-page site. It contains about eight paper pages worth of text explaining how to participate in a popular email discussion list.

22

FIGURE 22.1

A good table of contents can make a lengthy page easy to navigate.

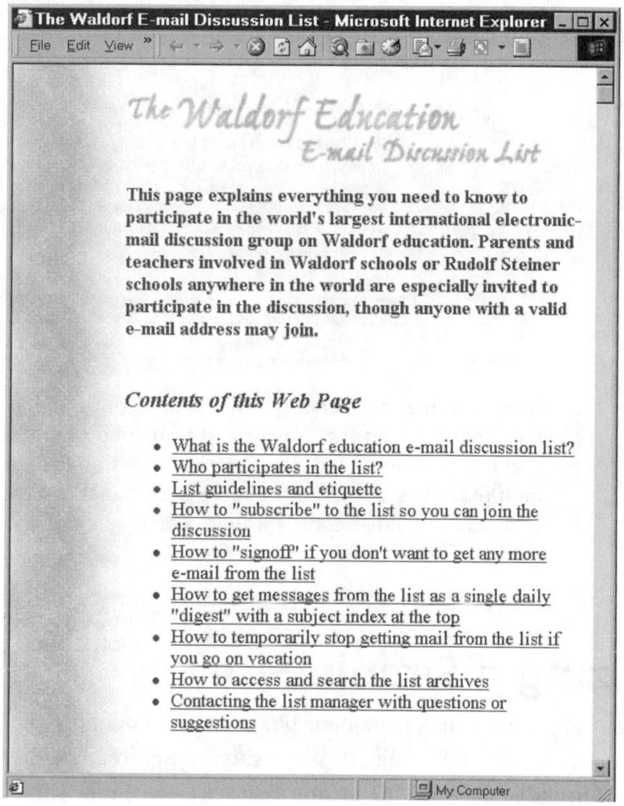

The page begins, as most introductory pages should, with a succinct explanation of what the page is about and who would want to read it. A detailed table of contents allows readers to skip directly to the reference material in which they are most interested. (Refer to Hour 7, "Email Links and Links Within a Page," for a refresher on how to build a table of contents.)

As Figure 22.2 shows, each short section of the page is followed by a link back up to the table of contents, so navigating around the page feels much the same as navigating around a multi-page site. Since the contents of the page are intended as a handy reference, its readers will definitely prefer the convenience of being able to bookmark or save a single page instead of 8 or 10 separate pages.

FIGURE 22.2

Always provide a link to the table of contents after each section of a long Web page.

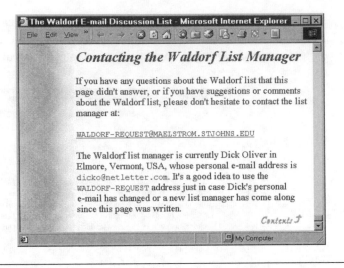

Having seen all the fancy graphics and layout tricks in the book, you may be tempted to forget that a good old-fashioned outline is often the clearest and most efficient way to organize a Web site. Even if your site does require multiple pages, a list like the table of contents in Figure 22.1 may be the best way to guide people through a relatively small Web site—or subsections of a larger one.

Organizing a Simple Site

Although single-page sites have their place, most companies and individuals serve their readers better by dividing their sites into short, quick-read pages with graphical navigation icons to move between the pages. That way, the entire site doesn't have to be downloaded by someone seeking specific information.

The goal of the home page in Figure 22.3, like the goal of many Web sites today, is simply to make the organization "visible" on the Internet. Many people today immediately turn to the World Wide Web when they want to find out about an organization, or find out whether a particular type of organization exists at all. A simple home page should state enough information so that someone can tell whether she wants to find out more. It should then provide both traditional address and telephone contact information and an electronic mail address, either directly on the home page or via a prominent link (like the About New Visions button in Figure 22.3).

FIGURE 22.3

This small-business home page uses distinctive graphics and no-nonsense text to quickly convey the intended mood and purpose.

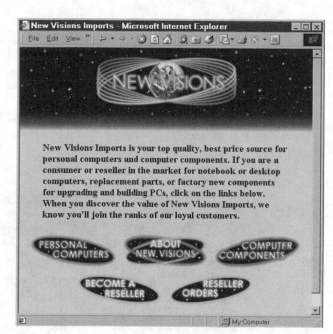

One of the most common mistakes beginning Web site producers make is having each page on the site look different than the one before. Another equally serious mistake is using the same, publicly available "clip art" that thousands of other Web authors are also using. Remember that on the Internet, one click can take you around the world. The only way to make your pages memorable and recognizable as a cohesive site is to make all your pages adhere to a unique, unmistakable visual theme.

For example, when someone clicks the Computer Components link in Figure 22.3, he is taken to the page in Figure 22.4. The visual reiteration of the link as a title and the repetition of the background, logo, and link graphics all make it immediately obvious that this page is part of the same site as the previous page. (Reusing as many graphics from the home page as possible also speeds display since these images are already cached on the reader's computer.)

The page in Figure 22.4 avoids another common disease that beginning Web authors too often catch; I call it the "construction site" syndrome. If you've looked around the Internet very much, I'm sure you're as sick as I am of cute little road worker icons and dead-end pages that say nothing but "Under Construction." Please remember that when you put your pages on the Internet, you are publishing them just as surely as if a print shop were running off 10,000 copies. No publisher would ever annoy readers by printing a brochure, book, or newspaper with useless pages saying only "Under Construction." Don't annoy your readers, either: If a page isn't ready to go online, *don't put it online* until it is ready, and don't put any links to it on your other pages yet.

Even though the page in Figure 22.4 does let the reader know that the site will offer an online parts database in the future, it also makes it clear how to price and order components today.

FIGURE 22.4

Clicking Computer Components in Figure 22.3 takes you here. The graphical theme makes it instantly clear that this is part of the same site.

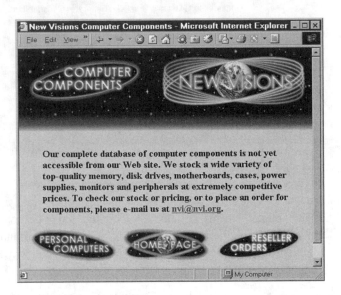

Organizing a Larger Site

For complex sites, sophisticated layout and graphics can help organize and improve the looks of your site when used consistently throughout all of your pages. To see how you can make aesthetics and organization work hand-in-hand, look at a site that needs to present a large volume of information to several different audiences.

Figure 22.5 shows the top part of the Center for Journal Therapy home page. This site currently provides access to the equivalent of about 75 paper pages of text, in the form of 25 electronic documents. As the Center for Journal Therapy continues to publish newsletters, directories, and instructional materials, the site is likely to expand to hundreds of paper pages' worth of information. (If you would like to view this site online, go to http://www.journaltherapy.com.)

FIGURE 22.5

The four links at the top of this page lead to a surprising wealth of information.

The first page a visitor sees should always begin by explaining what the site is about and provide enough introductory information to "hook" the intended audience while getting rid of anyone who really has no interest. The Center for Journal Therapy site does this with a photo and note from Kay Adams, whose face and name are well known by much of the target audience. After the welcome note, the home page offers brief sections with the headings, "What is Journal Therapy?," "About the Center for Journal Therapy," and "About Kathleen Adams," followed by the address, telephone numbers, and email address of the organization. This is a worthy model for any organization's home page to imitate, although in cases where a prominent personality is not a main feature of the site it's usually best to skip the "Welcome" and go straight into the "What is..." introduction.

If there's one thing I would change about the page in Figure 22.5, it would be the lack of emphasis on benefits to the reader. It is absolutely essential— especially for commercial sites or any site intending to serve the needs of some audience—to make the very first words on the page explain *why* it would benefit a reader to look further. Research shows that you have 3 to 5 seconds to convince visitors that your site is worth their attention before they head elsewhere, possibly never to return. Use those seconds wisely! (Hint: Is the phrase "Welcome to the Home Page of..." worth wasting two of those precious seconds on?)

The Center for Journal Therapy site is intended to serve at least three distinct groups: therapists and laypersons just discovering journal therapy, professionals who already use journal therapy in their practice, and journal therapy instructors. Many other Web sites are similar in that they need to address both newcomers and people who are already knowledgeable about the site's subject.

The site in Figures 22.5 and 22.6 is organized into four main categories, accessible through the four "hand written" link icons that appear at the top of each page. It's important to notice that these icons were chosen to give each of the three different audiences a choice that would clearly meet their needs. Always organize the main links on your site according to the questions or desires of your readers, not the structure of the information itself. For example, some of the same information is available in the Resource Center and in the Instructor Center on this site. This redundancy serves both audiences well because it gives them a place to find everything they need without wading through material they aren't interested in.

Figure 22.6 is the page you would get if you clicked Instructor Center, the imagemap in Figure 22.5. The graphics at the top provide a strong visual relationship to the original page, and provide quick access to the rest of the site, including the home page. All the contact information is also repeated at the bottom of the page; it's almost never a bad idea to put your name, address, and phone number on all the major pages of your site if you want to encourage readers to contact you.

The page in Figure 22.6 serves as a passage from the home page to all the resources on the site that are likely to be of interest to journal therapy instructors. Providing topic-specific link pages like this one is a much less confusing way of organizing large quantities of information than some of the alternatives that beginning Web publishers often choose instead. It's all too common to see home pages with a dozen or more links arranged in a long list or string of buttons. That many links all in one group will inevitably confuse readers and make your site hard to use.

In all aspects of your site design, keep in mind the following fact: Studies have repeatedly shown that people become confused and annoyed when presented with more than seven choices at a time, and people feel most comfortable with five or fewer choices. Therefore, you should avoid presenting more than five links (either in a list or as graphical icons) next to one another and never present more than seven at once. When you need to present more than seven text links, break them into multiple lists with a separate heading for each five to seven items.

FIGURE 22.6

You get this page when you click Instructor Center in Figure 22.5.

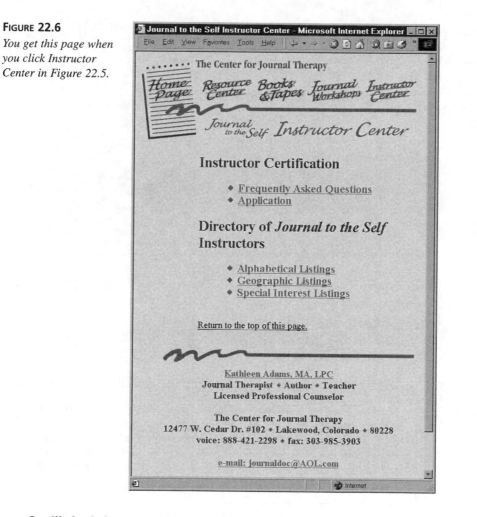

It will also help your readers navigate your site without confusion if you avoid putting any page more than two (or at most three) links away from the home page and always send readers back to a main category page (or the home page) after reading a subsidiary page. Figure 22.7 shows the page you would get by clicking the "Alphabetical Listings" link in Figure 22.6. This page, like all pages in the Center for Journal Therapy Site, is never more than two clicks away from the home page, even though it can be reached by multiple routes.

FIGURE 22.7

Subsidiary pages don't include all the graphics links in Figures 22.5 and 22.6, but they do follow the same visual theme.

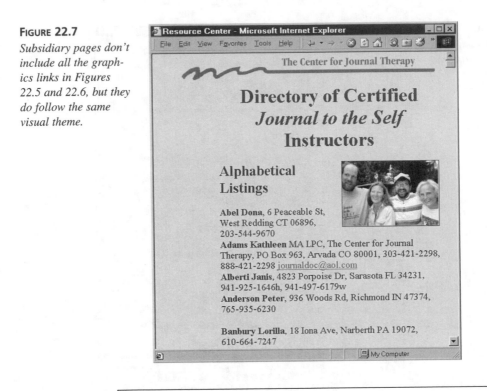

Clicking "The Center for Journal Therapy" at the very top of Figure 22.7 will take the reader back to the home page. The link uses an absolute address (`http://www.journaltherapy.com/`) instead of a relative address (`welcome.htm`), so that anyone who saves the page on his hard drive can still go to the online site by clicking this link. See Hour 3, "Linking to Other Web Pages," for a review of absolute and relative addresses.

Including Comments in a Page

Whenever you type an HTML page, keep in mind that you or someone else will almost certainly need to make changes to it someday. Simple text pages are easy to read and revise, but complex Web pages with graphics, tables, and other layout tricks can be quite difficult to decipher.

As you saw in Hour 20, "Setting Pages in Motion with Dynamic HTML," you can enclose comments to yourself or your co-authors between `<!--` and `-->` tags. These comments will not appear on the Web page when viewed with a browser, but can be read by anyone who examines the HTML code with a text editor, a word processor, or the Web browser's View, Source command.

To include comments in a JavaScript script, put // at the beginning of each comment line. (No closing tag is needed for JavaScript comments.) In style sheets, start comments with /* and end them with */.

The HTML <!-- and --> tags will not work properly in scripts or style sheets!

You can and should, however, include one <!-- tag just after a <script> or <style> tag, with a --> tag just before the matching </script> or </style>. This hides the script or style commands from older browsers that would otherwise treat them as regular text and display them on the page.

To Do

It will be well worth your time now to go through all the Web pages, scripts, and style sheets you've created so far and add any comments that you or others might find helpful when revising them in the future.

1. Put a comment explaining any fancy formatting or layout techniques before the tags that make it happen.

2. Use a comment just before an <img /> tag to briefly describe any important graphic whose function isn't obvious from the alt message.

3. Always use a comment (or several comments) to summarize how the cells of a <table> are supposed to fit together visually.

4. If you use hexadecimal color codes (such as <font color="#8040b0"> or <span style="color: #8040b0">), insert a comment indicating what the color actually is (bluish-purple).

5. Indenting your comments helps them stand out and makes both the comments and the HTML easier to read. Don't forget to use indentation in the HTML itself to make it more readable, too.

Summary

This hour has given you examples and explanations to help you organize your Web pages into a coherent site that is informative, attractive, and easy to navigate.

This hour also discussed the importance of making your HTML easy to maintain by adding comments and indentation to your HTML code.

Q&A

Q **I've seen pages that ask viewers to change the width of their browser window or adjust other settings before proceeding beyond the home page. Why?**

A The idea is that the Web page author can offer a better presentation if he or she has some control over the size of reader's windows or fonts. Of course, nobody ever bothers to change his settings, so these sites always look weird or unreadable. You'll be much better off using the tips you learn in this book to make your site readable and attractive at any window size and a wide variety of browser settings.

Q **Won't lots of comments and spaces make my pages load slower when someone views them?**

A All modems compress text when transmitting it, so adding spaces to format your HTML doesn't usually change the transfer time at all. You'd have to type hundreds of comment words to cause even one extra second of delay when loading a page. It's the graphics that slow pages down, so squeeze your images as tightly as you can (refer to Hour 13, "Page Design and Layout"), but use text comments freely.

Q **Will you look at my site and give me some suggestions on how to improve it?**

A I'd like to, really. Truly I would. If I looked at all my readers' sites and offered even a tiny bit of wisdom for each, however, I would be at it for hours every day. (Go to http://24hourHTMLcafe.com/mysite.htm for a form in which to tell me your site address. No promises, but I usually find time to take a peek.) I have looked at hundreds of reader sites, and my advice usually amounts to this: Your site looks pretty or ugly and you have the basic idea of HTML, but you need to make it more clear, first, who your site is intended for—in the first sentence or heading; second, what earthly good your site is going to do them; and third, what you want them to do as a result of visiting your site. All the great graphics and HTML-manship in the world can't substitute for clearly and consistently answering those three questions for yourself and for your site's visitors.

Workshop

Quiz

1. What are three ways to help people stay aware that all your pages form a single site?

2. What two types of information should always be included in the home page that people encounter at your site?

3. If you want to say, "Don't change this image of me. It's my only chance at immortality," to future editors of a Web page, but you don't want people who view the page to see that message, how would you do it?

Answers

1. Use consistent background, colors, fonts, and styles.

   Repeat the same link words or graphics on the top of the page the link leads to.

   Repeat the same small header, buttons, or other element on every page of the site.

2. Enough identifying information so that she can immediately see the name of the site and what it is about.

   Whatever the most important message you want to convey to your intended audience is, stated directly and concisely.

3. Put the following immediately before the `<img />` tag:

```
<!-- Don't change this image of me.
     It's my only chance at immortality. -->
```

Exercise

- Grab a pencil (the oldfangled kind) and sketch out your Web site as a bunch of little rectangles with arrows between them. Sketch a rough overview of what each page will look like by putting squiggles where the text goes and doodles where the images go. Each arrow should start at a doodle icon that corresponds to the navigation button for the page the arrow leads to. Even if you have the latest whiz-bang Web site management tools, sketching your site by hand can give you a much more intuitive grasp of which pages on your site will be easy to get to and how the layout of adjacent pages will work together—all before you invest time in writing the actual HTML to connect the pages.

Hour **23**

Helping People Find Your Web Pages

The HTML tags and techniques you discover in this hour won't make any visible difference in your Web pages, but they will help make your Web pages much more visible to your intended audience. For most Web authors, this may be the easiest—but most important—hour in the book. You learn how to make links to your pages appear at all the major Internet search sites whenever someone searches for words related to your topic or company. There are no "magic secrets" that guarantee you'll be at the top of every search list, but there are many reliable and effective techniques you can employ to make sure your site is as easy to find as possible.

This hour also shows you how to make one page automatically load another, how to forward visitors to pages that have moved, and how to document a page's full Internet address.

Publicizing Your Web Site

Presumably, you want your Web pages to attract someone's attention or you wouldn't bother to create them. If you are placing your pages only on a local network or corporate intranet or are distributing your pages exclusively on disk or by email, helping people find your pages may not be much of a problem. If you are adding your pages to the millions upon millions of others on the Internet, however, bringing your intended audience to your site is a very big challenge indeed.

To tackle this problem, you need a basic understanding of how most people decide which pages they will look at. There are basically three ways that people can become aware of your Web site:

- Somebody tells them about it and gives them the address; they enter that address directly into their Web browser.
- They follow a link to your site from someone else's site.
- They find your site listed in a search site such as Yahoo! or HotBot.

You can make all three of them happen more often if you invest some time and effort. To increase the number of people who hear about you through word-of-mouth, well, use your mouth—and every other channel of communication available to you. If you have an existing contact database or mailing list, announce your Web site to those people. Add the site address to your business cards or company literature. Heck, go buy TV ads broadcasting your Internet address if you have the money. In short, do the marketing thing.

Getting links to your site from other sites is also pretty straightforward—though that doesn't mean it isn't a lot of work. Find every other Web site related to your topic and offer to add a link to those sites if they add one to yours. If there are specialized directories on your topic, either online or in print, be sure you are listed. There's not much I can say in this book to help you with that, except to go out and do it.

What I can help you with is the third item: being visible at the major Internet search sites. I'm sure you've used at least one or two of the "big six" search sites: Yahoo!, Alta Vista, HotBot, Excite, InfoSeek, and Lycos. (The addresses of these sites are just what you'd think: `yahoo.com`, `altavista.com`, `hotbot.com`, and so on.)

These sites are basically huge databases that attempt to catalog as many pages on the Internet as possible. They all use automated processing to build the databases, though some (such as Yahoo!) emphasize quality by having each listing checked by a human. Others (such as HotBot) prefer to go for quantity and rely almost entirely on programs called robots or spiders to crawl around the Internet hunting for new pages to index.

NEW TERM A *robot* (also called a *spider*) is an automated computer program that spends all day looking at Web pages all over the Internet and building a database of the contents of all the pages it visits.

As the spiders and humans constantly add to the database, another program, called a search engine, processes requests from people who are looking for Web pages on specific topics. The search engine looks in the database for pages that contain the key words or phrases that someone is looking for and sends that person a list of all the pages that contain those terms.

NEW TERM A *search engine* is an automated computer program that looks in a database index for pages containing specific words or phrases. Some people use the term *Internet directory* to indicate a search engine whose database was built mostly by people instead of robots. (Lately, it's become vogue in some circles to call search engines *portals*.)

23

Listing Your Pages with the Major Search Sites

If you want people to find your pages, you absolutely must submit a request to each of the six major search sites to index your pages. Each of these sites has a form for you to fill out with the address, a brief description of the site, and in some cases a category or list of keywords with which your listing should be associated. These forms are easy to fill out; you can easily do all six of them in an hour with time left over to list yourself at one or two specialized directories you might have found as well. (How did you find the specialized directories? Through the major search sites, of course!)

Even though listing with the major search engines is easy and quick, it can be a bit confusing: Each of them uses different terminology to identify where you should click to register your pages. Table 23.1 may save you some frustration; it includes the address of each major search engine, along with the exact wording of the link you should click to register (as of mid-1999).

TABLE 23.1 Registering Your Site with a Search Engine

Search Engine Address	How to Register Your Page
yahoo.com	Go to the category you want to be listed under and click "Suggest a Site" at the bottom of the page.
altavista.com	Click "Add a Page" in the lower-right corner of the Alta Vista home page.

continues

TABLE 23.1   continued

Search Engine Address	How to Register Your Page
hotbot.com	Click the Add URL button on the far left side of the HotBot home page, just beneath the Advanced Search button.
infoseek.com	Click the "Add URL" link under Tools in the bottom-right corner of the InfoSeek home page.
excite.com	Click "Add URL" in the lower-left part of the Excite home page.
lycos.com	Click "Add Your Site to Lycos" in the bottom center part of the Lycos home page.

NEW TERM   *URL* stands for Uniform Resource Locator, which is just a fancy name for the address of a Web page.

There are sites that provide one form that automatically submits itself to all the major search engines, plus several minor ones. (www.submit-it.com and http://www.liquidimaging.com/submit/ are popular examples.) Many of these sites attempt to sell you a "premium" service that lists you in many other directories and indexes as well. Depending on your target audience, these services may or may not be of value, but I strongly recommend that you go directly to each of the six most popular search sites and use their own forms to submit your requests to be listed. That way you can be sure to answer the questions (which are slightly different at every site) accurately, and you will know exactly how your site listing will appear at each of them.

Wait! Before you rush off this minute to submit your listing requests, read the rest of this hour. Otherwise, you'll have a very serious problem, and you will have already lost your best opportunity to solve it.

To see what I mean, imagine this scenario: You publish a page selling automatic cockroach flatteners. I have a roach problem, and I'm allergic to bug spray. I open my laptop, brush the roaches off the keyboard, log on to my favorite search site, and enter *cockroach* as a search term. The search engine promptly presents me with a list of the first 10 out of 10,254 Internet pages containing the word *cockroach*. You have submitted your listing request, so you know your page is somewhere on that list.

Did I mention that I'm rich? And did I mention that two roaches are mating on my foot? You even offer same-day delivery in my area. Do you want your page to be number 3 on the list, or number 8,542? Okay, now you understand the problem.

Providing Hints for Search Engines

Fact: There is absolutely nothing you can do to guarantee that your site will appear in the top 10 search results for a particular word or phrase in any major search engine (short of buying ad space from the search site, that is). After all, if there were, why couldn't everyone else who wants to be number 1 on the list do it, too? What you can do is avoid being last on the list and give yourself as good a chance as anyone else of being first.

Each search engine uses a slightly different method for determining which pages are likely to be most relevant and should therefore be sorted to the top of a search result list. You don't need to get too hung up about the differences, though, because they all use some combination of the same basic criteria. The following list includes almost everything any search engine considers when trying to evaluate which pages best match one or more keywords. The first three of these criteria are used by every major search engine, and all of them also use at least one or two of the other criteria.

- Do the keywords appear in the `<title>` tag of the page?
- Do the keywords appear in the first few lines of the page?
- How many times do the keywords appear in the entire page?
- Do the keywords appear in a `<meta />` tag in the page?
- How many other pages in my database link to the page?
- How many times have people chosen this page from a previous search list result?
- Is the page rated highly in a human-generated directory?

Clearly, the most important thing you can do to improve your position is to consider what word combinations your intended audience is most likely to enter. I'd recommend that you not concern yourself with common single-word searches; the lists they generate are usually so long that trying to make it to the top is like playing the lottery. Focus instead on uncommon words and two- or three-word combinations that are most likely to indicate relevance to your topic. Make sure those terms and phrases occur several times on your page, and be certain to put the most important ones in the `<title>` tag and the first heading or introductory paragraph.

Some over-eager Web page authors put dozens or even hundreds of repetitions of the same word on their pages, sometimes in small print or a hard-to-see color, just to get the search engines to sort that page to the top of the list whenever someone searches for that word. This practice is called *search engine spamming.*

Don't be tempted to try this sort of thing—all the major search engines immediately delete any page from their database that sets off a "spam detector" by repeating the same word or group of words in a suspicious pattern. It's still fine (and quite beneficial) to have several occurrences of important search words on a page. Make sure, however, that you use the words in normal sentences or phrases, and the spam police will leave you alone.

Of all the search engine evaluation criteria just listed, the use of <meta /> tags is probably the most poorly understood. Some people rave about <meta /> tags as if using them could instantly move you to the top of every search list. Other people dismiss <meta /> tags as ineffective and useless. Neither of these extremes is true.

A <meta /> tag is a general-purpose tag you can put in the <head> portion of any document to specify some information about the page that doesn't belong in the <body> text. Most major search engines allow you to use <meta /> tags to give them a short description of your page and some keywords to identify what your page is about. For example, your automatic cockroach flattener order form might include the following two tags:

```
<meta name="description"
 content="Order form for the SuperSquish cockroach flattener." />
<meta name="keywords"
 content="cockroach, roaches, kill, squish, supersquish" />
```

Always place <meta /> tags *after* the <head>, <title>, and </title> tags but *before* the closing </head> tag.

According to the new XML and XHTML standards, <title> must be the very first tag in the <head> section of every document.

The first of these tags ensures that the search engine has an accurate description of your page to present on its search results list. The second slightly increases your page's ranking on the list whenever any of your specified keywords are included in a search query.

You should always include <meta /> tags with name="description" and name="keywords" attributes in any page that you request a search engine to index. Doing so may not have a dramatic effect on your position in search lists, and not all search engines look for <meta /> tags, but it can only help.

In the unlikely event that you don't want a page to be included in search engine databases at all, you can put the following `<meta />` tag in the `<head>` portion of that page.

`<meta name="robots" content="noindex">`

This causes some search robots to ignore the page. For more robust protection from prying robot eyes, ask the person who manages your Web server computer to include your page address in his or her `robots.txt` file. (She or he will know what that means and how to do it.) All major search spiders will then be sure to ignore your pages.

To give you a concrete example of how to improve search engine results, consider the page in Figures 23.1 and 23.2. This page should be fairly easy to find since it deals with a specific topic and includes several occurrences of some uncommon technical terms for which people interested in this subject would be likely to search. However, there are several things you could do to improve the chances of this page appearing high on a search engine results list.

The contents of the page in Figures 23.3 and 23.4 look to a human being almost the same as the page in Figures 23.1 and 23.2. To search robots and search engines, however, these two pages appear quite different. The following list summarizes the changes and explains why I made each modification:

1. I added some important search terms to the `<title>` tag and the first heading on the page. The original page didn't include the word *fractal* in the first heading—a key position.

2. I added `<meta />` tags to assist some search engines with a description and keywords.

3. I added an `alt` attribute to the first `<img />` tag. Not all search engines read and index `alt` text, but some do.

4. I took out the quotation marks around technical terms (such as `"fractal"` and `"iterated"`) because some search engines consider *"fractal"* to be a different word than *fractal*. I could have used the HTML character entity `&quot;` to make the quotation marks, in which case the search robot would have disregarded them, but I chose instead to simply italicize the words.

5. I added the keyword *fractal* twice to the text in the order form box. I also rearranged the table so this box didn't appear in the HTML code before the `<h1>` heading or the main body text. Since search sites give special importance to words occurring early in the HTML document, it's important not to put table columns (or `<script>` or `<style>` tags) before the text containing your most important search words.

```
<html><head><title>Fractal Central</title></head>
<body background="bacfrac.jpg" text="#003399">
<div align="center">
<img src="fraccent.gif" height="149" width="320" /></div>
<table cellspacing="10">
<tr><td valign="top">
  <table border="2" cellpadding="10" width="133">
  <tr><td align="center">Discover the latest software, books
  and more at our online store.<br /><a href="ordform.htm">
  <img src="ordform.gif" border="0" height="55" width="111" />
  </a></td></tr></table>
</td><td valign="top"><h2>A Comprehensive Guide to the<br />
Art and Science of Chaos and Complexity</h2>
<p>What's that? You say you're hearing about "fractals" and
"chaos" all over the place, but still aren't too sure what they
are? How about a quick summary of some key concepts:</p>
<ol><li><p>Even the simplest systems become deeply complex and
richly beautiful when a process is "iterated" over and over,
using the results of each step as the starting point of the
next. This is how Nature creates a magnificently detailed
300-foot redwood tree from a seed the size of your
fingernail.</p></li>
<li><p>Most "iterated systems" are easily simulated on
computers, but only a few are predictable and controllable.
Why? Because a tiny influence, like a "butterfly flapping it's
wings," can be strangely amplified to have major consequences
such as completely changing tomorrow's weather in a distant
part of the world.</p></li>
<li><p>Fractals can be magnified forever without loss of
detail, so mathematics that relies on straight lines is useless
with them. However, they give us a new concept called "fractal
dimension" which can measure the texture and complexity of
anything from coastlines to storm clouds.</p></li>
<li><p>While fractals win prizes at graphics shows, their
chaotic patterns pop up in every branch of science. Physicists
find beautiful artwork coming out of their plotters. "Strange
attractors" with fractal turbulence appear in celestial
mechanics. Biologists diagnose "dynamical diseases" when
fractal rhythms fall out of sync. Even pure mathematicians go
on tour with dazzling videos of their research.</p></li>
</ol><p>Think all these folks may be on to something?</p>
<div align="center"><ahref="http://netletter.com/nonsense/">
<img src="findout.gif" height="20" width="150" border="0" />
</a></div>
</td></tr></table></body></html>
```

It is impossible to quantify how much more frequently people searching for information on fractals and chaos were able to find the page in Figure 23.3 versus the page in Figure 23.1, but it's a sure bet that none of the changes could do anything but improve the page's visibility to search engines. As is often the case, the improvements made for the benefit of the search spiders probably made the page's subject easier for humans to recognize and understand as well.

FIGURE 23.2

The first part of the page in Figure 23.1, as it appears in a Web browser.

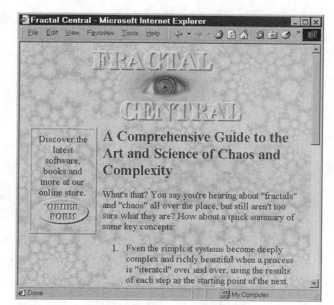

23

FIGURE 23.3

This page will be easier for people interested in fractals and chaos to find than the page in Figure 23.1.

```
<html><head><title>Fractal Central:
A Guide to Fractals, Chaos, and Complexity</title>
<meta name="description"
 content="A comprehensive guide to fractal geometry,
          chaos science and complexity theory." />
<meta name="keywords"
 content="fractal, fractals, chaos science, chaos theory,
          fractal geometry, complexity, complexity theory" />
</head>
<body background="bacfrac.jpg" text="#003399">
<div align="center">
<img src="fraccent.gif" height="149" width="320"
 alt="Fractal Central" />
<h2>A Comprehensive Guide to Fractal Geometry, Chaos Science
and Complexity Theory</h2>
</div>
<table cellspacing="10"><tr><td valign="top">
<p>What's that? You say you're hearing about <i>fractals</i>
and <i>chaos</i> all over the place, but still aren't too sure

    ...blah, blah, blah...

on tour with dazzling videos of their research.</p></li>
</ol><p>Think all these folks may be on to something?</p>
<div align="center">
<a href="http://netletter.com/nonsense/">
<img src="findout.gif" height="20" width="150" border="0" />
</a></div></td>
<td valign="top">
 <table border="2" cellpadding="10" width="133">
 <tr><td align="center">Discover the latest fractal software,
 books and more at the <b>Fractal Central</b> online store.
 <br /><a href="ordform.htm">
 <img src="ordform.gif" border="0" height= "55" width="111" />
 </a></td></tr></table>
</td></tr></table>
</body></html>
```

FIGURE 23.4

The first part of the page in Figure 23.3, as it appears in a Web browser.

If you read the popular science and computer magazines, you have probably found claims that XML, the "HTML of the future," will make it much easier to find what you're looking for on the Internet. You might be wondering how to get the Web pages you create hooked up to this magical new searching miracle.

The good news is that XML will indeed eventually make online searching easier and more efficient. You'll read more about how XML works and how it achieves this and other goals in Hour 24, "Planning for the Future of HTML." The bad news is that neither XML nor its young offspring, XHTML, can make it any easier for people to find your pages today or even this year.

While you're waiting for The Next Big Thing to hit, you might want to keep an eye on future developments in Web searching by stopping by the Search Engine Watch site at http://www.searchenginewatch.com every month or so.

Loading Another Page Automatically

When you are managing a Web site, it may become necessary to move some pages from one address to another. You might decide, for example, to change the service provider or your whole site's domain name. You might just reorganize things and move some pages into a different directory folder.

What happens, then, when someone visits his or her favorite Web page on your site after you've moved it? If you don't want your visitor to be stranded with a Not Found error message, you should put a page at the old address that says, "This page has moved to..." with the new address (and a link to it).

Chances are, you've encountered similar messages on the Internet yourself. Some of them probably employed the neat trick you're about to learn; they automatically transferred you to the new address after a few seconds, even if you didn't click a link.

In fact, you can make any page automatically load any other page after an amount of time you choose. The secret to this trick is the <meta /> tag, which goes in the <head> section of a page and looks like the following:

```
<meta http-equiv="refresh" content="5; nextpage.htm" />
```

Replace 5 with the number of seconds to wait before loading the next page and replace *nextpage.htm* with the address of the next page to load.

For example, the page listed in Figure 23.5 looks like Figure 23.6 when viewed in a Web browser. After 5 seconds (during which a GIF animation counts down from 5 to 0), the <meta /> tag causes the page at http://netletter.com/nicholas/ (Figures 23.7 and 23.8) to appear.

For the impatient, I also included a link to the netletter.com/nicholas page, which someone could click before the five seconds are up. Also, some very old Web browsers don't recognize <meta />, so you should always put a normal link on the page leading to the same address as the <meta /> refresh tag.

FIGURE 23.5

The <meta /> tag causes the Web browser to automatically load the page shown in Figure 23.7 after five seconds.

```
<html><head><title>New Address Notice</title>
<meta http-equiv="refresh"
 content="6; URL=http://24hourHTMLcafe.com/hour23/there.htm" />
</head>
<body bgcolor="black" text="silver" link="red" vlink="white">
<div align="center">Nicholas' home page is now located at
<a href="http://24hourHTMLcafe.com/hour23/there.htm">
24hourHTMLcafe.com/hour23/there.htm</a>.
<h2 style="color: red">You will arrive in</h2>
<p><font color="red"><img src="countdn.gif" /></p>
<h2 style="color: red">seconds.</h2>
</div></body></html>
```

FIGURE 23.6

This is the page listed in Figure 23.5. I used a GIF animation (countdn.gif) to entertain readers while they're waiting for the next page.

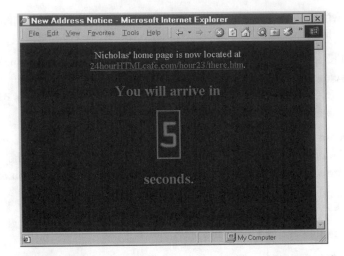

FIGURE 23.7

The <base /> tag in this page has nothing to do with page forwarding. (<base /> is discussed in the next section of this hour.)

```
<HTML><HEAD><TITLE>New Arrival Notice</TITLE>
<BASE HREF="http://24hourHTMLcafe.com/hour23/there.htm">
</HEAD>
<BODY BGCOLOR="black" TEXT="silver" LINK="red" VLINK="white">
<DIV ALIGN="center">
<H2><FONT COLOR="red">You have arrived.<P>
<IMG SRC="nicholas.jpg"><P>So has Nicholas.<BR>
(Age zero and counting.)</FONT></H2>
</DIV></BODY></HTML>
```

Advanced Header Tags

The <meta /> tag can actually be used for a wide variety of purposes. You can use it to specify any information you want about the document, such as the author or a page ID number. How and why you do this is beyond the scope of this introductory book, and very few Web page authors ever use the <meta /> tag for anything other than making their pages easier to find on the Internet.

There are also three other advanced tags for locating and interlinking documents that you may occasionally see in the <head> section of Web pages. Two of them, <isindex> and <nextid>, are considered obsolete and are rarely used by Web page authors today. <link /> is most often used to link a style sheet to a Web page (see Hour 16, "Using Style Sheets"), but can also theoretically be used to document an association between one Web page and another.

FIGURE **23.8**

This is the page listed in Figure 23.7. The page in Figures 23.5 and 23.6 forwards to this page automatically after the five-second delay.

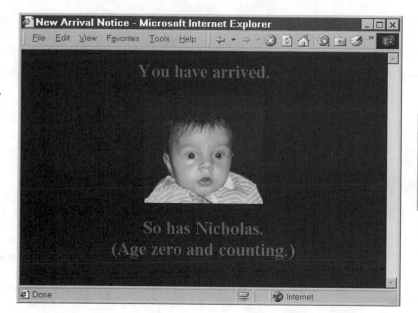

23

This hour's final section discusses one more tag that goes in the <head> section of a document, and one that you may sometimes find useful.

Documenting the Full Address of a Page

Suppose you create a Web page advertising your business, and a customer likes your page so much that she saves it on her hard drive. A couple of days later, she wants to show a friend your cool site, but guess what? She forgot to bookmark it, and of course the page doesn't contain a link to itself. She clicks the links to your order form, but they are only filename links (such as <a href="orderform.htm">); they don't work from her hard drive unless the order form is on her hard drive, too. You have lost two eager customers.

One way to avoid this heartbreaking scenario is to always use complete addresses starting with http:// in all links. However, this makes your pages difficult to test and maintain.

You could also include a link to your home page's full address on every page, including the home page itself. Yet there's a more elegant way to make a page remember where it came from.

The <base /> tag lets you include the address of a page within the <head> section of that page, like this:

```
<html><head>
 <title>My Page</title>
 <base href="http://www.myplace.com/mypage.htm" />
</head>
<body> ...The actual page goes here... </body>
</html>
```

For the HTML authors whose job is to maintain this page, the <base /> tag provides convenient documentation of where this page should be put.

Even more importantly, all links within the page behave as if the page was at the <base /> address—even if it isn't. For example, if you had the page in Figure 23.7 on your hard drive and you opened it with a Web browser, all images on the page would be loaded from the online site at http://netletter.com/nicholas/ rather than from the hard drive. The links would also lead to pages in the nicholas directory at http://netletter.com, instead of pages on the hard drive.

Few Web page authors use (or even know about) the <base /> tag. Many who do know about it don't like the hassle of changing it when they want to test a page (including images and links) on their hard drive. I've tried to give you enough information in this chapter to choose for yourself whether the <base /> tag is worthwhile for you—although I will mention that I never use it myself, nor do any of the professional Web page designers I have worked with.

If you do choose to use the <base /> tag, don't put it in your pages until you're ready to upload them to the Web server. That way you can test them with all the images and link pages on your hard drive and then add the <base /> tag at the last minute, to enjoy the benefits it offers once your pages are online.

Summary

This hour showed you how to make a page remember its own address and how to make a page load another page automatically. It also taught you how to provide hints to search engines (such as HotBot, Alta Vista, Lycos, and Infoseek) so that people can find your pages more easily on the Internet. Table 23.2 lists the tags and attributes covered in this hour.

TABLE 23.2 HTML Tags and Attributes Covered in Hour 23

Tag	Attribute	Function
`<meta />`		Indicates meta-information about this document (information about the document itself). Most commonly used to make a page automatically load another page or reload itself. Used in the document `<head>`.
	`http-equiv="..."`	Gives a command to the Web browser or server. For example, `http-equiv="refresh"` will cause a new page to load automatically.
	`name="..."`	Can be used to specify which type of information about the document is in the content attribute. For example, `name="author"` means the author's name or ID is in `content`.
	`content="..."`	The actual message or value for the information specified in `http-equiv` or name. For example, if `http-equiv="refresh"`, then content should be the number of seconds to wait, followed by a semicolon and the address of the page to load.
`<base />`		Indicates the full URL of the current document. This optional tag is used within `<head>`.
	`href="..."`	The full URL of this document.
`<isindex />`		Indicates that this document is a gateway script that allows searches (very seldom used).
`<nextid />`		Indicates the "next" document to this one (as might be defined by a tool to manage HTML documents in series). `<nextid />` is considered obsolete.
`<link />`		Indicates a link from this entire document to another (as opposed to `<a>`, which can create multiple links in the document); see Hour 16.

23

Q&A

Q I have lots of pages in my site. Do I need to fill out a separate form for each at each search site?

A No. If you submit just your home page (which is presumably linked to all the other pages), the search spiders will crawl through all the links on the page (and all the links on the linked pages, and so on) until they have indexed all the pages on your site.

Q I submitted a request to be listed with a search engine, but my page never comes up, even when I enter my company's unique name. What can I do?

A All the big search engines offer a form you can fill out to instantly check whether a specific address is included in their databases. If you find that it isn't, you can submit another request form. Sometimes it takes days or even weeks for the spiders to get around to indexing your pages after you submit a request. Yahoo! is particularly infamous for being way behind on index requests because they employ human beings to check every page they list.

Q When I put keywords in a `<meta />` tag, do I need to include every possible variation of spelling and capitalization?

A Don't worry about capitalization; almost all searches are entered in all lowercase letters. Do include any obvious variations or common errors in spelling as separate keywords.

Q Can I use the `<meta />` tag to make a page automatically reload itself every few seconds or minutes?

A Yes, but there's no point in doing that unless you have some sort of program or script set up on your Web server computer to provide new information on the page.

Workshop

Quiz

1. If you publish a page about puppy adoption, how could you help make sure the page can be found by people who enter *puppy*, *dog*, and/or *adoption* at all the major Internet search sites?

2. Suppose you recently moved a page from `http://mysite.com/oldplace/thepage.htm` to `http://mysite.com/newplace/thepage.htm`, but you're not quite sure if you're going to keep it there yet. How would you automatically send people who try the old address to the new address, without any message telling them there was a change?

3. What are three ways to make sure that people who save one of your pages on their hard drive can find your site online from it, even if they forget to add it to their Bookmarks or Favorites list?

Answers

1. First, make sure *puppy*, *dog*, and *adoption* all occur frequently on your main page (as they probably already do), and title your page something like Puppy Dog Adoption. While you're at it, put the following `<meta />` tags in the `<head>` portion of the page:

```
<meta name="description"
content="dog adoption information and services" />
<meta name="keywords" content="puppy, dog, adoption" />
```

Finally, put your page online and go to yahoo.com, hotbot.com, altavista.com, lycos.com, excite.com, and infoseek.com to fill out each of their page submission forms.

2. Put the following page at http://mysite.com/oldplace/thepage.htm:

```
<html><head><meta http-equiv="refresh" content="0;
http://mysite.com/newplace/thepage.htm"></head>
</html>
```

To accommodate people using older browsers that don't support `<meta>`, it would be a good idea to also include the following just before the `</html>` tag:

```
<body><a href="http://mysite.com/newplace/thepage.htm">
Click here to get the page you're after.</a></body>
```

3. Include a link to the site, using the full Internet address, on every page. Here is an example:

```
The address of this page is:
<a href="http://mysite.com/home.htm">
http://mysite.com/home.htm</a>
```

Use full Internet addresses in all links between your pages. Here is an example:

```
This is my home page. From here you can
<a href="http://mysite.com/personal.htm">
find out about my exciting personal life</a>, or
<a href="http://mysite.com/work.htm">
find out about my boring work life</a>.
```

Use the `<base />` tag to specify the full Internet address of a page. Here is an example:

```
<head><base href="http://mysite.com/home.htm" />
<title>My Home Page</title></head>
```

23

Exercises

- Can you think of some fun and useful ways to employ automatically changing pages (with the `<meta http-equiv="refresh">` tag)? I bet you can.

- Now that you've made it through all the HTML tutorials in this book, you probably have some fantastic Web pages online. Get on over to those search sites and let the world know you exist!

Hour **24**

Planning for the Future of HTML

Almost everything you have learned in this book is likely to work flawlessly with HTML-compatible software for many years to come. There are tens of millions of pages of information written in standard HTML, and even as that standard evolves, tomorrow's Web browsers and business software will retain the capability to view today's Web pages.

Some of the most exciting applications of HTML, however, are still rapidly developing. This hour introduces the latest HTML extensions and helps you understand what these new capabilities will enable you to do.

To Do

When this hour was written, "now" meant mid-1999. Because you are living in "the future," you can check to make sure my crystal ball wasn't too cloudy, with the help of the following Web sites.

- Your best two sources for the latest HTML standards (and proposed future standards) are the World Wide Web Consortium site

▼   (http://www.w3.org) and the HTML Compendium (http://www.
     htmlcompendium.org).

   • To see how the standards are actually implemented in the latest Web browsers, and
     to see what nonstandard HTML extensions might be available, visit the Microsoft
     (http://www.microsoft.com) and Netscape (http://home.netscape.com) Web
     sites .

▲   You can also get copies of the latest Web browser updates from these two Web sites.

HTML Beyond the Web

The intimate familiarity with HTML you gained from reading this book will be one of
the most important (and profitable) skills that anyone can have in the next few years.
However, most of the HTML pages you create in your lifetime will probably not be Web
pages.

To understand why, and to see the big picture of where HTML is headed, consider the
following features of the latest HTML standard:

   • Through style sheets and scripting, HTML now gives you precise control over the
     appearance and functionality of virtually any textual and graphical information.

   • All major programming languages, interactive media, and database formats can
     also be seamlessly integrated with HTML.

   • HTML's extended character sets and fonts can now be used to communicate in the
     native script of almost any human language in the world.

   • New data security standards are finally making it practical to carry out financial
     and other sensitive transactions with HTML, and to manage confidential or
     restricted-access information.

   • All future versions of the Microsoft Windows operating system will use HTML
     as a fundamental part of the user interface. Nearly all current versions of office
     productivity software also support HTML.

All this adds up to a very near future where HTML will, without a doubt, play a central
role—it might even be accurate to say the central role—in the display and exchange of
almost all information across all computers and computer networks on Earth. This
sounds important because it is important. However, this hour will make a case that
HTML will have an even more important role than that to play. To understand how
that can be so, we'll need to take another step back to see an even bigger picture: the
changing role of the computer itself in our society.

From Calculators to Communicators

The computer was once considered a device for accounting and number crunching. Then it evolved into a device for crunching all types of information, from words and numbers to graphics and sounds. Today and tomorrow, the computer is above all a communications device; its primary use is the transmission of information between people.

In many workplaces today, you can use a computer to access business information every day without knowing much more than how to click links and scroll through long pages—and you can do so without knowing which information is coming from your computer, which is coming from the server down the hall, and which is coming from other servers perhaps thousands of miles away.

Users who become used to seeing highly readable and attractive pages of information on their computer screens are losing the tiny bit of tolerance they have left for cryptic icons, unadorned text messages, and idiosyncratic menu mazes. They will soon expect their computer screens to always be as easy to read and interact with as is the Web.

24

Those who make their millions supplying computer software are well aware of that expectation, and are expending an unprecedented amount of research and development effort toward fulfilling it. Along the way, the central metaphor for interacting with computers has changed from the "window" of the 1980s "desktop" to the "page" of the 1990s "World Wide Web."

HTML as the New User Interface

As the role of the computer evolves, HTML is becoming more and more central to nearly everything we do with computers. HTML is the de facto global standard for connecting all types of information in a predictable and presentable way.

HTML gives you a painless and reliable way to combine and arrange text, graphics, sound, video, and interactive programs. Unlike older proprietary page layout standards, HTML was originally designed for efficient communication among all kinds of computers worldwide.

The prominence of HTML, however, does not mean that Web browsers will be a major category of software application in the coming years. In fact, the "Web browser" as a distinct program has already nearly disappeared. Microsoft Internet Explorer 5, for instance, does much more than retrieve pages from the World Wide Web. It lets you use HTML pages as the interface for organizing and navigating through the information on your own computer, including directory folders and the Windows Desktop itself. In conjunction with HTML-enabled software such as Microsoft Office 2000, HTML becomes the common standard interface for word processing, spreadsheets, and data-bases. Netscape Communicator is also much more than a Web browser. It uses HTML to integrate all types of media into email, discussion groups, schedule management, business documents, and collaborative project management.

Meanwhile, HTML support is being included in every major software release so that every program on your computer will soon be able to import and export information in the form of HTML pages. In a nutshell, HTML is the glue that holds together all the diverse types of information on our computers and ensures that it can be presented in a standard way that will look the same to anyone in the world.

In a business world that now sees fast, effective communication as the most common and most important task of its workers, the "information glue" of HTML has the power to connect more than different types of media. It is the hidden adhesive that connects a business to its customers and connects individual employees to form an efficient team. Knowing how to apply that glue—the skills you gained from this book—puts you in one of the most valuable roles in any modern organization.

The Digital Media Revolution

The most important changes in the next few years might not be in HTML itself, but in the audience you can reach with your HTML pages. Many Web site developers hope that Internet-based content will have enough appeal to become the mass-market successor to television and radio. Less optimistic observers note that the global communications network has a long way to go before it can even deliver television-quality video to most users, or reach a majority of the world's populace at all.

I won't pretend to have a magic mirror that lets me see how and when HTML becomes a mass-market phenomenon, but one thing is certain: All communication industries, from television to telephony, are moving rapidly toward exclusively digital technology. As they do so, the lines between communication networks are blurring. New Internet protocols promise to optimize multimedia transmissions at the same time new protocols allow wireless broadcasters to support two-way interactive transmissions. The same small satellite dish can give you both Internet access and high-definition TV.

Add to this the fact that HTML is the only widely supported worldwide standard for combining text with virtually any other form of digital medium. Whatever surprising turns digital communication takes in the future, it's difficult to imagine that HTML won't be sitting in the driver's seat.

More than a million people can already access the Internet without a "real computer"— via TV set-top boxes and from WebTV, Inc., cable TV companies, digital satellite services, and even telephones and pagers. These devices are only the first wave of much more ubiquitous appliances that provide HTML content to people who wouldn't otherwise use computers.

> The prospect of mass-market HTML access is obviously a great opportunity for HTML page authors. However, it can also present a number of challenges when designing HTML pages because many people might see your pages on low-resolution TV screens or on small hand-held devices. See this hour's "What You Can Do Today to Be Ready for Tomorrow" section for some pointers on making sure your HTML pages can be enjoyed and understood by the widest possible audience.

24

XML: Unity in Diversity

So far in this hour I've noted how HTML is in the right place at the right time to enable several key changes in business and interpersonal communication. As the people and companies of the world become more connected and dependent upon one another, HTML's capability to make all information technology easier to use and less constrained by geography seems almost magical.

Even more magically, HTML has enabled an explosion of new media formats and incompatible file types, while at the same time providing the first truly universal format for exchanging all types of information. The limitations of the HTML language itself have stood in the way of it truly fulfilling this important role, however. To address these limitations, the World Wide Web Consortium has created a new language called *XML*, or *eXtensible Markup Language*.

Before you can understand what XML is and why it may be a key to the future of computer communication, you first have to meet its mother. Her name is *SGML*, or *Standard General Markup Language*. She is a venerable, time-worn standard for describing other mark-up languages. HTML is just one of many languages that can be defined in SGML. Others include specialized languages for library indexing, print publications management, mathematical formulas, molecular chemistry, and so on. Although no one SGML browser can render all these specialized document types, any SGML browser can read the *document type definition* (*DTD*) and figure out how to render those elements of the document type that it understands while ignoring the rest.

It would be ideal if Web browsers could read any SGML document type instead of being limited to HTML documents. The problem with this idea is that SGML is so complex and powerful that it can be very difficult to learn and implement. If this book were about SGML, the title would be something like *Sams Teach Yourself SGML in a Year and a Half*.

XML was created to bridge the gap between HTML, which is easy to learn but kinda wimpy, and SGML, which gives you God-like powers but may require several reincarnations to master. Like SGML, XML allows you to define your own special-purpose tags and implement complex link relationships between documents. Like HTML, XML is simple enough to learn fairly quickly because it avoids all the more esoteric (and least commonly used) aspects of SGML.

XML is a general-purpose language, which includes all the HTML tags but also allows specialized extensions of the language to be easily defined without losing compatibility with the core language. XML standardizes the format of the most common types of information while freely allowing unlimited special cases for proprietary formats and new technology. This means that you can both ensure complete compatibility between the widest variety of software and easily develop unique information formats to meet your individual needs.

The ability to extend HTML pages with custom data types is far more than a way to embed a nifty movie or virtual reality scene into your Web page. To show how much more, the next section of this hour highlights some of the most exciting up-and-coming uses of XHTML and XML.

 Microsoft Internet Explorer 5 is the first widely used Web browser to support some XML capabilities. Netscape is working on a version of its browser, which also implements some or all of the XML 1 standard. For more information on XML, its capabilities, and its implementations, go to the W3C Web site at www.w3c.org.

XHTML, the New HTML

XML does pose a few problems, not the least of which is that the HTML and XML standards are almost—but not quite—compatible with one another. To smooth out these technical bumps, the W3C created a 100 percent XML-compliant version of HTML 4, called (you guessed, didn't you?) XHTML 1.

(Does that mean there will never be an HTML 5 standard? Sort of. There will undoubtedly be more tags and attributes added to HTML in the future, but the result will probably be called XHTML 2 instead of HTML 5.)

The most important thing for you to know about XHTML? How to write your Web pages for compatibility with it, while still remaining compatible with HTML-based Web browsers. If you learned HTML from this book, you have nothing to worry about because every example in the book and on the accompanying Web site (`http://24hourHTMLcafe.com`) is fully compatible with both HTML 4 and XHTML 1. If you have some older HTML pages that you need to convert for XHTML and XML compatibility, the following checklist will get you there:

1. In HTML, it doesn't matter whether tags are uppercase, lowercase, or a mixture of both. In XHTML, all tags must be lowercase. For example, use `<body>` instead of `<BODY>`.

2. Closing tags are often optional in HTML, but are always required in XHTML for any tag that *encloses* (refers to) some content. For example, every paragraph must begin with a `<p>` tag and end with a `</p>` tag. Likewise, every `<li>` list item must have a closing `</li>`, every `<td>` table data cell must have a closing `</td>`, and so forth.

3. HTML tags that don't enclose any content (such as `<br>`, `<hr>`, and `<img>`) must now contain a slash (examples: `<br />` `<hr />` `<img src="pic.gif" />`). This tells XHTML interpreters not to expect a closing tag.

4. In XHTML, all attribute values must be enclosed in quotation marks. For example, `<img src=pic.gif border=1>` was valid HTML, but it must be written as `<img src="pic.gif" border="1" />` to be valid XHTML.

5. All attributes must have values in XHTML. For example, `<input type="checkbox" checked>` should technically now be written as `<input type="checkbox" checked="checked">`.

The preceding XHTML value rule is the only one that causes problems in some current Web browsers, especially pre-1998 Macintosh versions of Microsoft Internet Explorer. You may want to continue to use the old HTML form of valueless attributes for a while longer, until all the people clinging to their hopelessly antiquated, non–XHTML-compatible ways just give up and stop using computers altogether (or until they upgrade their software, whichever comes first).

6. For technical reasons (read: bizarre and confusing reasons we don't need to get into), XHTML uses `<a id="AnchorName"></a>` instead of `<a name="AnchorName"></a>` to create a named anchor. (See Hour 7, " Email Links and Links Within a Page," if you don't quite remember what an anchor is.) This is the only direct contradiction between HTML 4 and XHTML 1, but it's easy enough to be compatible with both. Simply use `<a id="AnchorName" name="AnchorName"></a>`. (This redundancy is a bit of a hassle to type, and to be honest I haven't strictly followed the rule on this one in some of the examples in this book or on my own Web sites, since I doubt anyone will ever actually write software that fails to recognize `name` as meaning the same thing as `id` in this context.)

7. Certain special characters are not allowed in HTML because in context it might be hard to tell if they were meant as part of a mark-up tag. XHTML forbids the same characters, but is much more strict about not allowing them to appear in embedded style sheets and scripts. The forbidden characters and the codes you must replace them with are shown in Table 24.1.

(This is another case where I deserve a little slap on the wrist for not following religiously; for clarity I have used the single quotation mark character instead of `#39;` in some of the JavaScript examples in this book.)

TABLE 24.1 Characters You Should Avoid Using in XHTML Pages

Replace This...	With This...
& (ampersand)	&amp;
" (quotation/inch mark)	&quot;
< (open angle-bracket)	&lt;
> (close angle-bracket)	&gt;
[(open square bracket)	&#91;
] (closed square bracket)	&#93;
' (apostrophe/single-quote)	&#39;

If you have a number of HTML pages that you'd like to convert to XHTML-compatible format, I strongly recommend that you download the free HTML-Kit software from `http://www.chami.com/html-kit/`. This free program includes a module called HTML-Tidy, which automatically changes HTML to conform to the rules mentioned here and also reports any other problems or incompatibilities it finds.

HTML-Kit is also a friendly and well-designed text editor with many handy features for writing new HTML and XHTML pages. I used HTML-Kit 1 to convert and edit every example file in this book, and didn't encounter any bugs or errors; you shouldn't hesitate to trust your precious pages to it. (One caveat: HTML-Tidy changes the line breaks and spacing of your code, so you may have to do some reformatting by hand if you like to neatly indent your code.)

HTML Applications of the Future

The near-universal compatibility of HTML and XML provides a big incentive to format any important document as a Web page—even if you have no immediate plans for putting it on the World Wide Web. You can create a single page that can be printed on paper, sent as an email message, displayed during a board meeting presentation, and posted for reference on the company intranet. You can also take the traditional route and format the page separately for each of these applications—and edit each file with a different software program when the information needs to be updated. Now that most business software supports the HTML standards, many organizations are trying to get employees to consistently use it for all important documents.

Yet the great migration to HTML goes beyond what you might have thought of as "documents" in the old days. Combined with XML, Java, ActiveX, and other new technologies, HTML-based presentations can in many cases replace what was once done with proprietary data formats, specialized software, or more traditional programming languages. Here are a few of the other areas where HTML is finding application beyond the Web:

- *Kiosks* with HTML-based interactive content are popping up everywhere. They look like ATMs on steroids, and they're helping sell records and theme park tickets, expand department store displays, and even automate the paying of parking tickets.

- Information-rich CD-ROM titles are fast migrating to HTML. *Encyclopaedia Britannica* is already entirely HTML-based, which enables it to offer the content on CD-ROM, the Web, or a combination of both for maximum speed and up-to-the-minute currency. Because CD-ROM drives display multimedia so much faster than most Internet connections, dynamic HTML presentations that just couldn't be done on today's World Wide Web become possible. The new DVD-ROM drives will be even faster and will hold much more information, making them ideally suited to large multimedia "sites."

24

- Corporate HTML-based newsletters are now often created in HTML for the company intranet, then printed on paper for delivery to employees or customers who won't see them on the Web. The traditional difference between online and paper presentations was that graphics needed to be high-resolution black-and white for printing and low-resolution color for computer screens. Today's inexpensive color printers, however, do a great job making low-res color images look great in an HTML-based newsletter.

- Teachers are finding that tests and educational worksheets are easier to admin-ister as HTML pages and can include many types of interactive content that isn't possi-ble on paper. Simple HTML documents can be passed out on floppy disks for stu-dents who lack access to the Internet.

- Vertical market users often buy a computer specifically to run a certain custom-designed application or set of applications. The Value-added Resellers and systems integrators that provide these systems are delivering machines configured to start displaying HTML pages. This can help step users through the use of the machine or replace old-fashioned *idiot menus* with a more attractive and sophisticated interface without sacrificing ease of use.

I could list many more creative and beneficial uses of HTML beyond run-of-the-mill Web pages, but the point is clear: If you need to present any type of information, seri-ously consider HTML as an alternative to the specialized software or programming tools that you would have used for the job a couple of years ago.

What You Can Do Today to Be Ready for Tomorrow

If you've made your way through most of this book's hours, you already have one of the most important ingredients for future success in the new digital world: a solid working knowledge of HTML and XHTML.

Chances are that your primary reason for learning HTML at this time was to create some Web pages, but I hope this hour has convinced you that you'll be using XHTML for far more than that in the future. Here are some of the factors you should consider when planning and building your Web site today so that it will also serve you well tomorrow:

- Whenever you run into something that you'd like to do on a Web page, but can't with HTML as it stands today, include a comment in the page so you can add that feature when it becomes possible in the future. The multimedia and interactive portions of your site are likely to need more revisions to keep up with current technology than will the text and graphics portions. When possible, keep the more cutting-edge elements of your site separate and take especially good care to document them well with the `<!--` and `-->` comment tags.

- Although new technologies such as Java and ActiveX might be the wave of the future, avoid them today except when developing for disk-based media or a fast local intranet. Even when everyone is using 56Kbps or faster modems, many people will move on to a different site before they'll wait for an applet or interactive movie to download, initialize, and start working.

- Because style sheets give you complete control over the choice and measurements of type on your Web pages, it is a good idea to study basic typography now if you aren't familiar with it. Understanding and working with things such as *leading*, *kerning*, *em spaces*, and *drop caps* have long been essential for producing truly professional-quality paper pages. It will soon be essential for producing outstanding Web pages, too.

- The potential of JavaScript and other Web page scripting languages is currently hobbled by incompatible and buggy implementations. This should change fast when the new *Document Object Model* (*DOM*) standard comes out in 1999. Learning basic scripting now will put you one step ahead when the first truly standardized version of the language makes a much greater variety of interactive scripting applications possible.

- When you design your pages, don't assume that everyone who sees them will be using a computer. Televisions, video telephones, game consoles, and many other devices might have access to them as well. Some of these devices have very low-resolution screens (with as few as 320×200 pixels). Although it's difficult to design a Web page to look good at that resolution, you'll reach the widest possible audience if you do.

- As older Web browsers fall out of general use, you will be able to layer images and text on top of each other more reliably. That means that many things you need large images for today you will be able to do much more efficiently with several small image elements tomorrow. Always keep copies of each individual image element that goes into a larger graphic, without any text. This will let you easily optimize the graphics later without re-creating everything from scratch.

- Several new standards have been issued or are about to be issued by the World Wide Web Consortium. These include:

   Synchronized Multimedia Interface Language (*SMIL*)

   Mathematics Markup Language (*MathML*)

   eXtensible Style Sheet Language (*XSL*)

   Some early proposals for a graphics markup language

24

On the privacy and security front, new standards include:

Platform for Internet Content Selection (PICS)

Platform for Privacy Preferences (P3P)

Digital Signature standard (*Dsig*)

Since these advances are likely to both expand the potential capabilities of your Web site and change some of the methods you currently use to build Web pages, you should visit the www.w3c.org site and take the time to learn a little about each of them.

> You'll find links to several online reference and learning resources at the *24-Hour HTML Café* at http://24hourHTMLcafe.com.
>
> In addition to providing an easy way to review all the sample pages and HTML techniques covered in this book, this site offers many example pages this book didn't have room for.
>
> You'll also find links to hundreds of Web sites created by this book's readers. You're sure to pick up some great ideas for your own pages!

Summary

This hour has provided a bird's-eye view of the future of HTML. It discussed the new roles that HTML will play in global communications and briefly introduced how HTML relates to the new XML standard. Finally, it offered some advice for planning and constructing Web pages today that will continue to serve you well into the future.

Q&A

Q What is the difference between *digital communication* and other communication, anyway? Does *digital* mean it uses HTML?

A When information is transferred as distinct bits of information, which are essentially numbers, it's called *digital*. It's much easier to store, retrieve, and process information without losing or changing it when it is transferred digitally. Any information from a computer (including HTML) is by its nature digital, and in the not-too-distant future, telephone, television, radio, and even motion picture production will be digital.

Q **How soon can I start designing Internet Web pages that aren't limited by what I can transfer over a 28.8Kbps modem?**

A That depends on who you want to read your pages. There will be millions of 28.8Kbps modems (and the marginally faster 33.6Kbps and 56Kbps modems) in use for many years to come. A growing number of people will have 128Kbps ISDN lines, 400Kbps satellite dishes, and 1Mbps (1,000Kbps) or faster cable, copper-optic, and wireless connections, too. Before long, the number of 1.4Mbps users will just about match the number of 14.4Kbps users. That difference of 100× in speed will lead more and more Web page publishers to offer separate high-speed and low-speed sites.

Q **Man, I'm ashamed of you for not mentioning VRML in an hour about the future of the Internet! What gives?**

A Hey, everyone, did I mention that interactive, immersive three-dimensional worlds will be the future of the Internet? Virtual Reality Modeling Language (VRML) 2 is the current standard for making it happen, and it's compatible with your Web browser today. Unfortunately, VRML isn't quite ready for mass consumption and it's well beyond the scope of this book. If you don't think it's going to change the world, think again. Go to `http://www.vrml.org` to read all about it.

Workshop

Quiz

You've taken 23 quizzes in 24 hours! Instead of taking another, may I suggest that you congratulate yourself for a job well done, take a break, and treat yourself to something special? You deserve it.

Exercise

- Back from your break yet? Now that you've learned HTML and have your Web site online, this book can still help you make it better and better. You may want to review the Q&A sections throughout the book and Appendix A, "Readers' Most Frequently Asked Questions." Be sure to also stick a bookmark at the beginning of Appendix C, the "Complete HTML 4 Quick Reference." Exploring the "Exercises" sections that you might have skipped the first time around will help build your HTML skills as well.

  I'm sure you haven't yet explored all the oodles and oodles of entertaining examples and tutorial tips at the *24-Hour HTML Café*. That's 24hourHTMLcafe.com, where the JavaScript is hot and the HTML never stops flowing. See you there!

24

Part VII

Appendixes

APPENDIX A

Readers' Most Frequently Asked Questions

I have read and carefully collated over 1,000 questions and suggestions sent to me by readers of this book's previous editions. This feedback has influenced everything in this edition, from the overall outline to the specific notes, tips, and quiz questions. I've tried to incorporate the answers to readers' questions into the text at just the point in each hour when you would have found yourself asking those questions.

This appendix is for those times when you may have overlooked or forgotten a key point in the book. It's also a chance for me to answer those questions that just didn't fit under any particular topic. These questions are presented in order of frequency: Number 1 is the most commonly asked question, number 2 is the next, and so on down to number 24. (A good number. I had to stop somewhere!)

In cases where the answer is clearly explained in the book, I just refer you to the relevant part of that hour. In cases where you might need a little more from me, I provide a succinct answer here and may also refer to an online resource that can help.

If you have a question that isn't answered here (or in the rest of the book), please email it to me at `askme@netletter.com`. I can't promise a personal response to every reader (there are a lot of you!), but I will add new questions to the online version of this appendix at the *24-Hour HTML Café* site at `http://24hourHTMLcafe.com/faq.htm`.

The 24 Top Questions from Readers of *Sams Teach Yourself HTML in 24 Hours*

1. **What should I read next?**

   Try *Sams Teach Yourself JavaScript 1.3 in 24 Hours* or *Sams Teach Yourself Paint Shop Pro 6 in 24 Hours*. You can find out more about both books and buy them online at `www.mcp.com`.

2. **I'm stuck on my first page. It didn't work. What did I do wrong?**

   The first page is always the hardest. If you see all the HTML when you try to view the file (by selecting File, Open in your Web browser), or if you see some weird characters at the top of the page, you haven't saved the file in plain text or ASCII text format. If you can't figure out how to do that in your word processor, use the Notepad or SimpleText editor that came with your computer instead. (WordPad is especially problematic in this regard.)

   For more guidance on making your first page, carefully go over the first To Do section and "A Simple Sample Page" in Hour 2, "Create a Web Page Right Now."

   Also, remember that you don't have to be connected to the Internet to edit and view Web pages on your hard drive. (If your Web browser tries to connect to the Internet every time you start it, change the home page in the Edit, Preferences settings to a page on your hard drive.)

3. **Graphics or media files don't work/don't show online.**

   There are several common pitfalls you may encounter when putting graphics on a Web page:

   - Make sure the graphics file is in the same folder as the HTML document that refers to it. (If you're trying to refer to it in a different folder, review the "Relative Addresses" section of Hour 3, "Linking to Other Web Pages.")
   - Make sure the graphics file is saved in GIF or JPEG format. Open the file with Paint Shop Pro (or another graphics program) and use File, Save As to save it again just to be sure.

- Make sure the capitalization of the filename and the `src=` attribute in the `<img />` tag match. `MyImage.gif` and `myimage.GIF` are not the same to most Web servers!

- To get rid of the blue line around a graphic, put `border="0"` in the `<img />` tag.

- This one's unlikely, but possible: Do you have Automatically Load Images turned off under Edit, Preferences, Advanced in Netscape Navigator, or Show Pictures turned off under View, Internet Options, Advanced in Microsoft Internet Explorer?

- True story: One reader spent four days trying to figure out why none of his images worked. He was typing `<img scr=` instead of `<img src=` every single time. Don't laugh—just check *your* page for typos.

Refer to Hour 10, "Putting Graphics on a Web Page." If you're having trouble arranging graphics on the page, you'll find many helpful hints in all four chapters of Part IV, "Web Page Design."

Audio and video files are trickier and more prone to problems. There's no practical way to make them work in every version of every popular browser, but refer to Hour 17, "Embedding Multimedia in Web Pages," for as much help as I can give.

4. **How do I get forms to work on my server?**

   Ask your ISP to help you set up a forms-processing script. If the ISP can't do it, you either need to find an ISP that is willing to actually provide some service or use a third-party form-processing service, such as `www.freedback.com`.

5. **How do I put a counter on my page?**

   You probably don't need one, since most ISPs send you a detailed report each week, summarizing exactly how many times each of your pages was accessed. You should expect (read: demand) this, but some Web hosting services (especially free ones, or those outside North America) just won't provide it. In that case, you need to set up a CGI script on your server. That isn't terribly difficult, and you'll find the code and some advice on how to do it at `www.developer.com` and other Web development sites.

6. **I'm confused about frames. Mine don't work, and I don't understand why. Do you?**

   Frames are tricky. It may take a couple readings of Hour 21, "Multipage Layout with Frames" and some experimentation before something clicks and you see how the whole thing works. Here are some tips that may help:

A

- Remember that you can right-click in any frame and pick View Frame Source in Netscape Navigator or View Source in Microsoft Internet Explorer to see the HTML for that frame. Selecting View, Source from the main menu shows you the HTML for the frameset document.

- The only way to make a link change the contents of two or more frames at once is to link to a new frameset and include `target="_top"` in the `<a>` link tag.

- You also use `target="_top"` when you want to "break out" of all the frames and go back to a regular single-page document.

7. **How do I pursue a career in Web page design, and how much should I charge to make someone a Web page?**

   As in any competitive business (and Web page design is a very competitive business), you need a solid marketing plan to be successful. If you've already found some clients, the amount you charge them is obviously up for negotiation. As a general rule, the going rate for experienced Web developers is between $25 and $50 per hour. If you are still learning, expect to charge less than that, unless you are already a professional graphics or publications designer with a loyal client base.

8. **How do I make password-protected pages?**

   The easiest way is to make up a weird directory name, put the pages in that directory folder on the Web server, and tell the address of the pages only to those who are authorized to access them. More secure methods abound, but all of them require some kind of prewritten script or advanced server software. Consult your ISP to see what kinds of security options it may have available.

9. **Where can I find Java applets/prewritten JavaScript?**

   Try `www.developer.com` and `www.infohiway.com/javascript/indexf.htm`, or look in any of the major Internet search sites under *Java* or *JavaScript*.

10. **I can't get a link to work. What could be wrong?**

    Check the spelling and capitalization of the `href` link and the file to which you're trying to link. Some links will work on your hard drive, but fail on the Web server if the capitalization doesn't match. (This is because Windows doesn't care about capitalization of filenames, and UNIX does.) Also, review Hour 3 to make sure you understand the finer points of relative and absolute addressing.

11. **I am having trouble getting JavaScript/Java/ActiveX code to work, even though I'm pretty sure I got the syntax right.**

Please don't imagine for a moment that Microsoft and Netscape could possibly have bugs in their Web browsers, especially in the sacred Java and JavaScript modules. You are the problem. To redeem yourself, you must build a shrine next to your computer, paste gilt-edged pictures of Bill Gates and Marc Andreessen to it, and humbly offer it cold pizza thrice daily. If you do this with a clean heart and pure mind, all problems with code implementation will still be your own darn fault, but at least Microsoft may decide not to take legal action against you for it.

12. **Where can I get more help creating graphics and multimedia?**

If you use Paint Shop Pro for graphics, try the tutorials at www.jasc.com or read *Creating Paint Shop Pro Web Graphics*, which is available through the JASC online store. Learning to work with audio and video is a more ambitious endeavor, but my *Web Page Wizardry: Wiring Your Site for Sound and Action* gives you a good head start. I also contributed chapters on working online audio and video to *Web Publishing Unleashed: Professional Reference Edition*. Both books can be purchased at www.mcp.com.

13. **How do I put more "bells and whistles" on my site (a chat room, a hit counter, password protection, interactive sound, a pull-down list of links, and things of that nature)?**

Most of those involve JavaScript or CGI scripting (advanced stuff) to make them work. To help you go beyond what this book teaches, I've assembled a list of advanced developer resources at
http://24hourHTMLcafe.com/hotsites.htm#developer.

14. **How do I get a message to scroll along the bottom?**

You'll find JavaScript for that at both www.developer.com and www.infohiway.com/javascript/indexf.htm.

15. **How do I put files on a Web site for download?**

Just upload the file in the same place you put your Web pages and use a regular HTML link, like the following:

```
<a href="bigfile.zip">Click here to download bigfile.zip.</a>
```

16. **How do I put a browser on a disk? Do I need to if I publish Web pages on a disk?**

Most people have a Web browser on their computer these days, but if you want to provide one just in case, you need permission from the browser company. I recommend Opera (www.opera.no), which is small enough to fit on a single 1.4MB floppy disk and allows distribution of free time-limited evaluation copies.

A

17. **When I try to download Paint Shop Pro or the FTP software you recommended, the download is deathly slow or stops altogether. Can you help?**

    I'm afraid there's not much I (or you) can do, except recommend that you try again later. And you thought you needed a car to get in a traffic jam?

18. **Should I use Java applets and other advanced stuff?**

    Not unless you need to do something you can't do any other way. Basic HTML is faster, more widely compatible, and easier to maintain.

19. **How do I make a form for people to fill out and print?**

    They can fill out and print any HTML form. Just tell them to do it. See the Q&A section at the end of Hour 8, "Creating HTML Forms."

20. **How do I justify text so it lines up with both margins?**

    If you have a flat-panel screen, you could try scissors and glue. The CSS2 style sheet standard does support `"text-align: justify"` as a style specification, but none of the popular Web browsers can display full-justified text yet.

21. **How do I publicize my site, and how do I find advertisers for my site?**

    The first section of Hour 23, "Helping People Find Your Web Pages," will help some, but mostly you'll need to come up with your own marketing/PR plan tailored to your specific situation.

    There are a number of Web advertising services and companies that will pay independent Web publishers like you to run ads or affiliate with them in other potentially profitable ways. Most pay you a small amount each time a visitor clicks one of their ads. (See `http://www.sitecash.com/guide.htm` for some possibilities.)

22. **How do I create HTML pages or links within email messages?**

    Just type regular HTML like you would to make a Web page. Most advanced email programs nowadays (especially those bundled with Microsoft Internet Explorer and Netscape Communicator) allow you to create and view HTML Mail. You format it just as you would a document—no HTML experience required.

23. **How do I open a link in a new window?**

    Use `target="_blank"` in your `<a href>` link tag.

24. **How do I link to a database and let people search my site?**

    You'll need to give a software company some money for a good answer to that one. The most common solution these days is to use the FrontPage 2000 server extensions along with a Microsoft Access 2000 database. NetObjects Fusion is another one of the more popular and powerful options. One of many online stores where you can comparison-shop for this type of software is `www.developerdirect.com`

HTML Learning Resources on the Internet

General HTML Information

The 24-Hour HTML Café—the companion site to Sams Teach Yourself HTML 4 in 24 Hours, 4th Edition, including an online version of this appendix:

`http://24hourHTMLcafe.com`

The MCP Web Publishing Resource Center:

`http://www.mcp.com/resources/webdesign/`

The World Wide Web Consortium (W3C):

`http://www.w3.org/`

The Compendium of HTML Elements:
`http://www.htmlcompendium.org/`

Microsoft Internet Explorer Web browser:
`http://www.microsoft.com/windows/ie/`

Netscape DevEdge Online:
`http://developer.netscape.com`

The Developer's JumpStation:
`http://oneworld.wa.com/htmldev/devpage/dev-page.html`

The HTML Writer's Guild:
`http://www.hwg.org/`

The Web Developer's Virtual Library:
`http://WWW.Stars.com/`

Web Page Design

Creating Graphics for the Web:
`http://www.widearea.co.uk/designer/`

Web Page Design Tips:
`http://stoopidsoftware.com/tips/`

Web Page Design Decisions:
`http://www.wilsonweb.com/articles/12design.htm`

Sun Guide to Web Style:
`http://www.sun.com/styleguide/`

A Guide to Creating a Successful Web Site:
`http://www.hooked.net/~larrylin/web.htm`

Web Pages That Suck:
`http://www.webpagesthatsuck.com/`

Software

Paint Shop Pro—a highly recommended Windows graphics and animation editor:
http://www.jasc.com

GIF Construction set—another alternative for creating animated graphics:
http://www.mindworkshop.com/alchemy/gcsdemo.html

Perl Library to Manage CGI and Forms:
http://www.bio.cam.ac.uk/cgi-lib/

Mapedit: A Tool for Windows and X11 for Creating Imagemap Map Files:
http://www.boutell.com/mapedit/

Shareware.com—best source for almost any type of free or inexpensive software for all types of computers:
http://www.shareware.com

The Ultimate Collection of Winsock Software:
http://www.tucows.com/

Dave Central Software Archive:
http://www.davecentral.com/

WinSite Windows Software Archive:
http://www.winsite.com/

Graphics

Cool Graphics on the Web:
http://little.fishnet.net/~gini/cool/

Barry's Clip Art Server:
http://www.barrysclipart.com

256-color square:
http://www59.metronet.com/colors/

Color Triplet Chart:
http://www.phoenix.net/~jacobson/rgb.html

Frequently Asked Questions from comp.graphics:
http://www.primenet.com/~grieggs/cg_faq.html

B

Multimedia and Virtual Reality

Sound Central—free sound files in a variety of formats:
http://www.soundcentral.com

MIDIworld—music files:
http://www.midiworld.com

Stock Video/Film Footage:
http://www.cinema-sites.com/Cinema_Sites_PROD4.html

RealAudio and RealVideo:
http://www.real.com

StreamWorks and XingMPEG:

http://www.xingtech.com

QuickTime:
http://quicktime.apple.com

VDOLive:
http://www.clubvdo.net/

Macromedia's Shockwave:
http://www.macromedia.com/

Multimedia Authoring:
http://www.mcli.dist.maricopa.edu/authoring/

The VRML Repository:
http://www.web3d.org/vrml/vrml.htm

Advanced Developer Resources

Webreference—tutorials and references to HTML and related technologies:
http://www.webreference.com

Cut N' Paste JavaScript—200-plus scripts to cut and paste into your pages:
http://www.infohiway.com/javascript/indexf.htm

Netscape's JavaScript Guide:
http://developer.netscape.com/docs/manuals/communicator/jsguide4/index.htm

Javasoft:
http://www.javasoft.com/

Developer.com Resource Directories:
`http://www.developer.com/directories/`

Tech Tools for Developers:
`http://www.techweb.com/tools/developers/`

NCompass ActiveX Plug-In for Netscape Navigator:
`http://www.ncompasslabs.com/`

A Webmaster's Guide to Search Engines:
`http://searchenginewatch.com/webmasters/index.html`

The TrueDoc Web Typography Center:
`http://www.truedoc.com/webpages/intro/`

Microsoft's TrueType Typography Pages:
`http://www.microsoft.com/truetype/`

HTML Validators

HTML-Kit and HTML Tidy—Web page editor that also converts to XHTML 1:
`http://www.chami.com/html-kit/`

Htmlchek—checks compatibility with older HTML 2 and 3 standards:
`http://uts.cc.utexas.edu/~churchh/htmlchek.html`

Weblint—paid-subscription HTML validation service:
`http://www.unipress.com/cgi-bin/WWWeblint`

B

Directories with HTML Information

Yahoo! World Wide Web:
`http://www.yahoo.com/Computers/Internet/World_Wide_Web/`

HotWired's WebMonkey:
`http://www.webmonkey.com/`

Cool Site of the Day:
`http://cool.infi.net/`

TechWeb's HTML Authoring Tools:
`http://www.techweb.com/tools/html/`

Web Site Services

The List—Internet Service Providers Buyer's Guide:
http://thelist.internet.com/

PointGuide's Partners Program—free personal search engine for your site:
http://www.pointguide.com/partners/

freedback.com—free form-processing service:
http://www.freedback.com

GuestPage—free guestbook service:
http://www.GuestPage.com/

The Counter—free Web counter/tracker:
http://www.TheCounter.com/

Affiliate Guide—info on companies that pay you to promote them on your site:
http://www.sitecash.com/guide.htm

CreditNet—accept and process credit card payments online:
http://www.creditnet.com/

BannerAd Network—advertise your site/exchange ads with other sites:
http://www.banneradnetwork.com/

Add It— register your pages with multiple search sites, free:
http://www.liquidimaging.com/submit/

Submit It!—register your pages with hundreds of search sites, paid service:
http://www.submit-it.com/

Free Web Site Hosting

Geocities:
http://www.geocities.com/

Angelfire:
http://www.angelfire.com/

Cybercities:
http://www.cybercities.com/

Tripod:

`http://www.tripod.com/`

Yahoo!—Free Home Page Service Listings:

`http://www.yahoo.com/Business_and_Economy/Companies/Internet_Services/Web_`
`Services/Free_Web_Pages/`

B

APPENDIX C

Complete HTML 4 Quick Reference

HTML 4 is an ambitious attempt to meet the needs of Web developers worldwide, both casual and professional. XHTML 1 is a reformulation of HTML 4 as an XML 1 application, allowing extensions to the language to be more easily defined and implemented. This appendix provides a quick reference to all the elements and attributes of HTML 4/XHTML 1.

This appendix is based on the information provided in the *HTML 4.0 Specification W3C Recommendation*, revised on April 24, 1998, and the *XHTML 1.0 Specification Working Draft*, revised on May 5, 1999. The latest versions of these standards can be found at `http://www.w3c.org/`.

To make the information readily accessible, this appendix organizes HTML elements by their function in the following order:

- Structure
- Text phrases and paragraphs
- Text formatting elements
- Lists
- Links
- Tables
- Frames
- Embedded content
- Style
- Forms
- Scripts

The elements are listed alphabetically within each section, and the following information is presented:

- Usage—A general description of the element
- Start/End Tag—Indicates whether these tags are required, optional, or illegal
- Attributes—Lists the attributes of the element with a short description of their effect
- Empty—Indicates whether the element can be empty
- Notes—Relates any special considerations when using the element and indicates whether the element is new, deprecated, or obsolete

 Several elements and attributes have been *deprecated*, which means they have been outdated by the current HTML version, and you should avoid using them. The same or similar functionality is provided by using new features.

Following this, the common attributes and intrinsic events are summarized.

> HTML 4 introduces several new attributes that apply to a significant number of elements. These are referred to within each element listing as core, i18n, and events.

Structure

HTML relies on several elements to provide structure to a document (as opposed to structuring the text within) as well as to provide information that is used by the browser or search engines.

\<bdo\>...\</bdo\>

Usage	The bidirectional algorithm element used to selectively turn off the default text direction.
Start/End Tag	Required/Required.
Attributes	core.
	lang="..." The language of the document.
	dir="..." The text direction (ltr, rtl). Mandatory attribute.
Empty	No.
Notes	Strict DTD.

> There are, in fact, three versions of HTML 4: Strict (pure HTML 4), Transitional (elements within the Strict DTD plus additional elements held over from HTML 3.2), and Frameset (Transitional plus frames). Each one relies upon a Document Type Definition to specify which elements and attributes are to be used, and the DTD is noted here.

\<body\>...\</body\>

Usage	Contains the document's content.
Start/End Tag	Optional/Optional.

Attributes	core, i18n, events.
	`background="..."` Deprecated. URL for the background image.
	`bgcolor="..."` Deprecated. Sets background color.
	`text="..."` Deprecated. Text color.
	`link="..."` Deprecated. Link color.
	`vlink="..."` Deprecated. Visited link color.
	`alink="..."` Deprecated. Active link color.
	`onload="..."` Intrinsic event triggered when the document loads.
	`onunload="..."` Intrinsic event triggered when document unloads.
Empty	No.
Notes	Strict DTD. There can be only one <body>, and it must follow the <head>. The <body> element can be replaced by a <frameset> element. The presentational attributes are deprecated in favor of setting these values with style sheets.

Comments <!-- ... -->

Usage	Used to insert notes or scripts that are not displayed by the browser.
Start/End Tag	Required/Required.
Attributes	None.
Empty	Yes.
Notes	Comments are not restricted to one line and can be any length. The end tag is not required to be on the same line as the start tag.

`<div>...</div>`

Usage	The division element is used to add structure to a block of text.
Start/End Tag	Required/Required.
Attributes	core, i18n, events.
	align="..." Deprecated. Controls alignment (left, center, right, justify).

> You will notice that the oft-used align attribute has been deprecated. This affects a large number of elements whose rendered position was controlled by setting the alignment to a suitable value, such as right or center. Also deprecated is the <center> element. The W3C strongly encourages users to begin using style sheets to modify the visual formatting of an HTML document.

Empty	No.
Notes	Strict DTD. Cannot be used within a P element. The align attribute is deprecated in favor of controlling alignment through style sheets.

`<!doctype...>`

Usage	Version information appears on the first line of an HTML document and is an SGML declaration rather than an element.

`<h1>...</h1>` through `<h6>...</h6>`

Usage	The six headings (h1 is uppermost, or most important) are used in the body to structure information in a hierarchical fashion.
Start/End Tag	Required/Required.
Attributes	core, i18n, events.
	align="..." Deprecated. Controls alignment (left, center, right, justify).

Empty	No.
Notes	Strict DTD. Visual browsers will display the size of the headings in relation to their importance, <h1> being the largest and <h6> the smallest. The align attribute is deprecated in favor of controlling alignment through style sheets.

`<head>...</head>`

Usage	This is the document header and contains other elements that provide information to users and search engines.
Start/End Tag	Optional/Optional.
Attributes	i18n.
	profile="..." URL specifying the location of meta data.
Empty	No.
Notes	Strict DTD. There can be only one <head> per document. It must follow the opening <html> tag and precede the <body> tag.

`<hr />`

Usage	Horizontal rules are used to separate sections of a Web page.
Start/End Tag	Required/Illegal.
Attributes	core, events.
	align="..." Deprecated. Controls alignment (left, center, right, justify).
	noshade="..." Displays the rule as a solid color.
	size="..." Deprecated. The size of the rule.
	width="..." Deprecated. The width of the rule.
Empty	Yes.
Notes	Strict DTD.

`<html>...</html>`

Usage	The html element contains the entire document.
Start/End Tag	Optional/Optional.
Attributes	i18n.
	version="..." URL of the document type definition specifying the HTML version used to create the document.
Empty	No.
Notes	Strict DTD. The version information is duplicated in the <!doctype...> declaration and is therefore not essential.

`<meta />`

Usage	Provides information about the document.
Start/End Tag	Required/Illegal.
Attributes	i18n.
	http-equiv="..." HTTP response header name.
	name="..." Name of the meta information.
	content="..." Content of the meta information.
	scheme="..." Assigns a scheme to interpret the meta data.
Empty	Yes.
Notes	Strict DTD.

C

`<span>...</span>`

Usage	Organizes the document by defining a span of text.
Start/End Tag	Required/Required.
Attributes	core, i18n, events.
Empty	No.
Notes	Strict DTD. This element is new to HTML 4.

`<title>...</title>`

Usage	This is the name you give your Web page. The `<title>` element is located in the `<head>` element and is displayed in the browser window title bar.
Start/End Tag	Required/Required.
Attributes	i18n.
Empty	No.
Notes	Strict DTD. Only one title allowed per document.

Text Phrases and Paragraphs

Text phrases (or blocks) can be structured to suit a specific purpose, such as creating a paragraph. This should not be confused with modifying the formatting of the text.

`<abbr>...</abbr>`

Usage	Used to define abbreviations.
Start/End Tag	Required/Required.
Attributes	core, i18n, events.
Empty	No.
Notes	Strict DTD. This element is new to HTML 4. The material enclosed by the tag is the abbreviated form, whereas the long form is defined by attributes within the tag.

`<acronym>...</acronym>`

Usage	Used to define acronyms.
Start/End Tag	Required/Required.
Attributes	core, i18n, events.
Empty	No.
Notes	Strict DTD. This element is new to HTML 4.

`<address>...</address>`

Usage	Provides a special format for author or contact information.
Start/End Tag	Required/Required.
Attributes	core, i18n, events.
Empty	No.
Notes	Strict DTD. The ` ` element is commonly used inside the `<address>` element to break the lines of an address.

`<blockquote>...</blockquote>`

Usage	Used to display long quotations.
Start/End Tag	Required/Required.
Attributes	core, i18n, events.
	cite="..." The URL of the quoted text.
Empty	No.
Notes	Strict DTD.

`<br />`

Usage	Forces a line break.
Start/End Tag	Required/Illegal.
Attributes	core, i18n, events.
	clear="..." Sets the location where next line begins after a floating object (none, left, right, all).
Empty	Yes.
Notes	Strict DTD.

C

`<cite>...</cite>`

Usage	Cites a reference.
Start/End Tag	Required/Required.

Attributes	core, i18n, events.
Empty	No.
Notes	Strict DTD.

`<code>...</code>`

Usage	Identifies a code fragment for display.
Start/End Tag	Required/Required.
Attributes	core, i18n, events.
Empty	No.
Notes	Strict DTD.

`<del>...</del>`

Usage	Shows text as having been deleted from the document since the last change.
Start/End Tag	Required/Required.
Attributes	core, i18n, events.
	cite="..." The URL of the source document.
	datetime="..." Indicates the date and time of the change.
Empty	No.
Notes	Strict DTD. This element is new to HTML 4.

`<dfn>...</dfn>`

Usage	Defines an enclosed term.
Start/End Tag	Required/Required.
Attributes	core, i18n, events.
Empty	No.
Notes	Strict DTD.

\...\

Usage	Emphasized text.
Start/End Tag	Required/Required.
Attributes	core, i18n, events.
Empty	No.
Notes	Strict DTD.

\<ins>...\</ins>

Usage	Shows text as having been inserted in the document since the last change.
Start/End Tag	Required/Required.
Attributes	core, i18n, events.
	cite="..." The URL of the source document.
	datetime="..." Indicates the date and time of the change.
Empty	No.
Notes	Strict DTD. This element is new to HTML 4.

\<kbd>...\</kbd>

Usage	Indicates text a user would type.
Start/End Tag	Required/Required.
Attributes	core, i18n, events.
Empty	No.
Notes	Strict DTD.

\<p>...\</p>

Usage	Defines a paragraph.
Start/End Tag	Required/Optional.

Attributes	core, i18n, events.
	align="..." Deprecated. Controls alignment (left, center, right, justify).
Empty	No.
Notes	Strict DTD.

<pre>...</pre>

Usage	Displays preformatted text.
Start/End Tag	Required/Required.
Attributes	core, i18n, events.
	width="..." The width of the formatted text.
Empty	No.
Notes	Strict DTD.

<q>...</q>

Usage	Used to display short quotations that do not require paragraph breaks.
Start/End Tag	Required/Required.
Attributes	core, i18n, events.
	cite="..." The URL of the quoted text.
Empty	No.
Notes	Strict DTD. This element is new to HTML 4.

<samp>...</samp>

Usage	Identifies sample output.
Start/End Tag	Required/Required.
Attributes	core, i18n, events.
Empty	No.
Notes	Strict DTD.

`<strong>...</strong>`

Usage	Stronger emphasis.
Start/End Tag	Required/Required.
Attributes	core, i18n, events.
Empty	No.
Notes	Strict DTD.

`<sub>...</sub>`

Usage	Creates subscript.
Start/End Tag	Required/Required.
Attributes	core, i18n, events.
Empty	No.
Notes	Strict DTD.

`<sup>...</sup>`

Usage	Creates superscript.
Start/End Tag	Required/Required.
Attributes	core, i18n, events.
Empty	No.
Notes	Strict DTD.

`<var>...</var>`

Usage	A variable.
Start/End Tag	Required/Required.
Attributes	core, i18n, events.
Empty	No.
Notes	Strict DTD.

C

Text Formatting Elements

Text characteristics such as the size, weight, and style can be modified using these elements, but the HTML 4 specification encourages you to use style sheets instead (see Hour 16).

`<b>...</b>`

Usage	Bold text.
Start/End Tag	Required/Required.
Attributes	`core, i18n, events.`
Empty	No.
Notes	Strict DTD.

`<basefont />`

Usage	Sets the base font size.
Start/End Tag	Required/Illegal.
Attributes	`size="..."` The font size (1 through 7 or relative, which is +3).
	`color="..."` The font color.
	`face="..."` The font type.
Empty	Yes.
Notes	Transitional DTD. Deprecated in favor of style sheets.

`<big>...</big>`

Usage	Large text.
Start/End Tag	Required/Required.
Attributes	`core, i18n, events.`
Empty	No.
Notes	Strict DTD.

`<font>...</font>`

Usage	Changes the font size and color.
Start/End Tag	Required/Required.
Attributes	`size="..."` The font size (1 through 7 or relative, which is +3).
	`color="..."` The font color.
	`face="..."` The font type.
Empty	No.
Notes	Transitional DTD. Deprecated in favor of style sheets.

`<i>...</i>`

Usage	Italicized text.
Start/End Tag	Required/Required.
Attributes	`core, i18n, events`.
Empty	No.
Notes	Strict DTD.

`<s>...</s>`

Usage	Strikethrough text.
Start/End Tag	Required/Required.
Attributes	`core, i18n, events`.
Empty	No.
Notes	Transitional DTD. Deprecated.

C

`<small>...</small>`

Usage	Small text.
Start/End Tag	Required/Required.
Attributes	`core, i18n, events`.
Empty	No.
Notes	Strict DTD.

`<strike>...</strike>`

Usage	Strikethrough text.
Start/End Tag	Required/Required.
Attributes	core, i18n, events.
Empty	No.
Notes	Transitional DTD. Deprecated.

`<tt>...</tt>`

Usage	Teletype (or monospaced) text.
Start/End Tag	Required/Required.
Attributes	core, i18n, events.
Empty	No.
Notes	Strict DTD.

`<u>...</u>`

Usage	Underlined text.
Start/End Tag	Required/Required.
Attributes	core, i18n, events.
Empty	No.
Notes	Transitional DTD. Deprecated.

Lists

You can organize text into a more structured outline by creating lists. Lists can be nested.

`<dd>...</dd>`

Usage	The definition description used in a `<dl>` (definition list) element.
Start/End Tag	Required/Optional.
Attributes	core, i18n, events.

Empty	No.
Notes	Strict DTD. Can contain block-level content, such as the <p> element.

<dir>...</dir>

Usage	Creates a multicolumn directory list.
Start/End Tag	Required/Required.
Attributes	core, i18n, events.
	compact="compact" Deprecated. Compacts the displayed list.
Empty	No.
Notes	Transitional DTD. Must contain at least one list item. This element is deprecated in favor of the <ul> (unordered list) element.

<dl>...</dl>

Usage	Creates a definition list.
Start/End Tag	Required/Required.
Attributes	core, i18n, events.
	compact="compact" Deprecated. Compacts the displayed list.
Empty	No.
Notes	Strict DTD. Must contain at least one <dt> or <dd> element in any order.

<dt>...</dt>

Usage	The definition term (or label) used within a <dl> (definition list) element.
Start/End Tag	Required/Optional.
Attributes	core, i18n, events.

C

Empty	No.
Notes	Strict DTD. Must contain text (which can be modified by text mark-up elements).

`<li>...</li>`

Usage	Defines a list item within a list.
Start/End Tag	Required/Optional.
Attributes	`core`, `i18n`, `events`.
	`type="..."` Changes the numbering style (1, a, A, i, I), ordered lists, or bullet style (`disc`, `square`, `circle`) in unordered lists.
	`value="..."` Sets the numbering to the given integer beginning with the current list item.
Empty	No.
Notes	Strict DTD.

`<menu>...</menu>`

Usage	Creates a single-column menu list.
Start/End Tag	Required/Required.
Attributes	`core`, `i18n`, `events`.
	`compact="compact"` Deprecated. Compacts the displayed list.
Empty	No.
Notes	Transitional DTD. Must contain at least one list item. This element is deprecated in favor of the `<ul>` (unordered list) element.

`<ol>...</ol>`

Usage	Creates an ordered list.
Start/End Tag	Required/Required.
Attributes	core, i18n, events.
	type="..." Sets the numbering style (1, a, A, i, I).
	compact Deprecated. Compacts the displayed list.
	start="..." Sets the starting number to the chosen integer.
Empty	No.
Notes	Strict DTD. Must contain at least one list item.

`<ul>...</ul>`

Usage	Creates an unordered list.
Start/End Tag	Required/Required.
Attributes	core, i18n, events.
	type="..." Sets the bullet style (disc, square, circle).
	compact="compact" Deprecated. Compacts the displayed list.
Empty	No.
Notes	Strict DTD. Must contain at least one list item.

Links

Hyperlinking is fundamental to HTML. These elements enable you to link to other documents, other locations within a document, or external files.

`<a>...</a>`

Usage	Used to define links and anchors.
Start/End Tag	Required/Required.

C

Attributes	core, i18n, events.
	charset="..." Character encoding of the resource.
	name="..." Defines an anchor.
	href="..." The URL of the linked resource.
	target="..." Determines where the resource will be displayed (user-defined name, _blank, _parent, _self, _top).
	rel="..." Forward link types.
	rev="..." Reverse link types.
	accesskey="..." Assigns a hotkey to this element.
	shape="..." Enables you to define client-side imagemaps using defined shapes (default, rect, circle, poly).
	coords="..." Sets the size of the shape using pixel or percentage lengths.
	tabindex="..." Sets the tabbing order between elements with a defined tabindex.
Empty	No.
Notes	Strict DTD.

\<base /\>

Usage	All other URLs in the document are resolved against this location.
Start/End Tag	Required/Illegal.
Attributes	href="..." The URL of the linked resource.
	target="..." Determines where the resource will be displayed (user-defined name, _blank, _parent, _self, _top).
Empty	Yes.
Notes	Strict DTD. Located in the document \<head\>.

`<link />`

Usage	Defines the relationship between a link and a resource.
Start/End Tag	Required/Illegal.
Attributes	`core`, `i18n`, `events`.

`href="..."` The URL of the resource.

`rel="..."` The forward link types.

`rev="..."` The reverse link types.

`type="..."` The Internet content type.

`media="..."` Defines the destination medium (`screen`, `print`, `projection`, `braille`, `speech`, `all`).

`target="..."` Determines where the resource will be displayed (user-defined name, `_blank`, `_parent`, `_self`, `_top`).

Empty	Yes.
Notes	Strict DTD. Located in the document `<head>`.

Tables

Tables are meant to display data in a tabular format. Before the introduction of HTML 4, tables were widely used for page layout purposes, but with the advent of style sheets, this is being discouraged by the W3C.

`<caption>...</caption>`

Usage	Displays a table caption.
Start/End Tag	Required/Required.
Attributes	`core`, `i18n`, `events`.

`align="..."` Deprecated. Controls alignment (`left`, `center`, `right`, `justify`).

C

| Empty | No. |
| Notes | Strict DTD. Optional. |

`<col />`

Usage	Groups individual columns within column groups in order to share attribute values.
Start/End Tag	Required/Illegal.
Attributes	core, i18n, events.
	span="..." The number of columns the group contains.
	width="..." The column width as a percentage, pixel value, or minimum value.
	align="..." Horizontally aligns the contents of cells (left, center, right, justify, char).
	char="..." Sets a character on which the column aligns.
	charoff="..." Offset to the first alignment character on a line.
	valign="..." Vertically aligns the contents of a cell (top, middle, bottom, baseline).
Empty	Yes.
Notes	Strict DTD.

`<colgroup>...</colgroup>`

Usage	Defines a column group.
Start/End Tag	Required/Optional.
Attributes	core, i18n, events.
	span="..." The number of columns in a group.
	width="..." The width of the columns.
	align="..." Horizontally aligns the contents of cells (left, center, right, justify, char).

`char="..."`   Sets a character on which the column aligns.

`charoff="..."`   Offset to the first alignment character on a line.

`valign="..."`   Vertically aligns the contents of a cell (`top`, `middle`, `bottom`, `baseline`).

Empty	No.
Notes	Strict DTD. This element is new to HTML 4.

`<table>...</table>`

Usage	Creates a table.
Start/End Tag	Required/Required.
Attributes	`core`, `i18n`, `events`.

`align="..."`   Deprecated. Controls alignment (`left`, `center`, `right`, `justify`).

`bgcolor="..."`   Deprecated. Sets the background color.

`width="..."`   Table width.

`cols="..."`   The number of columns.

`border="..."`   The width in pixels of a border around the table.

`frame="..."`   Sets the visible sides of a table (`void`, `above`, `below`, `hsides`, `lhs`, `rhs`, `vsides`, `box`, `border`).

`rules="..."`   Sets the visible rules within a table (`none`, `groups`, `rows`, `cols`, `all`).

`cellspacing="..."`   Spacing between cells.

`cellpadding="..."`   Spacing in cells.

Empty	No.
Notes	Strict DTD.

C

`<tbody>...</tbody>`

Usage	Defines the table body.
Start/End Tag	Optional/Optional.
Attributes	`core`, `i18n`, `events`.

`align="..."`   Horizontally aligns the contents of cells (`left`, `center`, `right`, `justify`, `char`).

`char="..."`   Sets a character on which the column aligns.

`charoff="..."`   Offset to the first alignment character on a line.

`valign="..."`   Vertically aligns the contents of cells (`top`, `middle`, `bottom`, `baseline`).

Empty	No.
Notes	Strict DTD. This element is new to HTML 4.

`<td>...</td>`

Usage	Defines a cell's contents.
Start/End Tag	Required/Optional.
Attributes	`core`, `i18n`, `events`.

`axis="..."`   Abbreviated name.

`axes="..."`   `axis` names listing row and column headers pertaining to the cell.

`nowrap="..."`   Deprecated. Turns off text wrapping in a cell.

`bgcolor="..."`   Deprecated. Sets the background color.

`rowspan="..."`   The number of rows spanned by a cell.

`colspan="..."`   The number of columns spanned by a cell.

align="..." Horizontally aligns the contents of cells (left, center, right, justify, char).

char="..." Sets a character on which the column aligns.

charoff="..." Offset to the first alignment character on a line.

valign="..." Vertically aligns the contents of cells (top, middle, bottom, baseline).

Empty	No.
Notes	Strict DTD.

\<tfoot\>...\</tfoot\>

Usage	Defines the table footer.
Start/End Tag	Required/Optional.
Attributes	core, i18n, events.

align="..." Horizontally aligns the contents of cells (left, center, right, justify, char).

char="..." Sets a character on which the column aligns.

charoff="..." Offset to the first alignment character on a line.

valign="..." Vertically aligns the contents of cells (top, middle, bottom, baseline).

Empty	No.
Notes	Strict DTD. This element is new to HTML 4.

\<th\>...\</th\>

Usage	Defines the cell contents of the table header.
Start/End Tag	Required/Optional.

Attributes   `core, i18n, events.`

`axis="..."`   Abbreviated name.

`axes="..."`   axis names listing row and column headers pertaining to the cell.

`nowrap="..."`   Deprecated. Turns off text wrapping in a cell.

`bgcolor="..."`   Deprecated. Sets the background color.

`rowspan="..."`   The number of rows spanned by a cell.

`colspan="..."`   The number of columns spanned by a cell.

`align="..."`   Horizontally aligns the contents of cells (`left, center, right, justify, char`).

`char="..."`   Sets a character on which the column aligns.

`charoff="..."`   Offset to the first alignment character on a line.

`valign="..."`   Vertically aligns the contents of cells (`top, middle, bottom, baseline`).

Empty   No.

Notes   Strict DTD.

`<thead>...</thead>`

Usage   Defines the table header.

Start/End Tag   Required/Optional.

Attributes   `core, i18n, events.`

`align="..."`   Horizontally aligns the contents of cells (`left, center, right, justify, char`).

`char="..."`   Sets a character on which the column aligns.

`charoff="..."` Offset to the first alignment character on a line.

`valign="..."` Vertically aligns the contents of cells (`top`, `middle`, `bottom`, `baseline`).

Empty	No.
Notes	Strict DTD. This element is new to HTML 4.

`<tr>...</tr>`

Usage	Defines a row of table cells.
Start/End Tag	Required/Optional.
Attributes	`core`, `i18n`, `events`.

`align="..."` Horizontally aligns the contents of cells (`left`, `center`, `right`, `justify`, `char`).

`char="..."` Sets a character on which the column aligns.

`charoff="..."` Offset to the first alignment character on a line.

`valign="..."` Vertically aligns the contents of cells (`top`, `middle`, `bottom`, `baseline`).

`bgcolor="..."` Deprecated. Sets the background color.

Empty	No.
Notes	Strict DTD.

C

Frames

Frames create new "panels" in the Web browser window that are used to display content from different source documents.

`<frame />`

Usage	Defines a frame.
Start/End Tag	Required/Illegal.

Attributes	name="..." The name of a frame.
	src="..." The source to be displayed in a frame.
	frameborder="..." Toggles the border between frames (0, 1).
	marginwidth="..." Sets the space between the frame border and content.
	marginheight="..." Sets the space between the frame border and content.
	noresize Disables sizing.
	scrolling="..." Determines scrollbar presence (auto, yes, no).
Empty	Yes.
Notes	Frameset DTD. This element is new to HTML 4.

<frameset>...</frameset>

Usage	Defines the layout of frames within a window.
Start/End Tag	Required/Required.
Attributes	rows="..." The number of rows.
	cols="..." The number of columns.
	onload="..." The intrinsic event triggered when the document loads.
	onunload="..." The intrinsic event triggered when the document unloads.
Empty	No.
Notes	Frameset DTD. This element is new to HTML 4. Framesets can be nested.

<iframe>...</iframe>

Usage	Creates an inline frame.
Start/End Tag	Required/Required.

Attributes	`name="..."` The name of the frame.
	`src="..."` The source to be displayed in a frame.
	`frameborder="..."` Toggles the border between frames (`0`, `1`).
	`marginwidth="..."` Sets the space between the frame border and content.
	`marginheight="..."` Sets the space between the frame border and content.
	`scrolling="..."` Determines scrollbar presence (`auto`, `yes`, `no`).
	`align="..."` Deprecated. Controls alignment (`left`, `center`, `right`, `justify`).
	`height="..."` Height.
	`width="..."` Width.
Empty	No.
Notes	Transitional DTD. This element is new to HTML 4.

`<noframes>...</noframes>`

Usage	Alternative content when frames are not supported.
Start/End Tag	Required/Required.
Attributes	None.
Empty	No.
Notes	Frameset DTD. This element is new to HTML 4.

Embedded Content

NEW TERM Also called *inclusions*, embedded content applies to Java applets, imagemaps, and other multimedia or programmed content that is placed in a Web page to provide additional functionality.

`<applet>...</applet>`

Usage	Includes a Java applet.
Start/End Tag	Required/Required.
Attributes	`codebase="..."` The URL base for the applet.
	`archive="..."` Identifies the resources to be preloaded.
	`code="..."` The applet class file.
	`object="..."` The serialized applet file.
	`alt="..."` Displays text while loading.
	`name="..."` The name of the applet.
	`width="..."` The height of the displayed applet.
	`height="..."` The width of the displayed applet.
	`align="..."` Deprecated. Controls alignment (`left`, `center`, `right`, `justify`).
	`hspace="..."` The horizontal space separating the image from other content.
	`vspace="..."` The vertical space separating the image from other content.
Empty	No.
Notes	Transitional DTD. Applet is deprecated in favor of the `<object>` element.

`<area />`

Usage	The `<area>` element is used to define links and anchors.
Start/End Tag	Required/Illegal.
Attributes	`shape="..."` Enables you to define client-side imagemaps using defined shapes (`default`, `rect`, `circle`, `poly`).

`coords="..."` Sets the size of the shape using pixel or percentage lengths.

`href="..."` The URL of the linked resource.

`target="..."` Determines where the resource will be displayed (user-defined name, `_blank`, `_parent`, `_self`, `_top`).

`nohref="..."` Indicates that the region has no action.

`alt="..."` Displays alternative text.

`tabindex="..."` Sets the tabbing order between elements with a defined `tabindex`.

Empty	Yes.
Notes	Strict DTD.

`<img />`

Usage	Includes an image in the document.
Start/End Tag	Required/Illegal.
Attributes	`core, i18n, events`.

`src="..."` The URL of the image.

`alt="..."` Alternative text to display.

`align="..."` Deprecated. Controls alignment (`left`, `center`, `right`, `justify`).

`height="..."` The height of the image.

`width="..."` The width of the image.

`border="..."` Border width.

`hspace="..."` The horizontal space separating the image from other content.

`vspace="..."` The vertical space separating the image from other content.

`usemap="..."` The URL to a client-side imagemap.

`ismap="ismap"` Identifies a server-side imagemap.

Empty	Yes.
Notes	Strict DTD.

`<map>...</map>`

Usage	When used with the `<area>` element, creates a client-side imagemap.
Start/End Tag	Required/Required.
Attributes	core.
	`name="..."` The name of the imagemap to be created.
Empty	No.
Notes	Strict DTD.

`<object>...</object>`

Usage	Includes an object.
Start/End Tag	Required/Required.
Attributes	core, i18n, events.
	`declare="declare"` A flag that declares but doesn't create an object.
	`classid="..."` The URL of the object's location.
	`codebase="..."` The URL for resolving URLs specified by other attributes.
	`data="..."` The URL to the object's data.
	`type="..."` The Internet content type for data.
	`codetype="..."` The Internet content type for the code.
	`standby="..."` Show message while loading.
	`align="..."` Deprecated. Controls alignment (`left`, `center`, `right`, `justify`).

height="..."   The height of the object.

width="..."   The width of the object.

border="..."   Displays the border around an object.

hspace="..."   The space between the sides of the object and other page content.

vspace="..."   The space between the top and bottom of the object and other page content.

usemap="..."   The URL to an imagemap.

shapes="..."   Enables you to define areas to search for hyperlinks if the object is an image.

name="..."   The URL to submit as part of a form.

tabindex="..."   Sets the tabbing order between elements with a defined tabindex.

Empty	No.
Notes	Strict DTD. This element is new to HTML 4.

`<param />`

Usage	Initializes an object.
Start/End Tag	Required/Illegal.
Attributes	name="..." Defines the parameter name.
	value="..." The value of the object parameter.
	valuetype="..." Defines the value type (data, ref, object).
	type="..." The Internet medium type.
Empty	Yes.
Notes	Strict DTD. This element is new to HTML 4.

C

Style

Style sheets (both inline and external) are incorporated into an HTML document through the use of the `<style>` element.

`<style>...</style>`

Usage	Creates an internal style sheet.
Start/End Tag	Required/Required.
Attributes	i18n.
	`type="..."` The Internet content type.
	`media="..."` Defines the destination medium (`screen`, `print`, `projection`, `braille`, `speech`, `all`).
	`title="..."` The title of the style.
Empty	No.
Notes	Strict DTD. Located in the `<head>` element.

Forms

NEW TERM *Forms* create an interface for the user to select options and return data to the Web server.

`<button>...</button>`

Usage	Creates a button.
Start/End Tag	Required/Required.
Attributes	core, i18n, events.
	`name="..."` The button name.
	`value="..."` The value of the button.
	`type="..."` The button type (`button`, `submit`, `reset`).
	`disabled="..."` Sets the button state to disabled.
	`tabindex="..."` Sets the tabbing order between elements with a defined `tabindex`.

onfocus="..." The event that occurs when the element receives focus.

onblur="..." The event that occurs when the element loses focus.

Empty	No.
Notes	Strict DTD. This element is new to HTML 4.

\<fieldset>...\</fieldset>

Usage	Groups related controls.
Start/End Tag	Required/Required.
Attributes	core, i18n, events.
Empty	No.
Notes	Strict DTD. This element is new to HTML 4.

\<form>...\</form>

Usage	Creates a form that holds controls for user input.
Start/End Tag	Required/Required.
Attributes	core, i18n, events.

action="..." The URL for the server action.

method="..." The HTTP method (get, post). get is deprecated.

enctype="..." Specifies the MIME (Internet media type).

onsubmit="..." The intrinsic event that occurs when the form is submitted.

onreset="..." The intrinsic event that occurs when the form is reset.

target="..." Determines where the resource will be displayed (user-defined name, _blank, _parent, _self, _top).

C

<table>
<tr><td></td><td>accept-charset="..."   The list of character encodings.</td></tr>
<tr><td>Empty</td><td>No.</td></tr>
<tr><td>Notes</td><td>Strict DTD.</td></tr>
</table>

`<input />`

Usage	Defines controls used in forms.
Start/End Tag	Required/Illegal.
Attributes	core, i18n, events.

type="..."   The type of input control (text, password, checkbox, radio, submit, reset, file, hidden, image, button).

name="..."   The name of the control (required except for submit and reset).

value="..."   The initial value of the control (required for radio and checkboxes).

checked="checked"   Sets the radio buttons to a checked state.

disabled="..."   Disables the control.

readonly="..."   For text password types.

size="..."   The width of the control in pixels except for text and password controls, which are specified in number of characters.

maxlength="..."   The maximum number of characters that can be entered.

src="..."   The URL to an image control type.

alt="..."   An alternative text description.

usemap="..."   The URL to a client-side imagemap.

align="..."   Deprecated. Controls alignment (left, center, right, justify).

`tabindex="..."`   Sets the tabbing order between elements with a defined `tabindex`.

`onfocus="..."`   The event that occurs when the element receives focus.

`onblur="..."`   The event that occurs when the element loses focus.

`onselect="..."`   Intrinsic event that occurs when the control is selected.

`onchange="..."`   Intrinsic event that occurs when the control is changed.

`accept="..."`   File types allowed for upload.

Empty	Yes.
Notes	Strict DTD.

`<isindex />`

Usage	Prompts the user for input.
Start/End Tag	Required/Illegal.
Attributes	`core`, `i18n`.

`prompt="..."`   Provides a prompt string for the input field.

Empty	Yes.
Notes	Transitional DTD. Deprecated.

`<label>...</label>`

Usage	Labels a control.
Start/End Tag	Required/Required.
Attributes	`core`, `i18n`, `events`.

`for="..."`   Associates a label with an identified control.

`disabled="..."`   Disables a control.

C

accesskey="..."   Assigns a hotkey to this element.

onfocus="..."   The event that occurs when the element receives focus.

onblur="..."   The event that occurs when the element loses focus.

Empty	No.
Notes	Strict DTD. This element is new to HTML 4.

<legend>...</legend>

Usage	Assigns a caption to a FIELDSET.
Start/End Tag	Required/Required.
Attributes	core, i18n, events.

align="..."   Deprecated. Controls alignment (left, center, right, justify).

accesskey="..."   Assigns a hotkey to this element.

Empty	No.
Notes	Strict DTD. This element is new to HTML 4.

<optgroup>...</optgroup>

Usage	Used to group form elements within a <select> element.
Start/End Tag	Required/Required.
Attributes	core, i18n, events.

disabled="disabled"   Not used.

label="..."   Defines a group label.

Empty	No.
Notes	Strict DTD. This element is new to HTML 4.

`<option>...</option>`

Usage	Specifies choices in a `<select>` element.
Start/End Tag	Required/Optional.
Attributes	`core`, `i18n`, `events`.
	`selected="selected"` Specifies whether the option is selected.
	`disabled="disabled"` Disables control.
	`value="..."` The value submitted if a control is submitted.
Empty	No.
Notes	Strict DTD.

`<select>...</select>`

Usage	Creates choices for the user to select.
Start/End Tag	Required/Required.
Attributes	`core`, `i18n`, `events`.
	`name="..."` The name of the element.
	`size="..."` The width in number of rows.
	`multiple="multiple"` Allows multiple selections.
	`disabled="disabled"` Disables the control.
	`tabindex="..."` Sets the tabbing order between elements with a defined `tabindex`.
	`onfocus="..."` The event that occurs when the element receives focus.
	`onblur="..."` The event that occurs when the element loses focus.
	`onselect="..."` Intrinsic event that occurs when the control is selected.
	`onchange="..."` Intrinsic event that occurs when the control is changed.

C

Empty   No.

Notes   Strict DTD.

`<textarea>...</textarea>`

Usage   Creates an area for user input with multiple lines.

Start/End Tag   Required/Required.

Attributes   core, i18n, events.

                                                  name="..."   The name of the control.

rows="..."   The width in number of rows.

cols="..."   The height in number of columns.

disabled="disabled"   Disables the control.

readonly="readonly"   Sets the displayed text to read-only status.

tabindex="..."   Sets the tabbing order between elements with a defined tabindex.

onfocus="..."   The event that occurs when the element receives focus.

onblur="..."   The event that occurs when the element loses focus.

onselect="..."   Intrinsic event that occurs when the control is selected.

onchange="..."   Intrinsic event that occurs when the control is changed.

Empty   No.

Notes   Strict DTD. Text to be displayed is placed within the start and end tags.

Scripts

Scripting language is made available to process data and perform other dynamic events through the <script> element.

<script>...</script>

Usage	The <script> element contains client-side scripts that are executed by the browser.
Start/End Tag	Required/Required.
Attributes	type="..." Script language Internet content type.
	language="..." Deprecated. The scripting language, deprecated in favor of the type attribute.
	src="..." The URL for the external script.
Empty	No.
Notes	Strict DTD. You can set the default scripting language in the <meta /> element.

<noscript>...</noscript>

Usage	Provides alternative content for browsers unable to execute a script.
Start/End Tag	Required/Required.
Attributes	None.
Empty	No.
Notes	Strict DTD. This element is new to HTML 4.

Common Attributes and Events

Four attributes are abbreviated as core in the preceding sections. They are:

- id="..."   A global identifier.
- class="..."   A list of classes separated by spaces.
- style="..."   Style information.
- title="..."   Provides more information for a specific element, as opposed to the <title> element, which entitles the entire Web page.

C

Two attributes for internationalization (i18n) are abbreviated as i18n:

- `lang="..."`   The language identifier.
- `dir="..."`   The text direction (ltr, rtl).

The following intrinsic events are abbreviated events:

- `OnClick="..."`   A pointing device (such as a mouse) was single-clicked.
- `OnDblClick="..."`   A pointing device (such as a mouse) was double-clicked.
- `OnMouseDown="..."`   A mouse button was clicked and held down.
- `OnMouseUp="..."`   A mouse button that was clicked and held down was released.
- `OnMouseOver="..."`   A mouse moved the cursor over an object.
- `OnMouseMove="..."`   The mouse was moved.
- `OnMouseOut="..."`   A mouse moved the cursor off an object.
- `OnKeyPress="..."`   A key was pressed and released.
- `OnKeyDown="..."`   A key was pressed and held down.
- `OnKeyUp="..."`   A key that was pressed has been released.

HTML Character Entities

Table D.1 contains the possible numeric and character entities for the ISO-Latin-1 (ISO8859-1) character set. Where possible, the character is shown.

Not all browsers can display all characters, and some browsers might even display characters different from those that appear in the table. Newer browsers seem to have a better track record for handling character entities, but be sure to test your HTML files extensively with multiple browsers if you intend to use these entities.

TABLE D.1   ISO-Latin-1 Character Set

Character	Numeric Entity	Character Entity (if any)	Description
	`&#00;`–`&#08;`		Unused
	`&#09;`		Horizontal tab
	`&#10;`		Line feed
	`&#11;`–`&#31;`		Unused
	`&#32;`		Space
!	`&#33;`		Exclamation mark
"	`&#34;`	`&quot;`	Quotation mark
#	`&#35;`		Number sign
$	`&#36;`		Dollar sign
%	`&#37;`		Percent sign
&	`&#38;`	`&amp;`	Ampersand
'	`&#39;`		Apostrophe
(	`&#40;`		Left parenthesis
)	`&#41;`		Right parenthesis
*	`&#42;`		Asterisk
+	`&#43;`		Plus sign
,	`&#44;`		Comma
-	`&#45;`		Hyphen
.	`&#46;`		Period (fullstop)
/	`&#47;`		Solidus (slash)
0–9	`&#48;`–`&#57;`		Digits 0–9
:	`&#58;`		Colon
;	`&#59;`		Semicolon
<	`&#60;`	`&lt;`	Less than
=	`&#61;`		Equal sign

Character	Numeric Entity	Character Entity (if any)	Description
>	&#62;	&gt;	Greater than
?	&#63;		Question mark
@	&#64;		Commercial "at"
A–Z	A–Z		Letters A–Z
[	&#91;		Left square bracket
\	&#92;		Reverse solidus (back-slash)
]	&#93;		Right square bracket
^	&#94;		Caret
—	&#95;		Horizontal bar
`	&#96;		Grave accent
a–z	a–z		Letters a–z
{	&#123;		Left curly brace
|	|		Vertical bar
}	&#125;		Right curly brace
~	&#126;		Tilde
	&#127;–		Unused
¡	&#161;	&iexcl;	Inverted exclamation
¢	&#162;	&cent;	Cent sign
£	&#163;	&pound;	Pound sterling
¤	&#164;	&curren;	General currency sign
¥	&#165;	&yen;	Yen sign
¦	&#166;	¦ or &brkbar;	Broken vertical bar
§	&#167;	&sect;	Section sign
¨	&#168;	&uml;	Umlaut (dieresis)
©	&#169;	&copy;	Copyright
ª	&#170;	&ordf;	Feminine ordinal
«	&#171;	&laquo;	Left angle quote, guillemot left
¬	&#172;	&not;	Not sign

continues

D

TABLE D.1 continued

Character	Numeric Entity	Character Entity (if any)	Description
-	&#173;	&shy;	Soft hyphen
®	&#174;	&reg;	Registered trademark
¯	&#175;	&hibar;	Macron accent
°	&#176;	&deg;	Degree sign
±	&#177;	&plusmn;	Plus or minus
2	&#178;	&sup2;	Superscript two
3	&#179;	&sup3;	Superscript three
´	&#180;	&acute;	Acute accent
µ	&#181;	&micro;	Micro sign
¶	&#182;	&para;	Paragraph sign
·	&#183;	&middot;	Middle dot
¸	&#184;	&cedil;	Cedilla
1	&#185;	&sup1;	Superscript one
º	&#186;	&ordm;	Masculine ordinal
›	&#187;	&raquo;	Right-angle quote, quille-mot right
1/4	&#188;	&frac14;	Fraction one-fourth
1/2	&#189;	&frac12;	Fraction one-half
3/4	&#190;	&frac34;	Fraction three-fourths
¿	&#191;	&iquest	Inverted question mark
À	&#192;	&Agrave;	Capital A, grave accent
Á	&#193;	&Aacute;	Capital A, acute accent
Â	&#194;	&Acirc;	Capital A, circumflex accent
Ã	&#195;	&Atilde;	Capital A, tilde
Ä	&#196;	&Auml;	Capital A, dieresis or umlaut mark
Å	&#197;	&Aring;	Capital A, ring
Æ	&#198;	&AElig;	Capital AE diphthong (ligature)

Character	Numeric Entity	Character Entity (if any)	Description
Ç	&#199;	&Ccedil;	Capital C, cedilla
È	&#200;	&Egrave;	Capital E, grave accent
É	&#201;	&Eacute;	Capital E, acute accent
Ê	&#202;	&Ecirc;	Capital E, circumflex accent
Ë	&#203;	&Euml;	Capital E, dieresis or umlaut mark
Ì	&#204;	&Igrave;	Capital I, grave accent
Í	&#205;	&Iacute;	Capital I, acute accent
Î	&#206;	&Icirc;	Capital I, circumflex accent
Ï	&#207;	&Iuml;	Capital I, diercsis or umlaut mark
Ð	&#208;	&ETH;	Capital Eth, Icelandic
Ñ	&#209;	&Ntilde;	Capital N, tilde
Ò	&#210;	&Ograve;	Capital O, grave accent
Ó	&#211;	&Oacute;	Capital O, acute accent
Ô	&#212;	&Ocirc;	Capital O, circumflex accent
Õ	&#213;	&Otilde;	Capital O, tilde
Ö	&#214;	&Ouml;	Capital O, dieresis or umlaut mark
×	&#215;		Multiply sign
Ø	&#216;	&Oslash;	Capital O, slash
Ù	&#217;	&Ugrave;	Capital U, grave accent
Ú	&#218;	&Uacute;	Capital U, acute accent
Û	&#219;	&Ucirc;	Capital U, circumflex accent
Ü	&#220;	&Uuml;	Capital U, dieresis or umlaut mark
Ý	&#221;	&Yacute;	Capital Y, acute accent
þ	&#222;	&THORN;	Capital THORN, Icelandic

continues

D

TABLE D.1 continued

Character	Numeric Entity	Character Entity (if any)	Description
ß	&#223;	&szlig;	Small sharp s, German (sz ligature)
à	&#224;	&agrave;	Small a, grave accent
á	&#225;	&aacute;	Small a, acute accent
â	&#226;	&acirc;	Small a, circumflex accent
ã	&#227;	&atilde;	Small a, tilde
ä	&#228;	&aauml;	Small a, dieresis or umlaut mark
å	&#229;	&aring;	Small a, ring
æ	&#230;	&aelig;	Small ae diphthong (ligature)
ç	&#231;	&ccedil;	Small c, cedilla
è	&#232;	&egrave;	Small e, grave accent
é	&#233;	&eacute;	Small e, acute accent
ê	&#234;	&ecirc;	Small e, circumflex accent
ë	&#235;	&euml;	Small e, dieresis or umlaut mark
ì	&#236;	&igrave;	Small i, grave accent
í	&#237;	&iacute;	Small i, acute accent
î	&#238;	&icirc;	Small i, circumflex accent
ï	&#239;	&iuml;	Small i, dieresis or umlaut mark
∂	&#240;	&eth;	Small eth, Icelandic
ñ	&#241;	&ntilde;	Small n, tilde
ò	&#242;	&ograve;	Small o, grave accent
ó	&#243;	&oacute;	Small o, acute accent
ô	&#244;	&ocirc;	Small o, circumflex accent
õ	&#245;	&otilde;	Small o, tilde
ö	&#246;	&ouml;	Small o, dieresis or umlaut mark
÷	&#247;		Division sign

Character	Numeric Entity	Character Entity (if any)	Description
ø	`&#248;`	`&oslash;`	Small o, slash
ù	`&#249;`	`&ugrave;`	Small u, grave accent
ú	`&#250;`	`&uacute;`	Small u, acute accent
û	`&#251;`	`&ucirc;`	Small u, circumflex accent
ü	`&#252;`	`&uuml;`	Small u, dieresis or umlaut mark
ý	`&#253;`	`&yacute;`	Small y, acute accent
þ	`&#254;`	`&thorn;`	Small thorn, Icelandic
ÿ	`&#255;`	`&yuml;`	Small y, dieresis or umlaut mark

The following standard codes don't work reliably in most Web browsers. They are included here only because they are so darn handy when they do work.

Character	Numeric Entity	Character Entity (if any)	Description
	` `	` `	en space (wide space)
	` `	` `	em space (very wide space)
	` `	` `	thin space
–	`&#8211;`	`&ndash`	en dash (wide dash)
—	`&#8212;`	`&mdash`	em dash (very wide dash)
'	`&#8216;`	`&lsquo;`	left single quotation mark
'	`&#8217;`	`&rsquo;`	right single quotation mark
"	`&#8220;`	`&ldquo;`	left double quotation mark
"	`&#8221;`	`&rdquo;`	right double quotation mark
€	`&#8364;`	`&euro;`	Euro sign

D

GLOSSARY

ActiveX   A relatively new technology invented by Microsoft for embedding animated objects, data, and computer code on Web pages.

anchor   A named point on a Web page. (The HTML tag with the same name is used to create hypertext links and anchors, which explains why the tag is named <a>).

animated GIF   An animated graphic exploiting looping and timing features in the GIF89a format.

ASCII file   A text file that conforms to the American Standard Code for Information Interchange. All HTML files must be saved as ASCII text files (not in any other word processor format) or they will not appear correctly in Web browsers.

attributes   Special code words that are used inside an HTML tag and that control exactly what the tag does.

bandwidth   The maximum information-carrying capacity of an electronic connection or network.

binary file   An executable file or a file that is not in ASCII text format.

bookmarks   In Netscape Navigator, a list of your favorite Web pages and Internet resources. You can add items to this menu at any time. Bookmarks are equivalent to favorites in Microsoft Internet Explorer.

browse   To wander around a portion of the Internet looking for items of interest. Also known as *surfing* or *cruising*.

browser   A software program for viewing HTML pages.

cache   A temporary storage area that a Web browser uses to store pages and graphics that it has recently opened. The cache enables the browser to quickly load the same pages and images if they are opened again soon.

cascading style sheets   A new addition to HTML that allows page designers to have greater control over the rendering of a document. Browsers that support style sheets allow font and color attributes to be specified. CSS1 is the first phase of cascading style sheets. CSS2 is the second phase, which includes layer positioning and other new features.

CGI (Common Gateway Interface)   An interface for external programs to talk to a Web server. Programs that are written to use CGI are called *CGI programs* or *CGI scripts* and are commonly used for processing HTML forms.

client-side imagemaps   A new HTML method for linking an image to more than one address. The advantage of this approach is that the browser can display a region's destination URL when the mouse passes over it, and some network traffic is saved because the browser can directly request the new document when a click is made.

code   Anything written in a language intended for computers to interpret. *See* source *and* script.

comment   Text in an HTML document (or computer program) that will be seen only by the people who edit the source for that page. Comments are normally invisible when a page is viewed with a Web browser. Comments in HTML begin with <!-- and end with -->. Comments in JavaScript begin with //.

compression   The process of making a computer file smaller so that it can be copied more quickly between computers.

cyberspace   A broad expression used to describe the activity, communication, and culture occurring on the Internet and other computer networks.

definition list   An indented list without a number or symbol in front of each item. *See* ordered list *and* unordered list.

DHTML   *See* Dynamic HTML.

digital   Electronic circuits that use a sequence of on or off values to convey information.

digitized   Converted to a digital format suitable for storage.

direct connection   A permanent, 24-hour link between a computer and the Internet. A computer with a direct connection can use the Internet at any time.

directory service   An Internet service that maintains a database on individuals, including email, fax, and telephone numbers, that is searchable by the public.

DNS (Domain Name System)   An Internet addressing system that uses a group of names that are listed with dots (.) between them, working from the most specific to the most general group. In the United States, the top (most general) domains are network categories such as edu (education), com (commercial), and gov (government). In other countries, a two-letter abbreviation for the country is used, such as ca (Canada) and au (Australia).

DOM (Document Object Model)   A standard under development by the W3C that will govern the way scripting and programming languages refer to the elements on a Web page. Currently, Microsoft and Netscape use incompatible methods for referencing elements. It is hoped that the DOM standard will make it more practical to develop scripts and programs that work with all available Web browsers.

domain   The address of a computer on the Internet. A user's Internet address is made up of a username and a domain name.

download   To retrieve a file or files from a remote machine to your local machine.

DSig (Digital Signature)   A proposed standard from the World Wide Web Consortium for one organization or individual to vouch for the identity of another, which is currently the best that can be done to verify identities or statements online. May be used in conjunction with PICS or P3P for verification purposes.

Dynamic HTML   A somewhat loosely defined term for the integration of scripting, style sheets, and HTML to create animated, interactive Web pages.

email   An electronic mail system that enables a person to compose a message on a computer and transmit that message through a computer network, such as the Internet, to another computer user.

email address   The word-based Internet address of a user, typically made up of a username, an at sign (@), and a domain name (that is, user@domain). Email addresses are translated from the numeric Internet Protocol (IP) addresses by the domain name system (DNS).

encryption   The process of encoding information so that it is secure from other Internet users.

FAQ   Short for frequently asked questions, a computer file containing the answers to frequently asked questions about a particular Internet resource.

favorites   In Microsoft Internet Explorer, a list of your favorite Web pages and Internet resources. You can add items to this menu at any time. Favorites are equivalent to bookmarks in Netscape Navigator.

firewall   A security device placed on a LAN to protect it from Internet intruders. This can be a special kind of hardware router, a piece of software, or both.

form   A page that includes areas to be filled out by the reader. HTML forms allow information to be sent back to the company or individual who made (or maintains) the page.

frame   A rectangular region within the browser window that displays a Web page alongside other pages in other frames.

freeware   Software available to anyone, free of charge; this is unlike shareware, which requires payment.

FTP (File Transfer Protocol)   The basic method for copying a file from one computer to another through the Internet.

graphical editor   A program that allows you to edit an approximation of what a Web page will look like when viewed with a Web browser. Graphical editors usually hide the actual HTML tags they are creating from view. It is not recommended that you use a graphical editor when learning HTML with this book.

graphics   Digitized pictures and computer-generated images.

helper application   An application that is configured to launch and view files that are unreadable to a Web browser.

HTML (Hypertext Markup Language)   The document formatting language used to create pages on the World Wide Web.

HTTP (Hypertext Transfer Protocol)   The standard method for exchanging information between HTTP servers and clients on the Web. The HTTP specification lays out the rules of how Web servers and browsers must work together.

hypertext   Text that allows readers to jump spontaneously among onscreen documents and other resources by selecting highlighted keywords that appear on each screen. Hypertext appears most often on the World Wide Web.

image compression The mathematical manipulation that images are put through to squeeze out repetitive patterns. It makes them load and display much faster.

imagemap An image on a Web page that leads to two or more different links, depending on which part of the image someone clicks. Modern Web browsers use client-side imagemaps, but you can also create server-side imagemaps for compatibility with old browsers.

interlaced GIF An image file that will appear blocky at first, then more and more detailed as it continues downloading. Similar to a progressive JPEG file.

Internet A large, loosely organized integrated network connecting universities, research institutions, government, businesses, and other organizations so that they can exchange messages and share information.

Internet Explorer A popular Web browser created by Microsoft Corporation and integrated with the Windows operating system.

intranet A private network with access restricted to one organization, but which uses the same standards and protocols as the global public Internet.

ISDN (Integrated Digital Services Network) Essentially operates as a digital phone line. ISDN delivers many benefits over standard analog phone lines, including multiple simultaneous calls and higher-quality data transmissions. ISDN data rates are 56Kbps to 128Kbps.

ISP (Internet Service Provider) The company that provides you or your company with access to the Internet. ISPs usually have several servers and a high-speed link to the Internet backbone.

Java The Web-oriented language developed by Sun Microsystems.

JavaScript A Web page scripting language originally developed by Netscape. Many JavaScript commands are similar (but not identical) to Java commands. Unlike Java, however, you can include JavaScript directly in the text of HTML pages.

JScript The version of JavaScript implemented by Microsoft in Internet Explorer. JScript is almost, but not quite, compatible with Netscape's JavaScript.

Kbps Kilobits per second. A rate of transfer of information across a connection such as the Internet.

LAN (local area network) A computer network limited to a small area.

link An icon, a picture, or a highlighted string of text that connects the current Web page to other Web pages, Internet sites, graphics, movies, or sounds. On the Web, you skip from page to page by clicking links.

MathML (Mathematics Markup Language)   An XML-compatible formatting language for mathematical formulas.

Mbps   Megabits per second. A rate of transfer of information across a connection such as the Internet. Equal to approximately 1,000Kbps.

modem   An acronym for modulator/demodulator. A device that converts the digital signals of a computer to an analog format for transmission across telephone lines.

multimedia   A description for systems capable of displaying or playing text, pictures, sound, video, and animation.

navigation   Movement within a computer environment (for example, navigation of a Web site).

Netscape   Short for Netscape Communications Corporation, a software company that developed and markets a popular World Wide Web browser called Navigator, which is part of a software suite called Communicator. Some people casually refer to Navigator as Netscape.

network   A set of computers connected so that they can communicate and share information. Most major networks are connected to the global network-of-networks, called the *Internet*.

online   A general term referring to anything connected to or conveyed through a communications network.

ordered list   An indented list that has numbers or letters in front of each item. *See* unordered list *and* definition list.

P3P (Platform for Privacy Preferences)   A recent W3C standard concerning the security and privacy restrictions associated with Web pages.

Paint Shop Pro   PSP is a popular graphics program from JASC software for creating Web page images. PSP is used for the graphics examples in this book, although you can achieve the same results with many other graphics programs.

password   A secret code, known only to the user, that allows that user to access a computer that is protected by a security system.

PICS   Platform for Internet Content Selection is a new W3C standard protocol for rating Web page content according to any criteria a rating authority or company might choose. Applications include restricting access to confidential or adult-oriented material. *See* DSig.

pixel   An individual point of color in a computer graphics image.

Portal   A Web site intended to be used as a starting place for exploring and searching the World Wide Web, such as yahoo.com or infoseek.com.

POTS   Plain old telephone service.

PPP (Point-to-Point Protocol))   A communications protocol that enables a dial-up Internet connection.

progressive JPEG   An image file that appears blurry at first and then gradually comes into focus. Similar to an interlaced GIF file.

protocol   Specific rules and conventions defining how data can be exchanged between any two devices.

provider   A general reference to an Internet service provider.

public domain   Material that is freely usable by anyone, but still may be copyrighted.

relative address   An address describing the path from one Web page to another, instead of a *full* (or *absolute*) URL address.

resolution   The number of individual dots, or pixels, that make up an image.

resource   A generic term to describe the varied information and activities available to Internet users.

robot   An automated program that indexes Web pages for a search engine or carries out other repetitive tasks that humans would otherwise have to do.

script   A short computer program written in a simplified programming language such as JavaScript, VBScript, or Perl.

search engine   A program that provides a way to search for specific information. Often used to refer to popular sites such as Alta Vista or HotBot, where you can search for pages on the Internet containing certain keywords.

server   A networked computer that "serves" a particular type of information to users. *See* Web server.

server-side imagemaps   A technique for implementing Web page images that lead to more than one link, so that the server computer determines which link to go to. This method is now less commonly used than client-side imagemaps.

SGML (Standard General Markup Language)   A well-established international standard for defining text-based markup languages. HTML is one example of the types of languages that can be defined in SGML. *See* XML.

shareware   Software programs that users are permitted to acquire and evaluate for free. Shareware is different from freeware in that, if a person likes the shareware program and plans to use it on a regular basis, he is expected to send a fee to the programmer.

Shockwave   An interactive multimedia system for the Web that views applications developed using software from Macromedia, Inc.

SMIL (Synchronized Multimedia Integration Language)   A new W3C-recommended standard for controlling the timing of multiple audio, video, and interactive media presentations on a Web page. SMIL is not yet implemented in any Web browser software.

source   Also known as source code. The actual text and commands stored in an HTML file (including tags, comments, and scripts) that may not be visible when the page is viewed with a Web browser.

spider   An automated program that indexes Web pages for a search engine. Also called a *robot*.

surfing   Another term for browsing and cruising.

T-1 line   A digital circuit capable of transferring data at 1.544Mbps.

T-3 line   A digital circuit equivalent to 28 T-1 lines.

table   Text and/or images arranged into orderly rows and columns. HTML provides several tags specifically for creating tables.

tag   A coded HTML command used to indicate how part of a Web page should be displayed.

TCP/IP (Transmission Control Protocol/Internet Protocol)   The agreed-on set of computer communications rules and standards that allows communications between different types of computers and networks that are connected to the Internet.

text editor   Any program that allows you to edit text with your computer.

unordered list   An indented list with a special bullet symbol in front of each item. *See* ordered list *and* definition list.

URL   Also commonly called a *location* or *address*. A uniform resource locator is an addressing system that locates documents on the Internet.

username   Used with a password to gain access to a computer. A dial-up IP user typically has a username and password for dialing the access provider's Internet server.

VBScript   A script language developed by Microsoft. A technical competitor to Java and JavaScript applications.

visitor   A person who is viewing one of your Web pages. Also called a *user* or *reader*.

VRML (Virtual Reality Modeling Language)   A three-dimensional navigation specification used to simulate three-dimensional objects or worlds online.

W3C (World Wide Web Consortium)   The is an organization that drafts and recommends technical standards for the World Wide Web. HTML 4 and CSS2 are examples of W3C-recommended standards.

Web   Can be used to refer to the entire World Wide Web or to a particular Web site.

Web browser   A software program used for viewing Web pages, such as Netscape Navigator or Microsoft Internet Explorer.

Web page   An HTML document made available through the World Wide Web, along with any associated graphics or multimedia files.

Web server   A computer on the Internet that hosts data that can be accessed by Web browsers using the HTTP protocol.

Web site   One or more Web pages that are intended to be viewed and explored together as a cohesive presentation.

WWW (World Wide Web)   Also known as the Web. A set of Internet computers and services that provide an easy-to-use system for finding information and moving among resources. WWW services feature hypertext and multimedia information, which can be explored through browsers such as Netscape Navigator and Microsoft Internet Explorer.

XHTML (eXtended HyperText Markup Language)   New version of HTML, the standard document formatting language for the World Wide Web. XHTML 1 is essentially HTML 4, modified to be compatible with XML.

XML (eXtensible Markup Language)   A W3C-recommended standard for defining new document types, as well as user-defined or application-specific tags to extend the capabilities of HTML. Basically, a less powerful version of SGML.

XSL (eXtensible Stylesheet Language)   The W3C style sheet standard for XML. (XSL is related to XML in exactly the same way that CSS is related to HTML.)

INDEX

Symbols

24-Hour HTML Café Web site, 20, 32, 91, 175, 385
  animation resources, 181
  color resources, 160
  forms resources, 121
  frequently asked questions, 379-384
  graphics resources, 146
  imagemap resources, 208
  interactive scripts resource, 266
  JavaScript links, 289
  list links, 76
  multimedia resources, 252, 261
  style sheet resources, 241
  table designs, 223

256-color square Web site, 387

A

<a> tag, 38
  attributes
    OnClick, 306
    OnMouseOver, 283
  email address links, 102-105
  intrapage links, 97, 99
  link component, 411-412
  style sheet standard
    unvisited links, 239
    visited links, 239
<abbr> tag, 400
absolute addresses versus relative addresses, 41-42
<acronym> tag, textual structure, 400

ActiveMovie control (ActiveX), 272-274
ActiveX
  browser functionality, enhancing, 270-272
  Web page videos, embedding, 272-274
Add It Web site, 390
Add Text dialog box (Paint Shop Pro), 137
<address> tag, textual structure, 401
addresses
  links, importance of completeness, 357-358
  relative, 41-42
  Web pages
    copying, 38
    selecting, 49
Adobe PageMill, 54, 187-188

SAMS
Teach Yourself
in 24 Hours

When you only have time for the answers™

Sams Teach Yourself in 24 Hours *gets you the results you want—fast! Work through 24 proven one-hour lessons and learn everything you need to know to get up to speed quickly. It has the answers you need at the price you can afford.*

Sams Teach Yourself Microsoft FrontPage 2000 in 24 Hours

Rogers Cadenhead
ISBN: 0-672-31500-9
$19.99 US/$29.95 CAN